Re/Framing Identifications

Re/Framing Identifications

Michelle Ballif
University of Georgia

WAVELAND
PRESS, INC.
Long Grove, Illinois

For information about this book, contact:
Waveland Press, Inc.
4180 IL Route 83, Suite 101
Long Grove, IL 60047-9580
(847) 634-0081
info@waveland.com
www.waveland.com

CONTENTS

SECTION III   131

RE/FRAMING HISTORY, MEMORY, AND EVENTS

SECTION IV   185

RE/FRAMING EMBODIMENT AND RHETORICAL AGENCY

SECTION V   259

RE/FRAMING RACIAL, ETHNIC, AND CLASS IDENTIFICATIONS

SECTION VI 307
RE/FRAMING DISCIPLINARY IDENTIFICATIONS AND ASSUMPTIONS

EDITOR'S INTRODUCTION

Michelle Ballif

The fifteenth Biennial Rhetoric Society of America Conference convened at the Loews Philadelphia Hotel in Philadelphia, Pennsylvania with record-setting attendance numbers. Over the long weekend of May 25-28, 2012, more than twelve hundred attendees—with forty-seven of the United States, seven Canadian provinces, and eighteen other countries represented—gathered to address the convention's theme of *Re/Framing Identifications* and to participate in the nearly four hundred sessions devoted to our collective "rhetorical histories, theories, tactics, technologies, geographies, and practices" in an effort to "extend our roles as public intellectuals by discussing how to name, analyze, evaluate, teach, and take action rhetorically on challenges facing our world." The aforementioned theme posed by RSA President Krista Ratcliffe asked us to consider Kenneth Burke's notion of identification "as a place of perpetual reframing that affects who, how, and what can be thought, spoken, written, and imagined."

More specifically, Burke has asked us to reconsider "persuasion" as rhetoric's fundamental aim by reframing "persuasion" in terms of "identification"—as a process theorized as more complicated than simply an agonistic process between rhetor and audience, as traditional rhetoric has characterized it. In *A Rhetoric of Motives,* Burke acknowledges that rhetoric is the "region of . . . insult and injury," but he further contends that rhetoric is also the space of identification and consubstantiality, where humans come together despite their primordial and essential division one from the other (19, 22). In this way, rhetoric initiates and forges connections; in this way, "identification" invents and coheres social relations. Granted, not all rhetorically produced social relations are peaceful—war hovers on every horizon. That is, Burke insists that we are simultaneously "symbol-using" and "symbol-abusing" beings by nature. But in *Language as Symbolic Action,* he argues that we are "symbol-*making*" beings, as well (16; emphasis added).

In this spirit of invention—of generating new forms of rhetorical and social being—conference participants explored new rhetorical frames of identities and identifications. Some authors used Burke's theories explicitly to analyze specific social identifications; others used the notion of "identifications" more widely in order to explore how identities, whether national, gendered, raced, or otherwise embodied, have been framed or might be reframed.

1

Accordingly, this volume features a select representation of the many papers delivered at these sessions, and each attends to the conference theme in its own way. I have by necessity imposed an arbitrary categorization of the essays included here, dividing them into very general but thematic groupings. However, in the process of imposing such delineations I found myself empathizing with the delirium that Michel Foucault experienced when encountering "a certain Chinese encyclopedia" (*The Order of Things* xv). In any event, the deliriousness resulted in the identification of a rich substrata of themes regarding, for example, ethics, democracy, history, and embodiment—all to be detailed below.

Jacqueline Jones Royster inaugurates this collection as well as our first group of selected papers that address the theme of "Re/Framing National Identity."[1] Royster's plenary address, "Reframing Narratives of Nation: Women's Participation in the American Civil War," recounts the fascinating narrative of Sarah Emma Edmonds, who—as Frank Thompson—served as a "male nurse, a soldier, and a spy" during the American Civil War. The narrative serves to foreground and to make visible the very real work in which women engaged during the war, as well as to "account for all of our people" in our "multivariant nation" who have collectively participated in forging our national identity. Royster was prompted to investigate Edmonds's narrative by a keen sensitivity to the actual physical site that contextualized Edmonds's lived experience.

This attention to the historic site as a prompt to reinvestigate and reimagine our national identity is likewise apparent in David Zarefsky's essay, which analyzes two speeches that Lincoln delivered in Philadelphia—the site, of course, of the RSA convention but more primordially, the site of our nation's founding. In February of 1861, according to Zarefsky, Lincoln delivered "two unremarkable speeches" during that visit that—despite their "quotidian" nature—carried important rhetorical force in the face of the "secession crisis: to preserve the union yet also to constitute union by recommitment to the ideals of the Declaration of Independence." Lincoln's rhetoric thus attempted to frame American identity as the *united* states against the very real threat of its dissolution.

Analogously, America's national identity was reframed during the Cold War of the 1950s, when its citizens perceived the nation to be at risk against the communist threat of the Soviet Union. M. Elizabeth Thorpe analyzes the effort to add the words "under God" to the United States' Pledge of Allegiance, arguing that the resulting addition accomplished the rhetorical work of reframing American national identity as specifically "noncommunist." Jill M. Weber's essay suggests that American national identity is highly influenced by the powerful ideograph of "the family." By analyzing the rhetoric of "family values" in policy-making discussions, she demonstrates how effectively "the participants in these debates invoked family values language and images in a variety of ways, whether it was to help establish a need for the bill, to justify the bill's passage, or to respond to the bill's critics."

In the second section, "Re/Framing Deliberative Rhetoric, Democracy, and Ethics," the authors ask us to examine the difficult—if not impossible—questions attending to ethics in a national as well as a global community. As the ethical question is historically linked to deliberative rhetoric about the "best" action or the "best" policy, and as deliberative rhetoric is traditionally linked with "democracy," and as "democracy" presupposes human rights, we return—once again—to the question of ethics. Laura A. Sparks investigates the "ethically troubling" visual images of torture at Abu Ghraib but asks us to develop—via a comic frame of acceptance—a "proactive" rather than a "reactive attitude." This does not "mean ignoring the moral implications of an event; it can instead mean rethinking the human rights violations in light of the complex system in which they arise, challenging and complicating good and evil oppositions where there is room for misunderstanding." Geoffrey W. Bateman's essay discusses his community writing-center work at a day shelter for the homeless and economically disenfranchised, as an "ethical encounter in the ongoing efforts to secure and protect human rights for some of the most dispossessed people of our city." The literacy work, he argues, provides a site to "refashion the frames of reference that saturate our world, frames of reference that we can reinscribe with much more humane notions of what it means to be homeless, to be human, to write, and to have rights."

The next several essays investigate deliberative rhetoric and public discourse. William Duffy examines the rhetoric of Jon Stewart as deliberative insofar as it "is meant to engender accountability on the part of those who are responsible for mediating political debate in the news media." Specifically, Duffy analyzes Stewart's perspicuity as the key to his discourse's "deliberative virtue, its ability to contribute to the understanding necessary to actually evaluate arguments made in the course of debate." In contrast, Keith D. Miller interrogates a form of antidebate or "cunning projection" as identified by Patricia Roberts-Miller. In his analysis of the identity criticism of Barack Obama—"the claim that he was born outside the US and the claim that he is a Muslim," he argues that such antidebate debate is analogous to the rhetoric employed by proslavery defenders preceding the Civil War, as well as by the segregationist proponents in the mid-twentieth century. Foregrounding "its stubborn persistence and resurgence as a manifestation of long-standing white racial anxieties," he discusses possible rhetorical defenses against "cunning projection."

Randall Iden and Dale Cyphert argue that public debate needs informed citizens who practice prudence, or *phronesis*. They investigate Public Radio International's *This American Life* segment, "The Giant Pool of Money," which was produced to humanize the financial crisis beginning in 2008. Iden and Cyphert suggest that this segment manifests prudent rhetoric that "allow[s] members of the community to understand each other's motives, engage in reciprocal discourse, and perform a rhetoric that seeks their collective gain." A "public," they conclude, "that can discuss its own economic behavior will result in better public information, sharper public debate, and better policy decisions."

David M. Grant's contribution asks us to consider what a "public" is in our technological age, characterized by assemblages and nonhuman agencies, and how this affects rhetorical delivery. "[W]ho are the 'publics,'" he queries, "coalescing around the problem of getting a message out, circulating it, and even transmuting it across media platforms?" What are the material, distributed network systems not only in/through which "messages" are delivered but also through which agents are deployed and embodied? Grant concludes, "With posthuman, postconsumer, electronic, environmental thinking, we can neither so easily separate representations from being nor compartmentalize the rhetorical canons themselves."

Andrew Nicholas Rechnitz's contribution challenges the narrative that rhetoric flourishes in democratic political settings by rereading Gorgias's *Palamêdês*, which disentangles rhetoric and democracy, insofar as Gorgias—who is a noncitizen and hence would neither be part of the Athenian democracy nor be "equal" under the law—can "generate rhetorical activity, predicated on equality, without the sanction of an official politics." He further concludes, "[I]t is no longer possible to ignore the fact that foreigners are capable of doing so with as much (or more) rhetorical skill than citizens who are granted the right to speak based solely upon membership with the state." Erik Doxtader's essay provokes us to consider the (im)possibility of human rights by way of acknowledging that our humanistically theorized rhetoric (which presumes the notion of a "coherent speaking subject—whether in the form of an advocate, narrator, or witness—that remains somehow immune" to rhetoric's "own barbaric demands and desires") is "an intrinsic part of the violence that all sides in the debate [regarding human rights] claim to oppose." Doxtader urges us to move beyond the *agora*—the space of rational deliberation, as an *allegorical* rendering allows.

In the third group of essays, "Re/Framing History, Memory, and Events," the authors investigate historiographical methods as well as events and collective memories to theorize how such historical moments have been previously framed, what that framing ideologically reveals or obscures, and how these moments might be, alternately, reframed. Matthew Abraham's contribution examines the online debate on the Writing Program Administrators listserv (WPA-L) regarding the Rachel Corrie Award for Courage in the Teaching of Writing that foregrounded the Israel-Palestine conflict. He argues that the debate revealed an "abuse of history and historical memory" through a displaced "conception of anti-Semitism, a conception that had a particular meaning and resonance at a particular point in history" yet not in "contemporary debates about the Middle East." He urges us—as scholars and practitioners of rhetoric—not only to be "vigilant" against such displacements but also to intervene in public debates about the Israel-Palestine conflict.

Jerry Won Lee analyzes the "competing collective memories" of the Koreans and the Japanese regarding the controversial ownership and territorial proprietorship of a number of islets situated between the two countries, known in English as the Liancourt Rocks. He demonstrates the ideological power of such memories, arguing specifically that the "coexistence of two discrete collective memories, two discrete perspectives on the historical accuracy of the past, both of which aim to exist within a homogeneous framework of empirical knowledge, paralyzes transnational identification and enables the perpetuation of colonial tension in East Asia today." Whereas Lee investigates the relation between rhetoric and transnational identity, Jason A. Edwards examines the relation between rhetoric and citizenship by attending to the ideological power of collective apologies. In his analysis of such apologies from Australia, Canada, and Great Britain, he demonstrates how they not only "may work in opening up the boundaries of citizenship" but also work to limit the enactment of citizenship by marginalized groups such as "African-Americans, immigrants, women, [and] the GLBT community." Collective apologies are indicative, he suggests, of "democracies . . . who struggle in dealing with their present and future ideals and their past injustices" in the construction and possible deployment of citizenship.

The next two essays examine two events in American history, demonstrating how they had been framed by public discourse and offering alternative frames of understanding. In an essay marked by tragic timeliness, Katie Rose Guest Pryal reinvestigates the "predictable rhetorical patterns" of public discussion in the case of Jared Loughner, who pled guilty to a mass shooting spree in Tucson, Arizona, in January 2011. According to Pryal, these predictable rhetorical patterns ("we should have known!"; "how to identify the mentally ill?"; "what to do with the mentally ill?") have the underlying rhetorical purpose of "refram[ing] sanity as a culturally imposed division that can be used to forge identification among the sane after a traumatic event." This forged identification relies on scapegoating all the mentally ill, a divisive categorical construction based on the criminal acts of just a few. Reframing the rhetorical purpose of Jean Baudrillard's contribution to Verso Books' 9/11 book series, *Requiem for the Twin Towers*, Brian Gogan argues for an alternative reading of what was taken as an outrageous and even heartless text. Specifically, Gogan's analysis invites us to look at the text *as rhetorical* by turning our focus to the perlocutionary nature of the text as performative, as playing "the imaginary against the real." As such, when Baudrillard claims that "'[t]he Twin Towers were worth destroying,' he is not making a political claim or an ethical claim[;] he is making the weaker side of exchange, figuratively known in this architectural analogy as destruction, look the stronger. Thus, . . . destruction has the potential to trump construction and . . . the imaginary can still usurp the real—that is, until the next exchange." Shawn D. Ramsey's essay asks us to interrogate our very historiographical methods. Adapting Paul Prior's "cultural historic activity theory" as a methodological reparation for "neglected rhetorics situated in the past," Ramsey argues that this analytic "can provide more nuanced contextual examinations of rhetoric as an idea and a practice in the disparate times and places where it existed as a complex cultural edifice."

The fourth section, "Re/Framing Embodiment and Rhetorical Agency," features essays examining how bodies are framed—for example, as gendered or raced or queer—and how such bodies enact rhetorical agency contemporaneously, historically, and even posthumously, and through a variety of media—including Facebook, the theater, and the personal diary. Kaitlin Marks-Dubbs begins the section with her analysis of the SlutWalk movement by foregrounding the cultural script that problematizes "the rhetorical act of walking." That is, many rape victims are blamed merely because they chose to walk to or from a venue, rendering them a moving and potential target of rape. In protest, SlutWalk participants "write of, on, with, and through their bodies," carrying placards that ask the reader to reexamine foundational cultural scripts. Through an analysis of the online visual and text archives of Slut-Walk Facebook pages, Marks-Dubbs investigates how this "deployment . . . of visual, material, and embodied rhetorics" in the service of social activism "may simultaneously work to collude and undermine one another in challenging and changing common cultural scripts." Katherine Bridgman also looks to Facebook as a site of analysis. Specifically, she examines the page "We are All Khaled Said," which was mounted in response to the death of Khaled Said in 2010, a "threshold event in the mobilization of Egyptians for the [coming] revolution." According to Bridgman's detailed analysis, the Facebook page—the English-language version—effectively invited page followers to identify with the participants in the revolution (to experience "mutually embodied experiences of the revolution"), leading her to inquire into the rhetorical agency and "use of social media as a tool for social protest."

Elizabeth Tasker Davis presents us with the figure of Elizabeth Barry, a popular and successful performer and theater owner of the eighteenth century, who Davis believes could have exerted tremendous influence if "the venues of podium or pulpit had been available to her during her lifetime." Although traditional rhetorical agency was not available to her, "Barry's innovations in naturalistic elocution made a strong impression on the audiences and theatrical delivery techniques of her period."

M. Karen Powers's essay asks what identity and forms of identification the first three words of the preamble to the US Constitution, "We the People," invoke. To which bodies do these words refer—to those who framed the Constitution or to those in the present era? Powers examines one group—the Environmental Justice Movement, which "explicitly challenged the meaning of national identity in the contemporary United States by revising the Preamble to the Constitution in their 'Principles of Environmental Justice' to [read] 'We, the people of color,'" emphasizing that environmental issues are entangled with issues of race, class, and poverty. Powers contrasts the two documents to illuminate the rhetorical agency of a counter-public to reframe national identity.

Jessica L. Shumake's essay provokes us to think about *postmortem* rhetorical agency through her analysis of the deceased artist David Wojnarowicz's work and its censorship by the Smithsonian. Ironically, she contends, this censorship was precisely what fueled Wojnarowicz's postmortem rhetorical agency by "propelling him to national public recognition and visibility," allowing him—after death—to participate in social activism, arguing against homophobia and for gay rights.

In an analogous move, Heather Palmer also extends our conception of rhetorical agency beyond the motor of rational consciousness by including "affect and intersubjectivity" and "the reciprocity of body and soul." Her focus is the work of the early modern mystic Julian of Norwich, who— Palmer argues—"perform[s] the radically ethical work of unsettling repressive identity categories through a sustained engagement with the realm of affect, defined not as emotion, but as the intensity of textual becoming." The resulting form of rhetorical agency, then, is a function of "sensation and its representation in a discourse that does not separate the experience of its life from its expression."

By putting Aristotle, Burke, and Luce Irigaray in conversation with each other, Janice Odom argues that rhetorical agency—as defined by Aristotle and Burke—forecloses the feminine: "consubstantiality requires [that it is] possible to act collectively only in the moment that one shares substance with another or, as Irigaray would have it, in the moment one shares solids, which for her is the domain of the masculine." She continues: "Thus, in the process of constituting audiences, 'good' rhetoric will necessarily exclude from that scene the feminine, which is identified with fluids." Odom's essay explores how listening to Irigaray could teach rhetoric how to think about rhetorical agency in/through sexual difference.

In the final essay of this section, Sue Carter Wood looks specifically at the development of Ida B. Wells's rhetorical agency through her diary and autobiography. Using Kelly Myers's conception of "the relationship between *kairos*, or opportunity, and *metanoia*, or regret," Wood traces the embodied and lived experiences that impacted Wells's rhetorical voice to demonstrate how Wells "learned to re-frame rhetorical situations so as to open up a space in which to speak her mind."

The essays in the fifth section, "Re/Framing Racial, Ethnic, and Class Identifications," provide a fresh eye to the rhetorical ways and means—and political and social significance—of identifying race, ethnicity, and class. Malinda Williams's contribution investigates "our conceptions of race in this country, which on the one hand are perpetually fluid and, on the other, remain entirely static." As the public conversation regarding George Zimmerman—the accused killer of Trayvon Martin—reveals, "Hispanic" is commonly perceived as a *racial* as opposed to an *ethnic* term—a term which serves to mark someone "as *not* white." Through her careful review of the United States censuses, her essay responds to the questions: "[G]iven these common and widespread (mis)understandings of official ethnic and racial standards, what is the significance of a growing population [Hispanic] that rejects these notions and asserts its whiteness more than half of the time?" And, further: "[I]n a nation where historically 'one drop' of African blood has defined an individual as black, what does it mean to have a significant portion of society reject this notion?" Relatedly, Bryan Carr investigates how "whiteness" has been deployed in the superhero media, reinforcing white privilege by representing most superhero characters as white. His rhetorical analysis of the superhero media details the implications for how "these forms of media reflect and shape American popular culture."

Karen Ching Carter explores the theater as a site of cultural reinscription. The Chinese-themed club Forbidden City, which opened in San Francisco in 1938, featured dancers and performers from a variety of Asian cultures—but to American audiences, all Asian peoples were conceived of, pejoratively, as "Orientals." Carter argues that the theater served as an alternative public sphere, providing a unique site that transformed the negative American perception of the "Oriental" into the more humanized "Asian American." Nicholas S. Paliewicz's essay examines post-9/11 discourse that vilifies Muslims and Arab Americans through Burke's pollution-purification-redemption cycle. In his careful analysis of the representation of the 9/11 memorial and museum as detailed in the special edition of the *New York Times* on September 11, 2011, Paliewicz argues that the "post-9/11 discourse has been reframed by a terministic screen of cost[, which] reifies a religious orientation of capitalism because it demonstrates that there is a price to our symbolic order. . . . This frame is used to evaluate the cost-benefit of purification efforts."

K. Hyoejin Yoon argues that the early nineteenth century rise of the middle class was accompanied by a "desire for respectability," which in turn "created a market for consumers of genteel goods. Chinese goods, in particular, were sought after as Americans appropriated the aristocratic manners associated with tea service and other refined habits." Through her analysis of newspaper accounts of a certain Afong Moy, who was billed as the "Chinese Lady" in an advertisement for such Chinese goods, Yoon "considers the ways that the rhetoric of gentility coheres and divides the reading public and how a figure like Afong Moy became the medium for that social cohesion and division."

The essays in the sixth and final section, "Re/Framing Disciplinary Identifications and Assumptions," invite us to rethink a number of disciplinary assumptions—as do all of the contributions in this volume. But here, specifically, the authors ask us to examine our rhetorical foundations through the eyes of an alternate rhetoric—whether cross-cultural or cross-disciplinary. Dominic J. Ashby challenges Burke's theory of identification by contrasting it with the Japanese rhetorical tradition, exemplified by the "dynamic between *uchi* and *soto*, often translated as 'inside' and 'outside.'" Ashby contends that this dynamic moves fluidly between identification and disidentification and that presumes a shifting, contextual sense of self and that "presents self and social order as mutually constitutive." Ashby hopes that his analysis might "expand our range of tools and theories for understanding rhetoric in any number of contexts, global and local."

Similarly, Edward Karshner problematizes Burke's theorization of rhetoric through his analysis of Navajo rhetoric. The Navajo use a "rhetoric that reflects an epistemology based on experience and expressed as a symbolic practice validated by a ceremonial system." Karshner explains: "Thought, symbol, and action are synthesized through participation in these ceremonies that alter an individual's perception of reality, thus maintaining the balance between the individual and the metaphysical system." Karshner believes that elements of *Diné* rhetoric would positively modify the "practices of contemporary, Western rhetoric."

The concluding essay by Tonya Ritola argues that the field of rhetoric and composition and the field of communication "have much to learn from one another." For example, despite the coexistence of the Rhetoric Society of America convention and *Rhetoric Society Quarterly,* which both provide a space for "shared inquiry between the two fields," for the most part the disciplinary fields remain insulated from one another. Ritola argues that through more "scholarship that transgresses disciplinary boundaries" and through "[b]uilding a strong international and national coalition of rhetoric scholars regardless of disciplinary affiliation, rhetoric's power as a discipline will prosper."

All of the essays in this volume have challenged our collective identification as members of the Rhetoric Society of America to reconsider many of our most basic presumptions about rhetoric, including its relation to democracy and ethics, its power to frame and reframe history, its ability to enable and deny agency as well as to mark and re-mark bodies, its collusion with barbarism but also its responsibility for social activism. Indeed, in so doing, the authors have provoked us to continually reframe our identifications that determine "who, how, and what can be thought, spoken, written, and imagined."

NOTE

[1] The Keynote Speech, "Encapsulating the National Identity in Key Presidential Phrases," delivered by Kathleen Hall Jamieson and Karlyn Kohrs Campbell, likewise discussed the framing of national identity. Regrettably, we are unable to reproduce the text of that speech, as it is a part of a work in progress and "intended as an anchor chapter in a book in the early stages of development" (Jamieson).

WORKS CITED

Burke, Kenneth. *Language as Symbolic Action.* Berkeley: U of California P, 1966. Print.
---. *A Rhetoric of Motives.* Berkeley: U of California P, 1950. Print.
Foucault, Michel. *The Order of Things.* New York: Vintage, 1970. Print.
Jamieson, Kathleen Hall. Message to the author. 7 Jun. 2012. Email.

SECTION
I

RE/FRAMING
NATIONAL IDENTITY

REFRAMING NARRATIVES OF NATION

Women's Participation in the American Civil War

Jacqueline Jones Royster

Good afternoon, everyone. I'd like to thank Krista for inviting me to speak with you today and to share with you the general parameters of my new project, a book project, entitled: *Women's Work during the American Civil War.*

A primary feature of the project is that, in choosing it, I exemplify a point that many of us have persistently asserted over the years about rhetorical performance: context matters, including in our own scholarly performances. The context for this project certainly matters, beginning with my need to acknowledge the physical site at which I'm now located. If I weren't actually in this place on a daily basis—at the Georgia Institute of Technology in Atlanta, Georgia, I honestly don't believe that I'd be so continuously inspired to do this work.

Atlanta as a Site for Inquiry

So, what is this particular site of inquiry? And why is it now, at this particular moment in time, so compelling?

The answer begins with a turn west from my office, going just down the street to the end of the block. On the southwest corner of Marietta Street and Northside Drive stands a historical marker. It says:

> Georgia 1776
> Surrender of Atlanta
> September 2, 1864

> Gen. Hood, in person, with Stewart's A.C. & the Georgia Militia abandoned the city, Sept. 1, as a result of Hardee's defeat at Jonesboro August 31, and marched S. to Lovejoy's Station. Federal forces at Chattahoochee River crossings since Aug. 25, suspecting the evacuation of the city on hearing loud explosions, sent forward a reconnaissance to investigate. *At this point* [meaning at this spot] it met Mayor James M. Calhoun with a committee, who tendered the surrender of the city, asking protection for

citizens & property. Col. John Coburn, Vice Maj. Gen. H.W. Slocum, com'd'g 20th A.C., received the surrender.

Georgia Historical Commission 1958 (emphasis added)

This plaque memorializes the fall of Atlanta, as a key Confederate city, on September 1, 1864, after a very bloody summer. The years 2011-2015 mark a four-year period when our nation will recognize the sesquicentennial of the Civil War and constitute, thereby, a signal opportunity to reflect on our nation's past, present, and future by using this militarily grounded and culturally rich lens. Indeed, Atlanta has been engaging in several commemorative events.

The historical markers, though, as an environmental experience, are particularly worthy of consideration, not simply as a means of enlightenment about specific information about the war but also from an open-air literacy perspective. The plaque on the corner of Marietta and Northside is just one of many across the landscape of Metropolitan Atlanta, an urban space that now encompasses twenty counties instead of the one county of Fulton during the Civil War. Markers are everywhere.

On my way to lunch, I often pass markers for the Battle of Peachtree Creek, where now stands quite an affluent North Atlanta community, or a marker for the Augustus Hurt House, where the Carter Presidential Center now resides. On my way home, depending on the route that I choose (which varies tremendously given our Atlanta traffic patterns), I see markers commemorating the Battle of Ezra Church, or the Battle of Utoy Creek, or Fort McPherson—which any well-informed Spelman alumna knows is not just commemorating its current site but also memorializes its original encampment on what is now the Spelman College campus. Or I might see the plaque at Mt. Gilead United Methodist Episcopal Church, which, according to the Southwest Atlanta Heritage Trust, is Atlanta's oldest church, used as a hospital—at different times, of course—by both Union and Confederate troops. On yet another route, I might drive by John A. White Park, where I'm always reminded by the very landscape itself, even though there is no marker, that through this park runs the longest remaining line of Confederate trenches. This line of trenches is a symbol of the past that might very well be called "the last ditch," since, before Atlanta fell, it was indeed the last trench for the Confederacy, dug out with the labor of enslaved African American men, whose slaveowners were paid $1 per day for their services—in Confederate money.

The Southwest Atlanta Heritage Trust points out that this originally sixteen-mile trench stretched from Ashby and Fair Streets, where Morehouse College is currently located, through Cascade Springs, now a densely populated African American community, to the present site of Woodward Academy, a private school in East Point. This set of trenches was so well engineered for water runoff that there has been very little erosion during the past 150 years—in fact, it remains evident that the site where the Battle of Utoy Creek began (a site that is now a golf course) was a theatre of battle in

1864. Ironically, while there are several markers for the Battle of Utoy Creek, there is no marker at the park commemorating the contribution of enslaved African American men to this rather peculiar and quite interesting Civil War monument, now embedded so comfortably within the heart of one of the largest African American communities in the city.

In Fulton County alone (the site of the city proper), the Georgia Department of Natural Resources lists 229 plaques, with the overwhelming majority of these markers linked to the places and spaces of the Atlanta Campaign or its aftermath. In Atlanta these historical markers, these commemorations of our past, are deeply embedded in our urban landscape, part of the fabric of our lives, drawing for us a rationality and a sense of place. This particular war, the American Civil War, was very much a "backyard war" that has left behind legacies of presence on a quite densely packed urban landscape. The markers identify Atlanta, like many other contemporary sites around the nation and around the globe, as a place that has actually known civil war— recognizable now in Atlanta mainly through its historic markers.

By these means and others, we have memorialized one of the bloodiest contests in American history. According to James McPherson, documented casualties include 620,000 soldiers, 320,000 from Union forces and 260,000 from the Confederacy—figures, as he reports, that indicate losses greater than all the nation's other wars combined through the Vietnam War (854). McPherson also confirms that war-related civilian losses are unknown, but conservative estimates for the Confederacy as the larger theatre of the conflict indicate as many as 50,000 casualties, thus pushing the total to at least 670,000 (619).

With its prevailing image of brother fighting against brother, the inevitable impact of this bloodiest of American wars was a trauma that resonates these 150 years later, reminding us that this history is a living story that still exists in shadow and in flesh among us. In terms of operational identity, Atlanta was a specific and now iconic scene of the conflict—the Confederate city that in the public imagination General William Tecumseh Sherman and his troops burned to the ground.

What we know, then, is that in 2012 Atlanta is not just a vibrant, multicultural international city in the United States (as we may claim it to be, and I believe rightly so), but it is also very much a city of the South. Like the Phoenix, adopted as its symbol of prosperity, Atlanta has risen from its own ashes, from a burning that was not in truth just at the hands of Sherman's bombardments but, as the marker about the surrender indicates, also at the hands of the Confederates themselves who, with the loss of the battle in Jonesboro, were destroying their arsenals and infrastructure. What we really know, then, is that the city of Atlanta has now been reborn in twenty-first-century terms, not just despite this history but indeed because of it, as recorded in the open air by the historic markers that are so thoroughly imbedded in our midst. With them, we have rather organic opportunities to link sites and stories from the past to our present. They create a remarkable account of both continuity and change in our local, regional, national, and now international narratives of who we are as a city and indeed how our local stories significantly shape our larger narratives of who we are as a nation.

On a personal level, my interests and curiosities about this bloody conflict have been ensnared, not so much by the realities of the military conflict itself as by my wanting to know about the people, about the ways and means of their lives and work during the war. I'm taken in, for example, by the knowledge of the work of enslaved men on "the last ditch," but as a dedicated feminist researcher, I also must ask: With a war known as a "brother-against-brother war," what in the world were the women doing? How were they really functioning between 1861 and 1865, and not just in terms of what we have so nobly and boldly assigned to them quite mythologically by means of such iconic texts as *Little Women* or *Gone with the Wind*—even, sometimes, when we actually know better? Basically, I am compelled to ask: Instead of our images of Scarlet O'Hara, Mammy, Melanie, Jo, Meg, Beth, Amy, and Marmee, what did women actually do? How did they participate in these nation-forming and re-forming agendas? How do we enhance the capacity of our narratives of nation to generate a more textured and vibrant understanding of history with the inclusion of a broader swath of visions, voices, and experiences, rather than glossing over or marginalizing them?

Overview

So, in recursive fashion, permit me to tell this tale of discovery about the Civil War era again, with a springboard for looking more deliberately toward women at work during war.

I begin with two points. First is the fact that the Civil War is one of the most written-about moments in American history and, second, the related point that by 1860, while literacy was not universal, reading and writing had become a general tool of the masses.

Taking the second point first, for this project a particularly useful set of resources exists because of the industrial age and the systematic deployment of specific technological and logistical infrastructures. These mechanisms included a stable, nationwide transportation system (i.e., roads and trains); a nationwide postal service; a growing sense of the importance of education; an escalating sense that the United States was becoming a literate society with increasing access to reading and writing skills across all manner of communities, including both free and enslaved African American communities; and the availability of paper and writing instruments. As James McPherson notes:

> Civil War armies were the most literate in history to that time. More than 90 percent of the white Union soldiers and more than 80 percent of Confederate soldiers could read and write. Many of these three million soldiers were away from home for the first time during their military service. With strong ties to family and community, they stayed in touch by writing home and receiving letters in return—hundreds of millions of let-

ters during the four years of the war. . . . They are the best source for understanding the real war as experienced by the men who fought it. (Foreword xi)

As a historian, McPherson recognized the importance of literacy as a nineteenth-century asset, a factor that those of us in rhetoric, composition, and literacy also recognize—as demonstrated, for example, by Shirley Logan, Harvey Graff, and others (including myself). In these fields, we have established that literacy knowledge and practice were indeed a many-splendored thing. In this project, however, I want to go a step further to declare the fact that, given the availability of enabling technologies, material resources, and a broad range of reading/writing individuals, across race, class, and gender, we now have a legacy that in the United States had not existed before the Civil War. This legacy consists of not just letters but also journals, diaries, memoirs, and other writings, with men and women alike, both ordinary and extraordinary, making it their business to write their own stories and share their own points of view.

On the first point, then, the various written accounts of the Civil War from multiple points of view are a particularly useful asset. Generally, with the war being so "up close and personal" for so many, it has persistently captured the interest and imagination of an astounding number of people. In terms of scholars across several disciplines (including feminist scholars), we have documented and interpreted events, conditions, and circumstances; analyzed the tools and technologies that emerged as the instruments of war and ongoing national infrastructure; made visible the iconic places and spaces of the era; and interrogated the actions and achievements of various (albeit mostly male) individuals and groups. For non-academics, the story of inscription has been the same, with public and family historians, as well as creative writers and filmmakers (both popular and documentary) all representing this era multi-modally in narrative and image.

From a Google search, for example, the yield of available resources for "American Civil War" was 265,000,000 (18 May 2012); from Amazon books for the same term, the yield was 64,125 results, averaging in raw terms about 427 books per year for 150 years, a data point that is mind-boggling even when you take into account the inevitability of double counting. Notable, also, among the 64,000-plus books is a listing of 5,271 results on women in the civil war. These are sobering numbers, even if we modestly adjust the 427 books per year for 150 years to just one hundred (not counting, of course, an excruciatingly long list of articles and publications in other forms and genres). In other words, the base of available information, including information on women, academically accredited and otherwise, is substantial, filled with narratives, images, and analyses of a world at war, including the human dimensions of glory, trauma, tragedy, heroism, leadership, ingenuity, technological innovation, betrayal, endurance, and so forth. The abundance of information pulls into the sphere of popular understanding a sense of the individuals and groups who often acted with distinction and uncommon valor in geographical locations that we can still identify, that we still occupy.

Even when we assume this particular gaze, however, the apocryphal view has been that the white men of the nation—elite and poor—were at war and white women were keeping the home fires burning, both North and South. Further, quite interestingly, the default view of African Americans has been that both men and women were generally enslaved in the South. With precious few exceptions, African Americans are overwhelmingly represented in these diverse discourses as rather passive (and with considerable loyalty to former slave-owning families) at their plantation homes, struggling alongside their plantation mistresses to hold everything together. If not still working on the plantation, they were dislocated and on the move, roaming the cities and countryside or tagging along behind Union troops. In either case, however, whether on the plantation or on the move, they have been positioned mainly as pawns or instruments in a larger tale rather than as deliberately and actively involved in a national agenda.

The sesquicentennial, however, provides us with a unique opportunity to reconsider these easily defaulted images that continue to abound, despite a growing oeuvre of scholarship to the contrary. With this occasion, we have the opportunity to use the mound of now well-documented information to recast stories of involvement, active engagement, leadership, and impact. Toward this end, in my project I am focusing on the contributions of women (Union and Confederate, white, of several ethnicities—and African American, free and freed, the elite and non-elite), investigating explicitly what the actual lives, conditions, and work of women were like during the Civil War.

My intention is to use the auto-ethnographic texts of women to bring visibility and audibility to women's experiences in their own words, not simply as women at home but specifically as women at war, and to situate their voices within the larger sociopolitical context of "war work." Their diaries, letters, memoirs, autobiographies, and novels help to open new windows on specific, individual lives and experiences, as we use their words to reconsider our sense of history, to redefine our assumptions, and with these better-textured experiences to expand our sense of a far more complex world than we might have originally expected.

I would prefer to end today by sharing the words of several women who took advantage of the technologies and the opportunities that were available to them to write their own stories and to leave behind legacies of their thoughts and experiences. Unfortunately, I only have time to share very short excerpts from just one, the memoir of Sarah Emma Edmonds, a Canadian-born woman who in 1861 was already living and working in the United States, her adopted home, as a man. On May 25, 1861, in Detroit, Michigan, as Frank Thompson, Edmonds volunteered her services to the 2nd Michigan Infantry Regiment, where she served as a male nurse, a soldier, and a spy. "Frank" soon proved herself as a capable nurse and a valiant soldier. In a section discussed below she recounts the story of the process by which she became a spy, explaining her nomination and interview process for the job and the strategies that she used to prepare herself for this dangerous enterprise once she was selected. She says, "I had three days in which to prepare for my debut into rebeldom, and I commenced at once to remodel, transform and metamorphose for the occasion" (57).

What is striking about her strategies for transformation is that she chose to present herself in the disguise of what she referred to as a "real plantation style" African. She chronicles the steps of her transformation, highlighting her choice of "contraband" clothes and the fact that she shaved her head and managed to obtain a "wig of real Negro wool." In addition, she demonstrated how she shifted her dialect to reflect what she felt to be the language pattern of an uneducated ex-slave. Focusing on the moment after her transformation to her new disguise when she reenters her camp near Yorktown, Edmonds says:

> On my return, I found myself without friends—a striking illustration of the frailty of human friendship—I had been forgotten in those three short days. I went to Mrs. B's [who, with her husband, had been Edmonds's sponsor] tent and inquired if she wanted to hire a boy to take care of her horse. She was very civil to me, asked if I came from Fortress Monroe, and whether I could cook. She did not want to hire me, but she thought she could find someone who did require a boy. (57)

Edmonds's disguise worked, with the scene marking her second successful identity transformation. In this case, she had set aside her identity as a well-respected Union soldier to become a black male servant, an ex-slave, unrecognizable by her former friends. She slipped into her new role innovatively and creatively and went forward to do her job, again quite successfully, as a spy. Note that Edmonds's first transformation was from white woman to white man. In just three days, she further transformed herself from white cross-dressing/cross-performing woman to a male African American "contraband." Her account suggests, among many things, that her test of her Union comrades before entering her spy role among the Confederates, helped her to understand how seamlessly we can sometimes trigger the expectations of those whom we meet (and even know) when we evidence the symbols of those expectations. Obviously, there is so much more that could be said about gender, race, and the performance of identity as suggested by just this short excerpt, but I will stop with this basic highlighting and raise two last questions.

Conclusion

First, whose narratives are these? My response is that they are our narratives, the stories of a multi-variant nation, made so by race, gender, class, culture, ideology, and so many other factors. Second, why do these narratives matter in our master narratives of nation? From my perspective, they matter in a basic way. A nation is its human collective, and we won't really know our nation or its potential well enough until we acknowledge and act on the need to find better ways to account for all of our people—more fully rendered and more fully understood. We are advised, therefore, by the history that we do know, to pay attention to the many ways that all manner of people, regardless of race, gender, creed, or color, have been called upon to live and work, and in the case of the American Civil War to fight patriotically for both nations, the Union and the Confederacy. Most of all, at the end of the day, with the nations reunited since the war—back together again for 150 years as the United States of America, we are particularly obligated to use our knowledge and knowledge-generating skills to better effect. A basic challenge is to recognize continuity and change in terms of both the historical and contemporary fractures and fault lines of the nation and to acknowledge the people who occupy the land in time and space, whether we are looking at then or now—regardless of their race, gender, creed, or color. At this point of anniversary, the sesquicentennial offers a signal opportunity: to take a more critical view of the ways in which a fuller range of participants than we have heretofore accredited have been engaged in this transformative national moment, to use the knowledge generated to enrich our visions of who and how we are as a nation, and to fashion and implement strategic solutions to address our ongoing problems and issues. My view is that with such a good opportunity for reflection and action, we would be wise to take it.

WORKS CITED

Boyd, Belle. *Belle Boyd in Camp and Prison*. Baton Rouge: Louisiana State UP, 1998. Print.

Burgess, Lauren Cook, ed. *An Uncommon Soldier: The Civil War Letters of Sarah Rosetta Wakeman, alias Pvt. Lyons Wakeman, 153rd Regiment, New York State Volunteers, 1862–1864*. New York: Oxford UP, 1994. Print.

Edmonds, Sarah Emma. *Memoirs of a Soldier, Nurse, and Spy: A Woman's Adventures in the Union Army*. Dekalb: Northern Illinois UP, 1999. Print.

Georgia Historical Markers. *GeorgiaPlanning.com*. Georgia Department of Community Affairs, n.d. Web. May 2012.

Graff, Harvey J. *The Literacy Myth*. New Brunswick: Transaction P, 1991. Print.

Logan, Shirley Wilson. *Liberating Language: Sites of Rhetorical Education in Nineteenth-Century Black America*. Carbondale: Southern Illinois UP, 2008. Print.

McPherson, James. *Battle Cry of Freedom: The Civil War Era*. New York: Oxford UP, 1988. Print.

---. Foreword. *An Uncommon Soldier: The Civil War Letters of Sarah Rosetta Wakeman, alias Pvt. Lyons Wakeman, 153rd Regiment, New York State Volunteers, 1862–1864*. By Sarah Rosetta Wakeman. Ed. Lauren Cook Burgess. New York: Oxford UP, 1994. xi-xiv. Print.

Royster, Jacqueline Jones. *Traces of a Stream: Literacy and Social Change among African American Women*. Pittsburgh: U Pittsburgh P, 2000. Print.

"Southwest Atlanta Heritage Week: Historic Sites Tour." Southwest Atlanta Heritage Trust, Inc., n.d. Print

2

ABRAHAM LINCOLN
IN PHILADELPHIA

Defining and Deriving National Identity

David Zarefsky

Philadelphia symbolizes the nation's founding. The meeting place of the First and Second Continental Congresses and the Constitutional Convention, the site of the First and Second Bank of the United States, and of both the Declaration of Independence and the Constitution, it is the physical embodiment of the "imagined community" (Anderson) that is the American people. To participate in recollections of these events and to stand in these historic spaces is to reconstitute the American community by connecting those present at the moment with the founders and the generations in between. Those not alive at the time of the founding vicariously recreate it through participating in rituals of renewal here in Philadelphia.

Something of these feelings must have impelled Abraham Lincoln as he came to Philadelphia in late February, 1861, on his way to his first inauguration in Washington. This was the penultimate scheduled stop on a trip that began when the president-elect left Springfield, Illinois on February 11. In an era in which presidential candidates normally did not campaign and in which relatively few people could have seen them if they did, the primary purpose of Lincoln's trip was to allow him to see and be seen. It was not his plan to make formal addresses or policy pronouncements, only to exchange greetings and welcomes. He took a circuitous route in order to maximize his exposure to citizens of the North. In all, he traveled on eighteen different railroad lines, covered 1,900 miles, and delivered 101 speeches, on one occasion as many as thirteen speeches in one day (Holzer 389). These were not prepared addresses but largely extemporaneous remarks. Lincoln vacillated between offering hints of future policies in the guise of trial balloons and suppressing any comments about his plans until after his inauguration on March 4. In Indianapolis, he had raised the specter of rigorous enforcement of the law against South Carolina while denying that such measures would constitute coercion. Then in Columbus he proclaimed that nothing was going wrong and that the secession crisis was artificial, a view that was meant to calm the citizenry but that had the opposite effect.

By the time he spoke in Trenton to the New Jersey state legislature on February 21, Lincoln was invoking transcendent themes. Noting that he had not carried the state in the prior year's election, he appealed for support on the basis of their "devotion to the Union, the Constitution, and the liberties of the people" (Basler 236) and thereby sought to identify with people who actually were opposed to his policies.

Lincoln traveled from Trenton to Philadelphia on February 21. He received an enthusiastic welcome from 100,000 people and was lauded by Mayor Alexander Henry (White 54). In his response, Lincoln attributed this reception "not to me, the man, the individual, but to the man who temporarily represents, or should represent, the majority of the nation" (Basler 238). He promised to bring to his work "a serious heart" and ended by identifying his own political ideology with "the teachings coming forth from that sacred hall" (Basler 239) where the Declaration of Independence was issued, a theme to which he would return the next day.

The occasion for Lincoln's remarks on February 22 was ceremonial—the raising of a new 34-star flag outside Independence Hall. It was a joyous occasion, attracting a crowd of 10,000 and packing Chestnut Street from Sixth Street all the way down to Fifth (Holzer 387). Lincoln had expected to hoist the flag but not to make any remarks. He discovered, however, that a group of dignitaries had assembled inside the hall expecting him to speak. Lincoln did not disappoint. Then he also spoke very briefly outdoors before raising the flag.

The occasion called for epideictic, a genre of ceremonial address that strengthens community by making manifest and celebrating the ties binding speaker, audience, history, and place. Yet, as Chaim Perelman and Lucie Olbrechts-Tyteca remind us, epideictic is not purely ceremonial. In the choice of which bonds to strengthen and which to leave dormant, the choice of how to achieve presence (by which they mean something like salience), epideictic discourse advances argument (Perelman and Olbrechts-Tyteca 47-51). In Lincoln's case, it was an argument about what America's national identity was and from where it came.

It is worth noting briefly what Lincoln does not say in either the indoor or the outdoor speech. To begin with, the flag honored the admission of the 34th state to the union. That was Kansas—Bleeding Kansas of just a few years before, which had reignited sectional controversy by the prospect that it might come into the Union as a slave state. It was this prospect, in fact, that had brought Lincoln back into politics when the Kansas-Nebraska Act was passed in 1854. After having rejected admission in 1858 under the proslavery Lecompton constitution, Kansas remained a territory for another two and a half years. It was admitted as a free state in January of 1861 only because Southern Senators and Representatives, having resigned from Congress after their states seceded, gave up their chance to vote against the new state and reduced the number of free-state votes needed for a majority. The shifting status of Kansas must have been personally very meaningful for Lincoln. It could be taken as a sign of the country's future, as a commitment that slavery would not prevail—if it could not spread to Kansas, it probably could not spread anywhere. This would vindicate the 1860 Republican platform and augur well for Lincoln's political success. But he does not mention it!

In the indoor speech, Lincoln does not refer to the flag-raising at all, and outdoors he does not mention Kansas though he celebrates the steady growth in the flag from thirteen stars to thirty-four. He expressed the hope that the new star would remain (which it might not if unreconstructed Southerners returned to Congress and repealed the statehood act) and that "additional ones shall from time to time be placed there, until we shall number . . . five hundred millions of happy and prosperous people" (Basler 241-42). But this promise was contingent, dependent on "cultivating the spirit that animated our fathers, who gave renown and celebrity to this Hall, cherishing that fraternal feeling which has so long characterized us as a nation, excluding passion, ill-temper, and precipitate action on all occasions" (Basler 241). This was, to say the least, a selective reading of history. But mentioning Kansas would have been disruptive and divisive, calling to mind sectionalism and war. In contrast, mentioning national growth highlighted permanence, obscured the fact of secession (which at least theoretically *removed* stars from the flag), made permanence dependent on fidelity to the founders, located the founders in the place, and stipulated those attributes of the founders that were to be emulated. He did not need to mention that these attributes were incompatible with secession; this argument was made by implication.

Another omission is curious. The ceremony was held on February 22, George Washington's birthday. Washington was a national hero; the preceding decades had been years in which he was universally admired, and Lincoln himself had paid tribute to him (though noting, when he left Springfield, that he faced a task greater than that which had devolved upon Washington). Surely Lincoln would be helped by associating himself with Washington on this historic day. Yet Washington is not mentioned once, in either the indoor or the outdoor speech. Why not?

The answer may be suggested by Lincoln's references to Independence Hall, which he was seeing for the first time. Washington had been there for the Constitutional Convention; he was its presiding officer. But he had not been at the Second Continental Congress, which issued the Declaration of Independence—at that time he was commanding armies in the field. His mention on this occasion might have brought to mind the Constitution rather than the Declaration, whereas Lincoln's focus was on the latter. While the Constitution sanctioned slavery and made compromises with it, though carefully avoiding the term, the Declaration embodied the ideal that "all men are created equal." Lincoln clearly sought to tie the Declaration, not the Constitution, to Independence Hall and explicitly mentioning Washington might have interfered with that linkage.

These two omissions help to make clear what Lincoln was trying to do in his brief remarks: to derive American national identity from Independence

Hall and to define that identity through commitment to the ideals embodied in the Declaration of Independence. He challenges his listeners to commit to and to carry out these principles, and he offers the promise of a happy and prosperous future if they do. Without announcing specific policies—a task he explicitly deferred until the Inaugural Address—he made clear that he would not condone secession under any circumstances, certainly not for the purpose of violating the ideals of the Declaration. He could make his purpose clear without needing to say, as he had at Trenton, that "it may be necessary to put the foot down firmly" (Basler 237).

I want now to consider each speech individually. The indoor speech consists of four brief paragraphs, the first longer than the other three combined. In the long first paragraph, Lincoln acknowledges that his host, the president of the Philadelphia Board of Selectmen, had placed in his hands the task of restoring peace. In response, the president-elect mentioned that all of his political sentiments drew from sentiments "which originated, and were given to the world from this hall in which we stand" (Basler 241). The following sentence makes clear that he is referring to the Declaration. He never mentions that the Constitution, which sanctioned slavery, *also* originated in "this hall in which we stand."

Lincoln ruminates on the many hardships endured by the founders and considers what might have justified and sustained them in their trials and kept their work alive. Advancing an argument from proportionality, he surmises that such lasting fame could not have been achieved by "the mere matter of the separation of the colonies from the mother land" (Basler 240). This is a none-too-subtle reply to Stephen Douglas and others who had maintained that the Declaration did nothing more than separate the colonies from England. To Lincoln, the limited purpose claimed for the Declaration by this argument was disproportionately small for its extensive and long-lasting achievement. There must be something more, something beneath the surface animating the text and giving it a dynamic character, offering "hope to the world for all future time" (Basler 240). He unmoors the text from both its chronological and its geographical origins, and he finds in it the promise of eventual equality for all, the promise that "in due time the weights should be lifted from the shoulders of all men, and that *all* should have an equal chance" (Basler 240). In short, Lincoln has enlarged the Declaration from a situationally specific acknowledgment to a universal promise, from a text oriented toward the moment to the announcement of a timeless goal, from a political statement to a moral credo, from a pledge to the American people to a pledge to all people in the world. "That is the sentiment," Lincoln concluded, "embodied in that Declaration of Independence." He invites his audience to view the Declaration from a new perspective, yet he claims that his perspective comes from Independence Hall.

In the second paragraph, Lincoln asks a rhetorical question: whether the Union can be saved on the basis of the Declaration's principle. He elliptically raises the question of whether the country has moved so far from the Declaration that it has become merely a historical relic. Do its words and sentiment still animate American society? He does not answer the question but says (1) that he will be a very happy man if the answer to his question is yes, and (2) that if the country cannot be saved on the basis of the Declaration, the results would be "truly awful" because, as he implies, the country ultimately will not survive on any other basis.

But then Lincoln adds a step that has kept the psycho-historians busy: if the country cannot be saved by the ideals of the Declaration, he does not want to witness its demise. So he says, "I was about to say I would rather be assassinated on this spot" than yield the attempt to realize the Declaration's promise. It is not likely that this line is a foreboding of his assassination four years later. But it is very likely that he had on his mind the report he had received the previous night, that there would be an attempt on his life when he changed trains in Baltimore for the final leg of his journey to Washington. In the end this came to naught because Lincoln secretly changed his schedule and, some said, his clothing. When he said that he rather would die "on this spot," he not only emphasized the immediacy of the act—that he would be willing to die here and now—but also, of course, the reference to "this spot" refers literally to the inside of Independence Hall. This is a sacred space because of its association with the sentiments of the Declaration. Standing in that space, he is imbued with a sense of holiness and purpose. When he leaves that spot, he will need the Declaration's ideals to guide him and offer him the chance of success. Without them, it may be too big a risk.

Yet in these lines, Lincoln reveals his characteristic tentativeness and careful word choice. He did not say that he would rather be assassinated, but he reveals that he was "about to say" this. He distances himself from the full acceptance of this choice and yet, by raising the possibility, he gives it credence. In this paragraph, Lincoln reveals indirectly how strongly he feels about the need for a continuing connection between the country and the Declaration.

Saving the Union on the basis of the Declaration's ideals, some thought, would require a war. Lincoln devotes the short third paragraph of this speech to reassuring his listeners that this is not the case. He wisely eschewed the strong statement he had made in Cleveland that the crisis was artificial, but he does say, "[T]here is no need of bloodshed and war. There is no necessity for it" (Basler 240). One need not choose between dissolution of the Union, on one hand, and civil war, on the other. To give emphasis to his convictions, he committed himself not to strike first. Anticipating his Inaugural Address, he said, "[T]here will be no blood shed unless it be forced upon the Government. The Government will not use force unless force is used against it" (Basler 241). Neither those who would punish the errant Southerners, nor the Southerners themselves, need resort to war. All that is needed, Lincoln implies, is a common focus on the ideals of the Declaration. For its part, the Government will not initiate the use of force. In the Inaugural Address, Lincoln used the verb "assail" and probably realized that he could drop the "unless" clause because it was implicit in the statement, "the Government will not assail *you*." If disaffected Southerners turned their backs on the Declaration and persisted in their efforts to secede, a response by the national government hardly would count as assault; if anything, it would be an exercise in self-defense. As a result, in the Inaugural Address Lincoln could make the starker, more all-encompassing pledge, "the government will not assail *you*."

The final paragraph is in the nature of a brief apology for anything Lincoln might have misspoken, since he had not come with the intention of making a speech and had offered extemporaneous remarks. He feared that he might say something indiscreet, and for any mistake he might make he sought absolution. And yet he reassured listeners that he was speaking sincerely. So much did he believe his statements, he said, that he was willing to live by them or, if necessary, to die by them—another reference to his mortality. He used his own *ethos* to vouch for his convictions.

In short, this speech is the vehicle by which Lincoln derives and defines his sense of national identity, his justification for the course of action he would announce in Washington the next month. After his months-long silence, Lincoln only in Philadelphia began to reveal what, in fact, he was going to do.

The one-paragraph outdoor speech is not as interesting because there really is only one topic: national growth. Lincoln uses the flag as a synecdoche for the country. Its growth from thirteen to thirty-four stars "has given additional prosperity and happiness to this country until it has advanced to its present condition" (Basler 241). Interestingly, as a Whig Lincoln had favored the economic development of the existing states over the addition of new states, but here he associates expansion with increased prosperity and happiness. But he is not merely celebrating the path we already have traveled; the admission of Kansas is not the national apotheosis. Rather, this happy occasion is a milestone on a longer path, one that might continue "until we shall number . . . five hundred millions of happy and prosperous people" (Basler 242). But continued progress on the path is not inevitable. The future welfare of the country is placed in the hands of Lincoln's listeners; their actions will decide what happens. Here too Lincoln offers a contingent, not an absolute, promise.

The two speeches are mutually reinforcing. The indoor speech views the Declaration as transcending its historical moment, serving both to justify independence (the short-term goal) and to inspire future generations. The core idea of the Declaration is not the momentary speech-act of declaring independence but rather the establishment of equality as a goal constantly to be striven for even though not fully achieved. And the outdoor speech takes the act of adding a star to the flag, not just as cause for celebration now but also as inducement to further progress. Each speech transforms a moment into a force, yet in neither case does the force act of its own power. The nation's future is dependent on human agency, on decisions by his audiences to move these transitions along through their own right conduct.

Understood in this way, these two unremarkable speeches, on the surface altogether quotidian, do important work for Lincoln as he begins to reveal his approach to the secession crisis: to preserve the union yet also to constitute union by recommitment to the ideals of the Declaration of Independence. So, to allude to our conference theme, do these speeches frame or reframe national identity? Clearly, some of both. Lincoln is laying the foundation for a new identity in which the nation trumps the states, symbolized by the emergence after the war of "United States" as a singular rather than a plural noun. But to do so, he reframes the common understanding of older terms and events. There is no record that the framers of the Declaration understood what they were doing as making a promise for all future generations, the motive that Lincoln retrospectively attributes to them. If they had such an expansive vision of their goals, they left no evidence of it. It was Lincoln who reframed the historical moment to respond to the needs of his own moment. Moreover, although Lincoln preferred to see the addition of stars to the flag as evidence of happiness and prosperity, there is no evidence that the Declaration's signers saw it that way. In fact, the Declaration—unlike the Constitution—says nothing about national growth. These are cases of reframing on Lincoln's part in order to craft a vision of government that has historical resonance while also speaking to the exigence of the moment. Perhaps at least as much as in his formal speeches, quotidian discourses like these reveal the process of framing and reframing identifications. The work Lincoln did in Philadelphia is thus far more important than it might at first appear.

WORKS CITED

Anderson, Benedict. *Imagined Communities: Reflections on the Origin and Spread of Nationalism*. Rev. ed. London and New York: Verso, 2006. Print.

Basler, Roy P., ed. *The Collected Works of Abraham Lincoln*. Vol. 4. New Brunswick: Rutgers UP, 1953. Print.

Holzer, Harold. *Lincoln President Elect: Abraham Lincoln and the Great Secession Winter, 1860–1861*. New York: Simon and Schuster, 2008. Print.

Perelman, Chaim, and Lucie Olbrechts-Tyteca. *The New Rhetoric: A Treatise on Argumentation*. Trans. John Wilkinson and Purcell Weaver. Notre Dame: U of Notre Dame P, 1969. Print.

White, Ronald C., Jr. *The Eloquent President: A Portrait of Lincoln through His Words*. New York: Random House, 2005. Print.

3

"UNDER GOD"

An Epideictic Weapon in the Fight against Communism

M. Elizabeth Thorpe

On June 14, 1954, President Eisenhower signed a bill that added the phrase "under God" in the middle of the Pledge of Allegiance. Americans all over the nation knew and could recite the pledge without thinking, and yet the change was almost completely without controversy. In fact, Rep. Charles G. Oakman (MI) commented that in his "experience as a public servant and as a Member of Congress" he had never seen a bill "which was so noncontroversial in nature or so inspiring in purpose" (*Cong. Rec. HR* 7989).

Sen. Homer Ferguson (MI) explained the reason that he felt this change was so necessary and agreeable:

> We now live in a world divided by two ideologies, one of which affirms its belief in God, while the other does not. One part of the world believed in the unalienable rights of the people under the Creator. The other part of the world believes in materialism and that the source of all power is the state itself. (*Cong. Rec. S* 6348)

Ferguson, Oakman, and other lawmakers seemed to believe that there was some sort of crisis of identity on a worldwide scale. They believed that the world as they knew it was aligning itself in one of two ways and that their opposition, communism, was not just *the other* but a genuine threat to their way of life.

Rep. Jack Brooks of Los Angeles believed that free nations were battling "for their very existence." Brooks argued that "[i]n adding this one phrase to our pledge of allegiance to our flag we in effect declare openly that we denounce the pagan doctrine of communism" (*Cong. Rec. HR* 7758). Brooks's concern, it appears, had more to do with condemning communists than with a relationship with the Almighty. He and his colleagues were terrified of what they saw as dangerous ideologies encroaching on their lives, so they set out to try to make as distinct a separation between America and her enemies as possible.

This paper is an exploration of the arguments for adding the words "under God" into the Pledge of Allegiance and an analysis of the pledge post-addition. In public discourse, those words are often contextualized in a church-state conversation, but Congressional records indicate that the motivation for adding God to the pledge to the flag had less to do with our spiritual atonement and more to do with the Cold War and our enemy, the Soviet Union. Certainly, one cannot leave religion out of the conversation, but to think of the words "under God" as just a religious statement is a gross simplification of the power and purpose of the phrase. Lawmakers recognized that the Pledge of Allegiance provided a unique opportunity to reaffirm on a regular basis that America was very distinctly *not* communist. Adding "under God," they posited, cemented that contrast because our enemies were avowed atheists. I argue that, based on the arguments proposed by members of Congress, the addition of the words "under God" was an attempt to utilize the unique powers of epideictic rhetoric, using the Pledge of Allegiance as a divider between America and Soviet Russia. I will provide a brief history of the Pledge of Allegiance, a synopsis of the arguments provided by Congress for the addition of the words, a description of its importance as a specifically epideictic piece of rhetoric, and an analysis of the importance of the words "under God" themselves.

The pledge, written in the 1860s, had been a mainstay of school mornings and opening ceremonies of various lodges and clubs throughout the country for decades, but in that time, the political context in which it operated had changed. The pledge was as much a by-product of the Civil War as anything else, hence the emphasis on a unified Republic. If one posits that the Pledge of Allegiance was a rhetorical product of a particular context, then we may hypothesize that a change to the recitation itself is a response to a change in context, and the repetition of epideictic rhetoric, such as the Pledge of Allegiance, serves an important function: to display, praise, and affirm as truth certain communal values. The rhetorical situation that came after the Civil War required a particular response, so as America changed, the pledge did also.[1] Lawmakers chose very specific words and added them very carefully to what was already an acceptable definition of American identity. Discerning the importance of those words and how they were used tells us a good deal about the political turmoil of the Cold War and the powerful tools that words are in and of themselves.

Literature

Most of the available literature on the Pledge of Allegiance comes at the topic from perspectives very different than my own. The field that has given a good bit of attention to the Pledge of Allegiance is the education field. Books dealing either with how teachers can practically deal with classroom controversies or how they theoretically shape our understanding of education are myriad. For example, Joel Westheimer's *Pledging Allegiance: the Politics of Patriotism in America's Schools* covers a number of controversies dealing with the pledge but confines the discussion to the fields of education and politics. More pertinent to this study are the works of Anthony Hatcher's "Adding God: Religious and Secular Press Framing in Response to the Insertion of 'Under God' in the Pledge of Allegiance" in the *Journal of Media and Religion* and Ronald Bishop's "That is Good to Think of These Days: The Campaign by Hearst Newspapers to Promote Addition of 'Under God' to the Pledge of Allegiance" in *American Journalism.* Both approach the issue from a media or media ethics standpoint. They analyze the ways in which the Knights of Columbus and the Hearst newspapers framed their arguments to add "under God" to the pledge. Both found that the idea originated with the Knights but was championed by Hearst. Bishop finds that the campaign had much less to do with religion than it did with patriotism in the face of the communist threat, as well. Their histories of the controversy point to a much more politically oriented statement than a theological one in "under God."[2]

Richard J. Ellis's history of the Pledge of Allegiance *To the Flag: An Unlikely History of the Pledge of Allegiance* is an indispensable aid to a study of the pledge because of its thorough history.[3] Ellis's book is an engaging narrative of the evolution of the pledge and the characters that shaped it. Ellis is quick to point out that it is unlikely that Frances Bellamy left religion out of the pledge for any notable purpose other than he just didn't think it necessary to include. Bellamy was, after all, a member of the clergy and very adamant that America had a special relationship with God.[4] Still, the fact remains that God was not a part of the original pledge and that the germinal text focused on the indivisibility of the nation.[5]

However, none of these works approaches the pledge as a piece of rhetoric, and this analysis focuses on the pledge itself as a rhetorical weapon specific to its historical context. The bulk of the research comes from historical, primary sources. The literature about the pledge is ultimately not as useful as records from Congress detailing the process that actually got "under God" added to the pledge, so that is the starting point for my analysis. The real story, I believe, is the one that lawmakers themselves argued in the Capitol.

Changing the Pledge of Allegiance

In 1892, Frances Bellamy wrote the Pledge of Allegiance, but the phrase "under God" did not appear in the pledge until sixty-two years later.[6] His original pledge was "I pledge allegiance to my flag and to the Republic for which it stands—One Nation indivisible—with liberty and justice for all" (Ellis 1). The movement to add "under God" actually began with a resolution by the Knights of Columbus in April of 1951, when they began adding "under God" to the pledge they recited at the beginning of each meeting. In 1952, they called for Congress to follow suit, but lawmakers did not champion the cause until 1953 when, on April 20, Rep. Louis Rabaut (MI) introduced the idea to Congress (Ellis 131-35).

Then on February 7, 1954, President Eisenhower heard a sermon by George Macpherson Docherty. Docherty warned that the Pledge of Allegiance was not truly American and could be mistaken for a pledge to any flag, even a Soviet one. Docherty claimed that adding the phrase "under God" would be an affirmation of the American way of life. Docherty argued that since atheism was at the heart of communism, proclaiming that America was united "under God" would make it abundantly clear that the pledge was an American one and that it could not be mistaken for a "Muscovite" oath. Eisenhower felt Docherty had a particularly good point and threw his support behind an already very popular piece of legislation. Docherty, the man who convinced Eisenhower that "under God" was a necessary addition to the pledge, may have been a preacher, but his argument for the addition came from a very political starting point. He was, indeed, eager to associate God and America but for the purposes of separating America from her communist enemies (Ellis 131-35).

Rep. Frank Addonizio described the importance of the pledge as a declaration of a very specific version of American: "[W]e who take the pledge of allegiance to the flag . . . should bear in mind that our citizenship is of no real value to us unless our hearts speak in accord with our lips; and unless we can open our soul before God and before Him conscientiously say, 'I am an American'" (*Cong. Rec. HR* 7765). To Addonizio, the pledge was not just a simple recitation, but an oath to something greater than himself—his country. The pledge was a public proclamation that the speaker was an American and a proud bearer of the qualities that "American" entailed.

That being said, while Americans and their elected leaders were anxious to solidify their nation "under God," they were not so eager to specify exactly what kind of God defined America. For example, Sen. Ralph Flanders tried to take things to the extreme and proposed an amendment that would proclaim that "[t]his nation devoutly recognizes the authority and law of Jesus Christ, Savior and Ruler of nations, through who are bestowed the blessings of the Almighty God," but the proposal never got out of committee (qtd. in Ellis 126). In fact, when the proposal was presented only one other person even showed up to listen (Ellis 126). Flanders's failed effort, which took place around the same time as the efforts to include "under God" in the pledge, indicates something significant about the understanding of "God" and his importance to being American: it was God that was important to lawmakers, not Christianity. A more generic God was easier to use as a kind of rhetorical unifier, whereas a specifically Christian God or a proclamation that Christ was what defined "America" made our national identity too narrow.

Still, American lawmakers worried that Rev. Docherty's concerns might be well founded, and so they found a convenient and concise way to contend with the problem. Simply adding the words "under God" satisfied Congress's concerns that the pledge could have been mistaken for a Russian oath, and so they argued for this addition in order to appropriately Americanize the pledge. Rep. Rabaut felt that if Congress made

> the addition of the phrase "under God" to the pledge of allegiance the consciousness of the American people will be more alerted to the true meaning of our country and its form of government. In this full awareness we will, I believe, be strengthened for the conflict now facing us and more determined to preserve our precious heritage. ("The Pledge of Allegiance to the Flag," *Cong. Rec. HR* 15828)

He believed that adding the phrase was not just a symbolic measure but would actively and continually remind people of the "true meaning" of their own nation—somehow God would remind people of a democratic republic.

On four different occasions, congressmen referred to the words of George M. Docherty concerning the pledge. Only two of these cite Dr. Docherty, but they all questioned the "American-ness" of the pledge:

> Has it ever occurred to you that the former wording of the pledge could serve any republic claiming to be indivisible and to insure liberty and justice for all? Remember, when you heard your own children recite the pledge of allegiance that these same words could have come from little Muscovite children standing before the Red hammer-and-sickle flag of Soviet Russia. You know and I know that the Union of Soviet Socialist Republics would not, and could not, while supporting the philosophy of communism, place in its patriotic ritual an acknowledgement that their nation existed under God. Indeed, the one fundamental issue which is the unbridgeable gap between America and Communist Russian is belief in Almighty God. (Rabaut, "The Pledge" *Cong. Rec.* 15829)[7]

Algier L. Goodwin of Massachusetts reaffirmed this statement in his commentary "'Under God' Would Help Combat Pagan Influences." Goodwin hailed a local writer, Shirley Munroe Mullen, for her history of the pledge and her support for this bill. Most importantly to both Mullen and Goodwin, this bill was so important because "pagan philosophies" had been "introduced by the Soviet Union," and therefore it was "a necessity for reaffirming belief in God" (Goodwin, *Cong. Rec. Appendix* A4067). The addition to the pledge could not be separated from the threat of communism—it was the heart of the issue. The pledge, with the addition, made an argument for the identity of America. If she were god-fearing, then she could not be communist. It was imperative to lawmakers that the pledge aid in their efforts to carefully separate Americans from communists.

John R. Pillion of the House of Representatives argued that the addition to the pledge "would serve to deny the atheistic and materialistic corruption of Communism. It would condemn the absolute and concentrated power of the communistic slave state with its attendant subservience of the individual" (*Cong. Rec. HR* 7590-91). Whatever the connection between individuality and God was, Pillion did not attempt to explain it. But part of the Cold War narrative was that in America we could be individuals, while in Russia the communist regime stripped its citizens of their individual personhood, so here was another way God delineated us from our enemies.[8] For reasons Pillion saw as clear, "under God" effectively separated Americans from communists because being united under God actually affirmed our individuality.[9]

Rep. Brooks of Louisiana went so far as to claim this was the primary thing that separated the two dueling philosophies. The phrase "under God" would publicly proclaim America's separation from the East. The pledge would be a specifically Western, American pledge with the addition of the phrase "under God":

> Free nations today battle for their very existence in many parts of the world. Communism with its siren voice of false appeal is heard round the world and many peoples and many nations fall prey to these false headlights of the shores of time. One thing separates free peoples of the Western World from the rabid Communist, and this one thing is a belief in God. In adding this one phrase to our pledge of allegiance to our flag, we in effect declare openly that we denounce the pagan doctrine of communism and declare "under God" in favor of free government and a free world. ("Amending the Pledge." *Cong. Rec. HR* 7757-66)

But it was Sen. William Langer, the Chairman of the Judiciary Committee, who made the argument most explicitly. Langer explained that "there was something missing in the pledge, and that which was missing was the characteristic and definitive factor in the American way of life" ("Pledge of Allegiance to the Flag—Report of a Committee," *Cong. Rec. S* 6231). The American way of life was at stake, hence the need to unify Americans in their opposition to communism. "Under God" would be the ultimate sign that the Pledge of Allegiance was a pledge to an American flag and could never be mistaken as a pledge by America's communist enemies. Langer's comments cement the relationship between "under God" and anti-communism. Certainly, "under God" indicated a connection to the divine, but that connection was important because it removed us even further from our enemies, the Soviets. A nation that was "under God" could never be a communist nation.

On May 10, 1954, the Senate unanimously passed the resolution and on June 7, the House completed the legislative process and sent the bill on to the President (Ellis 130-35).[10] Rarely does any bill receive such wide and bi-partisan support, but this bill united politicians from both sides of the aisle. Arguments in both the House and the Senate never really showed much more creativity than what Eisenhower heard from Docherty. The arguments largely just repeated themselves over and over again. But there was no real reason to strive for a great deal of variety when there was no real opposition to the original arguments. Repetition simply served to strengthen the resolve of lawmakers in both the House and the Senate.

Adding "under God" to the Pledge of Allegiance was a very public and straightforward way to try to refine what it meant to be an American. It is one thing to publicly announce it, but to add it to the Pledge of Allegiance was a particularly well-calculated move on behalf of Congress. The epideictic nature of the Pledge of Allegiance offered the perfect way to continually reaffirm America as distinct from communist nations.

Epideictic Rhetoric

One of the functions of epideictic rhetoric is to reaffirm values and standards of the community. The Pledge of Allegiance itself is a ceremonial speech, in which we pledge to be faithful to the flag, which itself represents an America that is described in that very pledge. A change in such an important ceremonial speech indicates that in 1954, Americans felt some tension in regards to their national identity. American lawmakers felt the need to emphasize they were "under God" in order to separate themselves from their enemies, the "godless Communists." The Pledge of Allegiance not only fulfilled this need, but because it was repeated in almost all schools, and at many club meetings and opening ceremonies at special occasions, on a daily basis, it continually constituted this version of American identity.

Epideictic rhetoric is performative, ceremonial and a matter of "display" (Consigny 281). Aristotle emphasized epideictic's "focus on values," publicly affirmed and accepted American values, which the pledge elucidates rather clearly: standing "indivisible" and defending "liberty and justice for all." Chaim Perelman notes that epideictic "is uncontroversial because the values it brings to the forefront are not available to dispute" (Duffy 81). The communal values in epideictic rhetoric are those that, supposedly, the community has already accepted and has ingrained into the very fabric of its being. The pledge highlights those virtues Americans hope to instill in those who recite it. It reminds participants of allegiance, unity, and "liberty and justice for all" that, as Americans, we are supposed to espouse above all other ideals. The pledge unifies Americans in thought and deed; after all, the indivisibility of the Republic was its main focus originally. Its very purpose is spelled out in the speech.

A rhetor utilizing epideictic rhetoric "delineates his task as one of advocating his own position in a manner that is fitting with the 'norms' of the discourse at hand" (Consigny 285). In this sense, epideictic reaffirms social norms and helps those norms reproduce themselves, and the pledge requires no interpretive effort because it provides an explicit list. The performance of the pledge is an act of constitution. Adding something to epideictic rhetoric that is already set and accepted is a somewhat radical move, then, for in that action the author is adding something to communal values and identity.

Epideictic rhetoric facilitates "the instilling of philosophically correct values," as they are presented by the rhetor (Duffy 85). A rhetor who engages in epideictic speech is tasked with proclaiming and embedding community values. Epideictic rhetoric is the verbalization of the ties that bind, so to speak. It "must amplify belief in the values which inform decision in every sphere of human activity," which creates a particularly powerful piece of discourse. If epideictic rhetoric encourages us not only to believe particular ideas but also to believe in ideas that will affect our behavior, then even small and subtle changes to ceremony cannot be taken lightly.

Part of the power of epideictic rhetoric, specifically in the case of the pledge, is the ceremonial nature of it. Since the pledge is a ceremony that is repeated frequently, the pledge continually reaffirms the explicit American identity it is spelling out. It praises American virtue and, as we participate, we literally pledge to be subject to those virtues because we *are* Americans, and so the cycle continues. The repetition of the pledge creates its own narrative that gets told and retold with every recitation. An epideictic rhetor has the option to prioritize persuasion and appearance over accuracy or the facts of a situation, and in the case of the Pledge of Allegiance the importance is not that all of America believes in God but that we create a collective identity (Duffy 81). The pledge has particular persuasive power because of its pervasiveness. The job of the pledge is to publicly normalize attitudes toward America and define what America stands for.

The Pledge of Allegiance was not only familiar and accepted as part of American tradition, but since it explains specifically what Americans should value, it was the perfect piece of discourse to use as a means to set up the opposition between America and communist Russia. More importantly, the pledge evolved. The pledge was used as a response to changing world politics. Rep. Homer Angell told the House in his argument for the "under God" addition that "leaders of world thought" were realizing that the conflicts facing the world were ones of values, and that "bombs and guns have been tried and have failed" to quell the storm, so other weapons were needed, weapons like the Pledge of Allegiance (*Cong. Rec. H* 6919). The weapon that Rep. Angell was proposing was the power of epideictic rhetoric.

The debates in Congress made it clear *why* the change was made. The records of Congressional hearings provide a helpful way to contextualize the phrase "under God" as a product of the Cold War and in response to a growing concern over our own identity. However, an analysis such as this would be incomplete without looking at the text itself. Congressional discussion makes it clear that there was a problem that lawmakers felt could be addressed by changing the Pledge of Allegiance. What remains is understanding the text itself.

The Pledge of Allegiance: Analysis of the Text

When we recite the pledge we proclaim our devotion to the flag first and foremost. Our initial allegiance is given to that thing that represents America, not America herself. At first glance this seems to confuse the issue—we technically give our allegiance to a piece of red, white, and blue fabric.

The flag is a symbol—and a symbol gives the rhetor more leeway to create a definition than "the Republic." Beginning with the flag gives us the opportunity to describe what that flag represents. So, the Pledge of Allegiance defines the nation by defining those things that represent the nation. By using a mediator the rhetor has more license to define her or his terms. It is interesting to note that this is not a matter of synecdoche. The flag is not used as a smaller thing to represent the Republic. The flag is something in and of itself and should not be diminished. The Republic was a related, but not interchangeable, entity. The language is not particularly metaphorical or poetic but rather straightforward and organized in a list fashion in simple, declarative clauses. I pledge to the flag, then to the Republic, which is represented by the flag. The flag serves a dual purpose here—on the one hand, it is physical, and we can easily see and understand it as an object, solidifying in our minds a concrete image; but on the other hand, it is symbolic, and the bulk of the pledge is spent defining what that symbol stands for.

Next in that list is "one nation under God." The phrase "one nation under God" acts as an appositive. The Republic for which the flag stands is renamed in the pledge as "one nation under God." "One nation under God" is not just a description; it is a renaming of the preceding noun phrase. So the Pledge of Allegiance has changed from a pledge to a flag and a unified Republic to a pledge to a flag and a Republic that is unified under God. Appositives are usually defined as a single noun that follows immediately after another noun, identifying or supplementing it, not a noun phrase. In the case of the Pledge of Allegiance, it is a complex version of the appositive. It is attached to a statement or clause and functions as an explanatory mark (Norwood 267). An appositional relationship is more than just the standard "an appositive could replace its antecedent noun." As Diane Blakemore points out, appositional structures can give the audience the opportunity to consider the differences and similarities between two things. The listeners get the opportunity to compare and contrast for themselves. An appositive can also encourage the reader to "explore the total set of contextual assumptions made accessible" by all parts of the sentence (Blakemore 54). In other words, an appositional phrase encourages a reader (or, in this case, speaker or listener) to consider all of the assumptions about the flag, America, and the Republic that are connected through the phrase. The words "under God" were not minor additions; they were adding to the identity that millions of people performed regularly.

The phrase "under God" is inserted between two descriptors: "one nation" and "indivisible." Together these might seem somewhat redundant but separating them with "under God" changes the meaning. The new sentence reads "one nation Under God." That is, we are united through a common God. Being under God is one of the bonds we all share as Americans, according to the pledge to the flag. Continuing with another descriptive, we are "indivisible," strengthening some idea of unity. When we say the pledge out loud we are effectively renaming the nation with each new descriptor. We pledge to be faithful to the flag, and that means being faithful to the nation, which in turn means liberty and justice for all. Adding "under God" does not change the nature of the appositive, but strengthens the nature of our indivisibility. We are not just one nation, but we are united through a specific idea—in this case, God. Calling ourselves a nation that walked with God or a nation that God favored would not have the same rhetorically unifying and definitive power as being identified as "under God," and in the face of an enemy like communism, such unification through the very force that made us "not" them was powerful and important.

The final part of the pledge assures us that the Republic will guarantee liberty and justice. Liberty and justice rank high in the pantheon of American god terms, and like most god terms, they have a completely malleable and vague definition, but regardless all other terms are defined in relation to them. The pledge reminds us that we stand whole and we stand for noble and glorious concepts, hard as they might be to define (Weaver, *Ethics* 212-24).[11] Richard Weaver makes a similar comment about Abraham Lincoln in his essay "Abraham Lincoln and the Argument from Definition." He describes Lincoln's tendency to argue from principle but more specifically from definition. This form of argument postulates that "there exist classes which are determinate and therefore predicable." That is, there is an assumption that something is so, and in making such an assumption, the rhetor defines the terms that set the parameters for an argument (Weaver 86-87). The pledge functions in just this way—it defines a state that we assume exists so that we may argue from that definition of the Republic.

Conclusion and Remaining Questions

Communism was scary for myriad reasons. First and foremost, communist Russia had the bomb. Let us not pretend that the Cold War was entirely rhetorical. Certainly there was an actual, physical threat to deal with. But they had achieved that kind of technological greatness by being *nothing like us.* Somehow, another country had become as imposing as America, but the fact that their philosophy, government, and economy were completely oppositional to our own was not only threatening politically, but as a nation we were also faced with doubts about our own exceptionalism. Our claims to superiority were weakening daily, and that was frightening. We had to find ways to maintain our rhetorically fashioned superiority for the sake of our own national well-being. While certainly this speaks mostly to America's inner turmoil and identity crisis, the congressional records point to the looming crisis that was settling over most of the world, as well. There was a clash of narratives beginning that would define the next several decades of politics, economics, pop culture, and art. The Cold War was not just an arms race but a battle of ideas. Those ideas played out on a rhetorical stage. The Pledge of Allegiance, with its epideictic power, was one of the most powerful weapons in America's rhetorical Cold War arsenal.

Congress wanted Americans and her enemies alike to know that America was united under God, and because we stood united under God, we were separate from our godless enemies. Adding "under God" to the Pledge of Allegiance drew the lines between "us" and "them" clearly and publicly—and daily recited.

Current discussions of the Pledge of Allegiance, both academic and political, all too often ignore the political context "under God." "Under God" was, indeed, an effort to rhetorically unite the country under a deific power, but ultimately it does not fit wholly within the "America is/is not a Christian nation" debate that has usurped this powerful phrase. Contextually, it is more a comment on America's attempts to distance itself from communist enemies. Regardless of church-state arguments or religious and political contests, what the entire situation does imply is that the Congressmen of the early

1950s were right in their assessment that the Pledge of Allegiance was a powerful tool. The words we use to describe ourselves, our loyalties, and our nation are important, and because of the epideictic nature of that oath, even two, small words can make a world of difference.

I would be remiss to ignore that the first part of my thesis, that "under God" had a great deal to do with America's global enemies, did not have some relevance to politics today. Whether accurate or not, there are many Americans now who would classify America's enemies in the "War on Terror," the defining conflict of our time, as Islamic first, and then as their nationality second. And many of those same Americans would claim that the Allah of Islam is a different deity than the Judeo-Christian God, which the majority of Americans believe is the God named in the pledge. I have not addressed in this paper whether this is important to the Pledge of Allegiance, for it was not within the scope of this study, but I fully recognize that this is the question to which my study leads. If we are united "under God," how significant is that identity now that communism has fallen, but the enemy that has taken its place is associated with a religious cause in the minds of much of the public? If the Pledge of Allegiance still holds the epideictic power that lawmakers felt it did in 1953 and 1954, the answer could be significant. It may well present a rhetorical problem that our enemy seems just as united under a god, even if some do not believe it is the same one "we" claim. Future studies have hefty questions to answer.

The fact remains that as a nation we are officially united under God. The Pledge of Allegiance does not explicitly claim that God favors us or that he grants us exceptional power, simply that under him we are indivisible. That, in and of itself, is enough to remind us that we are not the same as our enemies, who, at the time of the addition, had no such unifying power according to our understanding of them. The epideictic nature of the pledge itself united us with every recitation; the words themselves described how and why we were united, and what we believed in that united us. The enemy, then, was a bit clearer. By painstakingly drawing lines between the communists and ourselves we created a situation in which we were much more prepared to do the work of the Republic, to stand fast in the face of the enemy, and to defend liberty and justice for all.

NOTES

[1] For a complete explanation of the rhetorical situation, see Bitzer, "The Rhetorical Situation."

[2] There are countless articles and books dealing with the "under God" challenge from 2002, for example. This incident seemed to garner much more rhetorical attention than the original addition. However, the writing that deals specifically with "under God" in the year 1954 is limited at best.

[3] Similarly, see Kirby.

[4] In discussions about the Pledge of Allegiance, there are those who are often quick to point out that Bellamy publicly claimed to be a socialist, as well. I would be remiss if I did not note that there was a time when that kind of economic progressivism was not in any way seen as being antithetical to a Protestant and evangelical worldview.

[5] Allit's *Religion in American since 1954: A History* helps to understand the context under which the pledge was changed, but since the bulk of the book deals with the years after the addition, its usefulness is limited to an overall understanding of the Cold War. See also Herberg; Kirby.

[6] The only real resistance that "under God" faced was from teachers who felt it was too hard to remember and ruined the rhythm of the pledge (Ellis 139). Classrooms had grown accustomed to the original way of reciting the Pledge, and teachers feared changes would be an unwarranted disruption. Given that school children are prone to say the Pledge of Allegiance more frequently than most other Americans, it is no surprise that teachers would be the most concerned about the change. That being said, disagreement from a group of teachers paled in comparison to the overwhelming support from other circles throughout the states.

[7] See also Rabaut, "Amending the Pledge of Allegiance to the Flag of the United States," *Cong. Rec. H* 7763; Rabaut, "Amend the Pledge of Allegiance to Flag to Include the Phrase '"Under God,'" *Cong. Rec. H* 6077.

[8] I am reminded of the notorious Cold War film *Invasion of the Body Snatchers* (distributed in 1956), which has been remade over and over again, usually during wartime. In the film, alien forces infiltrate an idealized human community and strip their free will from them. These alien forces turned human beings into automatons of a sort—they functioned just as humans do but without choice, emotion, or independence. The movie has long been recognized as a metaphor for communist influence in the United States.

[9] House Report 1693 overviewed the process of passing the "under God" bill. In the "Statement," it unequivocally asserted that the political climate was a reason for the pledge addition. The report claims that at that point in history the American way of life was under siege, and the addition of the phrase "under God" "would serve to deny the atheistic and materialistic concepts of communism with its attendant subservience of the individual" (2340). Again there was a connection between God and the individual. Since communism was supposedly opposed to the individual and God supposedly affirmed individual liberty, inserting God into the Pledge of Allegiance rhetorically divided America from communism. Supposed American values directly contrasted the perceived values of the USSR. This addition to the pledge verified something American, not just holy or religious but the main separation between the US and communist states.

[10] See Ellis 130-35. This is a brief summary of a much more detailed history of the addition of the phrase "under God."

[11] Weaver describes god-terms and devil-terms as those things by which we define other terms (*Ethics* 212-24). He specifically uses the words "American" and "un-American" in his description. If "American" is a god term and "communism" is a devil-term, then other terms are ranked by their proximity. For example, "capitalism" is better than "socialism" because one is associated with Americanism and the other with communism. While the original definitions of the god and devil terms might be a bit fuzzy, they serve as anchors by which we can organize other ideas.

WORKS CITED

Addonizio, Frank. *Cong. Rec. HR*. 1954: 7765. Print.

Allitt, Patrick. *Religion in America since 1945: A History*. New York: Columbia UP, 2003. Print.

"Amend the Pledge of Allegiance to Flag to Include the Phrase 'Under God.'" *Cong. Rec. HR*. 6077. Print.

"Amending the Pledge of Allegiance to the Flag of the United States." *Cong. Rec. HR*. 7 June 1954:7757-66. Print.

Angell, Homer. "One Nation Under God." *Cong. Rec.—HR*. 1954: 6919. Print.

Bishop, Ronald. "That is Good to Think of These Days: The Campaign by Hearst Newspapers to Promote Addition of 'Under God' to the Pledge of Allegiance." *American Journalism* 24.2 (2007): 61-85. Print.

Bitzer, Loyd F. "The Rhetorical Situation." *Philosophy & Rhetoric* 1.1 (Winter 1968): 1-14. Print.

Blakemore, Diane. "Apposition and Affective Communication." *Language and Literature* 17.1 (Feb. 2008): 37-57. Print.

Brooks, Jack. *Cong. Rec. HR.* 7 June 1954: 7758. Print.

Consigny, Scott. "Gorgias's Use of the Epideictic." *Philosophy & Rhetoric* 25.3 (1992): 281-97. Print.

Duffy, Bernard K. "The Platonic Functions of Epideictic Rhetoric." *Philosophy & Rhetoric* 16.2 (1983): 79-93. Print.

Ellis, Richard J. *To the Flag: The Unlikely History of the Pledge of Allegiance.* Lawrence: UP of Kansas, 2005. Print.

Ferguson, Homer. "Pledge of Allegiance to the Flag." *Cong. Rec. S.* 10 February 1954: 1600-01. Print.

---. "Pledge of Allegiance to the Flag." *Cong. Rec. S.* 11 May 1954: 6348. Print.

"Flag—Pledge of Allegiance." *H. Rept.* 11 May 1954: 2340. Print.

Goodwin, Algier. "'Under God' Would Help Differ Pagan Influences." *Cong. Rec. Appendix.* 1 June 1954: A4066-67. Print.

Hatcher, Anthony. "Adding God: Religious and Secular Press Framing in Response to the Insertion of 'Under God' in the Pledge of Allegiance." *Journal of Media and Religion* 7.1 (2008): 170-89. Print.

Herberg, Will. *Protestant Catholic Jew: An Essay in American Religious Sociology.* Chicago: U of Chicago P, 1983. Print.

Invasion of the Body Snatchers. Dir. Don Siegel. Allied Artists, 1956. Film.

Kirby, Dianne, ed. *Religion and the Cold War.* New York: Palgrave Macmillan, 2003. Print.

Norwood, J. E. "The Loose Appositive in Present-Day English." *American Speech* 29.4 (Dec. 1954): 267-71. Print.

Oakman, Charles G. "Pledge of Allegiance to the Flag." *Cong. Rec. HR.* May 1954: 7989. Print.

Pillion, John R. "Our Pledge of Allegiance." *Cong. Rec. HR.* 2 June 1954: 7590-91. Print.

"Pledge of Allegiance to the Flag." *Cong. Rec. S.* 10 February 1954: 1600-01. Print.

---. *Cong. Rec. S.* 22 June 1954: 6348. Print.

"Pledge of Allegiance to the Flag—Report of a Committee." *Cong. Rec. S.* 12 June 1954: 6231. Print.

Rabaut, Louis C. "Amend the Pledge of Allegiance to Flag to Include the Phrase 'Under God.'" *Cong. Rec. HR.* 5 May 1954: 6077. Print.

---. "Does the Addition of the Phrase 'Under God' to the Pledge of Allegiance to the Flag Endanger the First Amendment?" *Cong. Rec. Appendix.* 1 April 1954: A2527-28. Print.

---. "House Joint Resolution 243, to Amend the Pledge of Allegiance to Include the Phrase 'Under God.'" *Cong. Rec. HR.* 12 February 1954: 1700. Print.

---. "The Pledge of Allegiance to the Flag: 'Under God' This Nation Lives." *Cong. Rec. HR.* 20 August 1954: 15828-29. Print.

---. "Resolution of the United States Flag Committee Endorsing the Addition of the Phrase 'Under God' to the Pledge of allegiance to the Flag." *Cong. Rec. Appendix.* 1 April 1954: A2515-16. Print.

Weaver, Richard. "Abraham Lincoln and the Argument from Definition." *The Ethics of Rhetoric.* By Richard Weaver. Chicago: Regnery, 1953. 85-114. Print.

Westheimer, Joel. *Pledging Allegiance: The Politics of Patriotism in America's Schools.* New York: Teacher's College P, 2007. Print.

Wolverton, Charles A. "One Nation—Under God." *Cong. Rec. HR.* 17 Aug 1954: 14918-19. Print.

4

VOICING THE CONCERNS OF AMERICA'S FAMILIES

The Rhetoric of Family Values in the 1985-1990 "Family Policy" Debates

Jill M. Weber

During the recent healthcare reform debates, conservatives and liberals repeatedly appealed to images of American families to justify their respective positions. While the resulting bill represented a historical landmark in US domestic policy, it was not the first time that policy makers invoked a rhetoric of family values to advance their political agendas. This study analyzes the ways in which policymakers in the 1980s and early 1990s invoked family-values language and images in support of the *Tax Reform Act of 1986*, which reduced taxes for many working families, and the *1990 Child Care Bill*, the first comprehensive federal child-care bill.

Despite policy makers' employment of family-values language and images, few scholars have explored *how* the rhetoric of family values has functioned as a persuasive force in policy-making discussions. Dana Cloud asserts that "the family" is an ideograph, which Michael Calvin McGee has defined as a "high-order abstraction representing collective commitment to a particular but equivocal and ill-defined normative goal" (qtd. in Cloud 389). Cloud argues that "the family" is persuasive because, like other ideographs, it is "abstract, easily recognized" and evokes "near-universal and rapid identification within a culture" (389). In her analysis of the 1992 presidential campaign, Cloud finds that both Republicans and Democrats invoked "the family" ideograph and embraced a "traditional" conception of family life. She argues that this rhetoric functioned to scapegoat African Americans and the poor for their social inequalities and helped justify the privatization of social responsibility. Cloud's analysis challenged scholars' perception at the time that the rhetoric of family values had been "marginal to mainstream politics" or "unsuccessful in the long term" and helped to legitimize the study of the rhetoric of family values (Cloud 388).

Other rhetorical scholars have since studied how family-values language and images functioned rhetorically in particular policy contexts. Examining debates over welfare policy from the early 1900s to the 1970s, Robert Asen has found that portrayals of female-headed homes changed from positive depictions of single mothers deserving of government support to negative portrayals of allegedly undeserving, welfare-dependent mothers in the 1960s and 1970s ("Women"). Examining the hearings and debates over the *Personal Responsibility and Work Opportunity Act of 1996* (PRWOA), Lisa Gring-Pemble likewise has found that policy makers held up a "classic, normal family" as the ideal, thereby justifying a responsibility-based approach to the welfare reform legislation ("Legislating" 463; Gring-Pemble, *Grim Fairy Tales*). Like Cloud, these scholars reveal that the rhetoric of family values shapes US policymaking and, thus, warrants continued examination.

This study is not an encompassing analysis of the rhetoric within the 1985-1990 family policy discussions. Instead, it is a rhetorical history that illustrates how policy makers invoked family-values rhetoric and images in the congressional hearings and debates in an effort to justify their political agenda. By examining the congressional hearings and debates over the tax reform and child-care bills, this essay responds to recent calls to enhance our understanding of the policymaking formation process (Gring-Pemble, *Grim Fairy Tales*; Miller) and our knowledge of how rhetoric shapes public policy (Asen, "Reflections"). Congressional hearings and debates are valuable texts because they provide multiple voices and perspectives on an issue and policy. Additionally, they provide a formal record of the policy makers' intended policy goals and justifications. As Asen has noted, however, analyzing rhetoric in public policy can be a daunting task because the discussions include many authors, often extend over long periods of time, and are polysemous (Asen, "Reflections" 131-38). In an effort to mitigate those challenges, this essay draws upon Asen's method of "imagining others" to identify the rhetorical depictions of families employed within the 1985-1990 family policy policy-making debates ("Women" 286-88; *Visions of Poverty*). I identify the images of families within the rhetoric, reveal the ideological assumptions that underlay those depictions, and assess the implications of these depictions for family policy and, by extension, American families.

Although policy makers during the 1980s and 1990s offered widely disparate responses to the pressures working families faced, all of the proponents invoked similar compassionate depictions of American families. Moreover, advocates and opponents alike openly lamented the existing economic and employment policies that supposedly inhibited families' efforts to fulfill their familial responsibilities, and the policy makers argued that the federal government had an obligation to help families better address these needs. These debates not only endorsed the view that the federal government should enact new policies to help American families respond to the new pressures they faced, they established a justification for increased federal attention to family affairs.

"Unburdening" America's Working Families: The Rhetoric of Compassion in the 1985-1986 Tax Reform Debates

Ronald Reagan's election to the presidency laid the foundation for a dramatic change in the government's involvement in family affairs. Sweeping into office on a tidal wave of popular support, the Reagan administration pushed forward a vision of an America returning to the conservative values of an earlier era. In 1981, Reagan promoted the *Omnibus Budget Reconciliation Act* (Pub. L.97-35), which drastically cut social welfare spending. Four years later, he introduced a tax reform initiative designed to "promote more fairness for families" (Baker, "Statement," *Comprehensive* 18). The administration's plan included provisions designed to increase personal exemptions and dependent tax credits, remove many of the working poor from the tax rolls, and enhance tax benefits for a spouse "working in the home" (Baker, "Statement," *Comprehensive* 10). By allowing American families to keep more of their money, the administration reasoned, the federal government could reduce family stress and strengthen family life.

Tax reform supporters justified their plan with a rhetoric of compassion. They highlighted the inequalities in the nation's tax system, described the ways in which these inequalities allegedly inhibited working Americans' efforts to address their families' needs, and argued that the federal government had an obligation to promote families' economic stability. Portraying America's middle- and low-income working families as being burdened by unfair taxes, the proponents appealed to policy makers' sense of compassion and fairness.

The proponents maintained that American families were being treated "unfairly," insisting that low-income and middle-class families were forced to "subsidize excessive tax breaks for the wealthy" (Bourdette 45). These workers were simply "trying to get ahead" (Gephardt 13) and provide a better future for themselves and their families, but the system "penalize[d] work and saving and risk taking" (Feldstein 539). Although these injustices were most burdensome for the "working people," who were being driven "deeper into poverty" (Boxleitner 24), they negatively affected middle-class families who bore the "bulk of the tax burden" (Baker, "Statement," *Tax Reform* 18), stay-at-home spouses whose "valuable service to the family" (Baker, "Statement," *Comprehensive* 10) went overlooked in the tax system, low-income families who were "paying a larger share of their meager incomes" (Bourdette 41) in federal taxes, and working parents who watched as the system took from them the "resources they need[ed] to raise their children" (Coats 3). Emphasizing the urgent need to demonstrate the country's "commitment to American families" ("Address to the Nation") and "family values," President Reagan urged Congress to "give the family a break" ("Radio Address") and to restructure the tax system.

These family depictions helped to generate support for the bill and for the nation's middle- and low-income tax-paying families. These families appeared to be hardworking, moral, and law abiding. Unlike the corporations and the extremely wealthy who evaded their tax responsibilities, these families maintained steady employment, supported themselves and their children, and paid more than their "fair share" of the nation's taxes (Bradley 42). The bill's proponents maintained that many families required two incomes simply to keep themselves off welfare. Others gave up an extra income so that one spouse could remain in the home to care for their children. These families embraced the values of opportunity, hard work, and family. Thus, they "deserve[d] a break from high tax rates and a complex tax code" (Kasten 180). Invoking the image of the traditional family ideal, and arguing that Congress had an obligation to eliminate the barriers supposedly preventing families from achieving that ideal, the proponents helped convince the nation of the need for reform.

After a series of compromises, the House passed a tax reform plan on September 25, 1986, by a vote of 292 to 136, and the Senate passed the legislation two days later by a vote of seventy-four to twenty-three. On October 22, 1986, President Reagan signed into law the *Tax Reform Act of 1986* (Pub. L. 99-514). He lauded the bill's proposals and described the legislation as the "best anti-poverty bill, the best pro-family measure and the best job-creation program ever to come out of the Congress" (Reagan, "Remarks on Signing").

Barely beneath the surface of the tax-reform debates were concerns about the declining number of "traditional" breadwinner-homemaker families. Even though the administration publicly insisted that the tax plan was not intended to pit family "lifestyle against lifestyle" (Kronholm), the tax bill's provisions revealed an attempt to privilege the "traditional" family model and its ideals. The increase in the personal tax exemption and the reduction in the amount of taxes low- and moderate-income families faced was an apparent attempt to reduce the likelihood that more spouses—"who would rather stay home with their children"—would be "forced to go looking for jobs" (Reagan, "Remarks on Signing"). Similarly, the elimination of the two-earner deduction and an increase in a non-working spouse's allowable IRA contributions demonstrated an effort to eliminate the alleged discrimination against one-earner couples and homemakers. The increase in the child-care exemption reflected the administration's goal to "make it economical to raise children again" ("Remarks on Signing"). The removal of an estimated six million low-income families from the tax rolls marked an overt attempt to reward the "special effort and extra hard work" low-income families supposedly needed to make the "difficult climb up from poverty" and fulfill the traditional family ideal ("Remarks on Signing").

The passage of the *Tax Reform Act of 1986*, thus, marked an important moment in the contemporary family policy debates. Although Reagan claimed that the "taxing power of government . . . must not be used to regulate the economy or bring about social change" ("Address before a Joint Session"), the provisions belied the administration's attempt to reinforce the traditional family ideal and reduce the ways in which the government allegedly undermined "traditional" family life. Political scientists M. Stephen Weatherford and Lorraine M. McDonnell assert, "No president since Hoover had called for substantially diminishing the government's role in redistributive social programs; Reagan accomplished it" (131).

Improving Working Families' Child-Care Options: The Rhetoric of Compassion in the 1987-1990 Debates over a Federal Child-Care Bill

While many policy makers identified the existing tax code as one of the central issues of the 1980s, it was not the only issue US families faced. Liberal policy makers and social activists called upon the federal government to address the child-care needs of the growing number of employed mothers and wives (Cohen 93). In 1987, 126 representatives and twenty-two senators introduced the *Act for Better Child Care* (ABC), a progressive measure designed to provide federal funding to states to increase the number, affordability, and quality of child-care options available to low- and moderate-income families not on welfare (Cohen 94). By improving these families' child-care options, the bill's proponents maintained, the federal government could ensure a minimum level of stability for the nation's children and families, thereby reducing the pressures working parents faced.

Historically, the nation has resisted efforts to promote federal involvement in day care out of concern that it would either encourage families to abandon their care-taking obligations or compel mothers of young children to enter the workforce (Hunter 187; Zigler, Marsland, and Lord 40). The child-care advocates responded to these concerns with a rhetoric of compassion. They drew attention to the rising number of working mothers, highlighted the ways in which the lack of child-care options allegedly hindered both family and child well-being, and argued that the federal government had a responsibility to help American workers meet their familial obligations. Portraying the bill's intended recipients as hardworking families committed to their children's best interests, the proponents appealed to policy makers' sense of sympathy and concern.

The ABC was targeted toward low- and moderate-income female-headed and dual-income families that, the proponents claimed, were "most in need" of "affordable" and "quality" child care options (DeConcini 112). The majority of these mothers entered the workforce because they were the "sole providers for their children" or because their husbands' income was insufficient to meet their families' basic needs (Dodd 210). Many of these families did not have access to "relatives or parents or grandparents" (Martinez 6), who were willing or qualified to provide "quality" child care. As a result, millions of families were forced to subject their children to "marginal or inadequate" care (Zigler, "Statement" 36) or, worse, adopt "latchkey" arrangements (Seligson 13) in which the children had to care for themselves. These families were committed to providing "economic security" (Dodd 210) for themselves and their children. They just needed some assistance to ensure that their children received the quality child care the kids needed and deserved at a price they could afford.

These family depictions helped generate support for the bill and compassion for the nation's working families. These mothers were not entering the workforce out of choice or to achieve self-fulfillment. Nor were these families trying to surrender their child-care responsibilities. Instead, they were committed to the traditional family ideal and recognized that they had to make sacrifices to meet their families' economic needs. These depictions also served as a response to the critics' claims that the bill was a "middle-class entitlement that subsidize[d] child care for 'yuppie' professionals" (Dodd 211). The proponents acknowledged that the bill's call for increased federal regulation of child-care facilities would benefit "all working families," but they maintained that the bill gave "top priority" to the families at the "lowest income levels" (211). Insisting that the nation could not continue to "ignore the needs of the youngest segment of our population and their families" (Matsunaga 2), the ABC proponents implored Congress to enact the child-care bill.

After much compromise and negotiation, the Senate passed a federal child-care initiative by a voice vote on June 23, 1989, and the House of Representatives passed the bill on October 27, 1990, by a vote of 265 to 145. On November 5, 1990, President Bush approved the child-care initiatives as part of the *Omnibus Reconciliation Act of 1990* (Pub. L. 101-508). The five-year, $22.5 billion child-care package included tax credits for families with at least one employed parent, financial support for low-income families not on welfare, and funding for new state initiatives designed to improve the quality of child care.

Social policy scholar Sally Solomon Cohen argued that the 1990 child-care bill "marked the first time politicians in the executive and legislative branches of government reached an agreement about the role of the federal government in the child care arena" (134). This consensus, however, was largely built around support for the traditional value of family autonomy and parental "choice." For instance, the bill's proponents insisted that "every mother should have the right" (Blank 5) to stay home with her children, and, if "forced to work to make ends meet" (Schaefer 33), she should have a "range of day care options" (Abramson 12) from which to choose. Similarly, the bill's opponents insisted that one-earner couples should not be "force[d]" to "pay for the privilege of rearing their children" (Concerned Women for America 140) or subsidize married women who entered the workforce for extra spending money. The child-care bill's increased tax credits for single-earner couples—which were not a part of the initial Act for Better Child Care proposal—reflected more conservative policy makers' attempt to reward single-earner families for their "choice" to give up one income so as to allow one parent to remain in the home to care for a child.

The issue of parental choice was seemingly so central to justifying the bill's passage that President Bush singled out the child-care provision during his statement while signing the larger budget bill that enacted the child-care initiatives. Bush lauded the bill for increasing parents' opportunities "to obtain the child care they desire," including religious facilities "if the parents so choose," and for providing tax credits and block grants for new measures designed to "enable parents to exercise their own judgment" (Bush, "Statement on Signing") when choosing a child-care arrangement or program.

Conclusion: Rhetoric, Family Values, and US National Policy Making

Despite policy makers' invocation of family-values language and images, rhetoric scholars have paid limited attention to the rhetoric of family values. Cloud has suggested that these omissions may be because of a perception that such rhetoric has been "marginal to mainstream politics" or "unsuccessful in the long term" (388). This essay challenges these assumptions by revealing that "the family" has served as a potent political and rhetorical resource in debates ranging from tax reform to child care. Conservative and liberal policy makers and activists alike invoked family-values language and images as a means of promoting their respective causes. These constructs functioned rhetorically to reinforce the values of the "traditional" family ideal, solidified "the family" as an object of public policy, and underscored the view that the federal government had an obligation to address the pressures families faced.

The persuasiveness of family-values language and images shaped the rhetorical frameworks the advocates employed to promote their policies. Advocates in the debates used the rhetoric of compassion—in which the proponents tried to elicit sympathy for families or support for bills that supposedly helped "the family"—and the rhetoric of condemnation—in which the proponents criticized the families or policies that allegedly hindered family life. Although the compassion framework often dominated the discussions, both were present. During the debates over tax reform, for example, the bill's proponents condemned the nation's tax system that supposedly treated hardworking American families "unfairly" and suggested that the Reagan administration's tax reform proposals would increase family autonomy.

Whereas many Americans and scholars have discounted the significance of the rhetoric of family values, this essay illustrates the importance of recognizing its political and rhetorical influence. This analysis shows how the family can be used as a means to draw attention and support to an issue, to stifle discussion, or to silence critics. Conservative and liberal advocates invoked the image of the "hardworking" American family supposedly "struggling to get by" to generate support for their bills. Middle- and upper-class families had much to gain by the passage of these same bills, but the prospect of questioning the validity of the images of hardworking Americans made it difficult—although not impossible—to challenge the bill's intentions and benefits. In these instances, the opponents' most effective strategy was to introduce a counterproposal that more closely aligned with their views about the government's proper role in family life. This approach appears to have allowed them to support the goals of the policy in question without overtly subjecting themselves to being depicted as "anti-family." The apparent power of the "pro-family" and "anti-family" labels merely reinforces the need to interrogate the rhetoric of family values and its use in contemporary policy making.

The nature of policy making often results in the privileging of one group's interests over another. This study demonstrates the importance of critiquing the rhetoric of family values and the depictions policy makers invoke. The hegemonic assumptions about "the family" enabled policy makers to ignore the diversity of family life and to evade questions about how race, class, gender, and sexuality shaped families' experiences and posed additional challenges. As families become more diverse, it becomes more imperative that policy makers, activists, and citizens closely consider which types of families and family-values advocates of reform are promoting when they invoke family-values language and images in US national policy making.

This study analyzed the rhetoric in two different policy-making discussions in an effort to provide an overview of the rhetoric of family values between 1985 and 1990. The participants in these debates invoked family-values language and images in a variety of ways, whether it was to help establish a need for the bill, to justify the bill's passage, or to respond to the bill's critics. Further studies can analyze each of these debates in greater detail, drawing upon speeches and other texts to provide a richer description of the rhetoric in these debates and greater detail about policy makers' specific strategies. Studies of additional policy-making discussions could contribute to an even broader evolutionary scope, thereby further highlighting the important role that the rhetoric of family values has had in the policy-making process and in shaping American conceptions of family and the federal government's involvement in family life.

WORKS CITED

Abramson, Jerry E. "Statement." Subcommittee of the Education and Labor. HR 3660, *The Act for Better Child Care*. 100th Cong., 2nd sess. Washington: GPO, 1988. 12. Print.

Asen, Robert. "Reflections on the Role of Rhetoric in Public Policy." *Rhetoric & Public Affairs* 13.1 (2010): 121-43. Print.

---. *Visions of Poverty: Welfare Policy and Political Imagination*. East Lansing: Michigan UP, 2002. Print.

---. "Women, Work, Welfare: A Rhetorical History of Images of Poor Women in Welfare Policy Debates." *Rhetoric & Public Affairs* 6.2 (2003): 285-312. Print.

Baker, James A. "Statement." Committee on Ways and Means. *Comprehensive Tax Reform: Part 1*. 99th Cong., 1st sess. Washington: GPO, 1985. 18. Print.

---. "Statement." Committee on Finance. *Tax Reform Proposals—I*. 99th Cong., 1st sess. Washington: GPO, 1985. 18. Print.

Blank, Helen. "Statement." Subcommittee of the Committee on Ways and Means. *Child Care Needs of Low-Income Families*. 100th Cong., 2nd sess. 1988. 5. Print.

Bourdette, Mary. "Statement." Committee on Finance. *Tax Reform Proposals—IV.* 99th Cong., 1st sess. Washington: GPO, 1985. 45. Print.

Boxleitner, Monsignor Jerome. "Statement." Committee on Finance, *Tax Reform Proposals—IV.* 99th Cong., 1st sess. Washington: GPO, 1985. 24. Print.

Bradley, Bill. "Statement." Committee on Finance. *1985 Tax Reform.* 99th Cong., 1st sess. Washington: GPO, 1985. 42. Print.

Bush, George H. W. "Statement on Signing the Omnibus Budget Reconciliation Act of 1990." *The American Presidency Project.* Ed. John T. Woolley and Gerhard Peters. U of California—Santa Barbara, 5 Nov. 1990. Web. 22 May 2012.

Cloud, Dana. "The Rhetoric of <Family Values>: Scapegoating, Utopia, and the Privatization of Social Responsibility." *Western Communication Journal* 62 (1998): 387-419. Print.

Coats, Dan. "Statement." Select Committee on Children, Youth, and Families. *Tax Policy: What Do Families Need?* 99th Cong., 1st sess. Washington: GPO, 1985. 3. Print.

Cohen, Sally Solomon. *Championing Child Care.* New York: Columbia UP, 2001. Print.

Concerned Women for America. "Statement." Subcommittee of the Committee on Ways and Means. *Child Care Needs of Low-Income Families.* 100th Cong., 2nd sess. Washington: GPO, 1988. 140. Print.

DeConcini, Daniel. "Statement." Subcommittee of the Committee on Ways and Means. *Act for Better Child Care Services of 1987.* 100th Cong., 2nd sess. Washington: GPO, 1988. 112. Print.

Dodd, Christopher J. "Statement." Senate Subcommittee of the Committee on Ways and Means. *Act for Better Child Care Services of 1987.* 100th Cong., 2nd sess. Washington: GPO, 1988. 219-21. Print.

Feldstein, Martin. "Statement." Committee on Ways and Means. *Comprehensive Tax Reform: Part 1.* 99th Cong., 1st sess. Washington: GPO, 1985. 539. Print.

Gephardt, Richard A. "Statement." Committee on Ways and Means. *Tax Burdens of Low-Income Wage Earners.* 99th Cong., 1st sess. Washington, GPO: 1985. 13. Print.

Gring-Pemble, Lisa. *Grim Fairy Tales: The Rhetorical Construction of American Welfare Policy.* Westport: Praeger, 2003. Print.

---. "Legislating A 'Normal, Classic Family': The Rhetorical Construction of Families in American Welfare Policy." *Political Communication* 20 (2003): 473-98. Print.

Hunter, James Davison. *Culture Wars: The Struggle to Define America.* New York: Basic Books, 1991. Print.

Kasten, Jr., Robert W. "Statement." Committee on Finance. *1985 Tax Reform.* 99th Cong., 1st sess. Washington: GPO, 1985. 180. Print.

Kronholm, William. "Tax Bill Criticize[d] as Weighted Toward One-Earner Families." *AP Archive.* Associated Press, 15 June 1985. Web. May 2012.

Martinez, Matthew G. "Statement." House. Committee on Education and Labor. *Hearings on Child Care.* 101st Cong., 1st sess. Washington: GPO, 1985. 6. Print.

Matsunaga, Spark M. "Statement." Senate. Committee on Finance. *Federal Role in Child Care.* 100th Cong., 2nd sess. Washington: GPO, 1988. 2. Print.

Miller, M. Linda. "Public Argument and Legislative Debate in the Rhetorical Construction of Public Policy: The Case of Florida Midwifery Legislation." *Quarterly Journal of Speech* 85 (1999): 361-79. Print.

Reagan, Ronald. "Address Before a Joint Session of the Congress on the Program for Economic Recovery." *The American Presidency Project.* Ed. John T. Woolley and Gerhard Peters. U of California—Santa Barbara, 18 Feb. 1981. Web. 22 May 2012.

---. "Address to the Nation on Tax Reform May 28, 1985." *The American Presidency Project.* Ed. John T. Woolley and Gerhard Peters. U of California—Santa Barbara, 28 May 1985. Web. 22 May 2012.

---. "Radio Address to the Nation on the Major Legislative Achievements of 1985." *The American Presidency Project.* Ed. John T. Woolley and Gerhard Peters. U of California—Santa Barbara, 21 Dec. 1985. Web. 22 May 2012.

---. "Remarks on Signing the Tax Reform Act of 1986." *The American Presidency Project.* Ed. John T. Woolley and Gerhard Peters. U of California—Santa Barbara, 22 Oct. 1986. Web. 22 May 2012.

Rice, Robert M. *American Family Policy: Content and Context.* New York: Family Service Association of America, 1977. Print.

Schaefer, William Donald. "Statement." Subcommittee of the Committee on Labor and Human Resources. *Act for Better Child Care Services of 1989.* 101st Cong., 1st sess. Washington: GPO, 1989. 33. Print.

Seligson, Mickey. "Statement." Subcommittee of the Joint Economic Committee. *Latchkey Children.* 100th Cong., 2nd sess. Washington: GPO, 1988. 13. Print.

Weatherford, M. Stephen, and Lorraine M. McDonnell. "Ideology and Economic Policy." *Looking Back on the Reagan Presidency.* Ed. Larry Berman. Baltimore: Johns Hopkins UP, 1990. 122-55. Print.

Zigler, Edward. "Statement." Committee on Education and Labor. *Hearings on Child Care.* 101st Cong., 1st sess. Washington: GPO, 1985. 36. Print.

Zigler, Edward, Katherine Marsland, Heather Lord. *The Tragedy of Child Care in America.* New Haven: Yale UP, 2009. Print.

SECTION
II

RE/FRAMING DELIBERATIVE RHETORIC, DEMOCRACY, AND ETHICS

5

THE LAUGH OF RECOGNITION

Ethical Frames and Torture at Abu Ghraib

Laura A. Sparks

So come on boys
It weren't not for tryin'
It's called the laugh of recognition
When you laugh but you feel like dyin'

— Over the Rhine

[It] is an act for you to attempt changing your attitudes, or the attitudes of others.

— Kenneth Burke

This presentation takes up the question of how to view photographs of atrocity, particularly the ones depicting detainee abuse at Abu Ghraib. At the release of these photographs in 2004, the United States public responded with no small measures of disgust and shame. While the administration under former president George W. Bush sought to distance itself from the treatment captured on camera, journalists, politicians, scholars, and activists took this opportunity to question intelligence officers' interrogation techniques, including the extent to which the Abu Ghraib abuses might be implicated in a larger, state-sanctioned program of torture. And this conversation remains ongoing, particularly after new photographs were released to the public in 2006 and again in 2009. In March 2008, former US Army reservist Lynndie England claimed that the media were to blame for the Abu Ghraib scandal's aftermath. "If the media hadn't exposed the pictures to that extent, then thousands of lives would have been saved," she said. There have also been calls, like Susan Sontag's, to resist viewing images of torture at the risk of revictimizing the abused. Susie Linfield, however, has recently argued it is our ethical responsibility to engage with difficult and problematic images. The temptation when confronted with visual representations is to blame the image itself, to reject it, to censor it, to destroy it. (Or, in England's case, to blame those who publicize such images.) But Linfield suggests that exposure can also be ethical and productive. Taking up the question of how we might adopt an ethical viewing stance, I argue that Kenneth Burke's frames of acceptance and rejection offer new insights into these often-fraught interactions. What does it mean to view the Abu Ghraib abuses through frames of acceptance or rejection? Because it accounts for the responsibilities of the audience/viewer, as well as the possibility that abusers in the Abu Ghraib scandal are not simply "vicious" but "mistaken," I suggest here that Burke's comic frame, in particular, provides ethically invested and strategic possibilities for viewing photographs of atrocity.

To proceed, I will talk for the first half through what I see as the Bush administration's strategic frame of rejection, which I'll ultimately call a "pantomime" of sorts; then I'll think through what is entailed by rejection and acceptance by using Errol Morris's documentary *Standard Operating Procedure* to illustrate possibilities for the comic corrective. According to Burke, both "'acceptance' and 'rejection' . . . start from the problem of evil" (3). "Acceptance" and "rejection" characterize frames through which "the mind equips itself to name and confront its situation" (99). Frames of rejection attempt to "debunk" existing social structures, but for Burke they "tend to lack the well-rounded quality of a *complete* here-and-now philosophy" (28), containing no room for human error, for mistake, or for misunderstanding. An acceptance frame, on the other hand, is a system of meaning in which an individual, in Burke's terms, "gauges the historical situation and adopts a role with relation to it" (5). Acceptance frames give audiences a means for working within existing power structures.

I suggest that in its attempts to apportion responsibility for the abuses onto lower-ranking soldiers and to deflect attention from the scandal in favor of the larger goals of the War on Terror, the Bush administration created a frame of rejection from which to operate and organize public reactions to the abuses at Abu Ghraib. In this case, the rejection frame worked as a rhetorical construct in which the Bush administration rejected culpability by framing the perpetrators as sadistic outliers, as deviants. They could then reject and vilify the soldiers in the photographs and the ones behind the camera, while simultaneously aligning themselves with the outraged public and "debunking" those who attempted to identify what actually set the conditions for Abu Ghraib. President Bush, for example, expressed his shock and disgust at the Abu Ghraib photographs, explaining that Abu Ghraib "became a symbol of disgraceful conduct by a few American troops who dishonored our country and disregarded our values" (qtd. in Milbank). There were moves to disassociate the soldiers directly involved from the military, the government, and the nation itself. In a 2004 radio address to the nation, President Bush remarked that "All Americans know that the actions of a few do not reflect the true character of the United States Armed Forces." Defending the administration's detention and interrogation practices, Bush also asserted that "this government does not torture people." Then-Secretary of Defense Donald Rumsfeld contended that the abuses depicted in the Abu Ghraib photographs were committed by rogue soldiers rather than sanctioned by US policies. James Schlesinger, chairman of the four-member advisory panel appointed by Rumsfeld to investigate allegations of prisoner abuse, observed that "there was sadism on the night shift at Abu Ghraib, sadism that was certainly not authorized. It was kind of 'Animal House' on the night shift" (qtd. in "Report"). As these officials' comments suggest and as Susan Sontag notes in "Regarding the Torture of Others," "[T]he Bush administration and its defenders have chiefly sought to limit a public-relations disaster—the dissemination of the photographs—rather than deal with the complex crimes of leadership and of policy revealed by the pictures."

The administration's rejection frame not only apportioned blame, but it also distracted the public from the systematic use of torture in interrogation. As work by journalists like Seymour M. Hersh has revealed, of course, the Bush administration's role in creating and sustaining policies of prisoner abuse goes back years. Mark Danner, discussing the photographs' complex role in documenting detainee abuse, posits that Abu Ghraib is a

> peculiarly contemporary kind of scandal, with most of its plotlines exposed to view—but with few willing to follow them and fewer still to do much about them. While lower-ranking soldiers have been court-martialed for abusing detainees at Abu Ghraib, the United States has remained effectively insulated from the charge that the photographs are evidence of abuse derived from U.S. policy and sanctioned by the U.S. government. (47)

As Errol Morris has noted, "the Abu Ghraib photographs serve as both an exposé and a cover-up: an exposé, because the photographs offer us a glimpse of the horror of Abu Ghraib; and a cover-up because they convinced journalists and readers they had seen everything, that there was no need to look further." And while internal investigations have been underway, the trail of legal action has focused on the perpetrators depicted in the photographs themselves rather than on the policy makers who set the conditions for detainee abuse. Abu Ghraib's "surfacing" in the public consciousness temporarily forced a reckoning between the evil-doing "them" and the liberty-loving "us"—a self-and-other distinction the US had banked on for years. But the realization that we, too, were responsible for committing crimes against humanity was a realization of decidedly limited scope, as official narratives were worked and reworked to paint the perpetrators as sadistic individuals who acted alone. Thus, the release of the Abu Ghraib photographs—experienced through the rhetorical frames constructed by the Bush administration—while acting as the spark that ignited public furor and the spectacle that revealed our cruelty to us and the world, also strategically set the conditions for thinking about Abu Ghraib.

To comment a bit further on Burke's notions of rejection and acceptance, while I argue that the Bush administration operated from a frame of rejection, it did not, in doing so, reject any social or political structure itself. Instead, they mimicked, in some ways, the purging of evil that Burke associates with scapegoating—something generally understood as part of a more rigid frame of acceptance. So we have rejection and disassociation on the one hand and a purging that fits outliers into an already established system of crime and punishment on the other. The scapegoat is sacrificed for his or her deviance and order is, more or less, restored. But unlike Burke's scapegoating process, the situation of Abu Ghraib does not play out in essentially tragic forms. For example, Burke notes that tragic drama "deals *sympathetically* with crime. Even though the criminal is finally sentenced to be punished, we are made to feel that his offence is our offence, and at the same time the offence is dignified by nobility of style" (39). There is a kind of tragic sympathy associated with the criminal that is not apparent in the representations of the soldiers at Abu Ghraib. While they are certainly portrayed as villains, the scapegoat role seems incomplete. We are not, for example, witness to their punishment—this happens more or less in secret—nor is it clear there is any guilt on the part of the administration that is being exorcised. Instead, the vilification of the handful of individuals pictured in the Abu Ghraib photos serves as a distraction and an opportunity to shift the conversation from systematic abuse to sadism. Thus, symbolic rejection stands in for actual rejection, and Abu Ghraib becomes a strategic opportunity for the administration to reclaim American values and reaffirm the heroism of other US soldiers.

Understood in this way—as a separation from not only the soldiers but also the soldiers' actions—the administration rejected any understanding of the system that might recognize the soldiers as following orders. That is to say, the Bush administration's spin on Abu Ghraib entailed a rejection of both the soldiers and its own culpability in sustaining a system that endorses torture. In seeming to enforce the status quo by punishing the easy-to-identify wrongdoers, the administration attempted to distract the American public from the ways in which the established system actually works differently. But, as further inquiry has revealed, the soldiers held accountable for the detainee-abuse at Abu Ghraib were in a far more complex position than sadism or immorality could account for. So if we recognize frames of acceptance and rejection as ways of interpreting reality, preparing "us *for* some functions and *against* others, *for or against* the persons representing these functions" (4), as Burke himself explains, these systems of meaning are always provisional and always guided by particular motives. We might thus think of the administration's rejection as a reframing move as much as anything else.[1]

At the same time, if we understand frames of rejection and acceptance as not wholly one or the other, any rejection requires the acceptance of something else. In this case, old narratives about American values are made new by their opposition to and rejection of the crimes at Abu Ghraib. The crimes at Abu Ghraib were spun so as to reaffirm the rightness of the US cause. It's not a stretch to recognize that the Bush administration and its supporters were not rejecting and "debunking" a legitimate social system but instead mapping on good/evil distinctions to suit their purposes. In a sense, they pantomimed reform. But, as Burke explains, a frame can work deceptively "when it provides too great a plausibility for the writer who would condemn symptoms without being able to gauge the causal pressure behind the symptoms" (41). The administration's frame directed attention away from the causes that would create such a situation in the first place. The only explanation worth owning seemed to be that these soldiers were sadists.

To take this argument a step further, I suggest that Burke's comic corrective offers possibilities for transcending the kind of binary thinking reflected in the Bush administration's reaction to Abu Ghraib. The comic frame, for Burke, "is neither wholly euphemistic, nor wholly debunking—hence it provides the *charitable* attitude towards people that is required for purposes of persuasion and cooperation, but at the same time maintains our shrewdness concerning the simplicities of 'cashing in'" (166). According to Henry Bamford Parkes, Burke's comic frame refers to the "broadest possible development of consciousness and the maximum independence of all specific philosophies and ideologies" (117), making it an ideal perspective for critics. The comic frame clearly has Burke's favor here, as it "should enable people *to be observers of themselves while acting. Its ultimate [goal] would not be passiveness*, but *maximum consciousness"* (171). As William H. Rueckert puts it, the comic perspective is a frame of acceptance that reconciles individual lives in society "largely by means of knowledge of human error and a whole series of salvation and transcendence devices that stress a both/and rather than an absolutist either/or, US versus THEM attitude. It is a mindset committed to negotiation, education, and peace" (118). I argue that, for our purposes, it achieves a pliancy by accepting the flawed and the seemingly irreconcilable. The comic frame can thus provide a corrective to frames of rejection that both promote an "us" or "them" division and pantomime change. By responding to Abu Ghraib from within a comic frame, we have an arguably better chance of understanding both the human motivations at work and the possibilities for peace.

Errol Morris's 2008 documentary *Standard Operating Procedure* offers a potent example of the sort of comic corrective I'm talking about. His film documents the circumstances surrounding Abu Ghraib by examining the context of the photographs. "Why were they taken?" Morris asks. "What was happening outside the frame?" (Synopsis). Through interviews with the soldiers and other individuals involved in the prison, Morris seeks to understand who these people are, what they were thinking during the time, and how they perceived themselves as fitting into the larger military system. New narratives indeed emerge in the telling. Private Lynndie England, for example, who is best known for being photographed leading around a detainee by a leash, spends at least as much time in the film discussing her ill-fated love affair with Specialist Grainer as she does accounting for detainee abuse. In fact, for her, the narrative drama of her affair is inseparable from her activities of "softening up" detainees and being photographed with them. She remarks at one point that she "was blinded by being in love with a man" (Morris) and explains later that she didn't want to risk losing him. While it's clear that England understands in retrospect that her participation in the abuse of detainees was wrong, her contextualization of the abuses reveals her as a young and foolish figure who was, to put it mildly, in way over her head. Through various interviewees' retelling of the circumstances at Abu Ghraib, relations of power become more clear. The soldiers accused of abusing detainees were typically young, working-class people—England, for example, used to work nights at a chicken processing plant—and for the most part, naïve. "Softening up" detainees for interrogation became a way for them to do their part and possibly curry favor with their superiors and intelligence officers—it was their part to play in the larger narrative of information gathering in the War on Terror, and they saw their participation as a way of keeping US soldiers from being killed. Their dehumanizing treatment of prisoners was normalized to an extent that may seem inconceivable. But their representations in Morris's documentary exemplify, in many ways, the notion that the villains of a drama may not simply be vicious, but might also be mistaken. They are at times the fools, in other words, fooled by the notion that their superiors were looking out for them, fooled by their violent and paranoid surround, and fooled by the mystique of power surrounding the plain-clothed interrogators that walked among them. Recognizing these soldiers as fallible, mistaken figures opens up compelling questions about the network of power and responsibility of which they were a part.

But how does the comic corrective, as a frame of acceptance, function in relation to systems in which harm is being perpetrated? This, I think, is the crux of the matter. The abuses staged at Abu Ghraib were undeniably horrific—the public has seen those that are easiest to bear—and their graphic depiction in color renders them ever-present, despite our geographical distance from the prison. If we are to understand the Abu Ghraib photographs as documentations of the abuse, if not torture, of detainees in US-led detention centers, where in Burke's comic corrective—which is generally understood as a frame of acceptance—is there room for outrage and indignation? To what extent does a frame of acceptance inhibit the possibilities for change, in that it accepts and attempts to understand that which we may find ethically reprehensible? That is to say, how do we "accept" the perpetrators as not simply villainous, as the Bush administration does, but as "mistaken," the way a comic frame would have us do, while still condemning their actions? Can we still be angry at them?

In his discussion of the "rhetoric of outrage," Herbert Simons suggests that one way to get the rhetoric of outrage to "play well outside of the church of the already convinced" is to find balance. "Earned outrage, warrantable outrage, must be something more than righteous indignation; it must emerge out of Burke's stage of comedic irony as something that demands the cry of 'Thou Shalt Not' despite awareness of our own limitations; of our own foolishness." So perhaps one can be *both* vicious *and* mistaken—we needn't choose, necessarily. This needs, I suspect, more analysis than I can offer here. If we acknowledge the comic frame as a critical perspective, one that is undeniably difficult to work from and that demands our active participation, we should not expect to be able to ignore our outrage—just recognize it, for a start. In one sense, this might mean recognizing the human element of every person involved at Abu Ghraib. As the interviews in Errol Morris's documentary reveal, these soldiers could have been (nearly) anybody. Burke suggests that, through a perspective by incongruity, the comic corrective can help us "'remoralize' by accurately naming a situation already demoralized by inaccuracy" (309). Inaccuracies, in terms of who accepts blame and responsibility, certainly can have moral consequences. A perspective by incongruity means bringing together opposing concepts or terms in order to move beyond them—a "metaphorical extension" (309) that interrogates the limits of one or both orientations. It is to that extent a proactive attitude, rather than a reactive one. This is where our outrage meets our apathy. Thus, a comic frame of acceptance does not mean ignoring the moral implications of an event; it can instead mean rethinking the human rights violations in light of the complex system in which they arise, challenging and complicating good and evil oppositions where there is room for misunderstanding. From the perspective of ethics, it's apparent that Abu Ghraib is not a question of good versus evil, as the administration would have liked us to believe (and despite what we may see as the evil of torture). Rather, ethical questions remain in light of the abuses at Abu Ghraib (and other detention centers), and those considerations necessitate the most mindful of comic correctives.

Enacting a comic frame is, I argue, a way of approaching texts, particularly visual ones that we may find ethically troubling. It asks us to develop an attitude conscious of the system as a system rather than to simply reject the system and vilify its participants. A comic frame necessitates an expanded consciousness that, while recognizing the human rights violations depicted in the images, does not use that as an excuse to look away. As Burke explains, this is no easy task. By recognizing such a troubling situation as Abu Ghraib as the result of compounded human error, it means that we can no more vilify members of the Bush administration than we can the hapless soldiers. The goal is not sacrifice but dialogue. By recognizing that people can be both vicious and mistaken, we can certainly apportion blame, but we cannot neglect our own responsibilities. In one of his footnotes about what the comic frame entails, Burke writes that "[the comic frame] warns against too great reliance upon the conveniences of moral indignation" (147). So it's not enough to get steamed about Abu Ghraib and condemn the perpetrators. We must develop a new civic attitude that recognizes fairly (and not condescendingly) the fallibility of those whom we might consider evil, and, as Morris does in *Standard Operating Procedure*, we must ask what's happening outside the frame and seemingly beyond our recognition.

NOTE

[1] It's worth noting that some politicians and pundits took a different stance on the situation at Abu Ghraib, going so far as to applaud the mistreatment of detainees. In this case, good and evil are inscribed somewhat differently, with the soldiers as the good guys and the detainees as inherently bad.

WORKS CITED

Burke, Kenneth. *Attitudes Toward History.* 3rd ed. Berkeley: U of California P, 1984. Print.

Bush, George W. "Radio Address by the President to the Nation." *Iraqcoalition.org.* The Coalition Provisional Authority, 15 May 2004. Web. May 2012.

Danner, Mark. *Torture and Truth: America, Abu Ghraib, and the War on Terror.* New York: New York Review of Books, 2004. Print.

England, Lynndie. Interview. "Rumsfeld Knew." *Stern.de.* 2008. Web. 22 May 2012.

Hersh, Seymour M. "Torture at Abu Ghraib." *NewYorker.com.* Condé Nast, 10 May 2004. Web. May 2012.

Linfield, Susie. *The Cruel Radiance: Photography and Political Violence.* Chicago: U of Chicago P, 2010. Print.

Milbank, Dana. "Bush Seeks to Reassure Nation on Iraq." *Washington Post* 25 May 2004: A01. Print.

Morris, Errol, dir. *Standard Operating Procedure.* Sony Classics, 2008. Film.

---. "Standard Operating Procedure: Synopsis." *Errol Morris: Film.* n.d. Web. 29 April 2012.

Over the Rhine. "The Laugh of Recognition." *The Long Surrender.* Great Speckled Dog, 2011. CD.

Parkes, Henry Bamford. "Kenneth Burke." 1938. *Critical Responses to Kenneth Burke, 1924-1966.* Ed. William H. Rueckert. St. Paul: U of Minnesota P, 1969. 109-22. Print.

"Report: Abu Ghraib was 'Animal House' at Night." *CNN.* Cable News Network, 25 August 2004. Web. 4 May 2012.

Rueckert, William H. *Encounters with Kenneth Burke.* Champaign: U of Illinois P, 1994. Print.

Simons, Herbert. "Burke's Comic Frame and the Problem of Warrantable Outrage." *KB Journal* 6.1 (2009): n. pag. Web. 15 April 2012.

Sontag, Susan. *Regarding the Pain of Others.* New York: Farrar, Straus, and Giroux, 2003. Print.

---. "Regarding the Torture of Others." *The New York Times Magazine.* New York Times, 23 May 2004. Web. 29 April 2012.

6

ETHICAL ENCOUNTERS AT THE INTERSECTION OF EDUCATION AND ACTIVISM

Geoffrey W. Bateman

As historian Lynn Hunt suggests, the evolution of human rights depended, in part, on certain cultural practices that have their origins in the eighteenth century. "New kinds of reading (and viewing and listening)," she writes, "created new individual experiences (empathy), which in turn made possible new social and political concepts (human rights)" (33-34). In the early years of the twenty-first century, our continuing work to secure such rights universally challenges us to move beyond empathy, but the ethical valence of empathy—and its corollary, social recognition—still warrants consideration for its generative possibility in identifying social injustice and rectifying it in some way. To this end, this paper explores more fully our collaborative writing-center work at The Gathering Place, Denver's daytime, drop-in shelter for women, children, and transgendered individuals experiencing homelessness or poverty, and reads it as a significant kind of ethical encounter in the ongoing efforts to secure and protect human rights for some of the most dispossessed people of our city. It asks: What does it mean to situate ourselves ethically at the intersection of education and activism and work as community literacy sponsors to foster human rights for women who are homeless? As community writing center consultants, how do we—and our ways of reading and writing and framing individual experiences—transform the material and symbolic conditions of homelessness in Denver when we work with these women *as writers*?

To begin to answer these questions, let me reframe them somewhat through the words of Jessie Pedro, a woman who had been struggling with homelessness for two years in Seattle when oral historian Desiree Hellegers first interviewed her in 2006 for her project on women and homelessness. The "problem," as Pedro sees it, is that "society looks at the homeless as garbage. That's how I felt when I was homeless at times. I was nothing, you know? Because we're invisible to their eyes. Who I am is not homeless. I'm a human being named Jessie. That's who I am" (qtd. in Hellegers 133). Here, despite voicing her lived experience of not being seen, Pedro illustrates Hellegers's larger hope that her project will provide a "space to represent [these women's] lives on their own terms, rather than assuming that homelessness defined their lives or identities" (4), a hope to which our community-based writing centers also aspire. But Pedro's observation also reflects the sad reality of our cultural discourse on homelessness: By virtue of their experiences on the street, women like Pedro cannot fully embody their humanity in a culturally or politically legible way and must expend their already taxed emotional and physical resources to challenge this exclusionary logic as they lay claim to their status as a human being such that it resonates with the larger public.

In what follows, I'd like us to confront this dilemma and use our experiences to think through the collaborative scene of a writing consultation as a powerful means to securing a legible identity, one that could serve as a point from which larger political claims could be made.

According to Michel Foucault, since classical antiquity, "[t]aking care of oneself [has been] linked to constant writing activity. The self is something to write about, a theme or object (subject) of writing activity" (27). For the women I've worked with at The Gathering Place, writing represents a significant technology of the self: it's a means through which to make legible a self worth caring for. But in our attempts to make a space available for writers to represent their identities on their own terms, we've confronted a decidedly difficult double bind: On the one hand, writing is a powerful strategy through which socioeconomically disenfranchised people can account for themselves as fully human; on the other, our work to help foster a legible identity within this material and symbolic system re-inscribes the authority of the very system that has rendered them invisible and nonhuman in the first place. I submit, though, that the collaborative nature of the exchange—its dialogic and self-reflexive qualities—is central to transforming this problem, for the rhetorical agency that we promote also threatens to exceed the boundaries that limit these women.[1]

But here's the rub: the material conditions of living on the street and the discursive regime through which these women form and reform their identities inextricably ties them to something we've come to call "the homeless"—a term that forever ties these women's sense of self to its cultural and material displacement. Their very struggle to be seen as human remains a daunting challenge in our culture, as it does for anyone who lives in poverty or without housing. As a woman at The Gathering Place recently observed, what distinguishes this organization is that the staff there "treat us like we deserve respect, not like we're parasites" (Patty). Such respect, though, is sadly not the norm of their experiences, and considered alongside Pedro's story, this woman's comment suggests that to be recognized as a human being who is "homeless" threatens on many levels the very definition of what a human is in a world that values the economic agency of the individual and cloaks the dispossession of countless individuals within the discourse of moral responsibility.

As a city and county, Denver provides a rich opportunity to analyze the material and discursive conditions of homelessness and efforts to ameliorate it. Since 2005, Denver's Road Home, a city program funded through public and private partnerships, has been working to end chronic homelessness. Despite some initial success, the economic conditions of the past few years has inhibited these efforts, and Denver has seen an increase in people sleeping in public spaces, especially in our downtown corridor and in the park adjacent to our State Capitol and City and County Building, with as many as two hundred people sleeping on the 16th Street Mall last summer (Meyer, "Eviction"). This increase reflects both the residual efforts of Denver's Occupy Movement and the lack of resources for people who have become homeless in recent years. Since October, this increase in visibility has strained the patience of many in the business community, who have in turn pressed our new Mayor, Michael Hancock, and members of our City Council to take action on this issue (Meyer, "Call Made"). On May 14, Denver's City Council passed an ordinance—described by the *Denver Post* as a "homeless-camping ban"—that "forbids unauthorized camping on public or private property" with the hope that Denver police officers will now be able to use this ordinance to connect people living without shelter to service providers and get them off the streets (Meyer, "Camp Ban").

But in the debate leading up to the passing of this ordinance, those in favor of the ban framed their support in language that further ostracized individuals experiencing homelessness. Last October, when the camping ban was first being considered, Denver City Councilman Charlie Brown said, "I want to get them off of our Main Street. . . . We have to stand up for our businesses downtown and our women and children who are afraid to go downtown. Are we supposed to just give in?" (qtd. in Meyer, "Call Made"). In his testimony, Brown views the homeless as a threat to civic well-being, implying that they are primarily single men without children, and dangerous ones at that. His pitting homeless men against innocent women and children resonates falsely when we contrast it with data that the Metro Denver Homeless Initiative recently released, which documents that 44% of our homeless population is women and 64% of them are households with children (Metro Denver Homeless Initiative 7). Writing in support of the ordinance in April of this year, *Denver Post* columnist Vincent Carroll drew even deeper lines in the sand, urging the City Council to do "what it clearly must do: reclaim its premier downtown spaces." Agreeing with a city council member who argues that this ordinance should not be viewed as an attempt to "criminalize homelessness," he concludes, "[b]ut that doesn't mean we have to turn over downtown to them." It is perhaps this constant "them-ing" that most belies the supporters' supposed legal compassion for people living on the streets, relegating them instead to a material and discursive space external to some sanitized, supposedly "safe" middle-class zone of respectability. As Denver's mayor, Michael Hancock, told our local Commission on Homelessness in April, "The moment we lose downtown as a place people want to go for entertainment, recreation or a place to live, we lose the heart of Denver" (qtd. in "A Needless Delay").

Ultimately, the City Council's nine-to-one vote approving this ban revealed that the rhetoric supporting this ordinance proved effective, its success reinforcing a much larger exclusion of people experiencing homelessness from public space.[2] As Susan, a woman who accesses services at The Gathering Place, said about the ordinance, "It makes me feel like a piece of dirt. . . . We don't matter, we don't matter at all. . . . [I]t's just pushing me to outer areas, you know? Places that already have bans. . . . Where do I go where I am safe? . . . So where do I go? I'd like to ask." Susan's painful commentary renders visible what Judith Butler describes as a Foucauldian "regime of truth" that "offers the terms that make self-recognition possible" (22). As Butler argues, "what I can 'be,' quite literally, is constrained in advance by a regime of truth that decides what will and will not be a recognizable form of being" (22). For Susan and the many other men, women, and children who are homeless in Denver, what they can be and *where* they can be is largely out of their hands. They are being forced by our local government—despite all of its compassionate qualifications to the contrary—to be unrecognizable and invisible to the larger public. And even though such laws do not absolutely foreclose the possibility of self-recognition, they certainly inhibit and thwart it, making people like Susan largely unrecognizable to themselves.

How then can we work ethically with members of our community who find themselves in this troubling position? For Butler, the possibility of social recognition depends in large part on the framework of intelligibility. "If one is to respond ethically to a human face," she writes, "there must first be a frame for the human" (29). Within our local public sphere, the camping ban has clearly fractured our civic frame of reference for recognizing the human face of homelessness, serving as yet another instance of social erasure and dehumanization. This most recent form of displacement reasserts the ethical challenges for our work with writers who come to us for support in their efforts to put their lives and experiences into writing. As we continue to negotiate the social and economic differences that often distinguish consultant from writer, we find renewed urgency in resisting the dehumanizing frames and fostering each writer's claim to legitimacy as a social being. Our work dramatizes, in part, Butler's hope that

> the question of ethics emerges precisely at the limits of our schemes of intelligibility, the site where we ask ourselves what it might mean to continue in a dialogue where no common ground can be assumed, where one is, as it were, at the limits of what one knows yet still under the demand to offer and receive acknowledgement: to someone else who is there to be addressed and whose address is there to be received. (21-22)

This space of address is one of the more powerful manifestations of our collaborative endeavor, for it allows us and the writers to be present to the possibility of acknowledgment and to see each other across difference, especially when some of these women quite literally lack a material address. For Maria, a writer with whom we've worked for nearly four years, one of the most significant aspects of our work together is that our presence supports her and other women simply by attending to them as writers. As she said in an interview in March, "just acknowledging the value of the women writers here . . . that acknowledgment is important." Such recognition regrounds their common humanity, rendering their experiences visible, but also recasts it as valuable. "[S]ociety," she noted, "does not recognize women who have been targeted with homelessness or poverty, and so by having this writing program here, [it] validates the voices that are here . . . that the women here, on the streets, they have something to teach, as well." This mutual exchange between writers is central to how our work has evolved, for even though we spend most of our time as consultants working with the women on their writing, we do so in such a way as to respect their singular expertise even as we draw upon our own as writers, integrating both into our ongoing conversations. In this way, "the uniqueness of the other," as Butler writes, "is exposed to me, but mine is also exposed to her. This does not mean we are the same, but only that we are bound to one another by what differentiates us, namely, our singularity" (34).

To be fair, though, this ideal space of mutually exposed singularity is difficult if not impossible to achieve. As much as I might risk in such moments, the difference between our social positions highlights the women's vulnerabilities to a much greater extent than my own. But exposing their experiences collectively has also helped them to recognize more clearly what created these vulnerabilities in the first place, renewing their strength to survive these structural inequities. Perhaps most powerful has been the writing in which women have spoken against the various physical and sexual abuse that they've experienced. "[W]omen have suffered," Maria said, "and usually when a person is being abused in their life, they're being told that they're worth nothing, and so for the writer here to write, 'That person had no right to treat me this way . . . and how dare they,'" it reflects her dawning realization that "I'm a valuable human person." According to Caroline Heller, who worked with women writers living in poverty in the Tenderloin district in San Francisco in the early 1990s, "It was this very appetite for self-recovery that seemed to turn them into writers" (42). In contrast to other forms of social action, writing is particularly well-suited for such recovery and self-recognition, for as Maria argued, "we can't do exactly that on the street." For her, writing is instrumental in cultivating positive identities for women, "breaking through the labels and identities that society [has] put on [them] by establishing their own identity of how they wish to call" and "identify themselves." Because, as Maria admits, "we're frustrated and tired of being labeled, being denied human rights," writing provides these women a means to think of themselves differently and use such difference as a tool to challenge such denial.[3]

Ultimately, Maria knows better than any of us how difficult this challenge is. As she said, "I don't trust the system. . . . The system's not geared to hear my voice being a woman of color from poverty. . . . [T]hey don't really want me."[4] Yet, she perseveres. In the past year, she's returned to college to complete her degree. "I really want to improve myself," she explained, but she also recognized the inherent tension in wanting to succeed within a framework that really doesn't account for her. "[H]ow do we ethically say," she asked, "'send them to school, be part of the system,' but the system's not set up for it." As we reflected together on the ethical challenge we face supporting women in these kinds of situations, we didn't discover any new answers to these questions, but we still saw value in supporting women like her having their own opportunities to resolve these tensions. "[G]ive credit to the women," she reminded me, "we know. . . . [W]e know there are no fucking guarantees out there, because we do not trust what's going on." Despite this distrust, or perhaps because of it, Maria affirms her own "audacity to have hope." "So maybe," she concluded, "give yourselves the benefit of the doubt that it's important to encourage the women, and acknowledge and just own it, it's good."

In the end, Maria's comments may not fully account for the complexity of fostering human rights and for the push-pull tension between assimilation and transformation, but it does give us a possible path to follow as we continue to work with these writers and refashion the frames of reference that saturate our world, frames of reference that we can re-inscribe with much more humane notions of what it means to be homeless, to be human, to write, and to have rights.

NOTES

[1] Our view of rhetorical agency draws on the work of Linda Flower, who argues that we should attend to how *"everyday people"* who "stand outside the discourses of privilege and or power" . . . "take *rhetorical* agency not just by speaking up but by *acts of engaged interpretation and public dialogue carried out in the service of personal and social transformation*" (206; emphases in original). Flower's persuasive call for and defense of community literacy provides writing centers an important opportunity to revisit our core pedagogies, urging us to see our work as extending beyond the individual consultation and into a much broader engagement with the publics we enter into as we develop community-based writing center sites.

[2] Despite the efficacy of the rhetoric of those who supported the ordinance, a strong counter-discourse also emerged. See Parvensky; Foster, Curtis, and McVicker—all directors of non-profit organizations dedicated to serving and advocating on behalf of people experiencing homelessness in Denver—who published or spoke out against the camping ban.

[3] In this way, our work resonates with other feminist ways of theorizing and practicing critical literacy, supporting women as they develop critical and creative vocabularies that sustain their resistance to the norms that dehumanize and disenfranchise them, in turn leading all of us to transform our social and economic systems. Taking a "critical approach to women's literacy," we see

> reading and writing as a means for enabling women who have been conditioned to accept second-class status to affirm their aspirations as valid and their knowledge and views of life as genuine contributions to the net stock of human understanding. Merely enabling women to read and write without reference to their social standing and political inequity and its origins contributes materially to maintaining their oppression. (Bee 106).

See also hooks 107-15.

[4] As Deborah Brandt notes: "Poor people and those from low-caste racial groups have less consistent and less politically secured access to literacy sponsors—especially the ones that can

grease their way to academic and economic success" (170). Although distinct from Brandt's notion of sponsor—in that we intend our role to be more collaborative than a traditional literacy sponsor might—in many ways, we do work to grease these women's success if and when that's appropriate for them.

WORKS CITED

Bee, Barbara. "Critical Literacy and the Politics of Gender." *Critical Literacy: Politics, Praxis, and the Postmodern*. Ed. Colin Lankshear and Peter L. McLaren. Albany: State UP of New York, 1993. 105-32. Print.

Brandt, Deborah. *Literacy in American Lives*. Cambridge: Cambridge UP, 2001. Print.

Butler, Judith. *Giving an Account of Oneself*. New York: Fordham UP, 2005. Print.

Carroll, Vincent. "Take Back Downtown Denver." *The Denver Post.com*. MediaNews Group, 25 Apr. 2012. Web. 5 May 2012.

Flower, Linda. *Community Literacy and the Rhetoric of Public Engagement*. Carbondale: Southern Illinois UP, 2008. Print.

Foster, Leslie, Terrell Curtis, and Victoria McVicker. "Denver's Urban Camping Ordinance Should Consider Women." *The Denver Post.com*. MediaNews Group, 9 May 2012. Web. 21 May 2012.

Foucault, Michel. *Technologies of the Self: A Seminar with Michel Foucault*. Ed. Luther H. Martin, Huck Gutman, and Patrick H Hutton. Amherst: U of Massachusetts P, 1988. Print.

Hellegers, Desiree. *No Room of Her Own: Women's Stories of Homelessness, Life, Death, and Resistance*. New York: Palgrave MacMillan, 2011. Print.

Heller, Caroline E. *Until We Are Strong Together: Women Writers in the Tenderloin*. New York: Teacher's College P, 1997. Print.

hooks, bell. *Feminist Theory: From Margin to Center*. Boston: South End P, 1984. Print.

Hunt, Lynn. *Inventing Human Rights: A History*. New York: Norton, 2007. Print.

Maria. Personal interview. 20 Mar. 2012.

Metro Denver Homeless Initiative. "Homelessness in the Denver Metropolitan Area 2012: Homeless Point-In-Time Study." Denver Dept of Human Services, 7 May 2012. Web. 15 May 2012.

Meyer, Jeremy P. "Camp Ban Passes, Provokes," *The Denver Post* 15 May 2012: A1. Print.

---. "Call Made to Drive Homeless from Mall." *The Denver Post.com*. MediaNews Group, 21 Oct. 2011. Web. 21 May 2012.

---. "Eviction Notice." *The Denver Post.com*. MediaNews Group, 6 May 2012. Web. 21 May 2012.

"A Needless Delay on Homelessness." Editorial. *The Denver Post.com*. MediaNews Group, 23 April 2012. Web. 5 May 2012.

Parvensky, John. "Homeless Aren't Criminals." *The Denver Post.com*. MediaNews Group, 5 May 2012. Web. 5 May 2012.

Patty. Personal interview. 26 April 2012.

Susan. Personal interview. 20 April 2012.

7

PERSPICUITY AS DISCURSIVE ETHIC

Jon Stewart's Revival of Eighteenth-Century Rhetoric

William Duffy

> I think we always have to remember that people can be opponents but not enemies. And there are enemies in the world, we just need the news media to help us delineate. And I think that's where the failing is, that the culture of corruption that exists in the media doesn't allow us to delineate between enemies and opponents.
>
> — Jon Stewart

> The last thing I see every night, in addition to my husband and my cat, is your show. And I'm able to go to bed with the sense that there is sanity someplace in the world.
>
> — Terry Gross

The two quotations above come from an interview Jon Stewart gave to NPR's Terry Gross in 2010. The conversation primarily focused on Stewart's role as host of the Rally to Restore Sanity, but Stewart and Gross also discussed the current climate for political discourse in America, as well as Stewart's philosophy of satire and the functionality of humor on *The Daily Show.* Gross's comment about Stewart's sanity, which comes at the beginning of the interview, reflects what many media critics think about Stewart: that he is not *just* a comedian; he's also an invaluable resource for reason and rationality in the news media. Even President Obama, in a recent interview with *Rolling Stone* magazine, admitted he admires Stewart: "I don't watch a lot of TV news. I don't watch cable at all. [But] I like *The Daily Show.* . . . I think Jon Stewart's brilliant. It's amazing to me the degree to which he's able to cut through a bunch of the nonsense. . . . [H]e ends up having more credibility than a lot of [the] more conventional news programs" (Wenner). Scholars tend to agree. According to communication theorist Geoffrey Baym, *The Daily Show* is best understood "not as 'fake news' but as an alternative journalism, one that uses satire to interrogate power, parody to critique contemporary news, and dialogue to enact a model of deliberate democracy" (261), while rhetorician Robert Hariman opines that Stewart "continually calls the audience to informed participation, civil speech, and rational argument on behalf of sound public policy" (274).

Stewart's public image as a spokesperson for deliberative democracy solidified dramatically after his October 15, 2004 appearance on CNN's *Crossfire*. It was there Stewart for the first time publicly stepped away from his role as comedian and openly criticized mainstream news organizations for failing to be responsible arbiters of the public trust. As Lisa Colletta notes, "The blurring of entertainment and news is something satirized daily on Stewart's show, but on *Crossfire* Stewart unambiguously and without irony criticizes the media for abdicating their responsibility" (871). At the time, John Kerry was attempting to upset George W. Bush's reelection attempt, and the *Crossfire* producers obviously believed Stewart would inject some levity into discussion of this current event. But to the apparent surprise of the show's co-hosts, Tucker Carlson and Paul Begala, Stewart kept the discussion's focus on *Crossfire* itself and how programs like it turn the serious business of political debate into, as he put it, "theater" and "political hackery." In addition to asking Carlson and Begala to "stop hurting America," he told them that "what you do is not honest," a comment which prompted Carlson to effectively call Stewart a hypocrite. Stewart quipped he was unaware "news organizations look to Comedy Central for their cues on integrity," and then uttered one of the most memorable—and perhaps most rhetorically significant—lines from that exchange: "You're on CNN. The show that leads into me is puppets making crank phone calls."[1]

According to the president of CNN, Stewart's appearance on *Crossfire* played a factor in its decision to take the program off the air in early January 2005. Remarkably, this executive publicly acknowledged that he agreed with Stewart's assertion about *Crossfire* hurting public discourse (Carter). Such a turn of events is a noteworthy testament to Stewart's rhetorical power, especially given his transparent awareness that "puppets making crank phone calls" is the show which (at the time in 2004) leads into his own program. It is tempting to read Stewart's self-effacing humor in this context as a manifestation of his comedic style, which is to say that this kind of self-referential parody is how Stewart maintains his identity as a comedian. But if we are to understand Stewart's ethos as a media critic and social commentator, perhaps it is through this practice of self-deprecation that we actually see Stewart exercising his persuasive appeal. After all, the likes of journalists such as Larry King and Ted Koppel have tried to persuade Stewart to embrace the influence he obviously has on public discourse in America, only to find these suggestions the fodder for jokes about dancing monkeys and scat.

So what is it that gives Stewart his influence? Don Waisanen suggests that Stewart, as well as Stephen Colbert, bring a sense of playfulness to a Habermasian conception of the public sphere, thus "distinguishing themselves from a chorus of often mean-spirited media pundits, while also transcending concerns that they simply engage in meaningless entertainment" (120). In a similar vein,

Jamie Warner says "[b]y feigning ignorance and constantly insisting that *The Daily Show* is only for laughs, Stewart can operate stealthily" (31). Sandra Borden and Chad Tew, however, believe it is his style of parody—how Stewart actually "performs" the news—that gives him authority. Because he uses real news for the performance of his fake reporting, they suggest, Stewart can filter commentary through comedy. In this way, "we can observe how a Stewart or a Colbert separates himself through the use of comedy from the role of journalist to enhance his own voice and status. . . . That is how someone who inhabits the role of comedian can also perform the function of media criticism" (306, 307). In sum, then, Stewart's self-deprecation is simply a rhetorical tactic, a feigning of ignorance that is really a flaunting of influence. While these scholars are certainly correct in their explanation of how Stewart's ethos as a comedian gives him certain rhetorical liberties not available to other journalists, there is nothing stealthy about Stewart's rhetoric. For one, it does not operate under the radar; in fact, it is the transparency of Stewart's rhetorical strategy that warrants consideration from rhetoricians, because it is this strategy—rather than his self-deprecating humor—that gives Stewart his appeal.

The argument I pose here is that what gives Stewart authority is not the power of his satire but rather the perspicuous nature of his discourse. While Stewart's parody is certainly critical to his ethos as a comedian, it is the perspicuity through which Stewart frames his humor that engenders the deliberative qualities that so many ascribe to his work. Therefore I believe it is worthwhile to consider how Stewart's rhetorical practice might best be explained using the eighteenth-century rhetorical theory propagated by George Campbell and other belletristic rhetoricians influenced by Thomas Reid and the principles of Scottish common sense philosophy. While I do not intend to conflate belletristic rhetoric with a specific epistemology, I do suggest that in Campbell we have a rhetorician who believed perspicuity is the primary quality that links reason to eloquence; clearness of thought (and its presentation to an audience) is what gives a properly reasoned argument its aesthetic appeal. True reason pleases both the mind and the gut, Campbell might say. In Stewart, however, we have a rhetor for whom perspicuity is both means and ends, which is to say that what Stewart cultivates through his rhetoric is a performative argument for the virtue of perspicuous discourse in matters of public debate. In other words, Stewart's rhetoric promotes perspicuity as an ethic that delimits legitimate from illegitimate contributions to public discourse.

There are several implications for linking Stewart's discursive practice to eighteenth-century rhetorical theory, but first let me turn to George Campbell and the idea of perspicuity. I should note that because this essay is primarily about Jon Stewart, I refrain from a detailed review of Campbell's rhetoric and its antecedents. For my purposes here I will simply comment on the role of perspicuity as it relates to the common sense philosophy that underlies much of Campbell's work in *The Philosophy of Rhetoric*, his most important contribution to rhetorical theory.[2]

* * *

George Campbell published *The Philosophy of Rhetoric* in 1776, only a decade after his friend and colleague Thomas Reid published *An Inquiry into the Human Mind on the Principles of Common Sense*. Douglas Ehninger notes how Reid, the chief voice of Scottish common sense philosophy at the time, "asserted that human knowledge may be anchored on certain innate, self-evident laws of reason which are common property to all men" (271), an idea we see at work in Campbell's rhetorical theory. Ehninger explains it thusly:

> Now rhetoric, reasoned Campbell, is quite clearly a "human" art . . . [I]ts basic principles may be inferred from examining the ways in which mind knows, is led to believe, is agitated and moved. Let us, therefore, he said, follow in the path Reid has marked. Let us restudy the human understanding in the light of those laws which underlie all knowing and believing. (272)

One of the chief ends of discourse, Campbell explains, is to enlighten the understanding, so careful knowledge of the human mind naturally aids the practice of rhetoric.[3] It is here where the idea of perspicuity assumes its central place in Campbell's rhetoric, because an enlightened understanding requires a clear sense of how something works. As Campbell writes, perspicuity "results entirely from propriety and simplicity of diction, and from accuracy of method, where the mind is regularly, step by step, conducted forwards in the same track, the attention no way diverted, nothing left to be supplied, no one unnecessary word or idea introduced" (2). To appeal to the understanding, in other words, a rhetor must successfully present how the different parts of an idea come together to form the whole; he or she must be capable of outlining an argument's constitutive parts.

Thus Campbell's common sense approach to reasoning begins with perspicuity, or clearness of thought, one's ability to claim rhetorical precision as a quality of one's discourse. Perhaps this is why *The Philosophy of Rhetoric* is famous for Campbell's rejection of the syllogism as logic's chief trope. Campbell favors inductive reasoning to deductive speculation, explaining that audiences will usually favor particular examples rather than general assertions. Syllogistic reasoning does not promote knowledge acquisition as does induction, because as Campbell notes, "wherein experience is our only guide, we can proceed to general truths solely by the induction of particulars" (63). Moreover, and more to the point, syllogistic reasoning is an obstacle to perspicuity. "It is at once more indirect, more tedious, and more obscure," explains Campbell (63). In sum, says Ray McKerrow, Campbell holds "that the inductive process is the more profitable of the two methods since it produces knowledge and possesses the ability to test it against the particulars from which it is derived" (5). If the mind is naturally endowed to work in certain ways, which is the premise on which Scottish common sense philosophy is founded, this is why Campbell is ardent about induction being the most advantageous method for securing logical validation, because it promotes what he understandingly calls *natural* reason, the knowledge of "things themselves" we acquire experientially (202). To again cite McKerrow, "Since syllogisms do not depend on experience in the same fashion as the assimilation of particulars, they necessarily beg the question" (5). And to beg the question is a fallacy anathema to perspicuity, because as Campbell notes at the end of his chapter on the syllogism, to beg the question as the syllogism does "hinders us from discerning that we are moving in a circle all the time" (70).

So perspicuity is what allows one to guide the mind, step by step, toward reasoned conclusions. The most appropriate method for this kind of reasoning, the one that is itself most perspicuous, is the inductive because it begins with empirical truths already known and progresses forward without resting on generalized assumptions. When presented as a method of argumentation, this is—nearly to a tee—the method Jon Stewart regularly utilizes on *The Daily Show.*

While I believe we can apply this eighteenth-century rhetorical filter to most any of Stewart's regular performances, from how he reads the headlines, to his parodic dialogues with *Daily Show* correspondents, and even to his more circumspect interviews with writers and politicians, I want to focus on his interactions with other journalists, for here we see Stewart in full force when it comes to his perspicuous style of argumentation. Indeed, it is when he engages the criticism leveled against him by other journalists that Stewart so eloquently channels Campbell's ideal rhetorician: an orator who is audience-conscious, rhetorically precise, and completely transparent in his construction of an argument, beginning with concrete examples rather than generalized assertions. Stewart's confrontation with Tucker Carlson is an early example of this, but he has more recently clashed with Jim Cramer (CNBC), Bill O'Reilly (Fox News), Bernie Goldberg (Fox News), and Joe Scarborough (MSNBC), among others. In the case of Joe Scarborough, host of MSNBC's *Morning Joe,* Stewart ran a segment on *The Daily Show* in June 2009 in which he ridiculed Scarborough for signing a multi-million-dollar sponsorship with Starbucks. As part of that deal, not only do Scarborough and his co-anchors sip beverages from Starbucks cups, but also the text "brewed by Starbucks" now appears on the *Morning Joe* logo. For Stewart, this action amounts to a damning example of how corporations influence the news media, and he not-so-subtly suggests Scarborough is a "whore" because of the latter's willingness to sacrifice journalistic integrity for corporate sponsorship.

Obviously affected by this criticism, Scarborough attempts to deflect Stewart's remarks by lightheartedly suggesting that Stewart himself does not understand "irony and sarcasm." That is, rather than address Stewart's critique deliberatively, Scarborough laughs it off while questioning Stewart's chops as a comedian. From a rhetorical standpoint, Scarborough essentially digs his own grave because he forwards the suggestion that a journalist like himself understands comedy better than Stewart, the self-identified comedian. In response, Stewart begins his June 8, 2009, show by addressing Scarborough's reaction to his criticism.

Stewart: We showed you all the product placement and coffee drinking and ass-licking of the head of Starbucks when they did the interview with him, and insinuated that this deal made MSNBC's *Morning Joe* whores instead of reliable news providers. Well this morning over a couple prominently placed Starbuck's drinks, they set my sorry-ass straight.

[Cuts to clip of *Morning Joe*]

Scarborough: Apparently Jon Stewart, who should get jokes, ripped us on the Starbucks deal. And he showed a clip where [gestures like he is drinking a cup of coffee] we were being sarcastic. Don't you think a guy who gets paid to be a comedian should understand irony and sarcasm? [He holds up a Starbuck's cup and speaks directly to the camera, presumably to Stewart himself] That's a joe. Do you get it?

[Cuts back to Stewart]

Stewart: Oh, I'm such an idiot! You are not sponsored by Starbucks; you are "sponsored" [makes air quotations] by "Starbucks." You're not a sellout; you're a "sellout." Sarcasm! I get it now! See at the time I thought your jokey manner was just the way you were sublimating your shame over the discomfort you feel deep in your soul after extinguishing the last smoldering embers of any of your program's journalistic bona fides. But now I realize that wasn't the case.

Stewart's refutation of Scarborough hinges on the carefully outlined presentation of his original claim, followed by Scarborough's response to that claim, then concluding with Stewart's sarcastic, but thoroughly *un*-ironic, repetition of his initial claim. Moreover he plainly summarizes the constituent warrants from which this original claim was constructed, simultaneously reversing Scarborough's critique—that Stewart does not understand irony or sarcasm—making Scarborough, and not himself, appear the sap. Here, perspicuity is at work in Stewart's rhetoric on a number of levels. Not only does he transparently provide the context needed to understand Scarborough's remarks (Stewart admits he called Scarborough a "whore"), but he uses Scarborough's response as further evidence for his original claim, which is that Scarborough is not a reliable news provider. In other words, Stewart basically allows Scarborough to have his say, to which Stewart responds directly, enacting the deliberative debate (however artificial) Scarborough is unwilling to initiate himself.

In a more recent exchange, this time with Fox News commentator Bernie Goldberg, Stewart basically follows this same rhetorical strategy, one rooted in perspicuity, to illustrate why "professional" social commentators have so little authority when they attempt to ridicule *The Daily Show*. In this particular case, Stewart ran a series of clips on his April 15, 2010, show depicting Fox News personalities saying it is unfair to generalize about the Tea Party because generalizing about any political group is not only wrong (that is, presumably unethical) but also unproductive; and then Stewart shows another series of clips with the same commentators, but this time in every case they are generalizing about liberals. One of the commentators Stewart highlighted in the clips, Bernie Goldberg, appeared on *The O'Reilly Factor* shortly thereafter to address Stewart's charge of hypocrisy. Unlike Scarborough, Goldberg does not casually brush aside Stewart's criticism; instead he addresses Stewart directly in what amounts to a kind of open letter. Goldberg's fatal flaw, however, is that he suggests his own integrity (as a "social commentator" and not a comedian) is stronger than Stewart's. The following is a piece of Stewart's response, which aired on the April 20, 2010, broadcast of *The Daily Show*:

> *Stewart*: You see, last week I mentioned Fox was upset about the media generalizing who the Tea Party's [members] are, and I agree with them. And I may have at that point then shown some of the very same people at Fox giddily generalizing about liberals and the left, and I might have when presented with this rather bald hypocrisy, ah, I may have told them to go f-ck themselves.
>
> [Stewart then shows a clip of Bill O'Reilly asking Goldberg if he (Stewart) has a point, that Fox News commentators are guilty of generalizing. Goldberg actually assents to this claim, but says he wants to address Stewart directly.]
>
> *Goldberg*: If you just want to be a funny man who talks to an audience that will laugh at anything you say, that's okay with me. No problem. But clearly you want to be a social commentator more than just a comedian. And if you want to be a good one, you better find some guts.
>
> [Cuts back to Stewart]
>
> *Stewart*: Okay, two things. One, not all of us have your guts, Bernie. It takes a tough man to walk into O'Reilly's lion's den and criticize liberal elites. And two, to say that comedians have to decide whether they are comedians or social commentators, ahh, comedians do social commentary through comedy. That's how it's worked for thousands of years. I have not moved out of the comedian's box into the news box. The news box is moving towards me. I'm just doing what idiots like me have done for thousands of years. But I assume you have evidence that I've betrayed my craft.
>
> [Cuts to Goldberg]
>
> *Goldberg*: When you had Frank Rich on your show, who generalizes all the time about conservatives and republicans being bigots, you didn't ask him a single tough question; you gave him a lap dance; you practically had your tongue down his throat.
>
> [Cuts back to Stewart]
>
> *Stewart*: Guilty as charged. Was that televised? I didn't want to say anything, but Frank Rich hasn't been on the show since 2006. I mean, since I gave Frank Rich that lap dance, I don't know if you noticed, but I went back in the champagne room with Bill Kristol like five times. And if you

watch this show, which it appears you have, you must remember me and McCain f-cking like bunnies. But I guess that's beside the point. Here's the point: you can't criticize me for not being fair and balanced. That's *your* slogan. Which, by the way, you never follow. Which brings us back to the essence of the whole "go f-ck yourselves" piece.

In this particular segment, we see Stewart flexing his rhetorical muscle. That is, while he displays his typical self-deprecating humor, Stewart nonetheless delivers a scathing repudiation of Goldberg's criticism. Moreover we see Stewart's deliberative aim: he wants to be funny, but he also wants to enlighten his audience by presenting a clearly outlined defense of his criticism of Fox News.

So what does Stewart himself say about his rhetorical method? In her interview with him in 2010, Gross asks how he puts together what she calls "the hypocrisy videos," like the one of Goldberg and other Fox commentators saying one thing and doing another. He answers it is easy to "search on NexusLexus [*sic*] if you have an idea of what you want." But he also says, "It is all about just making connections, and then looking into it." When Gross suggests this is what all journalism should be about, Stewart disagrees. "We don't fact check, look into context, because of any kind of journalistic criterion that we feel has to be met; we do that because jokes don't work when they are lies." Moreover, he says, "We fact check so that when we tell a joke, it hits you at a kind of guttural level."

There is an obvious common sense quality to Stewart's explanation of how he presents the news while questioning the integrity, as well as the validity, of those who should be, but often fail to be, responsible managers of those spaces in the media where public debate and analysis transpire. For one, Stewart links the process of reasoning—what makes "sense"—to physicality and the idea that rationality is an affective quality just as much as a cognitive one. Take for example a segment from the May 1, 2012, episode in which Stewart shows several conservative commentators complaining that President Obama is politicizing the fact he ordered the strike that killed Osama Bin Laden. Several of these commentators use the metaphor of "spiking the football" to allude to Obama's supposedly indecorous speech in this regard. Stewart then shows a series of videos from 2004 in which Republicans are politicizing the death of Saddam Hussein in the exact same way, for which they are now accusing Obama. But it is the commentary Stewart delivers between these two juxtaposing clips that is particularly noteworthy for its allusion to an innate, biological standard for common sense:

> So let me get this straight. Republicans, you're annoyed by the arrogance and braggadocio of a wartime president's political ad? You think he's divisively and unfairly belittling his opponents. I see. I have a question: [yells] ARE YOU ON CRACK? Were you alive lo' these past ten years? It seems unseemly for the president to spike the football? Bush landed on a f-cking aircraft carrier with a football-stuffed codpiece! He spiked the football before the game had even started! Yes, your Republican cater-

wauling and outrage is the subject of our new segment: You are aware
that the frontal lobe of the cerebral cortex gives us the ability to store and
recall past events as they occurred, right?

Stewart's emphasis on the capacity to remember past events as a critical component for reasoning comes directly from common sense philosophy—the belief that reason is most "true" when it is rooted in the empirical
and experiential.

* * *

If we pause to ask the pragmatic question about what difference this
analysis of Stewart's rhetoric makes, we can consider what this kind of rhetoric says about the purpose of deliberation in matters of public debate. Surely
it is easy to agree with those in the media who tout Stewart as a kind of
refreshing balm in an otherwise fractured environment for mainstream news
and analysis. It is even tempting to agree with rhetoricians like Hariman who
suggest Stewart is a model for deliberative democracy and should be better
recognized as such. My own opinion of Stewart does not conflict with either
of these perspectives, but I do think that as rhetoricians we can better nuance
what Stewart does with his rhetoric and how what he promotes is not so
much a model for deliberative debate as it is a method for understanding the
value of deliberation itself within debate.

Let me explain this distinction.

Stewart often goes to great lengths, both on his show and in interviews
he gives (like the one with Terry Gross), to emphasize the apolitical ethos he
wants to inhabit as a comedian and critic. When we look at his methodology,
for instance, we see an emphasis on research and a concern for historical context. In moments of delivery, Stewart follows a rather transparent presentation of reasons and claims, usually in that order. And while it is possible to
occasionally discern Stewart's stance on certain policy or social issues, there
is actually very little "debate" that occurs on *The Daily Show.* When Stewart
disagrees with guests, and this does happen, it usually concerns a particular
statement or idea that has been presented and how best to interpret this statement or idea within a wider context. In other words, Stewart pushes his
guests to be perspicuous, to be transparent with the premises that inform their
claims so that we as an audience can better evaluate whatever argument is
under discussion. This push for perspicuity is also at work in the examples
I've shown where Stewart ridicules other journalists. What gives Stewart's
rhetoric its deliberative quality, then, is best understood by examining the
work Stewart expects deliberation to produce, which in all cases rests on
some manifestation of perspicuity. Put simply, Stewart uses his rhetorical
power to challenge obfuscation. As Stewart himself says, "The point of view
of this show is we're passionately opposed to bullshit. Is that liberal or conservative?" (qtd. in Jones 111). To be opposed to bullshit is of course neither liberal nor conservative; it is Stoic, which is where the Scottish philosophers
appropriate many of their ideas about the work of common sense. To suggest

that Stewart embraces perspicuity as a discursive ethic is to suggest that for Stewart winning an argument should be secondary to what, really, amounts to respect for one's audience. If we respect an audience, what we should offer them is the opportunity for understanding, and discourse that is perspicuous is what engenders understanding.

So what is the benefit of this analysis of Stewart's rhetoric? Is there a practical application for interpreting Stewart through an eighteenth-century rhetorical lens? On the level of pedagogy, Stewart offers a contemporary model for illustrating the topography of argument: how things like context, arrangement, and delivery affect both the power and persuasiveness of our claims. But this is obvious. What is particularly interesting is how Stewart positions perspicuity as its own argument, so to speak. Through careful research and artful arrangement, Stewart crafts occasions for perspicuity— rhetorical situations, we might call them, where it is impossible to obscure discursive intention from articulation.

To think about Stewart's rhetoric in a Scottish common sense frame also challenges those arguments posed by scholars who read Stewart as cynical and his "performance" of a journalist as postmodern. In "Political Satire and Postmodern Irony in the Age of Stephen Colbert and Jon Stewart," Colletta asks, for example,

> Can the social and political satire of television shows like *The Daily Show, The Colbert Report*, and *The Simpsons* really have any kind of efficacy beyond that of mere entertainment? Or does the smirky, self-referential irony that makes these shows so popular actually undermine social and political engagement, creating satiric critique and ironic, passive democracy to discerning, engaged politics? (859).

But Stewart's rhetoric is hardly postmodern when it is conceptualized as a defense of perspicuity, especially when perspicuity for Stewart is no different than it is for the belletristic rhetoricians who view it as an ethical component to argumentation. For Campbell, in particular, perspicuity should be the central quality of rhetoric meant to enlighten the understanding of an audience. As Lois Agnew writes, "Like the Stoics, who believe that the capacity for 'common sense' granted to everyone can either lie dormant or be developed through education, the Scottish philosophers perceive education as the crucial factor in leading people to the right application of the common sense that they have been given" ("The Stoic Temper" 77). She suggests that for Campbell, in particular, common sense "involves more than the static capacity to apprehend self-evident truth, because it serves as the foundation for the moral reasoning that enables people to make judgments about contingent matters in all areas 'concerning life and existence'" ("Perplexity" 82).

The Daily Show might be a "fake" news show, but to echo Jeffrey Jones, "being fake does not mean that the information it imparts is untrue. Indeed, as with most social and political satire, its humor offers a means of reestablishing common sense truths to counter spectacle, ritual, pageantry, artifice, and verbosity that often cloak the powerful" (183). In the end, one might argue that the deliberative quality of Stewart's rhetoric is meant to engender accountability on the part of those who are responsible for mediating political debate in the news media. The accountability Stewart's rhetoric thus demands is the accountability called upon by Campbell's defense of perspicuous argumentation. For if we agree with Stewart's methodology, it is perspicuity that gives discourse its deliberative virtue, its ability to contribute to the understanding necessary to actually evaluate arguments made in the course of debate.

NOTES

[1] The quotations from Jon Stewart's appearance on *Crossfire* are taken from a transcript of the program publicly available on the web; see "Jon Stewart Crossfire Transcript."

[2] Rhetoricians have debated about the sources that most influenced Campbell's rhetorical theory. While there is a persuasive line of literature that demonstrates the Stoic influence on Campbell, which speaks to the common sense quality of his rhetoric, scholars also point to Hume and the tradition of British empiricism as a significant influence as well; see, for example, Walzer; Benoit; Bevilacqua; Bitzer; and Ehninger.

[3] Campbell begins *The Philosophy of Rhetoric* with an explanation that all discourse proposes an end. As he writes: "All the ends of speaking are reducible to four: every speech being intended to enlighten the understanding, to please the imagination, to move the passions, or to influence the will" (1).

WORKS CITED

Agnew, Lois. "The Stoic Temper in Belletristic Rhetoric." *Rhetoric Society Quarterly* 33.2 (2003): 69-88. Print.

---. "The 'Perplexity' of George Campbell's Rhetoric: The Epistemic Function of Common Sense." *Rhetorica* 18.1 (2000): 79-101. Print.

Baym, Geoffrey. "*The Daily Show*: Discursive Integration and the Reinvention of Political Journalism." *Political Communication* 22 (2005): 259-76. Print.

Benoit, William L. "Campbell's *The Philosophy of Rhetoric* and the Advancement of Rhetorical Theory: The Integration of Philosophical Antecedents." *Communication Studies* 41.1 (1990): 89-100. Print.

Bevilacqua, Vincent M. "Philosophical Origins of George Campbell's *Philosophy of Rhetoric.*" *Speech Monographs* 32.2 (1965): 1-12. Print.

Bitzer, Lloyd. Introduction. *The Philosophy of Rhetoric.* Carbondale: Southern Illinois UP, 1963. vii-li. Print.

Borden, Sandra L., and Chad Tew. "The Role of Journalist and the Performance of Journalism: Ethical Lesson From 'Fake' News (Seriously)." *Journal of Mass Media Ethics* 22.4 (2007): 300-14. Print.

Campbell, George. *The Philosophy of Rhetoric.* 1776. Ed. Lloyd F. Bitzer. Carbondale: Southern Illinois UP, 1968. Print.

Carter, Bill. "CNN Will Cancel 'Crossfire' and Cuts Ties to Commentator." *New York Times* 6 January 2005: C5. Print.

Colletta, Lisa. "Political Satire and Postmodern Irony in the Age of Stephen Colbert and Jon Stewart." *The Journal of Popular Culture* 42.5 (2009): 856-74. Print.

The Daily Show with Jon Stewart. Episode 14076. Comedy Central, 8 Jun. 2009. Television.

---. Episode 15054. Comedy Central, 20 Apr. 2010. Television.

---. Episode 17097. Comedy Central, 1 May 2012. Television.

Ehninger, Douglas W. "Campbell, Blair, and Whately Revisited." *Southern Speech Journal* 28.3 (1963): 169-82. Print.

---. "George Campbell and the Revolution in Inventional Theory." *Southern Speech Journal* 15.4 (1950): 270-76. Print.

Hariman, Robert. "In Defense of Jon Stewart." *Critical Studies in Media Communication* 24.3 (2007): 273-77. Print.

"Jon Stewart Crossfire Transcript." *About.com.* About.Com, 2007. Web. 20 Apr. 2012.

Jones, Jeffrey. *Entertaining Politics: Satiric Television and Political Engagement.* 2nd ed. New York: Rowan and Littlefield, 2009. Print.

McKerrow, Ray E. "Campbell and Whately on the Utility of Syllogistic Logic." *Western Speech Communication* 40.1 (1976): 3-13. Print.

Stewart, Jon. "Jon Stewart: The Most Trusted Name in Fake News." Interview by Terry Gross. *Fresh Air.* Natl. Public Radio. WHYY, New York. 4 Oct. 2010. Radio.

Waisanen, Don J. "A Citizen's Guides to Democracy Inaction: Jon Stewart and Stephen Colbert's Comic Rhetorical Criticism." *Southern Communication Journal* 74.2 (2009): 119-40. Print.

Walzer, Arthur E. "Campbell on the Passions: A Rereading of the *Philosophy of Rhetoric.*" *Quarterly Journal of Speech* 85 (1999): 72-85. Print.

Warner, Jamie. "Political Culture Jamming: The Dissident Humor of *The Daily Show with Jon Stewart.*" *Popular Communication* 5.1 (2007): 17-36. Print.

Wenner, Jann S. "Ready for the Fight: Rolling Stone Interview with Barack Obama." *Rolling Stone.com.* Wenner Media, 25 Apr. 2012. Web. 5 May 2012.

8

CHARGING TREASON
WHILE COMMITTING TREASON

Patricia Roberts-Miller's Cunning Projection, Conspiracy Rhetoric, and the Identity Criticism of Barack Obama

Keith D. Miller

In her recent *Fanatical Schemes: Pro-Slavery Rhetoric and the Tragedy of Consensus*, Patricia Roberts-Miller proposes what she calls "cunning projection" as a theoretical framework for analyzing Southern, proslavery rhetoric during several decades prior to the Civil War.[1] Here I contend that Roberts-Miller's conception of cunning projection can profitably be used to explain other species of American rhetoric from different historical periods. I argue for this possibility by explicating her theory of cunning projection, briefly, in relation to Southern segregationist rhetoric of the 1950s and 1960s and, at greater length, in relation to the identity criticism of Barack Obama. I proceed, first, by explaining her conception of cunning projection and her analysis of proslavery argumentation. Second, I explore segregationist rhetoric as a more recent manifestation of cunning projection. Third, I elucidate the two main elements of identity criticism of Obama—the claim that he was born outside the US and the claim that he is a Muslim—as another species of cunning projection.

In the appeals that slaveholding rhetors offered between roughly 1830 and 1861, they characteristically refused to consider alternatives to slavery. They did not simply maintain that the necessities of Southern agriculture (or what Kenneth Burke might call an economic "Neo-Malthusian bottleneck") drove them to practice slavery; nor did their defense of slavery simply reflect complacency (or what Kenneth Burke might call "bureaucratization of the imagination") (*Attitudes* 225-227, 298-306). Instead, they regularly and happily proclaimed that slavery provided unalloyed glories and benefits to all. These appeals feature what Roberts-Miller spotlights as stark, recurring contradictions that, she argues, qualify as typical features of proslavery argumentation and that, through an Alice-in-Wonderland version of logic, helped construct a formidable web of argumentation that enveloped the antebellum white South. As she documents, a single proslavery speech can easily include an obvious logical contradiction that can resurface in another proslavery speech and again in a proslavery sermon and yet again in a proslavery editorial. One such often-repeated contradiction is the claim that slaves are happy and docile *combined* with the claim that slaves are war-like, antiwhite insurrectionists. Another frequently reiterated contradiction is the insistence that slavery is eternal *combined* with the assertion that slavery may eventually disappear. A third commonly recurring contradiction is the notion that slavery benefits everyone *combined* with the charge that the evil British wrongfully imposed slavery upon innocent, land-owning American colonists. A fourth recirculating contradiction is the harsh condemnation of sectionalism and factionalism *combined* with the ardent promotion of sectionalism and factionalism. Obviously, one task for critics of slavers' discourse is to account for such contradictions, which thrived for decades and became argumentative commonplaces in the white South.

Vigorously contesting historians' dominant view of the clash between abolitionist and proslavery rhetorics, Roberts-Miller challenges the assumption that, during this era, American political debate featured a balanced exchange of positions that competed for attention and consent in the public square. As she explains, prominent historians of this era, including Drew Gilpin Faust, presume that public discourse occurs in a "marketplace of ideas" in which people "are willing to examine, explain, modify, and even abandon any belief" after a careful process of public discussion and examination (19-20). According to Faust and numerous other historians, proslavery rhetors (many of whom hailed from South Carolina) produced discourse within a more-or-less routine process of reasonable public discussion until abolitionists issued feverish denunciations of slavery that, Faust and others conclude, spurred slavers to turn to increasingly alarmist, increasingly bellicose appeals. On the contrary, Roberts-Miller contends, slavers issued alarmist and bellicose appeals without regard to the tone of the national discussion of slavery and before polemical abolitionist voices gained prominence. Extending the scholarship of William Freehling, Roberts-Miller adds that, far from valuing open public discussion, slavers demanded that Northerners' critique of slavery, including polite and circumspect criticism, cease altogether. Despite the barbarity of slavery and despite their own self-contradictory arguments, proponents of bondage insisted that that institution stood above any possible criticism, insisting that, in her words, "free discussion of slavery in any public place was incompatible with slavery in slave states" (77). With the fervent, largely unqualified support of many Southern newspapers and pulpits, slavers fully expected to promote new policies—such as expanding slavery into the West—without national discussion. As she explains, slavers "wanted to change public policy regarding slavery without public debate. They wanted decision making without deliberation" (23). Freehling and Roberts-Miller add that, in addition to demanding Northern silence about slavery, slavers also disrespected the Bill of Rights—and its guarantee of freedom of speech and freedom of the press—when they prompted Southern state governments to pass laws to outlaw the criticism of slavery and, in contradiction to their insistence on states' rights, sternly demanded that Northern state governments enact similar legislation.

In an effort to stop debate, proslavery mobs repeatedly attacked abolitionist speakers; one such mob murdered antislavery editor Elijah Lovejoy (Curtis, Richards). White Southerners cheered openly when Preston Brooks, a Congressman from South Carolina, used a cane to pummel Senator Charles Sumner, an outspoken abolitionist, on the floor of the US Senate, injuring Sumner so badly that he spent years recovering from his wounds (Donald). In addition, over a period of several years, Southern members of the House of Representatives installed the "gag rule" in an attempt to prevent former President John Quincy Adams and other Northern members of the House from introducing antislavery petitions in Congress (William Miller). Slavers also intercepted antislavery pamphlets at the post office in Charleston, South Carolina, thereby halting the distribution of US mail; they also passed laws to stop the dissemination of David Walker's abolitionist pamphlet and other antislavery tracts (Roberts-Miller 1-17, 159-86). Many slave states also outlawed literacy among slaves, partly as an effort to discourage them from reading abolitionist texts.

Roberts-Miller ties proslavery rhetoric to a white Southern honor code that fostered dueling.[2] When one aristocratic white Southerner male verbally offended another aristocratic white Southern male, the offended man would often challenge the offender to a duel with pistols. Dueling clearly did not refute the offending comment or criticism; but, by fatally wounding the critic, a duel erased the criticism (Roberts-Miller 77, 114, 116, 200). She explicates the Southern code that fostered dueling: "In an honor culture, one is dishonored, not by one's actions, but by people speaking of those actions. . . . If something does not exist unless and until it is mentioned in public discourse, one need not control one's own behavior, as much as control others' talk about that behavior" (116). Like dueling, the effort to kill an offending speaker, maim an outspoken Senator, mob a disagreeable orator, squash troublesome petitions, and eliminate distasteful pamphlets, while not rebutting any criticism proffered about slavery, might erase present (and possibly future) criticism while salvaging the honor of "insulted" slavers, at least in their own eyes.

White Southerners sometimes evoked another means of preserving the personal honor that they thought abolitionists were besmirching: they threatened to secede from the Union. Beginning in 1828, Southern legislators and other proslavery rhetors regularly engaged in brinkmanship with the North by warning of their own possible secession. Then, finally, despite Abraham Lincoln's promise not to interfere with slavery in the South, Southern states seceded in 1861. By contrast, Northern states never seceded from the Union, nor did Northern legislators ever threaten to do so. But, as Roberts-Miller explains, slavers regularly reproached the North by claiming that the simple criticism of slavery rendered abolitionists blameworthy for pushing white Southerners to secede and thereby to break or dissolve the United States.

According to slavers' argument, opponents of slavery thereby proved disloyal to the Union. In other words, slavers faulted Northerners for slavers' own treasonous gesture of threatening to secede and of actually seceding, followed by slavers' initiation of the extremely bloody Civil War. As Roberts-Miller explains, "Calling abolitionists traitorous may, to a modern reader, look patently insincere, if not actively silly. It was, after all, a smear made by nullifiers who had . . . advocated secession" (36). Analyzing slavers' petulant and irrational rhetoric, she observes, "nullifiers specifically and proslavery politicians generally took the strongest criticisms of them—that *they* were not particularly loyal to the Constitution—and projected the accusation onto their [abolitionist] outgroup" (36).

Roberts-Miller coins the phrase "cunning projection" to designate the rhetorical process of shoving one's own flaws onto someone else (37, 38, 103-26, 221-22). Through cunning projection, she explains, "One takes the major and most damning criticism of one's own position and simply asserts that it is true of the opposition" (221). Citing the work of social psychologists Derek Rucker and Anthony Pratkanis, she remarks that cunning projection "serves to persuade people that the name-calling group must be innocent of the charge, as they condemn it with such vehemence" (39, 222). In this case, slavers engaged in cunning projection when they projected their own traitorous desire to secede onto Northern abolitionists. She elucidates cunning projection, in part, by building on Burke's definition of scapegoating, which she quotes:

> *Projection* device. The "curative" process that comes with the ability to hand over one's ills to a scapegoat, thereby getting purification by dissociation. This was especially medicinal, since the sense of frustration leads to a self-questioning. Hence if one can hand over his infirmities to a vessel, or "cause," outside the self, one can battle an external enemy instead of battling an enemy within. (Burke, *Philosophy* 173-74; qtd. in Roberts-Miller 38)

"Burke," she remarks, "emphasizes the psychologically soothing properties of scapegoating—that an individual feels strangely cleansed by projecting one's shames onto something ritually killed" (38). She adds that, when slavers engaged in cunning projection and scapegoated abolitionists, they discovered, "in Burke's terms, a perfect 'unification' device" that could foster solidarity among millions of white Southerners, including masses of poor whites who did not own slaves, while, in the minds of slavers, immunizing slavery from criticism (103).[3]

As Roberts-Miller maintains, advocates of slavery wallowed in insecurity while generating hugely overblown rhetoric alleging that white Southerners were innocent victims of the diabolical plans of crazed antislavery crusaders. By vastly inflating the numbers of abolitionists and grossly warping them into a monstrous threat, proslavery rhetors, Roberts-Miller argues, exemplified what Richard Hofstadter terms the "paranoid style" in American politics, a style that posits a huge, devilish conspiracy upon the innocent that requires a keen sense of emergency and deep solidarity among those who would resist it.[4]

Although Roberts-Miller provides only a few hints about other contexts for the curious antilogic of cunning projection, it unfortunately continued in American political life long after the conclusion of the Civil War. I contend that segregationists' responses to the civil rights movement of the 1950s and 1960s often exemplified cunning projection, scapegoating, and the paranoid style. Over many decades, throughout the South, white racists systematically violated African Americans' rights under the Fourteenth Amendment, which guarantees "equal protection under the law," including the rights to own property in good neighborhoods, to attend good public schools, to attend good public universities, to eat at lunch counters and restaurants, to rent rooms in hotels, and to read books in public libraries. When a crush of white segregationists killed two and injured more than four hundred others during a riot aimed at preventing James Meredith from integrating the University of Mississippi, the mob prevented Meredith from enjoying "equal protection under the law." When white police throughout the South routinely jailed activists for protesting segregation, they violated those activists' First Amendment right to freedom of speech. When segregationist mobs repeatedly and violently attacked reporters of major newspapers and camera crews of national television networks, they violated journalists' First Amendment right to freedom of the press (Roberts and Klibanoff). When lawless public officials (including Governor George Wallace of Alabama) and police countenanced the bombing of the homes and churches of those who objected to segregation, they promoted intimidation and murder.[5]

Further, segregationists throughout the South routinely and loudly defied the unanimous *Brown* decision of the Supreme Court that mandated the racial integration of all public schools in the US. One who flouted the *Brown* decision, Governor Orval Faubus of Arkansas, commandeered the National Guard for the purpose of preventing black children from integrating Central High School of Little Rock, spurring President Dwight Eisenhower's decision to dispatch the 101st Airborne Division of the US army to escort the children past segregationist mobs on their way to school. With the apparent sanction of Governor John Patterson and the police, a segregationist mob in Alabama violated the *Morgan* decision of the Supreme Court by pummeling Freedom Riders who, in concert with the *Morgan* decision, were peacefully integrating interstate commerce.

Despite segregationists' unconstitutional practices and often violent behavior—which climaxed with the murders of Medgar Evers, Michael Schwerner, James Chaney, Andrew Goodman, and Martin Luther King, Jr. (none of whom was afforded adequate police protection)—Southern governors, FBI Director J. Edgar Hoover, and others frequently ignored the lawlessness of white racists while routinely and falsely claiming that James Meredith, Evers, King, and other integrationists were Communists. Hoover devoted enormous time to spying on King and attempting to destroy his reputation (Garrow, *FBI*). Given American participation in a nuclear arms race and Cold War against Russia, China, and Cuba—three Communist nations—the charge of Communism amounted to an accusation of treason. That is, segregationists were asserting that advocates of racial equality were acting in concert with hostile foreign powers as part of a Communist conspiracy designed to overthrow the US. In doing so, segregationists exhibited a paranoid style while engaging in cunning projection and the scapegoating of African American avatars of Gandhian nonviolence. While blatantly disregarding the Constitution and the rule of law, white racist leaders and thugs projected their own treason onto exponents of civil rights, who, even when engaged in civil disobedience of local, racist ordinances, sought to implement American democracy for the first time in the South while acting in concert with the Constitution, the Supreme Court, and the dominant American religion of Judeo-Christianity (not the atheism of Karl Marx). Through cunning projection, segregationists succeeded, at least for awhile, in persuading some that, in Roberts-Miller's words, "the name-calling group must be innocent of the charge, as they condemn it with such vehemence" (222).

I maintain that Roberts-Miller's framework of cunning projection is also useful for explicating identity criticism of Barack Obama. By identity criticism, I do *not* mean criticism of the policies advocated by 2008 presidential candidate Obama or the policies espoused or enacted by President Obama since his inauguration in January 2009. (To anyone who will listen, I myself frequently rebuke Obama for many of his proposals and policies.) By identity criticism, I mean criticism of two of Obama's principal identity claims: his claim of birthplace and his claim of religious affiliation. I consider these below.

In 2008, a number of people criticized Obama's identity by declaring that he was not born in Honolulu, as he attested, but outside the US. Rebutting this claim, Senator Obama posted his Hawaiian birth certificate on his presidential campaign website of 2008.[6] In the same year Factcheck.org, a nonpartisan project sponsored by the Annenberg Public Policy Center, refuted the birthplace criticism by printing the same Hawaiian birth certificate, which *Newsweek* and the *Los Angeles Times* reprinted as well (Henig; Malcolm). Factcheck.org further declared that, a few days after Obama's birth in 1961, a prominent newspaper, the *Honolulu Advertiser*, publicly announced his birth in Honolulu. After posting the newspaper announcement on its website, Factcheck.org dispatched experts to personally inspect Obama's Hawaiian birth certificate, which they found to be valid (Henig). As of the day I am writing these lines, no evidence has been produced that would challenge the validity of that birth certificate or the contemporaneous newspaper announcement of Obama's birth. Nor has evidence surfaced to support the claim that Obama was born in any specific place other than Hawaii. Yet, relying on unalloyed speculation, skeptics (sometimes called "birthers") have persisted in disputing Obama's Hawaiian birthplace. In 2009, World Net Daily and talk-show hosts Rush Limbaugh, G. Gordon Liddy, Sean Hannity, and Lou Dobbs all asserted that Obama either was or might have been born outside the US; they sometimes stated or implied that his mother gave birth in Kenya. Prominent politicians—including former vice-presidential candidate Sarah Palin, Sena-

tor David Vitter, Senator Richard Shelby, and Representative Roy Blunt—
have all reiterated a version of this claim. Several polls suggest that many
Americans doubt that Obama was born in the US ("Barack Obama"). In
April 2011, after major news outlets trumpeted Donald Trump's revival of
the birthplace criticism, President Obama held a press conference in which
he distributed to reporters the "long form" of his Hawaiian birth certificate,
which he then placed on the White House website, where it remains. The *Los
Angeles Times* published this "long form" birth certificate (Memoli). Fact-
check.org responded to Trump by noting that, in 1961, along with the *Honolulu Advertiser*, another newspaper, the *Honolulu Star-Bulletin*, also announced
Obama's birth in Hawaii (Jackson and Kiely). Still, the birthplace criticism
persists. In October 2011, Governor Rick Perry of Texas, a Republican presidential candidate, recirculated the birthplace charge yet again (Geiger). In
May 2012, the well-known and controversial Sheriff Joe Arpaio of Phoenix—
sometimes deemed the "toughest sheriff in America"—held a press conference in which he charged that Obama was not born in the US (Forer).

The birthplace criticism matters because Article II, Section I of the US
Constitution appears to many to stipulate that only a person born in the US
qualifies to serve as President. For that reason Obama's birthplace scoffers
are either contending or strongly implying that he is constitutionally ineligible to serve in the White House.

World Net Daily and popular media figures Rush Limbaugh, G. Gordon
Liddy, Michael Savage, Pam Geller, Jim Quinn, and Rose Tennent all provide the second identity criticism of Obama: the claim that he is a Muslim
("Barack Obama"). In 2008, Senator Obama's campaign website also dismissed this charge, and Obama has repeatedly attested that he is a Christian.
However, as Limbaugh admits, for roughly two decades, Obama and his wife
and children regularly attended Trinity United Church of Christ, located in
Southside Chicago. During the presidential campaign of 2008, a large controversy erupted when journalists aired statements by Rev. Jeremiah Wright, the
pastor of Trinity Church, whose leftist Christian critique of the US resembled
that of the radical Martin Luther King, Jr. of 1967 and 1968. Limbaugh and
many others suggested that Obama shared Wright's leftist Christian views
and, therefore, did not deserve election to the White House.[7]

Note that World Net Daily, Limbaugh, Liddy, and others maintain *both*
that Obama was born outside the US *and* that Obama is a Muslim. These
identity critics do *not* simply claim or imply that Obama is a fascinating figure
because he is the first Muslim president. Appealing to Americans frightened
by the attacks of September 11, 2001, and fearful not only of al-Qaeda but
also of Muslims in general, critics who make these two identity claims—
when taken separately or, especially, when taken together—suggest, insinuate, hint, or imply that Obama is or might be a foreign plant who is not loyal
to the US, its democratic principles or its dominant religion.

I maintain that, by suggesting, insinuating, implying or hinting that
Obama is or might be an unconstitutional, foreign, anti-Christian, traitorous

presidential candidate, Obama's birthplace identity critics in 2008 sought to thwart national political debate and the national presidential election *not* by attempting to refute his ideas, but simply by disqualifying him from the campaign and removing him from the debate platform. By continuing to insinuate, hint, or imply that a foreign plant slipped into the Oval Office by means of a devious conspiracy, Obama's identity critics—especially those who continue to broadcast both identity criticisms after his election and inauguration—seek to undermine the democratic electoral process that allowed Obama to become president. They attempt to deny the validity of the 2008 primary election and general election, even though voters in November 2008 granted Obama a large popular majority plus a large electoral majority—a victory that included Obama's defeat of Senator John McCain in such normally Republican states as Indiana, Virginia, and North Carolina. These identity critics also insinuated, hinted, or implied that Obama's inauguration and subsequent occupancy of the White House were and are invalid. In other words, the identity critics insinuated or implied that Obama should be barred from running for the White House and now insinuate or imply that, as someone ineligible to serve as president, he should be banished from the White House. Instead of refuting his proposals and policies, they want to remove him initially from the political stage and now from the Oval Office.

By attempting to deny the legitimacy and success of Obama's candidacy—even after his triumphant campaign and inauguration—his identity critics consistently define themselves as patriots loyal to American ideals; like proslavery rhetors of the antebellum era, they object to factionalism while ardently promoting factionalism. Worse, Obama's identity critics, like the slavers, claim to support American democracy while actively rejecting it. Practicing cunning projection, they externalize their own rejection of democracy and their own treason, foisting that rejection and that treason onto their opponent, Obama. Roberts-Miller's analysis of proslavery rhetoric also fits the rhetoric of Obama's identity critics: "This cunning strategy of rhetorical projection rationalizes the bad behavior of the rhetor, in that it makes the aggressive behavior seem, at worst, defensive" (39). Through the cunning projection of slavers, Roberts-Miller explains, "those who support the Constitution are transmogrified into traitors, and those who wish to violate it are not" (125). This observation also describes Obama's identity critics. Like the cunning projection practiced by slavers, the cunning projection practiced by Obama's identity critics involves what Burke identifies as the unification strategy of scapegoating. Blue-collar, antiabortion Christian fundamentalists, Wall Street titans, and hunters in rural areas may have little in common; but Obama's identity critics attempt to unite all these people—and to distract them from policy debates—through a process of purification that they seek to achieve by scapegoating Obama.

Obama's identity critics also manifest what Hofstadter identifies as the paranoid style. Especially when combined, the two identity criticisms suggest, insinuate, or imply—or can be taken to suggest, insinuate, or imply—

that Obama was installed in the White House through an unconstitutional conspiracy for the purpose of aiding Muslim fanatics who wish to kill millions of Americans and to destroy the US. The implications of any such claim are huge. If Obama were a disloyal, foreign plant, then, anticipating that baby Obama would eventually run for the White House, Hawaiian officials and newspapers would, in 1961, be initiating the devilish plot when they conspired to attest falsely that Obama was born in Hawaii. Also wittingly or unwittingly furthering the conspiracy would be virtually the entire news media who, throughout 2007 and most of 2008, treated the alleged foreigner and/or alleged extremist Muslim as though he were a legitimate presidential aspirant whose prospects and ideas merited discussion. Also knowingly or unknowingly forwarding the conspiracy would be officials who prepared primary campaign ballots and general election ballots that included Obama's name alongside those of other contenders for the presidency.

Additional aware or unaware conspirators would be those other contenders—including Senator Hillary Clinton and Senator John McCain—who criticized Obama and who repeatedly debated him in formal, televised settings. The news media, ballot makers, Clinton, and McCain certainly treated Obama as someone qualified to pursue the highest office. Also fostering the conspiracy would be millions of seriously deceived Democrats who voted for Obama instead of Clinton or some other candidate in the Democratic primaries. Other witting or unwitting conspirators would be the millions of voters who picked Obama over McCain in the general election. Also intentionally or unintentionally facilitating the conspiracy would be everyone who participated in Obama's inaugural ceremony of January 2009, including John Roberts, the Chief Justice of the Supreme Court and a conservative Republican, who officially swore in Obama. The identity critics arguably imply that anyone who used or uses the phrase "President Obama" was or is knowingly or unknowingly promoting the same vast conspiracy.

In addition, many of these identity critics regularly contradict themselves. Limbaugh seems entirely unaware that he contradicts himself by charging *both* that Obama is a Muslim *and* that Obama is a leftist Christian. No one can be a bona fide Muslim and a bona fide Christian at the same time. Further, many of these identity critics, obviously including McCain's running mate Sarah Palin, strongly supported McCain's presidential bid. Palin and other birthplace critics of Obama failed to mention that McCain was incontrovertibly and by his own declaration born in Panama, where his father, a US military officer, was stationed. Simply stated, Palin and other right-wing birthplace critics cunningly projected any legitimate question about McCain's birthplace ineligibility onto Obama.[8]

Obama's identity critics also contradict themselves by refusing to notice that they themselves act in a way that furthers the alleged, anti-American foreign conspiracy. Whenever identity critics denounce Obama's proposals and policies—as they often do—they act under the assumption that Obama has the right to make proposals, sign legislation, and enact policies; that is, they act as though he were a bona fide president. By affirming Obama's standing as president, they themselves further legitimize the Obama presidency that they simultaneously suggest, hint, or imply is the illegitimate result of a diabolical, foreign conspiracy. Among Obama's identity critics are several members of Congress who, by attending his State of the Union addresses given before a joint session of Congress, also confirm his position as president and thereby appear to foster the same fiendish conspiracy that they detect underneath Obama's candidacy and election.

Antebellum white rhetors used cunning projection in an effort to promote and protect white supremacy and slavery. During the 1950s and 1960s, white racists used cunning projection in an effort to protect white supremacy and segregation. Since 2008, a group of white rhetors use cunning projection in an effort to discredit Obama, an African American, and to remove him from the political scene. White racial anxieties may factor into all three of these cases. In each of them, a vocal group of whites sought to maintain a stranglehold on subordinated African Americans by resorting to the sad, tortured logic of cunning projection. In the first two cases, vocal whites also resorted to violence aimed at physically eliminating proponents of African Americans rights.

Writing prior to Roberts-Miller, Sharon Crowley examines the paranoid style of contemporary, fundamentalist, and apocalyptic Christian rhetoric. Crowley briefly links this discourse to proslavery rhetoric when she quotes and reflects on Abraham Lincoln's comment (in his Cooper Institute speech of 1860) about the extreme difficulty of changing the minds of those white Southerners who displayed swaggering, conspiratorial proslavery discourse that seriously misrepresented his intentions with regard to slavery (164). Exploring the possibility of a more civil rhetoric that could bridge the current, yawning liberal-conservative divide in the US, Crowley forwards several suggestions. First, she asks her readers to attempt "to demonstrate" to fundamentalist, conspiracy-minded Christians "the superiority of alternative values" (200). Second, she advocates efforts "to demonstrate the contingency of . . . [fundamentalist] values by locating them in space and time, thus destabilizing the system of belief in which these same values are taken to be noncontingent" (201). Third, instead of prodding devotees of this rhetoric to immediately jettison their entire worldview, she advocates a piecemeal approach of "disarticulating a particular belief from the others with which it is articulated" in order to hold that belief up to inspection (201). She candidly admits that anyone who adopts her first two suggestions might find success either "not easy" or "very difficult" (200, 201). Her third suggestion, she adds, requires "discernment and skill" combined with "time and patience" (201). She concludes with, in her words, "the hope that my readers will find, or open, many more paths of invention" to reach conspiracy-minded fundamentalists than she has "been able to name here" (201).

I endorse Crowley's notions for engaging not only with the rhetoric that she analyzes, but also with the identity criticism of Obama and with any other new (yet, in some ways, distressingly old) manifestations of cunning projection that, unfortunately, may continue to surface in the public arena. But I also urge that, in addition to heeding her advice, we need to fathom cunning projection as an antidebate form of debate. We further need to understand its stubborn persistence and resurgence as a manifestation of long-standing white racial anxieties and to prevent those whom it targets from being removed from the national stage as the victims of false, self-contradictory charges and/or of physical violence.

NOTES

[1] Patricia Roberts-Miller is no relation to me.
[2] See Nisbett and Cohen.
[3] See Roberts-Miller 103-26; see also Cooper.
[4] See two books by Hofstader. See also Davis.
[5] For Wallace's knowledge about and tolerance of Ku Klux Klan bombings of African American homes and churches in Birmingham, see McWhorter.
[6] Hawaii became a state in 1959, two years before Obama's birth in 1961.
[7] For Limbaugh's linking of Obama to Wright, see rushlimbaugh.com/home/daily/site_031308/content/01125106.guest.html.
[8] Unlike Obama's birthplace critics, none of Obama's prominent supporters generated a "birther" argument against McCain or made an effort to disqualify him from the presidential race of 2008.

WORKS CITED

"Barack Obama Citizenship Conspiracy Theories." *Wikipedia.* Wikimedia Foundation, n.d. Web. 11 June 2011.

Burke, Kenneth. *Attitudes toward History.* 3rd ed. Berkeley: U of California P, 1984.

---. *Philosophy of Literary Form.* New York: Vintage, 1957. Print.

Cooper, William. *Liberty and Slavery: Southern Politics to 1860.* New York: Knopf, 1983. Print.

Crowley, Sharon. *Toward a Civil Discourse: Rhetoric and Fundamentalism.* Pittsburgh: U of Pittsburgh P, 2006. Print.

Curtis, Michael. "The 1837 Killing of Elijah Lovejoy by an Anti-Abolition Mob." *UCLA Law Review* 44 (April 1997): 1009-11; 1046-50. Print.

Davis, David Brion. *The Slave Power Conspiracy and the Paranoid Style.* Baton Rouge: Louisiana State UP, 1969. Print.

Donald, David Herbert. *Charles Sumner and the Coming of the Civil War.* New York: Knopf, 1960. Print.

Faust, Drew Gilpin. *The Ideology of Slavery: Proslavery Thought in the Antebellum South, 1830–1860.* Baton Rouge: Louisiana State UP, 1981. Print.

Forer, Ben. "Obama's Birth Certificate May Be Forged, Sheriff Joe Arpaio Says." *ABC World News.* ABC Internet Ventures, 1 May 2012. Web. 7 May 2012.

Freehling, William. *Prelude to Civil War: The Nullification Controversy in South Carolina.* New York: Harper, 1966. Print.

---. *The Road to Disunion: Secessionists at Bay, 1776–1854.* Vol. 1. New York: Oxford UP, 1990. Print.

Garrow, David. *The FBI and Martin Luther King, Jr.* New York: Penguin, 1981. Print.

Geiger, Kim. "Rick Perry Doesn't Know if Obama's Birth Certificate Is Real." *Los Angeles Times*, 24 October 2011. Web.

Henig, Jess, with Joe Miller. "Born in the U.S.A." *Factcheck.org*. Annenberg Public Policy Center, 21 Aug. 2008. Web. 10 June 2011. Rpt. in *The Daily Beast.com*. *Newsweek*, 20 Aug. 2008. Web. 10 June 2011.

Hofstadter, Richard. *Anti-Intellectualism in American Life*. New York: Knopf, 1963. Print.

---. *The Paranoid Style in American Politics and Other Essays*. New York: Vintage, 1967. Print.

Jackson, Brooks, and Eugene Kiely, with Michael Morse. "Donald—You're Fired." *Factcheck.org*. Annenberg Public Policy Center, 9 Apr. 2011. Web. 11 June 2011.

Limbaugh, Rush. "Barack Obama and Jeremiah Wright." *Rushlimbaugh.com*. Premiere Radio Networks, 13 Mar. 2008. Web. 11 June 2011.

Malcolm, Andrew. "Barack Obama's Birth Certificate Revealed Here." *Los Angeles Times*, 16 June 2008. Web. 7 May 2012.

McGough, Michael. "Rick Perry Doesn't Know whether Obama's Birth Certificate Is Real." *Los Angeles Times*, 25 Oct. 2011. Web. 5 May 2012.

McWhorter, Diane. *Carry Me Home: Birmingham, Alabama, the Climactic Battle of the Civil Rights Revolution*. New York: Simon and Schuster, 2001. Print.

Memoli, Michael. "As Campaign Heats Up, So Does Focus on 'Birthers.'" *Los Angeles Times*, 22 April 2011. Web. 6 May 2012.

Nisbett, Richard, and Dov Cohen. *Culture of Honor: The Psychology of Violence in the South*. Boulder: Westview, 1996. Print.

Richards, Leonard. *"Gentlemen of Property and Standing": Anti-Abolition Mobs in Jacksonian America*. New York: Oxford UP, 1970. Print.

Roberts, Gene, and Hank Klibanoff. *The Race Beat: The Press, the Civil Rights Struggle, and the Awakening of a Nation*. New York: Knopf, 2006. Print.

Roberts-Miller, Patricia. *Fanatical Schemes: Proslavery Rhetoric and the Tragedy of Consensus*. Tuscaloosa: U of Alabama P, 2009. Print.

Rucker, Derek, and Anthony Pratkanis. "Projection as an Interpersonal Influence Tactic." *Personality and Social Psychology Bulletin* 27.11 (Nov. 2001): 1494-507. Print.

9

THE NORMS OF (ECONOMIC) RHETORICAL CULTURE

Randall Iden & Dale Cyphert

Thomas B. Farrell begins his 1993 book, *Norms of Rhetorical Culture*, with a paradox. A rhetorical culture, he asserts, is "an institutional formation in which motives of competing parties are intelligible, audiences available, expressions reciprocal, norms translatable and silences noticeable" (1), a definition that cannot be reconciled with the popular view of rhetoric as undisciplined, partisan speech designed to obscure meaning for individual benefit. Farrell's notion of rhetorical culture requires belief in alchemy—a transmutation of creative and crafty spin control into the best hope for a civic life. Rhetoric is at once the demagoguery of the masses and the *phronesis* (practical wisdom) of speaking citizens.

Similarly, Deirdre McCloskey's *The Rhetoric of Economics* begins with the startling argument that even the most sophisticated quantitative analysis requires a proper rhetorical foundation. "Economics is scientific," she claims, "but literary too" (23), insisting that all scientific endeavor involves crafting arguments that do not merely fill out the space around the equation but also help to "reinstate wide and wiser reasoning" (164). Across the sciences, accepting the central place of rhetoric in the process of scientific inquiry has forced an acknowledgement that messy discourse is foundational to the creation and dissemination of ostensibly pure scientific knowledge (Bazerman; Prelli). Even the dark and dismal science of economics has not been immune to the "rhetorical turn" (Rorty).

McCloskey addressed economists as communicators within the technical sphere of their own discipline, avoiding the issues involved in the discussion of economics within the public sphere. Farrell discussed the public sphere at great length but, in keeping with the Enlightenment trifurcation of political, spiritual, and economic spheres, severed economic activity from the political, ignoring any need for the public debate of technical economic issues. In the years since both books were written, however, the intersection of economics and the public sphere has become increasingly important. We are acutely aware of the rhetorical behavior of politicians, bankers, media commentators, and market analysts as they explain and defend both state and individual policy and investment decisions.

The expectations of responsible citizenship now require that all individuals, not merely a wealthy few, make informed decisions that require economic understanding. For example, the shift from company-managed, defined-benefit pension plans to 401(k)s and IRAs has transferred responsibility for economic decision making from the company to the employed individual. Similarly, as post-secondary education becomes a prerequisite for a living wage, every parent must make informed decisions about savings plans, student loans, and college job-placement performances. Further, the global market has grown both more sophisticated and more interconnected. The financial crisis that began in 2008, in particular, forced the citizens of Main Street to pay attention to the issues of Wall Street. Awareness, in turn, has led to a realization that understanding the issues and making prudent political decisions requires economic sophistication. Government bailouts, tax policy, environmental regulation, monetary stimuli, deficits, and austerity plans have become crucial topics in political conversations around the globe.

Economic rhetoric as the undisciplined, partisan speech of ideologues is clearly not the rhetorical vocabulary from which emerges the *phronesis* of speaking citizens. But if alchemy is required to get from one to the other, where is our philosopher's stone? Farrell suggests that rhetoric becomes "the only-humane manner for an argumentative culture to sustain public institutions" because it "helps to define and so constitute such a culture by expanding the reach and scope of validity claims in practice and also by inviting audiences to think figuratively about their own place and conduct in unfolding historical episodes" (213).

We propose that the notion of a rhetorical culture can and must be extended to include the norms that govern economics and economic decision making. Our aim here is to examine one rhetorical attempt to explain our most recent financial crisis in a way that would allow broader public access to the "validity claims" of the economic sphere. An award-winning episode of NPR's *This American Life* successfully translated arcane technical information into language deemed effective and appropriate for public discussion. We claim that the rhetoric was successful on two levels and, further, that the interplay of these levels frames the substantive and effective public performance of economic decision making. First, the narrative format offers a vehicle by which financial and economic topics can be made meaningful to the citizenry, allowing individuals to judge economic decisions on the basis of narrative coherence and plausibility.

More importantly, those standards of coherence and plausibility necessarily invoke the norms of the rhetorical culture in which they operate. A closer reading of the text thus allows us to identify the rules of a rhetoric that might allow reasoned economic debate. By inviting audiences to "think figuratively about their place and conduct," the producers introduce information about the economy as a series of coherent, reasonable political and social claims. Rather than wallowing in ideological name calling and political pandering, our text illustrates the philosopher's stone, the alchemy by which a rhetoric of demagoguery can be turned into the *phronesis* of speaking citizens in a contemporary public sphere.

"The Giant Pool of Money"

In May of 2008, the radio series *This American Life* aired an episode through the Public Radio International (PRI) network of stations entitled "The Giant Pool of Money." *This American Life* is one of the most popular shows on public radio and uses a narrative model in each episode to tell several stories linked by a theme. The show is known for literate, funny, and touching storytelling, and most episodes deal with subjects such as memories of summer camp, lost loves, first jobs, experiences in war, and similar personal topics. The show works as both entertainment and commentary by taking disparate and often unconnected stories and weaving them into a coherent tapestry.

"The Giant Pool of Money" is an unusual episode in that two reporters, *This American Life* producer Alex Blumberg and NPR reporter Adam Davidson, used the entire hour to tell a single, if complex, story. The episode is also unusual because it takes on a serious topic; *This American Life* tilts toward entertainment and away from news. Further, airing in the midst of the financial meltdown during a time of great public anxiety, this episode was more temporally relevant than most *This American Life* stories.

Significantly, "The Giant Pool of Money" was one of the most popular episodes in *This American Life's* history. There were ten times as many downloads as normal for the show; it was aired by popular demand several times; and it has been used in a variety of educational settings. The episode's creators won the 2008 Polk Award for Radio Reporting, and PRI won the 2008 George Peabody Award. The success of the episode also inspired Blumberg and Davidson to form the Planet Money team for NPR.

An Analysis of Economic and Rhetorical Norms

Those who would study the processes by which humans allocate scarce resources include both economists, who have traditionally focused on the decision making of the individual agent, and rhetoricians, who seek to understand the means by which agents induce each other to decide. Either discipline aims to explain the means by which a community determines the relative values of material, intellectual, and social goods—and how its members are able to use, control, or exchange them. The economists' traditional preference for mathematical tools has stood in contrast to the rhetoricians' ancient roots in discourse, and academic structures prevent sufficient "familiarity with the other field's methods and findings" (Wildman 694). Still, advances in both economics and rhetorical theory highlight the degree to which every economic transaction can be understood as a site of rhetorical performance.

Textbooks continue to simplify and mathematize the decision-making model, presenting the classical economics of *homo economicus*, the rational, self-interested human who makes economic decisions to garner the most material gain with the least amount of effort. However, contemporary theorists have begun to address the more complex processes of economic decision making. The 2001 Nobel Prize in economics was awarded to three economists for their work in *information economics*, a field that attempts to codify, if not quantify, the degree to which economic choices are impacted by the amount of information available to parties in the transaction (Akerlof) and by signals that are given regarding the validity of information (Spence), and that asserts that an understanding of information exchange is fundamental to any kind of economic analysis (Stiglitz). The following year, the field of *behavioral economics* was recognized, with the Nobel awarded to Daniel Kahneman and Vernon L. Smith for their work to incorporate human judgment and decision making into theories of economics.

So, while it is still common for practitioners to discuss the economy and financial markets as the mathematically derived net of price/value calculations, economic theorists are searching for ways to incorporate the effects of communication among agents (Wildman 700) and the means of persuasion with regard to economic choices (Thaler and Sunstein), as well as to provide explanations for large-scale effects of discourse on economic outcomes (Pfeffer; Ferraro et al.; Akerlof and Shiller). Meanwhile, rhetorical scholars offer frameworks through which these collective economic decisions can be understood, explaining otherwise "irrational" behavior with the rhetorical tools of narrative and mimesis (Goodnight and Green), ethos and power (Lyon), and genre and style (Lanham). These theoretical efforts demonstrate the degree to which economics and rhetoric both study the process by which a community makes its economic decisions, but neither is primarily concerned with the alchemy of civil discourse.

Our investigation of the "The Giant Pool of Money" is thus concerned with understanding its rhetorical function. The broadcast created a multi-layered argument in and about the public sphere of economic discussions. Certainly the text makes claims as to the chain of events that led to the crisis, but it also humanizes the players, avoiding the ideologically based demonization of bankers, brokers, and consumers that appears in other accounts. As a highly acclaimed and usefully imitated narrative, it represents a template for rhetorically justified arguments and illustrates the possibility for reasonable discussion of economic issues in the public sphere.

Our analysis identifies an understanding of economic relationships that assumes the value of protective social relationships to counter the short-sighted errors inherent in the individual profit taking of the *homo economicus*. We find an epistemology of nuance and specific context rather than untempered reliance on abstracted and objectified numerical data, and we locate the norms of prudence that allow a performance of economic behavior that is both healthy and virtuous. We conclude that the compelling narrative of "The Giant Pool of

Money" shows how market machinations and technical information can be translated into discourse through which the public can understand and contribute to better economic policies. This broadcast might be seen as an eloquent philosopher's stone, a sample of the discursive alchemy that moves public rhetoric from the ideological demagogueries of invisible hands and econometric models toward the humanistic rhetorical norms that allow *phronesis.*

Adam Davidson introduces the broadcast by describing two events he has recently attended: an awards dinner for financial professionals and a seminar for homeowners facing foreclosure. Davidson asserts that these two groups of people are connected through a long chain of middlemen and that each group, aided by layers of agents between them, helped to bring about the real estate crisis. The trope that marks *This American Life* is the presentation of specific cases that stand for a topic; an accretion of stories creates understanding of the whole.

The scene begins with an epideictic moment, a black-tie dinner in lower Manhattan attended by Jim Finkle of Dynamic Partners, manager of a Collateralized Debt Obligation instrument nominated as CDO of the Year for Total Securitization's 4th Annual US Securitization Awards. The dialogue is critical of the proposed honor, with host Ira Glass and NPR's international business and economic correspondent Adam Davidson pointing out that the nominee instruments "included the one that nearly brought down the global financial system." Even the awarding organization was "aware that there's a certain irony" involved and had considered cancelling the event. Recordings from the Manhattan event are then juxtaposed with a Brooklyn gathering of "people on the opposite side of the mortgage crisis" who are facing foreclosure.

There is more going on, however, than a simple exposition of villains and victims. As Davidson describes it, "these two groups are connected" by the sub-prime crisis. In contrast with the polarizing rhetoric of the 99% who suffered mortgage losses throwing blame at the 1% who profited from their pain, this text explicitly aims to illuminate "this long chain of people that starts with these Wall Street guys and ends with people who stand to lose their homes." While there is assuredly bad behavior involved, the victim-villain dichotomy is not finely drawn. Instead, Glass declares "everybody along the chain kind of deluded themselves, thinking they could throw out the old rules of banking." The "old rules" are ultimately cast as the foundation for an enduring economic model, and in the implied relationships, epistemology, and decision-making performance, the public is offered a means to translate arcane economic policy into civil discourse.

The text of the broadcast avoids ideological shortcuts, adhering to Celeste Condit's recommendation for "empathic" critique that aims to "listen to as many voices as we can and to assume them to be sincere on their own terms" (188) in order to "locate pieces of common ground among various voices and to discover options for those compromises necessary for coexistence" (189). In short, easy ideologically motivated stereotypes do not lend themselves to civil discourse.

The nuance is illustrated in an interview with Clarence Nathan, who took out a $540,000 NINA loan while "working three part-time, not very steady jobs" for a total annual income of about $45,000. He says, "Nobody came and told me a lie, and told me a story, and said, oh, just close your eyes, and all your problems will go away. . . . The bank made an imprudent loan. I made an imprudent loan. So the bank and I are partners in this deal."

The rest of Act One traces the history of this new "imprudent partner-ship" between homeowners and banks to the early 2000s when a sudden expansion in the world's "giant pool of money" created a huge demand for "low-risk investment that paid some return." The language with which this is explained serves to humanize the players. Central banks are said to be "saving for whatever central banks save for" while "very nervous men and women" are left to watch over the pool of money." These men and women become characters in a recognizable narrative, no longer just abstracted financial data, and motivations can be understood in terms of moral human relationships.

Further, the source of the crisis is developed in terms of the Wall Street investment institutions' unwillingness to engage in authentic human relation-ships. "They didn't want to get mixed up with actual people, and their cata-strophic health problems, and their divorces, and all the reasons that might stop them from paying their mortgages." Nevertheless, they needed places to invest the giant pool of money, some $70 trillion globally, and pressure mounted at all levels of the mortgage industry to sell more mortgages to more homeowners, regardless of messy, context-bound considerations of prudence.

A second, equally important factor is the degree to which mortgage lenders did things they knew to be imprudent because they could make so much money doing it. Even though "guys like . . . Warren Buffett said the very logic was ridiculous" and individual mortgage brokers tried, at the beginning, to decline deals they thought badly underwritten, "people were laughing at us . . . to say, You're crazy. You're hurting your business. . . . [Y]ou could make $1 million a year." The commissions and fees motivated imprudent behavior, and reliance on bad data instead of real relationships made it possible for them to fool themselves.

The denouement of the program chronicles the unwinding of the finan-cial chain. First, Wall Street investors noticed their securities were not per-forming well and stopped purchasing the loans from the mortgage brokers, who, in turn, defaulted on the loans they had used to purchase them. The housing bubble burst, creating a sub-prime housing crisis, which became a credit crisis as those who tended to the giant pool of global money became obsessed with "avoiding anything with even the slightest hint of risk."

Norms of Economic Rhetoric

The elements of the story produce a plausible and coherent narrative, allowing listeners to believe they are hearing the truth about the economic crisis (Fisher). Most significantly for our purposes, they illustrate the rhetorical norms that have allowed the story to be reasonably told. We argue that by offering implicit evidence for specific norms within the bounds of the story, the broadcast illustrates a model for civil discussion of economic matters.

Given the responsibility of a public to collectively make its economic decisions, a sustainable civic rhetoric must define and maintain citizens' relationships to assure that they do, in fact, act toward each other in ways that foster economic health. When elite caretakers or an invisible hand are in charge, the demagogues can blame failure on them. For a public that would seek *phronesis*, rhetorical norms set the boundaries of moral relationships among its members. "The Giant Pool of Money" offers a model of mutual responsibility. The banker and the homeowner "are partners in this deal" with mortgage companies and investment firms that have ongoing business "relationships."

The promise made by the producers of "The Giant Pool of Money" is that understanding of the sub-prime crises comes from listening to the stories and explanations of real people. The reporting mission was undertaken because "in the coverage of all this, we hadn't heard that much from the people all along the chain. We wanted to know, what were they thinking. . . . [W]hy did they think it would work?" Analysis of the numbers provides ammunition for ideological debate, but the nuanced thinking, found only in conversation with real people, provides the basis for reasoned discussion.

The show explores expectations for the amount of information needed to make informed economic decisions. Economists work under the assumption that asymmetric information works in the favor of those with more information. Normal bankers attempt to verify an applicant's real income, even though borrowers might try to fudge the figures, and the invisibility cloak of credit scores gives the negotiating edge to the lender. Here, mortgage lenders (and ultimately the investment banks) were inventing ways to avoid having good information, relying instead on a "sort of theatre" through which they could pretend not to know that a creditor was shaky. Said one Morgan Stanley executive about the lending process, "We're telling you to lie to us."

Blumberg and Davidson ("The Giant Pool of Money") illustrate the sources of human failure: "It's easy to ignore your gut fear when you're making a fortune in commissions," highlighting the technocratic failure of "six computer screens connected to millions of dollars' worth of fancy analytical software designed by brilliant Ivy League graduates hired by the firm." Davidson calls the epistemological failure a "triumph of data over common sense," pointing out that the programs had been fed "historical data that was irrelevant" and were then used to rate the risk of mortgage defaults.

The story explains a collateralized debt obligation or CDO, as "the thing that took this problem and turned it into a crisis." Lest the audience begin to fade at the technical description of asset pools, tranches, and mortgage-backed securities, Blumberg pauses, "Let's translate some of that." The discussion then turns to risk and the financial industry's attempt to transfer the all-too-human risks of catastrophic health problems, lost jobs, and divorces into the mathematically calculated risks of structured junior tranches that returned a correspondingly higher return. In their single appeal to authority, the producers point out—as previously cited—that "[g]uys like billionaire investor Warren Buffett said the very logic was ridiculous," pitting the common sense of Main Street against Wall Street bankers who "were laughing at" those who did want to take advantage of the calculated returns.

Blumberg explores the underlying housing bubble, telling the stories of those caught when "property values started going down" and the "reverse chain reaction" began. Human beings are not, in general, very good at estimating probabilities of risk or reward, and while the skill of accurately calculating risk can be learned, the outcomes for complex, open-ended domains— economics, for instance—remain problematic (Evans). The alternative is discourse, and the rhetorical dynamic of speculative bubbles has been seen before, most recently in the dot-com crash. Thomas Goodnight and Sandy Green concluded that in any rhetorical community "imitation spreads across inexpert publics, knowledge degrades" (129), and action is driven by the narrative. On the way into a bubble, the story is one of gain; at the crash, "imaginations turn to see opportunities as limited" (128), and rhetorical movement pushes over the house of cards.

In keeping with the story-telling genre of *This American Life*, the narrators make no explicit claims regarding the proper epistemology of an economic public but instead "go downstairs to see Steve Pennington, the IT guy" whose software tracks every one of the sixteen million loans held in the Dynamic Partners CDO. Data had led the instrument into default, but now Pennington "sees lives" in the cells of the spreadsheet. Those lives are linked, in a long chain of human relationships, to the global investment managers whose pool of money is only half as giant as it had been three years earlier and whose sudden risk avoidance means that "everything's just kind of crappy . . . for the economy as a whole."

Most critiques of the market, the West's economic decision system, nibbles at its edges. More regulation, less regulation, changes in regulation, changes in accounting practices, changes in disclosure rules, and changes in the valuation of various resources, goods, or services are all seen as potential solutions to the market's inadequacies. Regardless of the specific regulations, accounting practices, or disclosure rules, the market is understood as an aggregator, masking the billions of individual decisions made each day behind a screen of exchange rates, stock prices, and statistical representations of national economies. The stories told in "The Giant Pool of Money" are all the more striking for their individuation and grounding in specific context.

On a daily basis, the public is bombarded with economic information. Whether it is the latest concern of the Euro Zone or an attempt at political gain by appealing to public naïveté about economic activity, full participation in public dialogue requires an understanding of the science of economics. While economists such as Paul Krugman offer expertise to facilitate discussion of complex metrics in the public sphere, the problem is not solved. As Plato noted in ancient times, those who remain unable (or unwilling) to "abstract the knowledge (*episteme*) necessary to secure truth" from the information are subject to "imitation (*doxa*)"; they "are misled because they merely repeat what is commonly said" (Goodnight and Green 120). Those who default to previously established ideological poles in order to process economic news are at the mercy of demagogues.

"The Giant Pool of Money" offers an alternative solution. The alchemy that moves a community from a rhetoric of undisciplined, partisan speech to a moment of *phronesis* involves the text's adherence to rhetorical norms that allow members of the community to understand each other's motives, engage in reciprocal discourse, and perform a rhetoric that seeks their collective gain. Farrell's framework for recognizing and using rhetorical norms calls for the active expression of *phronesis*.

In its stories of human beings making bad decisions, "The Giant Pool of Money" introduces prudence as the missing element in healthy economic relationships. There are no ideological stereotypes here, only the nuanced story of human beings doing what seems right in a given case. Abstracted, mind-numbing data is not allowed to take the place of the richly understood messiness of contextualized lives. Economic policy is not made in the distant conference rooms of Wall Street but in the daily performance of buying and selling, borrowing and loaning, and perhaps choosing to allocate resources for a sustainable future. Combined with the continuing effort to convince economists to discipline their science to these rhetorical norms, a public that can discuss its own economic behavior will result in better public information, sharper public debate, and better policy decisions.

WORKS CITED

Akerlof, George A. "The Market for 'Lemons': Quality Uncertainty and the Market Mechanism." *Quarterly Journal of Economics* 84 (1970): 488-500. Print.

Akerlof, George A., and Robert J. Shiller. *Animal Spirits: How Human Psychology Drives the Economy, and Why It Matters for Global Capitalism.* Princeton: Princeton UP, 2009. Print.

Bazerman, Charles. *Shaping Written Knowledge the Genre and Activity of the Experimental Article in Science.* Madison: U of Wisconsin P, 1988. Print.

Condit, Celeste Michelle. "The Critic as Empath: Moving Away from Totalizing Theory." *Western Journal of Communication* 57.2 (1993): 178-90. Print.

Evans, Dylan. "How to Beat the Odds at Judging Risk." *Wall Street Journal* 11 May. 2012: C3. Print.

Farrell, Thomas B. *Norms of Rhetorical Culture.* New Haven: Yale UP, 1993. Print.

Ferraro, Fabrizio, Jeffrey Pfeffer, and Robert I. Sutton. "Economics Langauge and Assumptions: How Theories Can Become Self-Fulfilling." *Academy of Management Review* 30.1 (2005): 8-24. Print.

Fisher, Walter R. *Human Communication as Narration: Toward a Philosophy of Reason, Value and Action.* Columbia: U of South Carolina P, 1987. Print.

"The Giant Pool of Money." Narr. Alex Blumberg and Adam Davidson. *This American Life.* PRI. Chicago: WBEZ, 9 May 2008. Radio.

Goodnight, G. Thomas, and Sandy Green. "Rhetoric, Risks, and Markets: The Dot-Com Bubble." *Quarterly Journal of Speech* 96.2 (2010): 115-40. Print.

Lanham, Richard A. *The Economics of Attention.* Chicago: U of Chicago P, 2006. Print.

Lyon, Alexander. "The Mis/Recognition of Enron Executives' Competence as Cultural and Social Capital." *Communication Studies* 59.4 (2008): 371-87. Print.

McCloskey, Donald [Deirdre] N. *The Rhetoric of Economics.* Madison: U of Wisconsin P, 1985. Print.

Pfeffer, Jeffrey. "Economic Logic and Language in Organization Studies: The Undermining of Critical Thinking." *Academy of Management.* Ed. Keynote address to the Critical Management Studies Groups. Address.

Prelli, Lawrence J. *A Rhetoric of Science: Inventive Scientific Discourse.* Columbia: U of South Carolina P, 1989. Print.

Rorty, Richard. "Science as Solidarity." *The Rhetoric of the Human Sciences: Language and Argument in Scholarship and Public Affairs.* Ed. John S. Nelson, Allan Megill and Donald N. McCloskey. Madison: U of Wisconsin P, 1987. Print.

Spence, A. Michael. "Signaling in Retrospect and the Informational Structure of Markets." *American Economic Review* 92 (2002): 434-59. Print.

Stiglitz, Joseph E. "Information and Economic Analysis: A Perspective." *The Economic Journal* 95 (1985): 21-41. Print.

Thaler, Richard H., and Cass R. Sunstein. *Nudge: Improving Decisions About Health, Wealth, and Happiness.* New Haven: Yale UP, 2008. Print.

Wildman, Steven S. "Communication and Economics: Two Imperial Disciplines and Too Little Collaboration." *Journal of Communication* 58.4 (2008): 693-706. Print.

10

CRAFT, PLENITUDE, AND NEGATION

Delivery in Post-Consumer Rhetorics

David M. Grant

In an article about the writing of William S. Burroughs, Marshall McLuhan describes how "men's nerves surround us; they have gone outside as electrical environment" (69). Further, McLuhan describes Burroughs's books *Naked Lunch* and *Nova Express* as "a kind of engineer's report of the terrain hazards and mandatory processes, which exist in the new electronic environment" (69), a characterization Burroughs himself makes (*Naked Lunch* 224). This bit of literary criticism by McLuhan points not only to the production and reception of messages but to the production and reception of *environment* as well. Having turned our insides out, we are confronted with a new awareness of our nervous system, its processes, circulations, effects, stimulations, affective registers, and speed.

Yet media theories often stop short of the point. McLuhan's student, Neil Postman, defined the phrase "media ecology" as "the study of transactions among people, their messages, and their message systems" (139). The phrase "media ecology" is often bandied about by consultants, theorists, professionals, and even professors who take the "ecology" portion of the phrase to mean the sum total of media outlets: social, print, and broadcast. In this sense, the word "systems" is used in a restricted sense to denote mainly the outlets rather than the technical hardware which makes those outlets possible. Take, for example, James Porter's excellent call to "resuscitate and remediate" delivery for the digital age. Important as Porter's reworking is, nowhere does he attend to the material. As part of his proposed theoretical framework, he lists a dimension of "distribution/circulation," which he defines as "concerning the technological publishing options for reproducing, distributing and circulating information" (208). He is correct in pointing to the array of "modes" we now have our disposal; our attunement to those modes in terms of timeliness, content, emotion, and ethos; and the difference between delivery and distribution (214). And yet the "technical knowledge" associated with this dimension pertains to "how audiences are likely to access, engage, and interact with information" so that rhetors can make critical decisions "about informational content, design, style, etc." (208). This is more dramatic in his discussion of "Body/Identity," where the bodies he talks about are constructed only through representations and even where he admits that the machines "we use to write and speak are closely merged with our flesh-and-blood bodies" (213). His posthumanism goes little beyond that we are able to attach our phone/computer to our ears.

So, while Porter is absolutely right, there are dimensions left out of his treatment of digital delivery. My only critique here is that the ideas haven't been pushed far enough. With posthuman, postconsumer, electronic, environmental thinking, we can neither so easily separate representations from being nor compartmentalize the rhetorical canons themselves. Rather, there are continual crossings of channels, modes, and heuristic categories. I want to call attention to a few ways these categories are crossed and repartitioned in new ways, not just severed and fragmented. Indeed, the repartitioning and reworking of what were once separate domains is precisely how I want to look at the notion of "craft" in an expanded, almost Burroughsian sense.

Hardware constitutes something of the cellular level of our own nerves surrounding us. Publishing outlets, the distribution of a message apart from its media, and the technical knowledge associated with these are organic processes and should not be confused with the externalized cellular processes themselves. When looking at systems of delivery, then, externalizing our nerves puts on display more of the corporate bodily processes—the processes of eating, digesting, and fucking, the organs of vein, nostril, and anus, the points and processes where technology meets environment. Like the good junkies we are, we are always looking for the next electronic fix. To turn a blind eye to this risks becoming the "grey, junk-bound ghost" of William Lee, "El Hombre Invisible" (Burroughs 61), inhabiting this earthly plane more as spirit than as body.

Like real bodies, corporate bodies must ingest raw material and process them into useful enzymes, proteins, aminos, peptides, or vitamins. All these organs are already on display with the mosquito mouth of every oil rig, Molycorp's great baleen mouths sifting for neodymium and scandium at the Mountain Pass Mine in California, the GIS-perfect rows of corn that hashtag the Iowa landscape, and the twirling windmill lungs helping to oxygenate the electrical blood that feeds the whole shebang. Let's not also forget, as Shawn and Kristi Apostel have argued, these bodies shit, too. In China, Ghana, and other developing countries, residents are appropriated like intestinal bacteria to smelt out the lead and gold from refuse heaps of sloughed off e-waste. These are all part of the delivery systems that we use and to which Burroughs points us. But they are the part of the delivery system we do not like to focus upon. It is understandable the ease with which we—and the corporate bodies with which we are entangled—might want to become ghostly.

Now, it would be easy to launch at this point into the tired, dystopian environmental scenarios that mutate from the DNA of *Frankenstein* and *Blade Runner.* I do think there are dire consequences for not paying attention, for turning into ghosts of a ruined world. However, I do not mean to launch a regressive environmental screed against industrialization and technology. It is not a question of a binary between one or the other. Our ecology has already become technology, or more accurately, our environment is continually becoming ourselves—in the literal sense, as well as in the form of our externalized organs. To argue against technology is to argue against who we have become.

While it is legitimate, perhaps necessary, to question who we have become, we must also accept who we are. I am neither entirely critical of nor entirely sanguine about that. As Colin Beavan writes in his book *No Impact Man*, environmentalists of recent years have done much to pivot away from the austerity-minded, smaller-versus-bigger, back-to-the-land thinking of "the old environmentalism of the 1970s" (216). Contemporary environmental activist organizations like Wes Jackson's The Land Institute are developing technology in ways that impact the environment differently with the understanding that existence itself implies impact. And, of course, there is the kind of thinking about environment and environmentalism exemplified by scholars like Timothy Morton, who said that ecological thought is "a matter of *how* you think. Once you start to think ecological thought, you can't unthink it: it's a sphincter—once it's open there's no closing" (4).

This strain of environmental thinking acknowledges and attempts to deal with "the negative" in much the same way John Muckelbauer attempts to deal with the negative in regards to invention and change. And Muckelbauer calls invention into question in ways I contend environmentalism and environmental rhetorics should with respect to delivery. He writes, "What is at issue in binary oppositions is not the abstract existence of opposite terms, but the pragmatic movement of negation through which such oppositions are generated and maintained" (5). Following Gilles Deleuze's critique of G.W.F. Hegel, Muckelbauer explains how advocacy of a concept, critique of the concept, and the synthesis between the two are styles of engagement ineffectual at producing real change. Each "repeats the structure of negation and reproduces the ethical and political dangers that accompany such movement" (9). For invention, then, Muckelbauer's project attempts to "move beyond" Hegelian dialectic, and I think such inventions would be good for delivery as well. So, it is not a question of switching to "green" technology or retrofitting current systems to work in ways that pollute less, recycling, or eschewing electronic hardware altogether. To get at real change, we need to move beyond solutions structured by binaries.

Indeed, there are rumblings that this project is already underway. However, because the thinking about this is not dialectical, the style of engagement allows for an understanding of how the more traditional concerns of Porter or the Apostels are linked with readings of Burroughs's manual for an electronic age. Put more simply, I argue that we can better follow the swirl of what Felix Guattari called the three ecologies: the natural, the social, and the mental. Technology spans all three, touching and affecting each in different ways. Jane Bennett's *Vibrant Matter* outlines the political ecology that might inform a more robust digital delivery. Reading John Dewey and Jacques Ranciére through a Latourian lens, Bennett outlines a potential alternative to our current political ecology as well as extending Bruno Latour's call for a reassembling of the social. She writes:

> Theories of democracy that assume a world of active subjects and passive objects begin to appear as thin descriptions at a time when the interactions between human, viral, animal, and technological bodies are becoming more and more intense. If human culture is inextricably enmeshed with vibrant, nonhuman agencies, and if human intentionality can be agentic only if accompanied by a vast entourage of nonhumans, then it seems that the appropriate unit of analysis for democratic theory is neither the individual human nor an exclusively human collective, but the (ontologically heterogeneous) "public" coalescing around a problem. (108)

Transposing this to rhetorical delivery, we might then ask who are the "publics" coalescing around the problem of getting a message out, circulating it, and even transmuting it across media platforms. We may also ask who the nonhuman subjects are—as Porter does to a limited extent—but to press the question further: who else is linked to those nonhuman subjects in roles of maintenance, supply, or servitude whether willing or coerced? What do these publics do? Where do they get their fix? How do they shit and who is their shit good for? Such questions may not only broaden who we consider when delivering messages and ideas but may also refigure the idea of delivery itself.

Bennett argues further that achieving this will likely require a changing of perspectives via transgressive assemblages, much like the example she cites from Ranciére about the plebians' interruption of the Roman Republic. In that example, there is an assemblage that is not so much oppositional "in the manner of the Scythian slaves" (105) as much as parallel with their own speeches, imprecations, oracle consultation, and representatives. In this way, "the plebs managed to repartition the regime of the sensible" (106). Such a repartitioning is necessary for us as a public to see the alien mugwumps and alien objects who carry our messages, to see how delivery is distributed, and to open up space for a re-identification of alien allies. Burroughs may not be the most rhetorically or pedagogically effective manual to use at this point. But he has pointed the way.

Economist Juliet Schor has similarly argued for the establishment of a more decentered, autonomous, yet parallel, set of economic markets that are now possible through social media sites like eBay, Etsy, and Dawanda as well as through community links to farmers markets, craft goods, and local products. By switching, as much as possible, to local and craft markets linked electronically, she argues that we may reap a host of benefits in the form of downshifting, alternative transportation, and community involvement, all part of what she calls "the new plentitude." Underneath the surface of her data, I think there are signs of rhetorical delivery in the materialist way I have suggested here. According to the American Craft Council in Minneapolis, whom I would like to thank for their generous research assistance, sites like Etsy have grown from $181 million in sales in 2009 to $314 million in 2010, have about fourteen million members, and serve about 2.2 million US citizens per month. The materials sought out and used by individual craftspeople range from specialty hops and grains to wools and dyes, pigments, and heirloom seeds. No longer aiming for a catchall variety of seed like Yellow Dent #5 corn, we now also aim for Black Aztec, Mandan Bride, and Country Gentleman varieties. It is not a rejection of capital, but a shift in the space of commodification. It is a material diversity that has an impact and yet avoids the paradox because its impact is different. These are repartitioned regimes of the sensible, telling new tales and offering new lessons.

From this vantage point, crafts become more than simply objects, processes, heuristics, or knowledge. Craft becomes spatialized with the potential to rework our material networks. Such action cannot come by negating the status quo but must build upon it, nondialectically. As Schor argues, true wealth is found in lots of time at parks, in public gatherings, in working around 21 hours per week, and perhaps even in taking in a pint at the local watering hole and reviewing such activities online later that day. Craft, then, is not only an aesthetic object, form, or activity, but also a political and social actant. It doesn't replace art or posit heuristics, but it is a dynamic and fluid category enmeshed with our material lives. As theorist Peter Dormer calls it, craft is "the workmanship of risk" (150).

With contemporary rhetorical delivery, we need to confront our expanded means on 1) visual display, 2) embedded coding, and 3) material support of circulation, but we also need to remain open to happenstance. How might each of these engage risk in productive, perhaps even transgressive, ways? By looking at the material support of delivery and circulation, what kinds of risks, transgressive or not, are we willing to take? Who and what do we identify or want to identify as engaged in each of these? Who gets left out?

Both the workmanship of risk and attention to who is enmeshed in one's delivery are increasingly important considerations as we think about and teach rhetoric. But, finally, any consideration of one canon from my perspective can't be channeled solely to a single one. As we think about and teach delivery in new ways, we need to also cross our wires, so to speak, and admit that rhetoric as a whole is changing as both exigency and response.

Changes in how we approach delivery will affect how we approach style and arrangement. Ben McCorkle points out in *Rhetorical Delivery as Technological Discourse* how paragraphs spatialize the printed page but are grounded in earlier, oratorical markings of texts (115-16). As does Porter, he traces this into contemporary rhetoric with attention to design and the more visual features of print. But he also traces how delivery has crawled out quite a bit from its subordination in the belletristic tradition. McCorkle notes how Hugh Blair theorized the text as primary to the speech. As a result, with so much attention placed upon how the stylistic effects played in the minds of the audience, the notion that handwritten texts imitated printed ones on a material level—what we might call a nascent or invisible form of delivery—was not given overt treatment. Rather, these rules got hidden, conflated with principles of style and arrangement, and were theorized as "natural" forms of persuasive writing. (112)

So, we are caught in a swirl of objects, aliens, nightmarish creatures, and ghosts. Once ascribed to our inner workings and psyche, this menagerie is more and more externalized in very real and material ways, across distributed networked systems. But we might take some comfort in that we can see them with different eyes or read a different set of manuals on them. Rather than with the eyes of the modernist who sees only orcs and ringwraiths and who longs for the comforts of a quiet home, rather than the corporate Hollywood eyes of *Monsters, Inc.* who make a world of monsters that are just like people, we might look out with more childlike eyes and see Wild Things on a distant shore, knowing we can dance with them, be hailed by them as their king, but still return to find our dinner waiting.

WORKS CITED

American Craft Council. *The Craft Organization Development Association Review (2011): Craft Artists, Income and the U.S. Economy.* Minneapolis: American Craft Council, 2011. Print.

Apostel, Shawn, and Kristi Apostel. "Old World Successes and New World Challenges: Reducing the Computer Waste Stream in the United States." *Technological Ecologies and Sustainability.* Ed. Danielle DeVoss, Heidi McKee, and Richard Selfe. Computers and Composition Digital P, 2009. Web.

Beavan, Colin. *No Impact Man: The Adventures of a Guilty Liberal Who Attempts to Save the Planet, and the Discoveries He Makes About Himself and Our Way of Life in the Process.* Boston: Farrar, Straus, and Giroux, 2009. Print.

Bennett, Jane. *Vibrant Matter: A Political Ecology of Things.* Durham: Duke UP, 2010. Print.

Burroughs, William S. *Naked Lunch.* New York: Grove, 1959. Print.

Dormer, Peter. "Craft and the Turing Test for Practical Thinking." *The Culture of Craft.* Ed. Peter Dormer. Manchester: Manchester UP, 1997. 137-57. Print.

Guattari, Felix. *The Three Ecologies.* Trans. Ian Pindar and Paul Sutton. London: Continuum, 2000. Print.

McCorkle, Ben. *Rhetorical Delivery as Technological Discourse.* Carbondale: Southern Illinois UP, 2012. Print.

McLuhan, Marshall. "Notes on Burroughs." *William S. Burroughs at the Front: Critical Reception, 1959-1989.* Ed. Jennie Skerl and Robin Lydenberg. Carbondale: Southern Illinois UP, 1991. 69-74. Print.

Morton, Timothy. Ecology *Without Nature: Rethinking Environmental Aesthetics.* Cambridge: Harvard UP, 2007. Print.

Muckelbauer, John. *The Future of Invention: Rhetoric, Postmodernism, and the Problem of Change.* Albany: State U of New York P, 2008. Print.

Porter, James. "Recovering Delivery for Digital Rhetoric." *Computers and Composition* 26.4 (Dec. 2009): 207-24. Print.

Postman, Neil. "The Reformed English Curriculum." *High School 1980: The Shape of the Future in American Secondary Education.* Ed. A. C. Eurich. New York: Pittman, 1970. 160-68. Print.

Schor, Juliet. *Plenitude: The New Economics of True Wealth.* New York: Penguin, 2010. Print.

11

DEMOCRACY AS DISCURSIVE INSURGENCY

Entering and Breaking

Andrew Nicholas Rechnitz

Of the various historical narratives that have attempted to explain the relationship between rhetoric and democracy, one of the most common in circulation today is the traditional rise-and-fall narrative (or what I shall hereafter refer to as the *genetic* narrative), which essentially suggests that the degree to which a government endorses the principles of democracy ultimately regulates the degree to which rhetoric flourishes or fails to flourish. "Under democracies," writes George Kennedy in *A New History of Classical Rhetoric*, "citizens were expected to participate in political debate, and they were expected to speak on their own behalf in courts of law"; as a result, "[a] theory of public speaking evolved, which developed an extensive technical vocabulary to describe features of argument, arrangement, style and delivery" (3). What often follows from this logic is the general notion that Athens was the first to manifest a truly progressive political structure or, more specifically, that it was the first to successfully implement a form of social organization that "recognized the need to entertain opposing views when expressed with rhetorical effectiveness" (Kennedy 3).

If accurate, perhaps the advent of democracy and the rise of its attendant political institutions help to explain why, from roughly 425-380 BCE, Gorgias of Leontini took up residence in Greece, was given license to discourse in a number of public venues, and seems to have been a regular feature at festivals, funerals, and athletic contests. At least from the perspective of the genetic narrative, with a flourishing democracy as the political context, Gorgias's extraordinary rhetorical production during the years he spent in Athens makes perfect sense. Upon a closer examination of the context itself, however, we might note that while Gorgias was apparently given free rein to discourse "on any subject" in a number of public venues, as a foreigner living in Athens he was also strictly forbidden from participating in any of the recently established appellate courts (Sprague 82 A 1a). Given his exclusion from speaking in such venues, my sense is that there may have been something particularly *risky* and *unsettling* about the defense Gorgias mounts on behalf of the mythological trickster, Palamêdês.

Although many of you in attendance today are familiar with the story of Palamêdês from the Troy legend, for the sake of context it bears briefly repeating here. Essentially, at the outset of the Trojan War, Palamêdês is tasked with locating Odysseus and persuading him to join the Greek campaign. Odysseus has absolutely no interest in going to battle, so when Palamêdês and the rest of the troops arrive at his home, Odysseus feigns madness by yoking together two ill-matched beasts (one a horse, the other an ox) and wildly hot-hoofing it around his fields while salting the earth. The trick fools everyone but the mythological trickster himself, and once Palamêdês sniffs out the ruse, he decides that the most effective way to expose it is to toss Odysseus's son, Telemachos, in front of the raging horse-ox cart, whereupon Odysseus, who of course loves his son, is forced to halt his escapades and join the war party. Apparently, Odysseus never forgave Palamêdês for exposing his cowardice; thus, when the opportune moment presents itself, Odysseus exacts his revenge at the Greek camp by publicly accusing Palamêdês of treason. Although various iterations of this myth exist, the most popular explains that Odysseus hired a crony to plant a specific sum of gold in Palamêdês's tent. He then forged a letter in King Priam's hand verifying that, in exchange for some strategic intelligence that could potentially bring down the Greek army, Palamêdês would receive exactly the sum of gold that was hidden in his tent. As a result of the evidence set against him, the Greeks find Palamêdês guilty as charged, and he is ultimately sentenced to death by stoning.

Now, as I mentioned earlier, because Gorgias was a foreigner, he was prohibited from speaking in the Athenian law courts; and although this prohibition was not extended to the practice of logography, which some scholars suggest may have been used by foreigners as a means to influence public policy in Athens, unlike several of Gorgias's contemporaries (e.g., Antiphon, Lysias, Isocrates, and Demosthenes), we find no record of Gorgias having written speeches for actual cases, with real defendants, that would have been delivered in front of Dikastic court officials. Nevertheless, because sophistic rhetorical training at this time often culminated in declamations on deliberative and judicial subjects, it would have been rather odd for Gorgias to have excluded these kinds of speeches from his own rhetorical pedagogy—and in fact, as Michael Gagarin suggests, Gorgias's *Defense on Behalf of Palamêdês* stands as an exemplary model for studying the rhetoric of *apologia*, since it displays "every possible argument for the defense in one speech" (287). Gagarin lists the arguments as follows:

> a sample of common arguments, including a proem (1-5) . . . then (6-12) a point-by-point demonstration of the improbability of the accuser's scenario of betrayal; next, (13-21) a catalogue of his possible motives with probability arguments refuting each possibility; then (22-27) a list of specific weaknesses in the prosecution's case; then (28-32) a description of his own accomplishments and character; and finally an epilogue (33-37) with generalizations about justice and injustice. (287)

Given the unusual diversity of these arguments, Gagarin ventures the follow-ing conclusion:

> A real forensic speech would concentrate on those few arguments that were most persuasive, but *Palamêdês*, despite its forensic setting, is in essence an epideictic speech. Its primary aim is not to persuade but to demonstrate Gorgias's skill to the audience, who are not jurors in court at Palamêdês's trial but intellectuals, students and others. (287)

Although Gagarin's conclusion perhaps underestimates the scope of persua-sion in epideictic discourse, I believe it nevertheless places Gorgias's *Palamêdês* within a fascinating rhetorical situation. As Susan Woodford explains, while the Troy legend positions the vengeful Odysseus as the princi-pal agent in Palamêdês's demise,

> In the fifth century BC a more complicated scenario, one which impli-cated *all* the Greeks in a judicial murder, was invented . . . [and the] con-clusion of the story was as *inevitable* as it was cruel: once the treasonable contents of the forged letter appeared to be confirmed by the discovery of the planted gold, Palamêdês was found guilty *by a majority of the Greeks* and executed by stoning. (165; emphasis added)

With the invention of this scenario, which coincidentally signals a shift from *dikē* (or a citizen prosecution initiated by Odysseus) to *graphē* (which would be a public prosecution initiated by "all the Greeks" in the name of the *polis*), it seems likely that a contemporary audience for Gorgias's *Palamêdês* would have known, in advance, that no matter how persuasive the arguments could be made in Palamêdês' defense, he still would not have been exoner-ated by a majority of the citizen population. Had Palamêdês been Greek—or, better yet, a Greek of high birth, like Odysseus—perhaps his fate would have been otherwise. But the fact remains that nationalist identifications seem to determine the outcome of the story *ipso facto*, and it would appear that this fact fundamentally complicates the logic that rhetoric flourishes because a democratic politics "recognize[s] the need to entertain opposing views when expressed with rhetorical effectiveness" (Kennedy 3).

If we return to the genetic narrative for a moment, we might find that while it is certainly persuasive in many contexts, its general historiography appears to eschew an important question: namely, if we are to believe that the level of democracy present in a politics is the necessary cause for rhetoric to flourish, then why do instances of rhetorical activity, which seem to be predi-cated on some vision of equality, occasionally appear to flourish without political sanction? To put it a bit differently, if democracy is ultimately reduc-ible to a formal politics, and if rhetorical activity predicated on equality is generated and regulated by the structural operations of democratic institu-tions, such as the appellate law courts, then how does the narrative account for rhetorical activity that appears to be coextensive with democracy but is not an effect of the social form of organization that *is* democratic politics?

What is at stake in Gorgias's *Defense*, I submit, is nothing less than the concept of equality itself, and building on the work of Jacques Rancière, my purpose will be to identify the *Palamêdês* as an example of rhetorical discourse wherein democracy occurs. As paradoxical as it may sound, I believe that it becomes possible to read the *Palamêdês* in this way—that is, as an *event* in which democracy occurs—precisely to the extent that the text's rhetorical patterns are able to distinguish themselves from the political tropes of the operative democracy in fifth-century Athens.

I am fairly sure that the preceding statements will provoke a general concern over the use of the term "democracy." If, as I am suggesting, democracy is not reducible to an official politics, then what else can it signify? What else can it do? Of course, etymologically the word derives from the Greek elements for "people" and "force," and it is generally translated into English as "rule of the people," but exactly how to interpret this word in relation to politics and government has recently become a point of contention for a number of contemporary thinkers, including Alain Badiou, Chantal Mouffe, and Jacques Rancière. The latter's *Hatred of Democracy* embarks on an analysis of the word with an unexpected and highly problematic philological account:

> [Democracy] was, in Ancient Greece, originally used as an insult by those who saw in the unnameable government of the multitude the ruin of any legitimate order. It remained synonymous with abomination for everyone who thought that power fell by rights to those whose birth had predestined them to it or whose capabilities called them to it. (2)

It is not difficult to recognize in this insult the stentorian voice of a Socrates, whose stratifying agenda in *The Republic* guards against the democratic impulse to assign social positions by lot, or that of an Aristotle, whose rationalist agenda in the *Politics* guards against the democratic impulse to dispense with explicit rules for social organization. Of greater *rhetorical* import, however, is that the insult substitutes "democracy" for "unnameable government," which signals the main definitional problem: the metonymy suggests what appears to be a paradox, for a government, by definition, always *names* the structure of its politics. In response to this apparent contradiction in logic, Rancière explains that, while democracy is not *indifferent* to juridico-political forms, it nevertheless cannot be *identified* with them (54) because "[u]nder the name democracy, what is being implicated and denounced is politics itself" (33). The following passages from Rancière help to clarify this apparently absurd claim:

> Democracy is not a type of constitution, nor a form of society. The power of the people is not that of a people gathered together, of the majority, or of the working class. It is simply the power peculiar to those who have no more entitlements to govern than to submit. . . . The scandal [of democracy] lies in the disjoining of entitlements to govern from any analogy to those that order social relations, from any analogy between human convention and the order of nature. It is the scandal of a superiority based on

no other title than the very absence of superiority. . . . Democracy really
means, in this sense, the impurity of politics, the challenging of governments' claims to embody the sole principle of public life and in so doing
be able to circumscribe the understanding and extension of public life.
(46; 42; 62)

Following Rancière's formulation, the "challenge" initiated by democracy
can be read as operating in the form of a discursive *insurgency*, an insurgency
that unsettles entitlements to legitimacy founded on totalizing political
claims. Furthermore, because this challenge signifies the impurity of politics
rather than a type of constitution or a form of society, democracy as insurgency tends not to name the activities of *progressive movements* that militate in
order to seize the state form but, rather, *particular moments* of discursive unsettling that happen to occur when essentialized tropes are made to confront
their own contingency. Crucial to this distinction is that progressive movements (e.g., social revolutions, protests, uprisings, and so forth) tend to consider their challenges successful only insofar as they can be identified as
correctives to established political structures. This is not always the case, and
other identifications are certainly possible, but in contradistinction to the corrective aim, particular moments of democracy as insurgency distinguish
themselves foremost as *events*, which is to say that they herald *a breakdown of
the counting practices* that structure an official politics by way of unsettling
essentialized tropes.

   With this definition of democracy in mind, if we consider the fact that
both Gorgias and Palamêdês were foreigners to the Greeks of their respective
times, perhaps what Gorgias's retelling of the myth points out is that, even
with the recent invention of this supposedly progressive democratic institution
called the law court—which should, according to the logic of the genetic narrative, ensure a reasonably fair trial wherein the accused is afforded the opportunity to generate rhetorical activity that might persuade a successful
defense—we find that no argument, however "rhetorically effective," would
have been persuasive *enough* to have absolved Palamêdês. The particular manner of his execution notwithstanding, this much is clear: though *all* Greeks
know he is innocent, Palamêdês will be put to death . . . over and over again.

   An interesting question to ask is whether it could have been Gorgias's
own *Defense* that initially gave rise to the new scenario. And if so, what might
have motivated him to take the risk of implicating *all* of the Greeks in a judicial murder? Although these questions would of course be difficult to answer
definitively, I argue that what is of democratic value in Gorgias's *Defense* is, in
fact, the antilogy it offers. Consider that when Gorgias produces what
appears to be "every possible argument for the defense," because this speech
issues from an illegitimate speech position (that of the foreigner who is not
only forbidden from speaking in court but who is also guilty of treason *a priori*), it exposes the fact that Palamêdês's speech, even when expressed with
Gorgias's famed rhetorical effectiveness, simply will not *count* as a legitimate
defense. Thus, the risk involved in generating this kind of speech appears to

be substantial, for the defense requires *presupposing* that all of the individual *logoi* of the *kategoria* [prosecution] are *equally available* to *all* speakers for figuration in an *apologia*. The antilogy thus points out that a speaker who is forbidden from participating in the institution of the law court nevertheless can generate legitimate *apologia* from an illegitimate speech position by presupposing equality with an opposing *logos*.

In other words, we might say that Gorgias's *Palamêdês* risks presupposing equality between noncitizen and citizen, between accused and accuser, or between *apologia* and *kategoria*. While the *apologia* itself almost certainly would have failed to *persuade* a Dikastic court to exonerate Palamêdês given the sociopolitical atmosphere in fifth-century Athens, once the event of Gorgias's discourse occurs, it is no longer possible to ignore the *fact* that foreigners are capable of generating rhetorical activity, predicated on equality, without the sanction of an official politics. Furthermore, it is no longer possible to ignore the fact that foreigners are capable of doing so with as much (or more) rhetorical skill than citizens who are granted the right to speak based solely upon membership with the state. These facts would appear to herald a breakdown in official counting practices; unlike progressive political movements, however, they bring no guarantee that the guardian institutions of democracy will correct themselves as a result. They simply affirm the following: rhetorical activity can be generated from speech positions that are not accounted for according to the counting practices of democratic politics.

Thus, I believe Gorgias's *Palamêdês* stands as an example of rhetorical discourse in which an event of democracy occurs as a discursive insurgency. The *Palamêdês*, I submit, mounts its discursive insurgency by performing a twofold operation: *entering* a discourse that has been reified through statist politics and, then, *breaking* the metaphysical arrangement of signifiers that sustains the binary citizen/noncitizen. Paradoxically, of course, it becomes possible to read the *Palamêdês* in this way precisely to the extent that its rhetorical patterns will have challenged and unsettled the counting practices that structure an institution of Athenian democracy. By pointing out an inequality legitimated by the concept of citizenship, which is the essentialized trope *par excellence* in the myth, democracy occurs in the *Palamêdês* precisely because Gorgias's rhetorical pattern presupposes equality with an institutional discourse that *a priori* disavows the legitimacy of foreign speech—because it risks confronting the contingency of an essentialized trope by speaking in the genera of *apologia* reserved exclusively for Athenian "citizens" with "full rights," and because it successfully challenges the counting practices of a politics built on nationalist identifications.

WORKS CITED

Gagarin, Michael. "Did the Sophists Aim to Persuade?" *Rhetorica: A Journal of the History of Rhetoric* 19.3 (2001): 275-91. Print.

Kennedy, George. *A New History of Classical Rhetoric.* Princeton: Princeton UP, 1994. Print.

Rancière, Jacques. *Hatred of Democracy.* Trans. Steven Corcoran. London and New York: Verso, 2009. Print.

Sprague, Rosamond Kent, ed. *The Older Sophists.* Trans. of *Die Fragmente der Vorsokratiker.* Ed. H. Diels and W. Kranz. Columbia: U of South Carolina P, 1972. Print.

Woodford, Susan. "Palamedes Seeks Revenge." *The Journal of Hellenic Studies* 114 (1994): 164-69. Print.

12

Coming to Terms with a Declaration of Barbarous Acts

Erik Doxtader

We must start questioning again.

— Maurice Blanchot

There must be a human estate that demands no sacrifices.

— Theodor Adorno

1. The (im)possibility of human rights has long appeared as a question of the angels. The question hovers. Neither here nor there, neither now nor then, it inquires into the beginning of an allegorical expression, a breaking with the rule of language and slipping from *apophansis* in a way that discloses an unspeakable violence.[1] Appearing between the divine and the natural, thus without certain subject or object, the question asks after the terms that betray the ongoing wreckage of the word's barbarism. Of the angels, it seeks the passing of a message, a language of passage in which the experience of coming to terms in the midst of the unspeakable is an experience of discovering the (im)potentiality of a recognize-ability that renders history otherwise.

History looms. In 1496, Giovanni Pico della Mirandola invoked the angels as he prefaced his attempt to answer some nine hundred (potentially heretical) questions with "An Oration on the Dignity of Man." Here, Pico articulates one version of renaissance humanism, a call toward the possibility of peace that inheres in the angel's message to forge the terms of "seamless friendship," a union that "passes expression" and which natural philosophy can neither propagate nor fully explain (21-22); the human condition takes form within a faith sustained equally by prayer and rigorous study of the liberal arts, both of which provide a humble grasp of the fact that human beings are not self-sufficient, that we are "neither of heaven nor earth" and that we arrived (too) late, with no intrinsic properties and no endowments to call our own (7-8). For Pico, the beginning of becoming human is not a moment of divine or historical fate so much as a hinge, a turning between animality and

116

humanity in which dignity emerges through an abiding experience of vulnerability (41). More precisely, dignity arrives only as we give ourselves to words that are not our own; it arrives only as we are able to suspend our canon of self-understanding and listen to philosophical and religious discourses that have long been dismissed as sources of error and corruption. As Pico hears it, the question of the angels brings the so-called barbarian into the light of recognizability in the name of recognizing that our own idiom is neither the first nor the last word. Today, however, we well know the ambivalent legacy of this gesture. Even as Pico offers a way to rethink the character and caricature of humanism, the question of the angels marks the thin divide between an ethics of shared vulnerability that underwrites what we now call human rights and that "seamless friendship," which serves as a pretense for conversion, domination, and eradication.

2.   The inspiration that heralds the promise of human rights is seemingly indissociable from the force that enacts its limit. As Samuel Moyn has suggested, the search for a way out of this circle, the manic hope for a sign of pristine origin, a glint of sunlight from the mirror below, has supported the manufacture of myths whose "deep roots" have been used variously to validate and discredit the contemporary human rights agenda. The cost of such "usable pasts" is a feedback loop, an endless debate over the meaning and value of human rights in which competing schools of thought share a proclivity to presuppose precisely that which remains open to question (12). Even so, Moyn's objection to the habits of historicism is rooted in a closely guarded piety of its own, a rather quaint desire to expose the false pillars of the human rights debate in the name of revealing the "true story." A demonstration of how the field of history not infrequently covers its allergy to expression's contingency with the faculty of narration, Moyn's tale peddles the sacred belief that the reality of human rights will appear only as the rhetorical is weeded from the picture; the word is mere prelude and the symbolic only a hollow pretense of public relations efforts dedicated to hiding the actual operations of power (56-61).

This is an old tactic. Since Jeremy Bentham, at least, one history of human rights is the respective attempt by advocates and opponents to completely sever or fully unify the "rhetoricity" and "actuality" of human rights. Both cases are warranted by more or less explicit appeals to barbarism—the horrors of our times demand action not idle proclamation; human rights discourse is simply a horde of words affording thin cover for imperial aspirations. If it is tempting to turn the tables, to dismiss these claims as solecisms or naïve barbarisms, the more important point is that they obscure if not deny the ways in which language is an intrinsic part of the violence that all sides in the debate claim to oppose. This was Richard McKeon's prescient argument in the 1940s, one that went largely unheard.[2] A bit later, Theodor Adorno put the matter more elegantly, when he claimed at the beginning of *Negative Dialectics* that rhetoric is "on the side" of dialectic content and that "it is in the rhetorical quality that culture, society, and tradition animate the thought; a stern hostility to it is leagued with barbarism" (56). Even so, haunted by his own claim as to how the writing of poetry after Auschwitz was nothing less than barbaric, Adorno closes *Negative Dialectics* with a warning—rhetoric will not arrive just in time:

> All post-Auschwitz culture, including its critique, is garbage. In restoring itself after the things that happened without resistance in its own country-side, culture has turned entirely into the ideology it had been potentially. . . . Whoever pleads for the maintenance of this radically culpable and shabby culture becomes its accomplice, while the man who says no to culture is directly furthering the barbarism which our culture showed itself to be. Not even silence gets us out of the circle. (367)

At a moment in which the terms of culture have been turned to the task of (self) negation, there is no avenue for rescue; save for their *ex nihilo* creation, there are no grounds, no *topoi* on which to stand, no way to speak adequately to the unspeakable even as the silence compounds the horror. There is then no question in the aftermath, no question of the "rhetoric of human rights," as if these concepts were given. If anything, the wake of atrocity (and its pre-lude) betrays a language of suffering language: a suffering wrought by the word given to violence and, simultaneously, a language suffering the violence of its appropriation by humans whose potential it may well hold.

3.   In the "monstrous events" of World War I, Walter Benjamin foresaw the emergence of this norm. He grasped the exception that takes form when expression refuses to ask after let alone relinquish its dependence on tragic law and the law of tragedy, a commitment to self-certain meaning that impov-erishes experience, not least the experience of language as such, in whose lament may (yet) appear the possibility of what Benjamin called a "positive barbarism" (2: 232). Benjamin put the matter succinctly. Indeed, it is now increasingly difficult to find a more or less critical reflection on human rights discourse that does not, early in the game, muster a passage from Thesis VII of Benjamin's 1940 essay "On the Concept of History." Here, just months before his death and relying heavily on a recent elaboration of his path-break-ing 1916 reflection on language (1: 62), Benjamin writes, "There is no docu-ment of culture which is not at the same time a document of barbarism" (4: 392). And, he continues, "just as such a document is never free of barbarism, so barbarism taints the manner in which it was transmitted from one hand to another" (4: 392). In some sense, the culmination of Benjamin's indictment of historicism's conformist empathy with the legacy of the victor, the "trium-phal procession in which current rulers step over those who are lying pros-trate" (391), both explains Benjamin's warning about the normalization of emergency by juridical institutions quick to forget the contingency of their founding law and sets the stage for his turn to the dialectical image of Paul Klee's *Angelus Novus* and its allegory of the past's wreckage, an accumulating and unfolding catastrophe that calls on us to "brush history against the

grain" in the name of exposing that moment (*Jetztzeit*) in which its word is not given, in which language discloses its unspeakable defeat.[3]

Benjamin was well aware of the classical roots of barbarism. Not least from the work that set the stage for his study of *Trauerspiel,* he knew that the *barbaroi,* the figure of the barbarian, was first and foremost a reference to language, an invention of the early fifth century that emerged from the concepts of *heterophone* and *barabarophonos*—non-Greek and foreign speech (Hall 7-9). With the "babble" of its (the question of the pronoun is open) "bar-bar," the barbarian arrives with unintelligible sounds and appears without words to make sense (Pagden 16). Aeschylus's *Persae* takes pains to identify the strange and estranging nature of the barbarian's clamoring tongue—a varying set of rough and unfamiliar words, an awkward if not incorrect diction, and a pain-inducing pitch.[4] As imagined and then mythologized in the name of codifying Hellenism's *homotropia,* the barbarian sits at the edge of *logos* and the culture that it claims to sponsor. Sometimes inside and sometimes outside, the barbarian's barbarism can mark an animal or inhuman lack of language, an incompetent, gibberish-sounding performance of language, an infelicity that corrupts language's law and value, and an attack on language—a violence against the word wrought by an incomprehensible voice. These renderings, of course, enable and sustain a so-called "barbarian effect," a codification of *ethnos* and shared cultural understanding that emerges with and through the naming of the barbarian. Through an attribution and then a discourse that pronounces an unwillingness to listen and which takes the (im)possibility of expression as cause to deny recognition, this effect stands as the very refusal that supported enlightenment's self-sure and colonizing sanctification of civilized progress (Hall 99; Todorov; Neilson).

The documents do not make for easy reading. Facing culture's self-constituting barbarism and barbarian-making culture, Benjamin's is not a simple reminder that progress rests on the exploitation of the toiling masses and that it gathers steam through the combustion engineered by imperial-military campaigns (Löwy 49). Nor does he believe that history's unfolding and enfolding violence can be redeemed on the register of tragic guilt, an appeal to law whose arbitration is simply more of the same, an assumption of the word's finitude that warrants its plausibly deniable appropriation and instrumental deployment against those who breach its externally secured contract. While there is nothing comic about it (though happiness may be a different story), the work of brushing history against its grain entails hearing the indistinguishability of documents of culture and documents of barbarism as an "iterative disturbance" that calls forth the question of language (Neilson 86). In Benjamin's view, this work is not dedicated to parsing meaning so much as asking after the way in which the documents on which we depend for meaning betray a lack of care for language, a refusal of hospitality rooted in a self-serving denial of our own rhetorical (in)capacity. Thus, at one level, the barbarisms that inhere in culture's documents are assertions that miss the mark of meaning—words go unheard and yield little apparent interest; expression falls out of control and into incomprehensibility; the sound of discourse serves only to grate. Yet, at another level, the mark itself is barbarous, a sign of an inherent lack of proficiency, an assumption of a gift that remains outside of our interest and our control, and an indication that the professed universality of culture's language is wholly particular, if not idiosyncratic, and fully dependent on that which would have it fall silent. Suddenly then, the *logos* is heterophone, a turn on which tragedy's fateful motion depends but which Benjamin seeks to recast as an experience of language. This experience is fleeting, a flash of the word's (un)recognizability that appears here, that appears now, before the dénouement, before the word is *spoken* (accounted) *for.*

Not: what have we said wrong? Not: what wrong follows from what we say or the way in which we have said it? Rather, before these limits that presuppose the traction of the law's speaking subject, the experience of language is a fleeting glimpse of expression's violence against language itself, of the saying and the said that sets language to lament its own loss. The very sliver of messianic power to which Benjamin aspires, this experience marks his hope for a "positive barbarism" in which the interiority of expression sets us outside language just as much as our habitation of language displaces the possibility of (its) expression.

This experience is an experience of the exception that our words introduce into language. At the hinge of culture and barbarism, a lacking *logos* professes universality, a commitment to commonality, in a way that strips being from (its) language and language from (its) being.[5] As a barbarous act, the production of culture's document is simultaneously an incomprehensible gesture *and* an attack on the integrity of language itself, the very power in which being may discover the power to become human (Todorov 18-20). In these terms, even as Adorno saw it teetering on the edge of mysticism and Scholem worried over its secularization of Judaism, Benjamin's claim both anticipates and subtly explains Arendt's profound concern for radical evil and the attending paradox of human rights, in which the expression of legal violence strives simultaneously to destroy the speech-action that holds "the potentialities of human power" and to enforce a discourse that relegates the being of language to a fate of endless becoming, an eternal sacrifice in the name of that which is (never) to come (Arendt, *Origins*; Arendt, *Human* 241, 246, 176). Wedding the ontological and the ethical, Benjamin's seventh thesis thus asks what is to be done in light of the indissociable connection between language whose expression forecloses recognition and expression that refuses to recognize language. What can be said in the midst of (un)speakable violence and the violence that inaugurates (un)speakability?

4.   The appearance of barbarism beckons the question of language—as a question. With this claim, Benjamin refuses to set the barbarian outside culture at the same time that he resists collapsing culture to outright barbarism. Never far from a concern for Schmitt, Benjamin turns away from the question of the friend and the enemy, the subject and object of politics, by turning

the problem of the "normality" of exception to the question of language itself, an inquiry in which the (im)potential for a "real state of emergency" is no different from the discovery of a "positive" sense of barbarism, an experience of language, an experience of enmity for language on which rests the (im)possibility of friendship. What is the threshold of an (in)capacity for expression? What are the grounds and rules of (proper) expression? What violence has been done with language? How is violence done to it? These questions must be joined and thought simultaneously—ascribed by the "inside," a lack from the "outside" portends a loss on the "inside" that renders it "outside." In the word, the wall comes down.

Eight years after Benjamin's death, at a moment in which his seventh thesis seemed to hold far more truth than promise, the Universal Declaration of Human Rights (UDHR) began with the question of the word.[6] With "recognition" as its first word, the Declaration opens with a Preamble of uncertain status, a more or less official "passage" that announces the beginning of a world that holds the promise of free speech in the aftermath of "barbarous acts." Here, although perhaps not now, in a transition that is both prefigured and yet to come, the opening of human rights is figured in the tension between barbarism and speech, a set of implicit questions as to the status of humanity's language in the wake of brutality. What damage to language has been wrought by barbarous acts? Has language gone missing? How has it been damaged? In what ways is it now distorted? Was the wound self-inflicted, a turning of language against itself?[7] In reply, the Preamble offers the warmth of a (re)turn to language, a promise that language has (re)turned. This assurance is set out in two "official" languages, French and English, both of which have long been the subjects of cultural campaigns to demonstrate their respective universality. With it, the work of debarbarization is held out as both compensation for language gone missing and a warrant for human(izing) "rights talk." Faced with a(n) (ontological and ethical) loss of language, the Preamble both announces and performs an (im)potential for expression, a power that marks both a condition and fulfillment of human rights—speaking being (re)turns to human being and back again; the human subject has a language to speak and speaking has the human as its object. If this makes good on the Declaration's first word, if the (re)turn of speech underwrites recognition, the equation is cemented by an appeal to an already existing rule of law, a protection that precludes barbaric backsliding and deters revolution (the two are conflated). The lingering difficulty, however, is whether this formulation allows the (re)turn of the first word—recognition—to (conceptually and temporally) jump the question of its own beginning. Then and now, the Preamble appears to foreclose the question of speech by invoking a prior word—the abiding (and pre-given) word of law's rule, a word that may indemnify language from the question of its (im)potential and figure the question of language as incomprehensible, except insofar as the question marks a return to barbarism.

The issue is not *what* can (not) be said or *how* it can (not) be said. Framed by its Preamble, the UDHR does not so much foreclose opposition to its announced promises as it pre-empts the deep discomfort (if not terror) that attends the experience of language, the anxiety entailed in giving one's words away and finding (discovering) a way to a language that one's words may well damage. This tactical gesture comes at cost, an inability to consider the question of what barbarism may unfold in the midst of self-certain expression, from within the comforts of culture. Before both content and form, blurring their difference, the Preamble constitutes a nearly explicit prohibition against the unloosing of the word's (in)capacity, a recollection of the way in which its gift is not a given, the way in which one of the defining qualities of being human is not our own. This prohibition is enacted and enforced by the rule of law, a prior word whose integrity is not in doubt; there is no question about the provision of law, the conditions under which its words arrive or its capacity to withstand the force (or temptation) of barbarism. Thus, as it installs sanctions against revolution and recasts barbarism as an offence that invokes the necessity of law's force, the Preamble sets precedent—it erases the question of the word as a question. Its (re)turn of speech is a promise of recognition whose dignity is a function of the rule of law, a rule whose formation and expression is not open to question precisely because it appears only at the hinge of culture and barbarism, the question of the relationship between (un)speakability and violence that the law claims to have already answered—once and for all.

The (law-making *and* conserving) force of the UDHR, even as it did not itself have the status of law, is rooted in a (re)turn of expression (a speaking *through* language) that affords recognition, on the condition that its enabling rule of law is freed from the (constitutive-revolutionary) question of its rule of recognition, a question of the threshold beyond which its force is unjustified. This means, for one, that "legal violence" remains wholly and uncritically legal, an allowance secured in the Preamble and further confirmed by the General Assembly's decision to exclude the act of petitioning and the protection of minorities from the UDHR. For another, it means that the American Anthropological Association may have misunderstood the issue at hand (or simply performed the field's guilty conscience) in 1947, when it publicly wondered how the proposed declaration could be anything but a "statement of rights conceived only in terms of values prevalent in countries of Western Europe and America."[8] This is bedrock, the fundament of so many objections to contemporary human rights. And yet, no matter how compelling, this *topoi* takes the "statement" for granted. The UN may not have the standing to make a universal declaration. It may make a declaration that inflicts a selective ideology on the world or which does nothing at all. But, declare it can. The capacity to speak is up, running, and backed by law. The very question of (un)speakability, the saying of what can(not) be said (as being human turns on the word) is set aside as resolved and replaced with the foundation for an endless *logomachia,* a war of words over what the said says about its relative universality and the ways in which its shortfall counts as hypocrisy.

5. The Universal Declaration of Human Rights beckons progress. Yet, when approached in light of Benjamin's thesis on the entwinement of culture and barbarism, this turn from past to future discloses a lament, a sadness that appears beneath its tragic form and its tragic formulation of the word that (re)turns humanity's dignity. Less a memory of the past or a memorialization of that which has passed into history, this sadness is far less mournful than melancholic.[9] It is an open wound of language damage, the expression of a damaged language that appears (or sounds) when a promise to come to terms, a promise to find words that (re)turn humanity to itself, is set into the legal terms of a struggle for recognition in which declarations about the imminent arrival of the "better angels of our nature" serve to obscure and drown out a flash—a surprising moment between past and future in which an angel arrives and begins a self-interrupting hymn (or scream), a song (or siren) that offers not a word of redemption but an opening in which to ask after the recognizability of the word.

The tragic arc (if not premise) of the UDHR is apparent in the Preamble: with a (mis)appropriation of the word, barbarous acts create a breach in which appears a symbol of guilt, a figure fallen silent before the law to which it must then be sacrificed in the name of learning and promoting "reverence and gratitude for the word" (Benjamin, *Origin* 109). Thus, as Benjamin explains in his study of *Trauerspiel*, the law at play in tragedy seeks to redeem speechlessness with the promise of a "moral order of the world" that pronounces guilt but lacks any reference to its own "historical content" (*Origin* 101). With the future at stake, the tragic fate wrapped around the (mis)taken word is released and supplanted with a timeless justice, an act and verdict of law that simultaneously projects itself backwards and forwards, such that it can claim that the word is now safely given and ahead of itself.

In the face of the word held out variously as an error, a distraction, and a danger, the law appears and presents itself as a non-arbitrary sign. In the name of breaking the cycle of tragic fate and (re)inaugurating progress, it declares itself a word of words. This pronouncement, for Benjamin, marks the beginning of "mythic violence," a sovereign demand for sacrifice that conceals and begs the question of culture's fundamental implicature in barbarism. It is also the precise reason why, in the months after his first internment in the camps, Benjamin followed the seventh thesis with an argument about the emerging normality of exception. The language of law mediates the tragic violence of expression by sealing the question of the violence of its own judgment. Through the temporal projection of the precedent that legitimizes its rule, the taking place of the law's words is deemed intrinsic and extrinsic to itself, a movement of exception that turns the question of culture's barbarism, the threshold of the (un)speaking being and the threshold of being's (un)speakability, into a sovereign claim over the status of language as such. With this edict, as Benjamin puts it, language is "overnamed." Through an appropriation of the power to name *and* the appropriation of the name's object, language is turned from the translation of its spiritual character, an experience of nonidentical immediacy (a turning on its turning) to an idealizing symbol system through which to produce, differentiate, and mediate good and evil (Düttmann 41). The overnaming of language is a judgment in language that names language as outside of itself, a decision that reduces it to an "external content," an object of knowledge and a means of revelation (Benjamin 1: 73; Düttmann 64). In short, the question of language that marks the hinge between culture and barbarism, the question of an experience of a (self) lacking *logos,* is discarded as so much debris, a threat of contamination vanquished by the victors in history's battle to say what saying counts and for what. Now the figure that refuses to fall silently into the law, the barbarian sits at the very center of tragedy's stage, a testament to why "never again" cannot (yet) be true.

Benjamin's reply appears within the figure of an angel, the *Angelus Novus,* a painting by Klee that Benjamin counted as one of his most prized possessions and which he invokes in "The Concept of History" after constellating culture's barbarism with the logic of sovereign exception. Here, Benjamin draws together an idea that runs throughout much of his early and late work: the "overnaming" of tragedy must be met with the "undermeaning" of allegory, the *allêgoria* that pronounces an "other-speaking" with "undermeaning."[10] If the question of language has been written out of juridically enabled historical progress, what remains is a lament, the sadness of language that gives voice to precisely that which is silenced in the sovereign act of overnaming. This voice, the voice of *Angelus,* is not capable of being fully heard. From that which lacks a name, it may sound a hymn, a whisper, or a breath. Without clear referent, it resists full interpretation. It does not express a counterorder, a command from "on high" to render language otherwise. Its arrival constitutes a surprise, a moment to wonder about its source and a disruption of what has been thought to come next. The appearance of *Angelus* thus marks a temporal rift, a "taking place" of language in time that constellates and then blurs past and present.[11]

A beginning is present and presented. In this thin opening, the given word is interrupted with the question of the word's gift. This gift cannot be returned. Its arrival entails loss, an experience of receiving without the chance for reciprocity and offering to depart empty-handed; the bringing-forth of the word unfolds in a way that does not assure let alone fate its exchangeability. Spiritual but not a spirit, Klee's *Angelus* discloses a gap whose traversal announces the very experience of language as such, a being in between the creative word and the origin of (its) creation.[12] As Scholem put it in his poem, *Greetings from Angelus,* a portion of which Benjamin set as the epigraph to his reading of Klee's painting, the voice of the angel resounds with the message, "I am an unsymbolic thing" (Scholem, *Correspondence* 80). This is perhaps the very essence of allegory, for Benjamin: the other-speaking, a speaking otherwise with "undermeaning," an undermining if not a lack of meaning that discloses the word's mystery, the *heterophone logos* that cannot be located inside or outside itself.

Filled with sorrow, *Angelus* laments the loss of language in the name of language. It expresses the catastrophe in which it is caught, literally a "turning down," the turning down of that undermeaning which exposes the wreckage of language, shatters the integrity of its historical continuity, and opens it to question. Scholem thus gathers what Benjamin hears but cannot put into words: "I am an unsymbolic thing" is a refusal of recognition, an undermeaning that resists overnaming precisely as it recalls the damage that language has wrought on itself, the damage borne in a tragic desire for recognition that refuses the question of what "makes us relate to language."[13] To ask after this refusal is to ask a self-interrupting and likely proteptic question, an inquiry that calls forth a theoretical impulse, a turning back and forth, away from and toward the power by which and through which the word departs and returns (Gadamer).

6.   The turn from tragedy to allegory is not stable. This is a basic part of its importance, a turning between, a disclosing of turns between us, the turning between past and future in which we are called to "come to terms" in the midst of suffering language, a damage that is both a loss of words to the point of (in)comprehensibility and an experience of the anxiety that attends the word's infliction of (un)unspeakability. If so, in the light of *Angelus Novus,* the UDHR's tragic form appears as an emblem of catastrophe; it is a trace of language's (own) ruin that remains to be thought in the name of ethical life.

"The UDHR is a document of culture that *is* a document of barbarism." It's been easy enough to make this claim, particularly given the way in which multiculturalist politics have flattened the "dialectic of enlightenment" into an identitarian equation. Yet, if Horkheimer and Adorno wrote in Benjamin's debt, the significant risk of this judgment is that it figures the UDHR as little more than a register on which to discern and name the "hypocrisy" of human rights; the Declaration's terms are simply an ahistorical way to measure the disparity between the announced promise of human rights (as this promise appears both inside and outside the UDHR itself) and the "reality on the ground."[14] This tack fails Benjamin—and perhaps the very (im)potentiality of human rights. Its comfort is an endless debate that deters the revolutionary gesture against which the UDHR warns. Its cost, however, is that it legitimizes the Preamble's erasure of the very question of language with which it begins. We expect as much from sovereign power—such forgetting may be a necessary condition of its constitution. Yet, if the promise of human rights aims to exceed this exception, if it seeks to discover (to disclose and turn) the way in which legal violence has repeatedly sponsored conflict, atrocity, and genocide, then it may be important to approach the UDHR in allegorical terms, as a dialectical image in which a turning-down of language is a catastrophe in which appears a flash of language's own undermeaning, a lament over the loss incurred as the "falling short" of meaning in which its voice abides is devastated by expression's demand for the communication of "real" meaning. Put another way, the difference between a human rights culture predicated on the language of recognition and a human rights culture that emerges by asking after the recognizability of language is the difference between ceding to the demand to give up the word in the name of indemnifying the self-certain power of expression and an experience of giving the word back to itself in the name of hearing a question of expression's beginning to which we may all be bound.

Can we live with this? This question brings the matter home, to the question of the (dis)connection between rhetoric as an academic field and the problem of human rights. Neither angelic nor altogether timely, the field remains largely outside the orbit and gambit of human rights discourse. At some basic levels, its message has yet to be felt on earth. Today, the terms, objects, and subjects of human rights discourse are forged by policy makers who go to extravagant lengths to deny its rhetorical quality, and these terms, objects, and subjects are shaped by traditions of political, legal, and philosophical inquiry that cling with claws to strictures about rhetoric's irrelevance, instrumentality, and danger.[15] One wonders: at what point does a tolerance for such bungling begin to look more and more like an ethically dubious rationalization for nonconsensual masochism? Is there a point at which an unwillingness to reconsider the (im)potentiality of rhetoric counts as a barbarism? The corollary to this question is that the integrity if not the veracity of inquiry into "human rights rhetoric" may hinge on the advocacy of rhetoric—as a concept—to those who do not abide in the fold of its grammar. With respect to human rights, what are the conditions that govern rhetoric's (un)speakability? How does its unspeakability become speakable—and back again? What is the ethical (im)potential of this movement?

If these questions press, they may also hold an opening, a theoretical gesture that troubles the near-sacred separation of theory and practice that drives so much human rights discourse. Related closely to an aversion to rhetoric, this division animates the institutional and policy-making arms of human rights discourse and leads them to frequently condemn all theoretical inquiry as so much "postmodernism." The dogma is almost cute. It is also naïve, particularly as a tragic view gives just a bit of way to the allegorical, a shift in which it becomes possible to see how language instigates, perpetuates, and rationalizes (its) violence and the ways in which the (local) construction of human rights culture cuts open the exception that sponsors sovereign atrocity by posing the question of how to gather the inside and outside of the law's rule, the question of whether (not what) the word can yet mean in the wake of its suffering and its damage. What can be taken as given at the moment in which the gift betrays its proclivity for (self) destruction? Insight into this dynamic may well disclose that the universal-particular question that drives and paralyzes so much human rights discourse is something of a distraction, a failure to think the very question to which rhetoric has perhaps always been given.

* * *

None of this is to suggest that rhetoric will arrive just in time. We are late and we would do well to ask why. Our journals from the 1940s and 1950s are a mixed, if not somewhat depressing legacy, a testament to the fact that we did not have a great deal to say in the wake of the UDHR's appearance. This lack needs to be thought—however uncomfortable it might be—of in terms of Adorno's claim that silence in the wake of Auschwitz participates in its barbarism. It also needs to be thought in terms of the violence that may inhere in rhetoric's own culture. A significant portion of the American field still does not require its graduate students to learn a foreign language (at a moment when many are touting the virtues of "internationalism"). Moreover, the conceptual contours of "human rights rhetoric" may deserve reflection, particularly if it assumes the presence of a coherent speaking subject (whether in the form of an advocate, narrator, or witness) that remains somehow immune to the usurpations, distortions, and extractions of language wrought by atrocity. While this is partly a question of the word's (im)potential to turn being toward and from humanity, it is also a question of what, if anything, rhetoric is willing to relinquish in the name of participating in the unfolding of human rights culture. Does our very interest in human rights not present a call to challenge our canonical assumptions, the self-certain words about words that may yet give way to a view of rhetoric that remains (yet) incomprehensible and (yet) unrecognizable, not least to us? Are we willing to risk at least something of our own language? Through such an experience, we may arrive at a point where our questions move rhetoric into the fold of human rights discourse, a turn that moves beyond the walls of the city and offers hospitality to an angel's mysterious words—if not our own.

NOTES

[1] Within the question of human rights, Hamacher argues that this is partly a question of prayer.

[2] I have taken up the importance of McKeon's work on human rights elsewhere (see "The Rhetorical Question").

[3] This is partly to say that Benjamin's claim about the state of emergency deserves to be read through his "Critique of Violence" (1: 236) and his analysis of *Trauerspiel* (*Origin*). For insightful commentary on these and related issues, see the respective essays by Bahti and McLaughlin.

[4] Also see Hall's commentary (77), along with Pagden (71); Smith (291); Harrison.

[5] The question then is not about the "other" as such; the inside has become the outside and back again. For a difficult but helpful reading of this dynamic, see Badiou.

[6] The opening of the UDHR:

> *Whereas* recognition of the inherent dignity and of the equal and inalienable rights of all members of the human family is the foundation of freedom, justice and peace in the world, *Whereas* disregard and contempt for human rights have resulted in barbarous acts which have outraged the conscience of mankind, and the advent of a world in which human beings shall enjoy freedom of speech and belief and freedom from fear and want has been proclaimed as the highest aspiration of the common people, *Whereas* it is essential, if man is not to be compelled to have recourse, as a last resort, to rebellion against tyranny and oppression, that human rights should be protected by rule of law.

[7] For a very nuanced and difficult reading of these problems in the context of Nazi power, see Haidu.

[8] For a discussion of the Association's announcement, see Stanton (67).

[9] Düttmann usefully characterizes it as a gap in relation to what has been created (51).

[10] Benjamin (4: 392) sets out Klee's work as both a performance of allegory and a larger warrant for allegorical interpretation. For a useful but somewhat idiosyncratic commentary see Caygill.

[11] On the "taking place" of language, see Agamben (*Language*).

[12] This is partly to say that Thesis IX of "The Concept of History" relies heavily on Benjamin's 1916 essay on language, "On Language as Such and on the Language of Man."

[13] Düttmann (54) attributes this to Adorno but does not specify the passage.

[14] Elsewhere, I have taken up the question of how this hypocrisy-based approach may work at the cost of discovery (see "The Rhetorical Question").

[15] In the last five years, the emergence of transitional justice doctrine is tangible evidence of just this dynamic, not least as it features extended discussions of "norm entrepreneurs," whose task is to mobilize campaigns of instrumental persuasion that sell the value of law's rule beyond question. I have discussed this development elsewhere (see "Critique").

WORKS CITED

Adorno, Theodor W. *Critical Models: Interventions and Catchwords.* Trans. Henry W. Pickford. New York: Columbia UP, 2005. Print.

---. *Negative Dialectics.* Trans. E. B. Ashton. New York: Continuum, 1973. Print.

Agamben, Giorgio. *Potentialities: Collected Essays in Philosophy.* Ed. Daniel Heller-Roazen. Stanford: Stanford UP, 2000. Print.

---. *Language and Death: The Place of Negativity.* Trans. Karen Pinkus. Minneapolis: Minnesota UP, 1991. Print.

Arendt, Hannah. *The Origins of Totalitarianism.* Orlando: Benediction Books, 2009. Print.

---. *The Human Condition.* Chicago: U of Chicago P, 1998. Print.

Badiou, Alain. *Ethics: An Essay on the Understanding of Evil.* Trans. Peter Hallward. New York: Verso, 2002. Print.

Bahti, Timothy. "History and Rhetorical Enactment: Walter Benjamin's Theses 'On the Concept of History.'" *Diacritics* 9.3 (1979): 2-17. Print.

Benjamin, Walter. *The Origin of German Tragic Drama.* Trans. John Osborne. New York: Verso, 2009. Print.

---. *Walter Benjamin: Selected Writings, 1913–1926.* Ed. Marcus Bullock and Michael W. Jennings. Vol. 1. Cambridge: Belknap P of Harvard UP, 2004. Print.

---. *Walter Benjamin: Selected Writings, 1931-1934.* Vol. 2. Cambridge: Belknap P of Harvard UP, 2005. Print.

---. *Walter Benjamin: Selected Writings, 1938-1940.* Ed. Howard Eiland and Michael W. Jennings. Vol. 4. Cambridge: Belknap P of Harvard UP, 2003. Print.

Blanchot, Maurice. *The Space of Literature.* Trans. Ann Smock. Lincoln: U of Nebraska P, 1982.

Caygill, Howard. "Walter Benjamin's Concept of Allegory." *The Cambridge Companion to Allegory.* Ed. Rita Copeland and Peter T. Struck. Cambridge: Cambridge UP, 2010. 241-53. Print.

Doxtader, Erik. "A Critique of Law's Violence yet (Never) to come: United Nations' Transitional Justice Policy and the (Fore)closure of Reconciliation." *Theorizing Post-Conflict Reconciliation: Agonism, Restitution, Repair.* Ed. A. Hirsch. New York: Routledge, 2011. 27-64. Print.

---. "The Rhetorical Question of Human Rights—A Preface." *Quarterly Journal of Speech* 96:4 (2010): 353-79. Print.

Düttmann, Alexander Garcia. *The Gift of Language: Memory and Promise in Adorno, Benjamin, Heidegger, and Rosenzweig.* Trans. Arline Lyons. Syracuse: Syracuse UP, 2001. Print.

Gadamer, Hans-Georg. *Praise of Theory: Speeches and Essays.* Trans. Chris Dawson. New Haven: Yale UP, 1999. Print.

Haidu, Peter. "The Dialectics of Unspeakability: Language, Silence and the Narratives of Desubjectification." *Probing the Limits of Representation: Nazism and the "Final Solution."* Ed. Saul Friedlander. Cambridge: Harvard UP, 1992. 277-99. Print.

Hall, Edith. *Inventing the Barbarian: Greek Self-Definition Through Tragedy.* Oxford: Oxford UP, 1991. Print.

Hamacher, Werner. "The Right to Have Rights (Four-and-a-half Remarks)." *South Atlantic Quarterly* 103 (2004): 343-56. Print.

Harrison, Thomas, ed. *Greeks and Barbarians.* New York: Routledge, 2001. Print.

Löwy, Michael, and Chris Turner. *Fire Alarm: Reading Walter Benjamin's "On the Concept of History."* New York: Verso, 2006. Print.

McLaughlin, Kevin. "Benjamin's Barbarism." *The Germanic Review* (2006): 4-20. Print.

Mirandola, Giovanni Pico della. *Oration on the Dignity of Man.* Trans. A. Robert Gaponigri. Washington, DC: Gateway Editions, 1996. Print.

Moyn, Samuel. *The Last Utopia: Human Rights in History.* Cambridge: Belknap P of Harvard UP, 2012. Print.

Neilson, Brett. "Barbarism/Modernity: Notes on Barbarism." *Textual Practice* 13.1 (1999): 79-95. Print.

Pagden, Anthony. *The Fall of Natural Man: The American Indian and the Origins of Comparative Ethnology.* 1st ed. Cambridge: Cambridge UP, 1987. Print.

Scholem, Gershom, and Werner J. Dannhauser. *On Jews and Judaism in Crisis: Selected Essays.* Philadelphia: Paul Dry Books, 2012. Print.

Scholem, Gershom, and Anson Rabinbach. *The Correspondence of Walter Benjamin and Gershom Scholem, 1932-1940.* Trans. Gary Smith and Andre LeFevere. Cambridge: Harvard UP, 1992. Print.

Smith, Ian. *Race and Rhetoric in the Renaissance: Barbarian Errors.* 1st ed. New York: Palgrave Macmillan, 2009. Print.

Stanton, Donna. "Top-Down, Bottom-Up, Horizontally: Resignifying the Universal in the Human Rights Discourse." *Theoretical Perspectives on Human Rights and Literature.* Ed. E.S Goldberg and A.S. Moore. New York: Routledge, 2011. 65-86. Print.

Todorov, Tzvetan. *The Fear of Barbarians: Beyond the Clash of Civilizations.* Trans. Andrew Brown. Chicago: U of Chicago P, 2010. Print.

The Universal Declaration of Human Rights. *UN.org.* United Nations, 2013. Web. May 2012.

Section

III

Re/Framing History, Memory, and Events

13

REFRAMING IDENTIFICATIONS

Recognizing the Effects of the Past in the Present within Debates about the Israel-Palestine Conflict

Matthew Abraham

Burkean and postmodern conceptions of identification teach us that just as we inhabit history as situated subjects, history (with all its haunting) inhabits us. To speak of an "I" is to speak simultaneously of a "We." If, as Diana Fuss reminds us, identification is the name of the psychical mechanism through which one achieves self-recognition by detouring through the Other, position taking cannot be simply viewed as an individual "act" but emerges in negotiating the border between the inside and the outside, the border between the self and one's environment (49). To identify where one stands is to identify simultaneously where one stands in relation to a community of other voices, a community characterized by identification and division. As Kenneth Burke reminds us, "put identification and division ambiguously together, so that you cannot know for certain just where one ends and the other begins, and you have the characteristic invitation to rhetoric" (25). How we answer this "characteristic invitation" determines the conditions of possibility for achieving community.

As committed public intellectuals, rhetoricians have a great deal to contribute in elucidating how history, conscious and unconscious identifications, affective attachments, and the "embodied" shape one's understanding of—and the ability to make claims about—the Israel-Palestine conflict (including identifying how history and language all too frequently serve or obscure a particular politics). However, these uses (and possible abuses) of history and language to advance a particular viewpoint are not always in our conscious control, as I will try to elaborate. Indeed, history often "returns" to us like a boomerang with sometimes unexpected and startling effects.[1] By virtue of its returning to us in a different form, and within a potentially deformed context, this history necessarily becomes ripe for misrecognition and possibly illegitimate activation and deployment as part of (and within) a hegemonic politics.

Disavowals

How could the circumstances surrounding the death of an American college student in Gaza become the object of intense discussion on a listserv for

133

writing program administrators (WPA-L)? How could the politics surrounding the Israel-Palestine conflict and the Middle East, as the controversy over
this college student's act of seeming martyrdom, come to ever so briefly grip
the attention of our field? What seemed like a relatively straightforward decision to post a call for nominations for the Rachel Corrie Award for Courage
in the Teaching of Writing to WPA-L in May of 2006 quite unexpectedly led
to an interrogation of the values informing our professional organization and
its supposed politics.

What narrative, if any, was the umbrella convention for writing instruction—the Conference on College Composition and Communication
(CCCC)—forwarding about Rachel Corrie's death and Middle East politics,
some asked, by allowing the Progressive Special Interest Caucuses and Coali-
tions (PSCC) to promote the Rachel Corrie Award for Courage in the Teaching of Writing—an award seeking to recognize courage and risk taking in the
academy—and to present the award at the national conference (CCCCs)?
According to some critics of the award, to make a value judgment about Corrie's actions—that they were in fact courageous—and to accept a specific
reading of these actions as consistent with anti-colonial and liberationist
struggle improperly politicized an organization committed to writing and
rhetorical studies. To endorse a tendentious reading of Corrie's actions,
according to some, was to uncritically accept a pro-Palestinian politics, essentially confirming that Corrie had been deliberately killed by the Israeli
Defense Forces (IDF) in March of 2003 when she was supposedly defending
a Palestinian home in Rafah, Gaza against demolition. Could Rachel Corrie
necessarily be framed as a victim, some asked, implying that she may have
been responsible for her own death?

According to the nomination announcement, "Rachel [Corrie] was
attempting to block an Israeli military bulldozer from demolishing the house
of a pharmacist and his family when the driver of the bulldozer ran over her,
then backed up and ran over her again." Furthermore, "Wearing a bright
orange jacket and using a bullhorn, Rachel was, by all eyewitness accounts
and in horrifying photographs published on the Internet, exceptionally visible." For many participants on the WPA list, both of these claims were far
from factual. For some, claims that were being reported as factual by the
award creators were tendentious and partisan, deliberately slanted against
Israel. Perhaps equally controversial was the claim within the nomination
announcement that Corrie's "parents, some members of Congress, and grassroots organizations including several Jewish peace groups have called for an
independent US investigation into her death. Such an investigation has yet to
happen, and the US media virtually buried the story—though it was featured
prominently in the UK and in many other countries."

While Corrie's actions have been praised by certain members of the progressive community, others have described here as a naïve, idealistic young
woman who took her ideals too far, someone who had been duped by "left-
wing propaganda" on the conflict. For many participants, what justice looks

like in the Middle East is far from clear; therefore, the Rachel Corrie award is inappropriate because it presents the Palestinians as the only group with a legitimate grievance, portraying a complex situation in a simplistic binary of right and wrong. As one participant complained, the award supporters "treat extremely complex situations in simplistic manners and the price for doing so is continued conflict and lack of resolution." If one were to suggest that the circumstances around Corrie's death—and her parents' efforts to involve the US and Israeli governments in an investigation of those circumstances—had been underreported or purposely embargoed in the US, would one then be engaging in the classic anti-Semitic canard that "Jews control the media"? These were just a few of the questions encircling this debate one May morning in 2006 on the WPA list.[2]

Some critics of the award questioned whether Corrie's motives were as pure as her supporters believed, stating that they had read accounts portraying her as protecting terrorist tunnels in Gaza, and, as a member of the ISM (International Solidarity Movement), harboring and providing comfort to known terrorist organizations.[3] So, what some saw as an altruistic act of sacrifice, others viewed as anti-Israel activism. Given these disparate accounts of how Rachel Corrie died and what she represented, it is perhaps unsurprising that heated discussion ensued when a call for nominations for an award created in her memory came across a major listserv. The dynamics of this discussion in our field, among our colleagues, did surprise me, however. As Barbara Herrnstein Smith reminds us, "The dynamics of intellectual controversy often mirror, shadow, and predict quite closely the dynamics of larger human conflict" (vii). Smith's insightful observation certainly seems to ring true as we turn to an examination of some of the exchanges between participants on the WPA list about the Rachel Corrie Award for Courage in the Teaching of Writing.

Rachel Corrie as an Object of Transference

In a 2004 *JAC* article entitled "Edward Said in the American Imagination: Academic Controversy after 9/11," I sought to analyze debates within the public sphere around the Israel-Palestine conflict by examining how Edward Said's life and legacy tend to operate as transferential objects. I would like to extend my analysis in this article by looking at how transference also operates around the life and legacy of Rachel Corrie, specifically with respect to competing historical narratives of Palestinian and Jewish victimization as these rely upon and extend the uptakes that become activated in contemporary contexts.

The circumstances around Corrie's death came to represent a more general debate about the politics informing the Israel-Palestine conflict. In other words, Corrie became an object of transference in this controversy, representing a conduit through which the controversy could develop and play out.[4] Participants seemingly either strongly identified with her or completely disavowed that she could possibly stand for what the award claimed she did. Corrie's actions and legacy were also taken up in discussants' affective transmissions, with each message to the list seemingly escalating the political and professional stakes of the exchange. Furthermore, participants who agreed with one another solidified their identifications by identifying themselves as reasonable and compassionate, while seemingly characterizing those who supported or criticized the award as somehow biased or uninformed. In this debate, Corrie was either a victim of IDF aggression or a terrorist (Hamas, Hezbollah, etc.) sympathizer. In other words, she was either defending an innocent Palestinian's home or protecting a terrorist's stash.

When a contested figure such as Corrie becomes an object of transference, through which participants debating her legacy demonstrate a tendency to repeat the very problems they are supposedly subjecting to critique and analysis (the use and seeming repetition of violent metaphors to examine violence or the recycling of anti-Semitic tropes in a discussion about the Holocaust and Israel, for example), the debate itself becomes susceptible to resuscitating echoes (or "uptakes") of the past. These uptakes tend to seize upon a particularly affective-laden event or meaningful signifier from the past, which are then redeployed in the present for the purpose of maintaining unified meaning and coherence. While this strategy contributes to the circulation of a lachrymose narrative about all kinds of suffering, it simultaneously enables a conflation of memory, whereby supposed threats to Jewish memory in the present seemingly enable one to reach for events from the past, as part of an effort to suture together a rather fragmented history.[5]

According to many, the memory of Rachel Corrie had been taken up as part of a propaganda campaign to defame and delegitimize Israel, at a time of supposed increasing anti-Semitism through the world. To name after Corrie an award seeking to recognize courageous teaching and scholarship was a controversial idea because Corrie's actions were not necessarily courageous, particularly if her memorialization was being employed to be critical of Israel. Perhaps some found Corrie's actions, or at least the way in which they have been memorialized, potentially anti-Semitic.

Transferring the Past into the Present

The psychoanalytical concept of transference refers to the tendency to repeat the very problems one sets out to study and identify (e.g., using anti-Semitic tropes in the course of studying anti-Semitism or employing sexually violent rhetoric in the course of discussing sexual violence)—or, more directly related to the concerns of this chapter, the tendency to repeat the usage of warlike metaphors in the context of discussing various positions within the Israel-Palestine conflict. There indeed seems to be a tendency for interlocutors to adopt the same rhetorical stances as the actual disputants in the conflict, unwittingly repeating the very same problems they set out to discuss and solve. According to Dominick LaCapra in *Writing History, Writing*

Trauma, one can cope with the problem of transference either by engaging in greater empathic identification or by working through this tendency to repeat the very tendency one seeks out to analyze and study. As LaCapra explains, we tend to handle transference by either acting out these inappropriate feelings from the past in the present or by working through them. We either work through the past or allow the past to work through us.

The return of the past through the mention of a name or an event and the different memories that are evoked in the process of remembering those names and events represent a complex process of reconciling personal histories with events in the world. In other words, our libidinal investments (the ways our narcissistic identifications and attachments become mobilized) manifest themselves in the social field when we remember a controversial event or an individual associated with a controversial event. An analysis of libidinal attachments, then, requires us to suspend conceptions of justice and "right and wrong" and to concentrate on how individuals approach social antagonisms in the ways they do, noting how they create identifications with respect to social conflicts based on race, gender, ethnicity, religion, and class.

Inevitably, interlocutors seem to draw comparisons between Jewish and Palestinian suffering, without realizing that these comparisons are not only inappropriate but quite unnecessary. Herein resides the dilemma: the Israel-Palestine conflict brings together two distinct histories of oppression and suffering that are simply incompatible and incomparable, leading to easy conflations of memory—where both Hamas or Israeli settlers in the West Bank can be compared to either Nazis or freedom fighters depending upon the point to be made. Hamas can be compared to the Nazis because as an organization it is dedicated to the destruction of Israel as a Jewish state; however, one cannot simply state that Hamas is driven to destroy Israel because of anti-Semitism. Instead, one must recognize that Hamas seeks Israel's destruction because Israel is viewed as occupying and colonizing Palestinian land. The reason Palestinian resistance against Israeli occupation is often configured as anti-Semitic is because the occupiers of Palestinian land are Jewish. Just as American Indian resistance against European settlers in the New World could not be credibly framed as arising from "anti-Europeanism" or "anti-White-ism," we should be equally skeptical of framing Palestinian resistance to Israeli domination as arising from anti-Semitism.[6] We must carefully interrogate these easy conflations and transpositions.

The Affective Component

Far too often, interlocutors debating the Israel-Palestine conflict become enmeshed within affective environments within which it becomes extremely difficult to separate position taking from assignments of moral culpability. How does one achieve the necessary intellectual and affective distance from the complex issues surrounding the Israel-Palestine conflict before entering into an informed and good-faith discussion about them? Appropriate "distance" in this instance refers to the achievement of a certain ability to recognize and avoid the polarizing influences and affective transmissions that often infuse analyses of issues such as nationalism, occupation, ethnic exclusion, and the historical grievance of dispossession. These influences and transmissions, which often infuse defenses of nationalistic commitments, are often intense and irrational, verging on a type of fundamentalism. Indeed, these transmissions have a contagious quality to them, ensuring controversy once they are unleashed. In describing the affective dimension of the conflict, I am drawing upon the work of Teresa Brennan, who in her *The Transmission of Affect* defines affect as "the physiological shifts that accompanies a judgment" and "the energy transfer or exchange between aggressor and passive recipient" (49).

In her *Toward a Civil Discourse*, Sharon Crowley describes how fundamentalist ideologies develop, noting how "densely articulated belief systems" take root and preclude the kind of inventiveness that makes for flexible and contingent thinking. Fundamentalism interferes with one's capacity to process new information and to notice evidence that does not confirm one's strongly held perspective. A fundamentalist ideology literally gives one tunnel vision with respect to how one views the world and processes events within it. Drawing on Gerald Clore and Karen Gasper, Crowley argues that "densely articulated ideologies construct bad affective grammarians who pay intense notice to objects and events that can be threaded into the intricate tapestries of their belief system(s)" (85). As Crowley notes, "They notice because almost everything that is made legible by their belief system(s) is weighty with affect for them" (85).

When someone interprets an event through an interpretative framework weighty with affect, one can only view that event as either contributing to or undermining one's worldview because of how the structure of feeling that informs the event shapes one's very understanding of—and relation to—it. In other words, as the fundamentalist subject encounters an event within the social field, she processes this event as consistent with what she already believes, even if the event itself has no bearing on the belief in question. In this sense, the fundamentalist maintains her tunnel vision. If she were to lose it, she would lose her very identity. Crowley draws this conclusion: "If this account is correct, extremists have difficulty taking notice of events or objects that neither support nor attack their beliefs. That is to say, whatever is new and neutral in relation to their system of beliefs is likely to pass unremarked" (85). Crowley works, then, to build a rhetoric of fundamentalism by noting just how resilient and impervious to change some belief systems can become. We see such impervious belief systems at work within debates about the Israel-Palestine conflict.

The Return of the Past in the Present

It is a commonplace of psychoanalysis that the past frequently intrudes upon the present, often in unexpected and novel ways.[7] A bad romantic relationship, for example, can return and influence all future relationships, persistently exercising control over us and shaping how we view others, while all the while not announcing itself in any definable or visible way. The reason such experiences exercise such a hold on our attention and seemingly reappear in other contexts is because they have played a formative role in shaping our identities, establishing an important place in the solidification of our self-esteem and our ability to understand our positionality in the world. As Thomas Rickert's reading of Jean Laplanche reminds us, "It takes two traumas to make a trauma," by which he means that the first trauma instills in us the fear that we will re-experience the absence and loss of the original traumatic event (23). When the second trauma overtakes us, it has so much resonance because we experience and feel the second trauma through the framework created by the first.[8]

When certain traumatic experiences are reawakened in us because of a particularly painful memory, we tend to react quite defensively, insisting upon removing the conditions that have led us to revisit the past, or more precisely, that have led the past to revisit us. Certain triggers can quickly and quite unexpectedly bring the past "back" into the present, surprising even the most astute and critical observer of a particular social scene. That there is a degree of uncontrollability to these intrusions is consistent with the notion that the unconscious exercises its influence upon the conscious mind in slightly detectable ways, from a slip of the tongue to a particularly realistic dream that corresponds to or embellishes upon the events of the previous day or a particularly memorable moment. How the past will "return" to us is enigmatic, defying any easy explanation.

The past continually seeks to catch up with and exercise its hold on the present, erupting into the contemporary scene, even as we work diligently to keep this past at bay. As the past makes its way into the present either through unconscious language choices or conscious manipulation of certain tropes, we are often surprised at how quickly the past can literally dictate the unfolding of the present. This phenomenon (which Freud labeled "belatedness") or deferred action (*nachträglichkeit*), reminds us that past events take on more and more significance and often become more and more meaningful (affect laden) in our conscious minds because it takes time for the memory—particularly a memory about a traumatic event—to develop or catch up with the present ("From the History of Infantile Neurosis" 7-122). These belated memories seem to have a boomerang effect upon the psyche of the subject, "returning" the full force of the prior event with a particular energy and force.

Belatedness is certainly operative with respect to contemporary discussions of the Israel-Palestine conflict, as day-to-day events in the Middle East seem to inevitably become refracted through the prism of Jewish suffering leading up to and during the Holocaust. Perhaps it is only to be expected that this history of Jewish suffering should be invoked to contextualize and explain the violence and religious hatred that drives the "clash-of-civilizations" mentality of the disputants and partisans in the Israel-Palestine conflict.

Conclusion

As rhetoricians, we should be concerned by this possible misuse of history in these debates; indeed, the charge of anti-Semitism, if it is to be taken seriously, must be leveled with precision and not as a facile propaganda device employed to achieve cheap political points.[9] In this discursive environment, every statement introduced into the debate contains a hidden motive or at least a hidden rhetorical or historical resonance whereby nothing can be interpreted as being offered in good faith: "You claim that the Rachel Corrie Award for Courage in the Teaching of Writing is about X (rewarding courage, risk taking, innovation, etc.), but it is really about Y (anti-Israelism, pro-Palestinian politics, anti-Semitism)." It is this displacement of a particular conception of anti-Semitism, a conception that had a particular meaning and resonance at a particular point in history, which tends to confuse participants in contemporary debates about the Middle East. As rhetoricians, we should be much more vigilant about the prospects of importing this flawed conception of anti-Semitism into the field of rhetorical studies, particularly when doing so has the potential to hurt possibilities for dialogue and understanding.

As rhetoricians, we must make public interventions into debates about the Israel-Palestine conflict. Events such as the ones I have described in this essay are relatively representative of the opportunities that are available to those seeking to identity and clarify the kinds of psychological forces and energies infusing the rhetorical situations surrounding these debates. The abuse of history and historical memory in the service of politics does not enable productive dialogue but instead creates affective environments that disable the potential for experimentation, risk taking, and exchange. In such an environment, participants are particularly susceptible to the kinds of inappropriate transfers of the past into the present that I have examined. If we refuse to engage the relevant issues with respect to the Israel-Palestine conflict, particularly when these issues are directly part of our professional conversation (as the discussion of the Rachel Corrie Award for Courage in the Teaching of Writing clearly was), then we cede the discursive field to the past, without considering the demands for political and rhetorical action in the present.

NOTES

[1] In his *Multidirectional Memory,* Rothberg, drawing upon Arendt's *Origins of Totalitarianism* and Cesaire's *Discourse of Colonialism,* develops the notion of *choc en retour,* literally "boomerang effect," "backlash," or "reverse shock" (23).

[2] For a list of all the e-mails posted on the topic of the Rachel Corrie Award for Courage in the Teaching of Writing, see: condor.depaul.edu/~mabraha5/Chart (final).pdf.

[3] See Ticker, as well as Hammer. For a critique of Hammer's article, see Nguyen.

[4] See my "The Rhetoric of Academic Controversy after 9/11" for a discussion about how transference can develop around an individual or school of thought.

[5] See Sand.

[6] See Finkelstein's *Image and Reality in the Israel-Palestine Conflict.*

[7] See LaCapra's *History in Transit* and *History and Memory after the Holocaust.*

[8] According to Rickert in his *Acts of Enjoyment:*

> Zizek understands trauma to be our response to an impossible limit or radical antagonism; it is an experience of constitutive anxiety or unease at the terrifying prospect of the impossibility of achieving harmonious resolutions to personal and social relations. Furthermore, trauma is more intensified by the fact that is also "resists symbolization, totalization, symbolic integration" (*Sublime* 6). (219n 15)

[9] See Finkelstein's *Beyond Chutzpah.* For additional perspectives on the "New Anti-Semitism," see Cockburn and St. Clair. For a contrasting view, see Harrison.

WORKS CITED

Abraham, Matthew. "The Rhetoric of Academic Controversy after 9/11: Edward Said in the American Imagination," *JAC* 24.3 (2004): 113-42. Print.

Brennan, Teresa. *The Transmission of Affect.* Ithaca and London: Cornell UP, 2004. Print.

Burke, Kenneth. *A Rhetoric of Motives.* 1950. Berkeley: U of California P, 1969. Print.

Cockburn, Alexander, and Jeffrey St. Clair. *The Politics of Anti-Semitism.* London: AK, 2003. Print.

Crowley, Sharon. *Toward a Civil Discourse: Rhetoric and Fundamentalism.* Pittsburgh: U of Pittsburgh P, 2006. Print.

Finkelstein, Norman. *Beyond Chutzpah: On the Misuse of Anti-Semitism and the Abuse of History.* Berkeley: U of California P, 2005. Print.

---. *Image and Reality in the Israel-Palestine Conflict.* London and New York: Verso, 2004. Print.

Freud, Sigmund. "From the History of an Infantile Neurosis." *The Standard Edition of the Complete Psychological Works of Sigmund Freud.* Trans. James Strachey. Vol. 17. London: Hogarth, 1964. 7-122. Print.

Fuss, Diana. *Identification Papers.* New York: Routledge, 1995. Print.

Hammer, Joshua. "The Death of Rachel Corrie." *Mother Jones.com.* Mother Jones and the Foundation for National Progress, Sept./Oct. 2003. Web. 31 Aug. 2010.

Harrison, Bernard. *The Resurgence of Anti-Semitism: Jews, Israel, and Liberal Opinion.* Lanham: Rowman and Littlefield, 2006. Print.

LaCapra, Dominick. *History in Transit.* Ithaca: Cornell UP, 2004. Print.

---. *History and Memory after Auschwitz.* Ithaca: Cornell UP, 1998. Print.

---. *Writing History, Writing Trauma.* Baltimore: Johns Hopkins UP, 2001. Print.

McCarthy, Rory. "British Activist Saw Rachel Corrie Die under Bulldozer, Court Hears." *The Guardian.co.uk.* Guardian News and Media Limited, Mar. 2010. Web. 25 Aug. 2010.

Nguyen, Phen. "Mother Jones Smears Rachel Corrie Specious Journalism in Defense of Killers." *If Americans Knew.* If Americans Knew.org, 20 Sept. 2003. Web. 31 Aug. 2010.

Rickert, Thomas. *Acts of Enjoyment: Rhetoric, Zizek, and the Return of the Subject.* Pittsburgh: U of Pittsburgh P, 2007. Print.

Rothberg, Michael. *Multidirectional Memory: Remembering the Holocaust in the Age of Decolonization.* Stanford: Stanford UP, 2009. Print.

Sand, Shlomo. *The Invention of the Jewish People.* London: Verso, 2010. Print.

Smith, Barbara Herrnstein. *Belief and Resistance: The Dynamics of Intellectual Controversy.* Cambridge: Harvard UP, 1999. Print.

Ticker, Bruce. "The Case against Rachel Corrie." *Israel National News.com.* Arutz Sheva, 30 May 2004. Web. 31 Aug. 2010.

Zizek, Slavoj. *The Sublime Object of Ideology.* London and New York: Verso, 1989. Print.

14

RE/FRAMING TRANSNATIONAL COLLECTIVE MEMORIES

Dokdo/Takeshima, Korea/Japan

Jerry Won Lee

In this presentation, I explore how national identity and nationalist senti-ment are contested and fortified at the intersections of competing collective memories, which continuously re/frame transnational identifications. One of the most prolonged examples of this phenomenon is to be found embedded in the complex of sentiments that constellate around a small series of islets located in the Pacific Ocean between Korea and Japan; to the Koreans, they are called *Dokdo*, and to the Japanese, they are *Takeshima*. In an effort to maintain neutrality, I will refer to the islets by their English name, the Lian-court Rocks.

The Korean Peninsula was liberated from Japanese colonial rule at the end of World War II, and sovereignty over the islets has been disputed since. The dispute was notably exacerbated in July 2008, when the Japanese gov-ernment authorized the publication of history textbooks claiming Japanese ownership of the islets. The Korean ambassador to Japan was recalled, and a range of protests in Korea ensued, including demonstrations that involved Korean citizens cutting off their own fingers outside the Japanese embassy in Korea. Although Koreans occupied (and continue to occupy) the islets, the act signified an effort to historicize Japanese legitimacy: to authorize a hege-monic national history and to reify a homogenized transnational collective memory. The controversy, along with the collective memories re/authorized, continues to resuscitate the specter of Japanese colonization and threaten diplomatic relations in the region. The coexistence of two discrete collective memories, two discrete perspectives on the historical accuracy of the past, both of which aim to exist within a homogeneous framework of empirical knowledge, paralyzes transnational identification and enables the perpetua-tion of colonial tension in East Asia today.

Collective memory is, according to Lewis Coser, "not a given but rather a socially constructed notion" (22) sustained by, to use the words of Maurice Halbwachs, the efforts of "individuals as group members" (qtd. in Coser 22). Collective memories are critical to the maintenance of a shared national identification and hence are critical to the maintenance of the nation itself. Homi Bhabha, however, reminds us that "[a]s an apparatus of symbolic power, [nationness] produces a continual slippage of categories, like sexuality, class affiliation, territorial paranoia, or 'cultural difference' in the act of writing the nation" (201). National identity is tenuous—the emergent and constantly shifting product of a plurality of narratives, a plurality of collective memories. Yet an institutional document such as a history textbook poses the threat of silencing nonnormative discourses in an effort to provide an "official" narrative of the past.

The Liancourt Rocks controversy follows a narrative thread centering on the ethics of accurate historic representation. There is no physical evidence of legitimate ownership beyond various historical documents and maps, which predate modern geography and are in many cases circumstantial or anecdotal. Yet, both Korea and Japan claim to possess evidence of legitimate ownership of the territory: two collective memories, two "legitimate" histories. For Koreans, sovereignty over the islets is self-evident, and any Japanese claim is forcefully combated by arguments equating such claims as residually colonial. But my point is not to explore the intricacies of each state's claim and to endorse one over the other. Nor do I wish to further the common misconception of Japan as the "country that can never say sorry" (Berger 195). I merely wish to suggest how the insistence on a factual representation in the history textbook points to a general need to corroborate a collective national memory with an institutionally endorsed, legitimizing text, a byproduct of the modern political unit of the nation-state.

On the surface, legitimate ownership of the Liancourt Rocks determines designated fishing waters in the Pacific Ocean for Japan and Korea. But to understand more fully why the claim to the islets, whose area is scarcely one-tenth of a square mile, can breed such rancor, we must examine it within the context of a critical component of nationalism, which is territorial sovereignty of a nation's homeland. The islets operate as part of what Anthony Smith has called the ethnoscape, which is a landscape "endowed with poetic ethnic meaning through the historicization of nature and the territorialization of ethnic memories" (16). Although a nation may very well be an *imagined* community, to use Benedict Anderson's expression, it does not mean necessarily that the collective memory of a national imaginary is fortified organically. A nation's ties to its homeland are inextricably bound to imagined conceptions of antiquity, and the collective memory of an ancestral tie to an ethnoscape is itself capable of producing nationness. Therefore, each nation's claims to the Liancourt Rocks threatens the other's mytho-historic national narrative, and hence, both narratives of rightful ownership cannot exist simultaneously.

A point to be emphasized, however, is that a nation's claim to a particular ethnoscape has not always needed to be historically based. Take, for instance, the decision made in the early 19th century by Gia-long, then emperor of what is present-day Vietnam, to insist on adopting the name

"Nam Việt." The Manchu Son of Heaven (Chinese emperor), however, insisted on *"Việt Nam"* (Anderson 157). According to Anderson, such a reversal was driven by an imperative to deny the Vietnamese an anachronistic claim to antiquity:

> "Việt Nam" (or in Chinese Yüeh-nan) means, roughly, "to the south of Việt (Yüeh)," a realm conquered by the Han seventeen centuries earlier and reputed to cover today's Chinese provinces of Kwangtung and Kwangsi, as well as the Red River valley. Gia-long's "Nam Việt," however, meant "Southern Việt/ Yüeh," in effect a claim *to* the old realm. (157)

The antiquity of territorial claims is crucial to the construction of a national imaginary, but the collective memory of a nation involves a willful amnesia as well:

> That today's Vietnamese proudly defend a Việt Nam scornfully invented by a nineteenth-century Manchu dynast reminds us of [Ernest] Renan's dictum that nations must have "oublié bien des choses [forgotten many things]" but also, paradoxically, of the imaginative power of nationalism. (Anderson 158)

The commonly acknowledged fact that Amerigo Vespucci did not in fact "discover" America has not compelled an appellative overhaul in the US or in the Americas either. To quote Bhabha: "Forgetting, I would even go so far as to say historical error, is a crucial factor in the creation of a nation, which is why progress in historical studies often constitutes a danger for [the principle of] nationality" (11). Curiously, the emphasis on historical verification of collective memory that we often see today contradicts the systematic forgetting that in the past has been crucial to the formation of national solidarity.

In fact, I believe the Korean outrage over the Japanese government's decision to authorize, print, and use, *within Japan's borders*, history texts that claim the islets as their own suggests an ambivalence of Korean authority and an acknowledgement that a transnational articulation of Korean illegitimacy is essential to the international recognition of Korean legitimacy. Bhabha argues that, in the context of colonialist maintenance of authority, repetition exposes ambivalence and the precariousness of authority itself (126). I wish to suggest that the continual production and dissemination of claims to the islets reaffirms the ambivalence of the legitimacy of either state's claim to the islets—the insistent and recurring enunciation of legitimacy points to an ambivalence of the legitimacy claimed. Korean occupation and administration of the islets reveals, or at least suggests, an implied rightful ownership, a self-affirmed collective memory of the Liancourt Rocks as Korean territory— so a collective memory of Korean sovereignty over the islets remains intact. However, the fact that the publication of an alien textbook threatens Korean legitimacy, and the fact that these textbooks were authorized by a politically legitimate governmental body, the Japanese Ministry of Education, engenders a repetition of legitimacy and underscores the appeal of institutionalized collective memory, irrespective of its site of enunciation. Anderson confirms the weight of political and institutional power in the articulation of the nation. He argues that it is

> leaderships, not people, who inherit old switchboards and palaces. No one imagines, I presume, that the broad masses of the Chinese people give a fig for what happens along the colonial border between Cambodia and Vietnam. Nor is it likely that Khmer and Vietnamese peasants wanted wars between their peoples, or were consulted in the matter. (161)

It is through ideological engineering, such as through state-sponsored documents, in this case, history textbooks, that a citizenry is made to "give a fig."

In East Asia, the primary impediment to transnational identification is the reverence for institutionalized history. In exploring the dangers of history, Walter Mignolo argues that competing socio-epistemic conceptualizations of history are largely responsible for the colonization of the Americas by the Europeans. Mignolo traces the privileging of alphabetic written histories over oral and pictographic histories to the works of figures like Thucydides or Tacitus (129) and to Cicero's definition of history, which "became the standard definition during the European Renaissance and was often repeated by historians of the New World: *esse testem temporum, vitae magistram, vitam memoriae, veritatis lucen et vetustatis nuntian* (witness of time, model of life, life of memory, light of truth, and messenger of antiquity)" (136). Mignolo also reminds us that in the ancient Roman context, history, beyond merely reporting the past, operated as an agent of the imperial agenda: "Roman historians were mainly concerned with constructing the space and memories of Roman territoriality" (181).

The appeal of history has been its capacity as a collectivizing and legitimizing force, along with its alleged ideological neutrality. But we must proceed with caution. Sonia Ryang has identified the tendency of Korean historical research to serve nationalistic agendas (503). One can also look to C. Sarah Soh's influential study on the comfort women (euphemism for women from various territories of Japanese occupation, including Korea, who served as sex slaves for Japanese soldiers during Japan's imperial period). Soh disrupts the popular narrative that locates Korean women as victims of Japanese hegemony by identifying *Korean* nationalist patriarchy itself as a contributing force to the practice of sexual slavery during Japanese occupation. As Soh argues: "Most regrettably, the activists' master narrative has glossed over the more complex, wider-reaching narratives of women's oppression and has thereby failed to generate a sense of societal responsibility among Koreans for their compatriots' lifelong suffering," and adds that "in Korea's modern history feminism has generally been subordinated to nationalism" (237). Simply put, I hope we recognize the precariousness of privileging one narrative, even if it operates under the auspices of decolonization and emancipation of consciousness. In the instance of competing conceptualizations of history, the danger is that one will invariably subsume the other. When two concurrent narratives from different loci grapple for legitimacy, the result cannot be a symbiotic, co-compatible ecosystem of knowledges; the result is rather the subordination of one system in favor of another, as has been the symptom of colonial thought.

Despite any inherent limitations to conceptualizing a collective narrative on behalf of the nation, and despite the inherent limitations to any historiographical method, one may at least acknowledge the political force afforded to the articulation of a collective memory through an artifact of history. As O. Hugo Benavides reminds us, although there is no such thing as national history in the singular, what is presented in history textbooks for a nation's youth can nonetheless be used for dangerous political purposes (193). No matter how mythic, when presented in a document such as a history textbook, national narratives are reified as truth and are critical to the manufacture and maintenance of ideological consent.

So, where do we go from here? Mignolo advocates a "pluritopic hermeneutic" (15). According to Mignolo, a "pluritopic understanding implies that while the understanding subject has to assume the truth of what is known and understood, he or she also has to assume the existence of alternative politics of location with equal rights to claim the truth" (15). What we are bearing witness to with the Liancourt Rocks controversy is rather an instance in which only one representation of history may exist. Remember what happened in the Americas during European colonization: the conceptual friction produced by two competing ideologies of history compelled, or rather enabled, the colonizer to stratify varying modes of historical knowledge production; the outcome of the colonial project in the Americas was the depriviling, dismissal, and virtual obliteration of oral and pictographic systems of knowledge. And curiously—if the history textbook may be regarded as a quintessential artifact of modernity, because it is a tool of effecting ideological consent, because it aspires to present an authoritative, empirical narrative of the past (the pinnacle of the Western conceptualization of historical memory, perhaps)—one may argue that it is the collective subscription to modernity by both the Koreans and the Japanese that produces the sustained friction over details of historical accuracy.

The operative logic of institutionalizing memory through state-endorsed educational curricula is simple: if collective memory of occupation and ownership of a territory prefigures a legally sound right to said territory, the larger the community of those who remember, the more legitimate the claim is. The US occupation of its soil, for instance, depends on the fraudulent historical narrative of "discovery." Columbus is still said to have "discovered" America in 1492, and in the US our collective memory of the discovery is reinvigorated in October of every year. And it is in history textbooks that children are made to believe that the Americas were discovered, occupied previously by mere savage subhumans. The state of Arizona this year is celebrating its centennial. One cannot help but recognize that such commemoration resignifies indigenous peoples as subhuman, legitimates the narrative of colonial expansion, and justifies one of the greatest travesties in human history. Yet this and similar practices of commemoration continue shamelessly.

In a globalizing world, national collective memories can no longer be understood solely from their originary loci. They are tenuous, constantly re/framed, transnational and transhistorical phenomena. Collective memories are best understood dialectically, in relation not only to complementary narratives, but to competing ones as well. The problem, of course, is that the modernist conception of nationalist realization through state sovereignty allows for only one official collective memory. In other words, transnational identification hinges on a unitary perception of historical accuracy. In the ongoing controversy between Korea and Japan, we see that competing collective memories enunciated from the locus of institutional and political legitimacy shapes national identity, belonging, and consciousness, while simultaneously paralyzing the potential for collective identification between peoples of different nations. Transnational identification in East Asia might be possible, perhaps, but through a collective dismissal of history as it is practiced today, history as it emerged from the logic of Western modernity.

WORKS CITED

Anderson, Benedict. *Imagined Communities: Reflections on the Origin and Spread of Nationalism*. 2nd ed. New York: Verso, 2006. Print.

Benavides, O. Hugo. "Narratives of Power, the Power of Narratives: The Failing Foundational Narrative of the Ecuadorian Nation." *Contested Histories in Public Space: Memory, Race, and Nation*. Ed. Daniel J. Walkowitz and Lisa Maya Knauer. Durham: Duke UP, 2009. 178-96. Print.

Berger, Thomas U. "Of Shrines and Hooligans: The Structure of the History Problem in East Asia after 9/11." *Power and the Past: Collective Memory and International Relations*. Ed. Eric Langenbacher and Yossi Shain. Washington: Georgetown UP, 2010. 189-202. Print.

Bhabha, Homi K. *The Location of Culture*. New York: Routledge, 1994. Print.

Coser, Lewis. Introduction. *On Collective Memory*. Maurice Halbwachs. Ed. and Trans. Lewis A. Coser. Chicago: U of Chicago P, 1992. 1-36. Print.

Mignolo, Walter. *The Darker Side of the Renaissance: Literacy, Territoriality, and Colonization*. 2nd ed. Ann Arbor: U of Michigan P, 2003. Print.

Ryang, Sonia. "Historian-Judges of Korean Nationalism." *Ethnic and Racial Studies* 13.4 (1990): 503-26. Print.

Soh, C. Sarah. *The Comfort Women: Sexual Violence and Postcolonial Memory in Korea and Japan*. Chicago: U of Chicago P, 2008. Print.

Smith, Anthony D. *Myths and Memories of the Nation*. New York: Oxford UP, 1999. Print.

15

COLLECTIVE APOLOGIES AND RECONSTITUTING CITIZENSHIP

Jason A. Edwards

The subject of citizenship has received a good deal of attention from rhetorical scholars over the past decade or so. As Robert Asen explained, the fundamental question one should pose when thinking about citizenship is, "How do people enact citizenship?" (191). In answering this question there has been a focus on how politicians, particularly American presidents, constitute the ideals of citizenship (Beasley, *You, the People*; Beasley, *Who Belongs*; Murphy; Paulson; Stuckey). These studies offer a vocabulary of what citizenship can and should look like in America's political system. At the same time, the door has often been shut to a number of different groups (e.g., African Americans, immigrants, women, the GLBT community) who have been denied the ability to fully enact their citizenship. Accordingly, scholars have attempted to chronicle how some groups endeavor to become full members of the American polity (see Bennett; Cisneros; McDorman; Ray; Ray and Richards; Zaeske). Combined, this scholarship presents both the possibilities and limits of how citizenship can be accessed and enacted. I would like to add an additional layer to this scholarship by maintaining that a collective apology can provide a rhetorical space to understand how citizenship has been denied and reconstituted for certain victimized groups. This essay is of an exploratory nature into the potential power these apologies may have regarding citizenship within certain countries.

Since the end of the Cold War, there have been a plethora of political leaders from the United States to Sri Lanka, Japan to Great Britain, Canada to France, who have apologized for various historical injustices (e.g., the Holocaust and slavery). Typically, these apologies are directed from a governmental representative to a community who was the target of a particular government program and/or policy. These rhetorical acts are primarily focused on reconstituting, rebuilding, and strengthening relationships amongst communities that have been harmed by past wrongdoing (Edwards 62). Typically, the focus on this form of rhetoric is to explain how they are a distinct rhetorical genre, to analyze the components of said genre, and/or to analyze a specific case study to determine the effectiveness of a collective apology (see Edwards and Calhoun; Hatch; Izumi; Villadsen, "Speaking on Behalf").

However, these apologies can be (and are) more than merely reflections on past wrongdoing. They can also be, as Lisa Villadsen notes, about "civic reconstruction" ("Beyond" 231). Melissa Nobles further argues that a primary function of collective apologies, or as she termed it "official apologies," is the reconsideration of obligations and boundaries of membership within a national community (4-5). Furthermore, Brian Weiner asserts that American political identity is less than ideal. Relationships between individuals and groups within our polity can be vastly improved (187). Part of the need for improvement is the historical injustices committed against some groups and America's inability to confront this unsavory past. Accordingly, collective apologies can be a means to improve our basic identity. I maintain that collective apologies serve to fold victimized groups back into the polity from which they have been symbolically and materially exiled. In such apologies, the victims of these historical injustices are having their stories told. The apology resets the boundaries upon which they can stand. It recasts their identity from victims to, at least symbolically, equal players amongst the bricolage of groups that make up a national polity. At the same time, these apologies may also circumscribe the citizenship grounds upon which these groups stand. The apology may serve as a rhetoric of control: for once an apology is given, it may be more difficult for a victimized group to use their "other" status to leverage policy changes at the national level that may work in their favor. The apology, in a sense, strips a sense of agency that group could use to argue for further "rights."

In what follows, I examine collective apologies from Australia, Canada, and Great Britain to examine how collective apologies may work in opening up the boundaries of citizenship, but at the same time how those boundaries might be limited in certain areas.

Collective Apologies in Australia, Canada, and Great Britain

During the past fifteen years the prime ministers of Australia, Canada, and Great Britain have issued various apologies. In 2008, Australian Prime Minister Kevin Rudd issued an apology to the "stolen generations" for Australia's policy of removing aboriginal children from their parents and shipping them off to schools where they often never had any contact with their families again. In the same year Canadian Prime Minister Stephen Harper offered an apology to First Nations for Canada's "residential school program," which was similar to the program that created the stolen generations in Australia. Additionally, in 2006 Harper apologized to Chinese-Canadians for its "head-tax" policy, which made it financially impossible for many Chinese to immigrate to Canada, and for those who had immigrated to bring their families from China to join them. Finally, British Prime Minister David Cameron issued an apology concerning "Bloody Sunday" within Northern Ireland and the subsequent whitewash and cover-up of the event by the British government. In all of these apologies, these political leaders attempt to reset and recast the basic identities of these victimized groups from being an "other" to becoming part of the larger narrative of that particular nation. I argue this rhetorical work comes primarily in the acknowledgment sections of the apology.

Collective apologies are composed of three primary rhetorical strategies: mortification, corrective action, and perhaps most importantly, acknowledgment. Why acknowledgment? Because an embedded presumption of citizenship, as Brian Weiner convincingly argued, is that citizenship is often predicated upon a shared history that citizens can draw upon when discussing present and future policies, problems, and principles that affect a nation (23-27). Acknowledgment is the portion of collective apologies that often focuses on the history and memory of events. In terms of collective apologies, it consists of admitting a wrong has been committed in the past, typically by a previous government. Aaron Lazare asserted acknowledging wrongdoing was the most important aspect of an apology because a failure to be forthcoming about the past can render the overall apology's sentiment suspect (76). In acknowledging past wrongdoing, speakers delineate the injustices committed against their victims. Girma Negash referred to this accounting of injustices as "reckoning" (9). Reckoning is where the victimizer/apologizer puts the crimes on the historical record in an open, public fashion. By confessing and discussing the atrocities committed, both the injurer and injured can take stock of the event and what that has meant for the past, present, and future relationship between communities.

Additionally, rhetors typically specify the victims of these wrongs. Victims of historical wrongdoing are "the ghosts of the past that will not remain in their graves until their stories are told" (Nytagodien and Neal 468). Recognizing and naming the injured parties gives voice to the "ghosts" of the past and their descendents. These victims' stories are finally being told. Through acknowledging their past, their history, in some small way, is being recovered. Accordingly, this gives voice to the victimized group's humanity and de-emphasizes their status as an "other" in society. In recognizing another person's humanity, Donald Shriver noted, a rhetor "lays the groundwork for both the construction and repair of any human community" (8).

In each of these apologies, the prime ministers spend some time delineating the crimes committed, the victims affected, and consequences of these historical injustices. Australian Prime Minister Kevin Rudd, prior to acknowledging the specifics of Australia's "stolen generations" policy, noted:

> there comes a time in the history of nations when their peoples must become fully reconciled to their past if they are to go forward with confidence to embrace their future. Our nation, Australia, has reached such a time. That is why the parliament is today here assembled: to deal with this unfinished business of the nation, to remove a great stain from the nation's soul and, in a true spirit of reconciliation, to open a new chapter in the history of this great land, Australia.

Here, Prime Minister Rudd acknowledged something was not right with the nation's history. There was a "great stain from the nation's soul," which needed to be removed in order for a "new chapter" in the history of Australia to be written. As such, he recognized crimes committed against its aboriginal population in two ways. First, he told the story of one of its members, Nanna Nugala Fejo. He discussed how she had been forcibly removed from her family's care without warning, without any time to say goodbye. Nanna Fejo's family was broken up twice, and she never "saw her mum again." Her story symbolized the suffering of thousands of aboriginal children who experienced the same kind of pain, separation, and trauma at the hands of the Australian government. Moreover, Rudd quantified the number of stolen generation victims. As he put it, "Nanna Fejo's is just one story. There are thousands, tens of thousands of them: stories of forced separation of Aboriginal and Torres Strait Islander children from their mums and dads over the better part of a century." According to the prime minister, "between 1910 and 1970, between 10% and 30% of Indigenous children were forcibly taken from their mothers and fathers; that as result up to 50,000 children were forcibly taken from their families." As a result, these children suffered "hurt," "humiliation," "degradation," and the "sheer brutality of the act of separating a mother from her children" (Rudd). By telling Nanna Fejo's story, while also quantifying the larger tragedy Rudd fully disclosed the extent of these injustices caused by past governments. Without the government hiding any of its crimes, the current Australian government and the Aboriginal communities could come to a place of negotiation with a clean state, which would give their relationship "real respect."

Canadian Prime Minister Stephen Harper, in both of his apologies, outlined the atrocities committed by previous Canadian governments toward Chinese-Canadians and First Nation Canadians. For example, in his apology for Canada's "head-tax," Harper asserted, "the Canada we know today would not exist were it not for the efforts of Chinese labourers who began to arrive in the mid-nineteenth century." Their efforts in helping to build the Canadian Pacific Railway "helped to ensure the future of Canada. But from the moment that the railway was completed, Canada turned its back on these men." Canadians began turning their backs on Chinese immigrants with the passage of the "Chinese Immigration Act of 1885," which imposed a "head tax of $50" on "Chinese newcomers in an effort to deter immigration." Apparently, the head tax did not have a great enough effect because, as Harper explained, "the government subsequently raised the amount to $100 in 1900, and then to $500—the equivalent of two years' wages—in 1903." The head tax remained in place until 1923, when the "government amended the Chinese Immigration Act and effectively banned most Chinese immigrants until 1947." Similar legislation existed in the "Dominion of Newfoundland, which also imposed a head tax between 1906 and 1949, when Newfoundland joined Confederation." According to the prime minister, "the Government of Canada recognizes the stigma and exclusion experienced by the Chinese as a result." Harper went on to state:

[W]e acknowledge the high cost of the head tax meant many family members were left behind in China, never to be reunited, or that families lived apart and, in some cases, in poverty, for many years. We also recognize that our failure to truly acknowledge these historical injustices has led many in the community from seeing themselves as fully Canadian. ("Head Tax")

As did Prime Minister Rudd, Harper clearly demonstrates that the Canadian government's "head-tax" policy was wrong. He laid the groundwork for his apologetic efforts to be accepted by the larger Chinese-Canadian community.

Similarly, Prime Minister Harper admitted the extensive damage Canada's residential school policy had on First Nation children. Canada's Indian residential school policy, put into place in the 1870s, was supposed to "educate Aboriginal children" so it could "assimilate them in the dominant culture," a system designed to "kill the Indian in the child." In order to accomplish this task, Harper indicated these children were "forcibly removed from their homes." They were "inadequately fed, clothed, and housed." They were deprived of the care of their parents, grandparents, and communities. First Nations, Inuit, and Metis languages and cultural practices were prohibited in these schools. Tragically, some of these children died while attending these residential schools and others never returned home. They suffered "emotional, physical, and sexual abuse." Ultimately, "the legacy of Indian residential schools has contributed to social problems that continue to exist in many communities today" (Harper, "Residential School"). By offering a forthright assessment of Canada's wrongdoing, Harper gave more reasons for its First Nations to believe the sincerity of his contrition and made it much more likely they would accept his apologetic efforts.

Finally, British Prime Minister David Cameron delineated the injustices committed by Britain's military in what is commonly known as "Bloody Sunday" (Edwards and Luckie). After a review of more than decade, on June 15, 2010, Lord Saville and his tribunal issued its report concerning the events surrounding Bloody Sunday. Within hours of the report being issued, Prime Minister Cameron went to the British Parliament to discuss the findings of the inquiry. As he put it, "the conclusions of the report are absolutely clear. There is no doubt, there is nothing equivocal, there are no ambiguities. What happened on Bloody Sunday was both unjustified and unjustifiable. It was wrong." Cameron then proceeded to outline the specific crimes committed by British soldiers on Bloody Sunday. He identified that soldiers were given orders they should not have been given by their commander; the first shots fired were fired by the British army; not one of the people shot by British soldiers was armed; there was no justification for shooting civilians; soldiers did not give a warning they would open fire; there was a severe loss of self-control and training by the soldiers; and many soldiers gave false testimony to justify the firing onto unarmed civilians. Ultimately, as Cameron pointed out,

> Saville says that the immediate responsibility for the deaths and injuries on Bloody Sunday lies with those members of support company whose unjustifiable firing was the cause of those deaths and injuries. . . . There is no trying to soften or equivocate what is in the report. It is clear from the tribunal's authoritative conclusions that the events of Bloody Sunday were in no way justified.

For Prime Minister Cameron, there was no doubt that the actions taken by British soldiers on January 30, 1972 were fundamentally and absolutely wrong. His acknowledgment closed a chapter within the history of Northern Ireland and subsequently removed a further impediment to the larger peace efforts that began in 1998.

In all four of these apologies, Prime Ministers Rudd, Harper, and Cameron detail the atrocities, crimes, and consequences of the various injustices committed by past Australian, Canadian, and British governments. However, how does the acknowledgment of each set of atrocities help to reconstitute the citizenship of victimized communities? First, as noted earlier, I operated from the premise that citizenship is predicated, in part, on some aspect of a shared history between groups they draw upon to talk about the present and future. Communities that have been affected by past wrongdoing have largely been excluded from that larger history. The legacy of these atrocities, as Prime Minister Harper mentioned, made Chinese-Canadians not "fully Canadian" (and I would venture a similar sentiment is shared by all victimized communities). This recognition of past wrongdoing is what James Janack called "dystalgia." Dystalgia is a particular way to view the past. Unlike nostalgia, where political leaders talk of a golden age long past that they hope to restore in the present and future, dystalgia casts the past in a negative light. Dystalgia offers audiences lessons in what they should *not* do (Janack 38). Delineating the crimes, victims, and consequences of past governmental policy suggests these governments should be denounced. Their actions should be attacked and looked upon with disdain. Admitting these wrongs offered audiences tutorials of what should not be done in government. The exclusion of these collectives from national life can be corrected now that the historical record will be reshaped. By implication, admitting past wrongdoing reconfigures and recasts the history of these three nations. In one sense, this acknowledgment creates a "new" history of Australia, Canada, and Great Britain because the "ghosts'" stories of the past are finally being told—along with how these communities have contributed positively to the larger growth of the state. Including "their" account into the larger historical narrative of a particular nation symbolizes a shared history that all groups within a national polity can draw upon. In future recitations concerning the residential school policy, the Chinese head tax, and Bloody Sunday, previous understandings of these events must change to account for the apologies provided by the Australian, Canadian, and British governments.

Additionally, the acknowledgment of this past wrongdoing, in some small way, reshapes the identity of the "stolen generations," First Nation children, Chinese immigrants, and the fourteen people who were killed by British soldiers during a peaceful protest in Northern Ireland. These apologies alter the relational dynamic between victimized groups and victimizer. Australian Aborigines, Canadian First Nations, Chinese-Canadians, and Northern Irelanders can no longer be considered outliers within the larger polity of Australia, Canada, and Britain. Symbolically, at least, they are no longer "others" within the national bricolage of groups that make up these three nations. Rather, acknowledgment of these past atrocities demonstrates they should be recognized as full members of society. Accordingly, Australian Aborigines, Chinese-Canadians, Canadian First Nations, and the people of Northern Ireland can fully participate in the various mechanisms that make up national citizenship, which includes basics such as voting and access to better economic opportunities, but also includes having their history recognized, recorded, and perhaps even exalted as being part of the larger historical narrative of Australia, Canada, and Great Britain. Therefore, collective apologies hold the potential to reconstitute the boundaries of citizenship.

Despite the healing potential of collective apologies, it can also be said that they may have a negative side to them. When Prime Ministers Rudd, Harper, and Cameron all presented their apologies, there was an expectation that these apologies would mark a new chapter in the history of each nation-state. For example, Prime Minister Rudd asserted his apology was in part aimed at "[righting] past wrongs" but also "aimed at building a bridge between indigenous and non-indigenous Australians—a bridge based on real respect rather than a thinly veiled contempt." This bridge would allow all to "turn this page together: Indigenous and non-Indigenous Australias, government and opposition, Commonwealth and state, and write this new chapter in our nation's story together." Similarly, Prime Minister Harper asserted in both of his apologies that Canada "has a collective responsibility to build a country based firmly on the notion of equality of opportunity, regardless of one's race or ethnic origin" ("Head Tax"). Canadians must forge "a new relationship between aboriginal peoples and other Canadians, a relationship based on the knowledge of our shared history, respect for each other and a desire to move forward that . . . will contribute to a stronger Canada for all of us" (Harper, "Residential School"). Prime Minister Cameron expressed a similar outlook when he maintained that

> we should never forget or dismiss the past, but we must also move on. Northern Ireland has been transformed over the past 20 years and all of us in Westminster and Stormont must continue that work of change, coming together with all the people of Northern Ireland to build a stable, peaceful, prosperous and shared future.

Each of the sentiments by Rudd, Harper, and Cameron, on the surface, appear sycophantic and lend themselves to the power of a collective apology, which is primarily about rebuilding, strengthening, and extending damaged relationships caused by past hardship. It also confirms for these victimized communities that they finally will be allowed to fully participate in Australian, Canadian, and British society. With these apologies, they are being recognized as the true citizens they should have always been. At the same time, however, expressing a common and collective future that involves all groups may undercut the agency of these victimized groups. If the identity of a group has been built, in part, based upon a status as the "other," and if that status is rewritten with a collective apology, then there is an expectation from the government and the public that the suffering of these groups has been arrested. Accordingly, identifying oneself with a hyphen is no longer appropriate. Victimized groups can no longer demand more from their government and the general public because they have received the ultimate form of public contrition. The injustices of the past have been put on the historical record. The historical record has been rewritten. Aside from some potential small corrective action, these communities can no longer leverage their status as "others" to receive more contrition and/or corrective action from the government and from society at large. Consequently, a collective apology becomes a rhetoric of control over these victims. Their agency is, in some respects, stripped away. Now these communities are just like all others within the national polity, jostling for position to better their own interests within their specific collectives. Certainly, collective apologies are laudatory due to their potential healing effects, building of bridges to reconciliation, and broadening the boundaries of citizenship and national community members. At the same time, those apologies do close other doors. They close off the ability of these groups to use their "otherness" for potential gain for their community because they are now part of the national community. They are no longer the "other," which is of course is good. However, if that victimized group still suffers from the legacy of past injustices the public may be less apt to support measures to help that community because of the perceived help that was provided through the apology itself.

Conclusion

This short essay has been a meditation on how collective apologies can be used to redraw the boundaries of citizenships for national polities. Specifically, I have argued that collective apologies work to refold an outlying group back into the national community. The history of the victimized is being reconsidered. Their stories are being told. They become enveloped into the larger national narrative. Their identity is symbolically transformed. At the same time, these apologies may serve as a rhetoric of control. Once an apology is given, an expectation is created that reconciliation efforts will move forward. The "otherness" of those victims will melt away, and they will begin a new chapter with all other communities within a particular state. The ability to use that "otherness" to gain future considerations from the government and the public may be weakened. Therefore, it circumscribes the future grounds upon which they can argue for specific benefits for their particular community.

When thinking about the larger issue of rhetoric and citizenship, this essay brings to the fore, at least for me, the debate within the literature regarding what constitutes the enactment of citizenship? Can citizenship be just discursively constructed or is it only related to action? In the beginning of this essay, I noted that the literature on citizenship seems to focus on two opposite poles: scholars who discuss how the ideals of citizenship are constructed and those who examine how specific groups attempt to meet and operate within those ideals. Perhaps that is a false dichotomy because the enactment of citizenship requires both the symbolic and the material. Perhaps the question this essay brings up is: how do collective apologies meld the symbolic and material together? How are those items enacted together? Or are collective apologies merely discursive constructions of citizenship, which lay the groundwork for "others" to participate in larger society?

Additionally, this analysis can enlighten us about the communities from which they spring (Villadsen, "Speaking" 25). The apologies examined here were all from liberal democracies with very long histories. However, according to liberal democratic theory, democracies tend to be amnesiatic (Weiner 187). The past is not a subject that liberal democratic theorists often discuss. They focus more attention on theorizing how to improve democracy in the present and future. That said, these apologies do demonstrate that democratic states are attempting to deal with aspects of their shameful past. Even the United States, perhaps the most amnesiatic nation in the world, has apologized for a number of wrongful deeds during the past twenty-five years. The question is then what do these collective apologies say about liberal democratic theory and members of that particular society? Do these apologies represent a maturation process within these nation-states? Are they merely for political gain? How does this fit within a larger discussion regarding how Americans deal with the past, positively and negatively? I do not have the answers to these questions. But it is clear that collective apologies bring up interesting conundrums for democracies across the world who struggle in dealing with their present and future ideals and their past injustices. If Brian Weiner is correct concerning the weakness of American political identity, particularly as it relates to marginalized groups (e.g., American Indians, African Americans, etc.), then something must be done to improve relationships amongst communities, or the fractures within the national polity may become so large that bridging the gulf for the common good may be a venture that no politician or political party can bridge.

WORKS CITED

Asen, Robert. "A Discourse Theory on Citizenship." *Quarterly Journal of Speech* 98 (2004): 186-210. Print.

Beasley, Vanessa B. *You, the People: American National Identity in Presidential Rhetoric.* College Station: Texas A&M UP, 2004. Print.

---., ed. *Who Belongs in America?: Presidents, Rhetoric, and Immigration.* College Station: Texas A&M UP, 2006. Print.

Bennett, Jeffrey A. *Banning Queer Blood: Rhetorics of Citizenship, Contagion, and Resistance.* Tuscaloosa: U of Alabama P, 2009. Print.

Cameron, David. "Bloody Sunday: PM David Cameron's Full Statement." *BBC News.* BBC, 15 June 2010. Web. May 2012.

Cisneros, Josue David. "(Re)Bordering the Civic Imaginary: Rhetoric, Hybridity, and Citizenship in La Gran Marcha." *Quarterly Journal of Speech* 97 (2011): 26-49. Print.

Edwards, Jason A. "Apologizing for the Past for a Better Future: Collective Apologies in Australia, Canada, and the United States." *Southern Journal of Communication* 75 (2010): 57-75. Print.

Edwards, Jason A., and Lindsay R. Calhoun."Redress for Old Wounds: Canadian Prime Minister Stephen Harper's Apology for Chinese Head Tax." *Chinese Journal of Communication* 4 (2011): 73-89. Print.

Edwards, Jason A., and Amber Luckie. "British Prime Minister David Cameron's Apology for Bloody Sunday." The Rhetoric in Society III Conference. Antwerp, Belgium. 2010. Address.

Harper, Stephen. "Address by the Prime Minister on the Chinese Head Tax Redress." *Prime Minister of Canada.* Canada, 22 June 2006. Web. May 2012.

---. "Apology for Canada's Residential School Policy." *Canadian Broadcasting Corporation.* CBC, 11 June 2008. Web. May 2012.

Hatch, John B. *Race and Reconciliation: Redressing Wounds of Injustices.* Lanham: Lexington Books, 2009. Print.

Izumi, Mariko. "Asian-Japanese: State Apology, National Ethos, and the 'Comfort Women' Reparations Debate in Japan." *Communication Studies* 62 (2011): 473-90. Print.

Janack, James. "The Future's Foundation in a Contested Past: Nostalgia and Dystalgia in the 1996 Russian Presidential Campaign." *Southern Communication Journal* 65 (1999): 34-48. Print.

Lazare, Aaron. *On Apology.* New York: Oxford UP, 2004. Print.

McDorman, Todd. "History, Collective Memory, and the Supreme Court: Debating 'The People' Through the Dred Scott Controversy." *Southern Communication Journal* 71 (2006): 213-24. Print.

Murphy, Troy. "Romantic Democracy and the Rhetoric of Heroic Citizenship." *Communication Quarterly* 51 (2003): 192-208. Print.

Negash, Girma. *Apologia Politica: States and Their Apologies by Proxy.* Lanham: Rowman and Littlefield, 2006. Print.

Nobles, Melissa. *The Politics of Official Apologies.* Cambridge: Cambridge UP, 2008. Print.

Nytagodien, Ridwan, and Arthur Neal. "Collective Trauma, Apologies, and the Politics of Memory." *Journal of Human Rights* 3 (2004): 465-75. Print.

Paulson, Jon. "Theodore Roosevelt and the Rhetoric of Citizenship: On Tour in New England, 1902." *Communication Quarterly* 50 (2002): 123-34. Print.

Ray, Angela G. "The Rhetorical Ritual of Citizenship: Women's Voting as Public Performance, 1868-1875." *Quarterly Journal of Speech* 93 (2007): 1-26. Print.

Ray, Angela G., and Cindy Koenig Richards. "Inventing Citizens, Imagining Gender Justice: The Suffrage Rhetoric of Virginia and Francis Minor." *Quarterly Journal of Speech* 93 (2007): 375-402. Print.

Rudd, Kevin. "Apology to Australia's 'Stolen Generations.'" *The Australian.com.* The Australian, 13 February 2008. Web. May 2012.

Shriver, Donald. *An Ethic for Enemies: Forgiveness in Politics.* New York: Oxford UP, 1995. Print.

Stuckey, Mary E. *Defining Americans: The Presidency and National Identity.* Lawrence: U of Kansas P, 2004. Print.

Villadsen, Lisa Storm. "Beyond the Spectacle of Apologia: Reading Official Apologies as Proto-Deliberative Rhetoric and Instantiations of Rhetorical Citizenship." *Quarterly Journal of Speech* 98 (2012): 216-34. Print.

---. "Speaking on Behalf of Others: Rhetorical Agency and the Epideictic Functions in Official Apologies." *Rhetoric Society Quarterly* 38 (2008): 25-45. Print.

Weiner, Brian. *Sins of the Parents: The Politics of National Apologies in the United States.* Philadelphia: Temple UP, 2005. Print.

Zaeske, Susan. *Signatures of Citizenship: Petitioning, Anti-Slavery, and Women's Political Identity.* East Lansing: Michigan State UP, 2003. Print.

16

REFRAMING SANITY

Scapegoating the Mentally Ill in the Case of Jared Loughner

Katie Rose Guest Pryal

Rhetoric scholars have examined the rhetorical disempowerment of the mentally ill, whose perceived lack of reason isolates them from public discourse (Lewiecki-Wilson; Prendergast; Pryal). Such isolation can be explained using Kenneth Burke's theory of identification and its "ironic counterpart," division (*Rhetoric of Motives* 23). Division shows how the discursive markers of "sane" and "insane" function to create an in-group, the sane, whose existence relies upon the rhetorical and physical isolation—the scapegoating—of the insane. This article argues that the mentally ill make an ideal Burkean scapegoat. Furthermore, this article shows that the criminal acts of a few mentally ill people provide the necessary justification for the scapegoating of the entire group.

Using the case of Jared Loughner's spree killing in Tucson, Arizona, in January of 2011, this article examines reports of major US media outlets in the weeks following the shootings to show how the public response to such tragedies tends to follow predictable rhetorical patterns.[1] One group of articles looks to the past, arguing that "we should have known" that the perpetrator was mentally ill, blaming the mental health system for failing to identify the mentally ill person. A second group of articles looks to the present and focuses on identifying the mentally ill and dividing them from the "sane." A third group of articles looks to the future with a rhetoric of prevention that invokes the Burkean scapegoat, asking, "Now that we have identified the mentally ill, what can we do with them?" This third set of articles arises out of a desire for reassurance, arguing that future tragedies can be prevented—so long as we can identify, and isolate, the insane. In the end, these sets of public rhetoric reframe sanity as a culturally imposed division that can be used to forge identification among the sane after a traumatic event.

Notably missing from these articles are voices of the mentally ill themselves. However, in a few articles, a "talking back" occurs by those who are mentally ill or by their advocates. These articles, I suggest, do not seek to blame, divide, or scapegoat but rather to reframe our society's approach to mental health into one that is workable and actually capable of preventing violent tragedies.

Burkean Scapegoating and Division

Kenneth Burke describes scapegoating as, "in its purest form, the use of a sacrificial receptacle for the ritual unburdening of one's sins" (*Permanence and Change* 16). The scapegoat is a "'representative' or 'vessel' of certain unwanted evils"; it is a "sacrificial animal" (*The Philosophy of Literary Form* 29). For Burke, then, the scapegoat provides a symbolic place wherein a social group can unload its worst: worst thoughts, worst deeds, or worst group members. This unloading ritualistically cleans the social group. Thus, as James Jasinski explains, Burke saw the scapegoat as a means of purifying society of its sins, or of removing its guilt, through a process of "externalization" (504). This externalization often takes place in the realm of rhetoric, of storytelling and mythmaking.[2]

C. Allen Carter argues that the scapegoat serves a necessary function in society's mythmaking: "We tell stories of redemption that give us a sense of direction and orient us with respect to a system of moral values—but often at the expense of innocent victims" ("Kenneth Burke" 363). In this way of thinking, society *needs* a scapegoat to unify itself, in order for its disparate constituents to find ways to identify with one another. Carter asks, "Does this mean that our directionless Babel can only be given a common direction when we all blame a more or less blameless surrogate? . . . Can our identities only form around a scapegoat? Burke's answer is yes" (363). Carter points out the blamelessness of the scapegoat. Similarly, Barry Brummett notes that "[s]capegoating is a particularly poignant symbolic form because the goat is attacked for its ability to represent the sins of the attackers more than for its own transgressions" (66). In other words, the scapegoat is—usually—innocent in some fashion. Indeed, as Carter points out, "The Christian myth [involving the sacrifice of the Creator's own son] provides the classic model" of the scapegoat (364). Christ is the ultimate, innocent scapegoat.

When Carter asks whether our identities can only form around a scapegoat, he invokes Burke's notion of identification. Burke points out that identification occurs when one's "interests are joined" with another's (*A Rhetoric of Motives* 20). The "ironic counterpart" to identification is "division" (23). Indeed, "[i]dentification is affirmed with earnestness precisely because there is division" (22). Because we are not perfectly identified with one another, rhetorically we must work to craft identification. "If men were not apart from one another, there would be no need for the rhetorician to proclaim their unity" (22). Furthermore, division of others from ourselves allows us to create identification among those that remain. And, as Shane Borrowman and Marcia Kmetz observe, "[D]ivision is necessary for aggression, physical or rhetorical" (279).

In this way, scapegoating and division appear to work hand in-hand. Once individuals have, through the process of identification, formed a social group, those external to the group are divided, cast out, and ripe for scapegoating to protect the cohesion of the identified group. This, I argue, is the rhetorical process that follows killing-spree tragedies perpetrated by the mentally ill. Although I believe the killers are guilty of horrible crimes and deserve to be punished, the public rhetoric surrounding these events shifts focus from the *crimes* of a single perpetrator to focus on the *mental illness* of the perpetrator and, from there, the mental illness of *anyone* with a psychiatric disability. News reports and opinion pieces create an in-group of the "sane" and then divide the "insane." This division allows for rhetorical aggression toward the insane.

This aggression takes the form of scapegoating. Rather than focusing on the major societal change required to provide just and necessary health-care services to those with mental illness—services that are often expensive and politically unpopular—the "insane" are publicly scapegoated to relieve the in-group's guilt over the lack of these very services because, in the end, it is these services that might have prevented the tragedies in the first place.

With this theoretical framework in mind, let us turn to the news reports that exploded after the Tucson shootings to see how division and scapegoating manifest in public discussions of the mentally ill. As noted above, the news reports and other texts on Jared Loughner's spree killing in Tucson tend to fall into three categories: (1) those that look to the past and rue the lack of prevention; (2) those that operate in the present by providing "helpful" means of identifying the insane; and (3) those that look to the future, scapegoating all mentally ill persons to assuage society's guilt. A small set of articles do "talk back" to the dominant voices, providing a more nuanced critique of the mental health system and pointing out the changes that would need to occur (but are unlikely to occur for various political reasons) in order to prevent spree killings in the future.

Looking to the Past: Rhetoric of Prevention

The articles that look to the past and narrate the story of Jared Loughner often strike a tone of regret, of "we should have known." They point out ways that the tragedy could have been, or should have been, prevented. They argue that this prevention would have occurred had the killer, in this case Loughner, been identified sooner as a person who was mentally ill. Schools, police, or family should have recognized his illness and involuntarily committed him. Thus, in most cases, these articles note a failure of intervention, as demonstrated below.

Mark Goulston, a psychiatrist writing for the *Huffington Post*, notes that there was "a long trail of 'red flags'" surrounding Loughner and his behavior, red flags that ostensibly should have been noted by persons in power—teachers, parents, law enforcement officials—in time to prevent the tragic spree killing. Similarly, in "Red Flags at a College, but Tied Hands," Benedict Carey (writing for the *New York Times*) notes, "He was coming undone, that much is clear. Sometimes surly, sometimes seemingly unhinged, he was unpredictable in a way that made fellow students in a community college class want to leave the room." Carey notes, then, that Loughner's "coming undone" was "clear"—and ostensibly should have been acted upon by those around him.

"Red flags"—and the failure to follow through on them—pop up in many articles about Loughner. For example, Dean Reynolds writes for *CBS.com*, "Loughner was deemed a problem at school by teachers. . . . But there is no record of him ever getting treatment, or of anyone calling the mobile acute-care teams available there." Neil Katz and David Freeman point out in *Time*, "From what we know so far, Loughner was never evaluated by a mental health professional, despite erratic behavior at school and with friends." Reynolds, along with Katz and Freeman, thus observe a failure of intervention.

Megan H. Chan, writing for *USA Today*, notes that Loughner's teachers at the community college he attended feared his strange behavior and believed he would be a "threat." Chan reports that "[a]fter just one week of classes, Jared Loughner proved so disruptive and belligerent," Loughner's math teacher recalled, "that I remember going home and thinking to myself, 'Is he going to bring a weapon to class?'" Furthermore, Loughner's "classmates also noticed that he seemed at odds with the world around him." One classmate called him "creepy." Most damning in the eyes of these authors, it appears that Loughner's behavior at school led to an encounter with mental health enforcement before the Tucson shooting, an encounter that did not stop Loughner from committing his violent crime: "officials at the college" sent "campus police officers to the home of Loughner's parents in September with a letter suspending him from the school." The school told Loughner that "he could not return without providing a letter from a mental health professional to show that 'his presence at the College does not present a danger to himself or others.'" Loughner agreed not to return to the school, and no further intervention occurred.

In retrospect, it appears that red flags abounded. Adam Klawonn, writing for *Time*, points to the landscaping of the Loughner home as a red flag: "Neighbors say the Loughners kept to themselves, but weren't exactly unfriendly. . . . Still, Dawn Cook, 33, says she and her daughter avoided the house. 'We go selling Girl Scout cookies door-to-door,' says Cook, . . . 'But we didn't go there,' she says of the Loughners' house, because it appeared foreboding with its unkempt plants." Dennis Romero, writing for the *LA Weekly*, points to drugs, writing that Loughner "was a 'habitual drug abuser'" in that he smoked marijuana, and Romero notes a correlation between marijuana use and mental illness.

These articles that look toward the past essentially rue society's failure to identify the perpetrator as mentally ill and dangerous or, rather, as mentally ill and *therefore* dangerous. The red flags of drug use or odd behavior should have been acted upon, these articles argue. The overarching tone, then, is one of guilt, regret, and anxiety. In Burkean terms, these articles describe a failure of division: it was clear, after all, that Loughner did not belong in the group marked "sane"; these articles ask why he was not placed into the group marked "insane" *before* the tragedy in Tucson. Although these articles express guilt and anxiety, they also express identification at the expense of Loughner, a voice of "we're not like him," with his pot habit and "foreboding" home.

This identification and division at the expense of Loughner does not seem misplaced; Loughner did, after all, commit a terrible crime. Rhetorical trouble arises, however, when writers expand their purview and craft identification at the expense of all persons with mental illness, as they often do, especially in the other two types of articles examined below.

Looking to the Present: Rhetoric of Division

In order to assuage the anxiety of the failure of police, school officials, or others to identify the potential killer, another set of articles provides methodologies for identifying the mentally ill. These articles often take the form of checklists, and they are some of the least nuanced articles on the Tucson tragedy. These articles seek to simply identify, and therefore divide, the sane from the insane, at whatever cost to the mentally ill. They also seek to reassure readers by ostensibly arming them with tools to protect themselves from the mentally ill (who are presumably also violent).

Mark Goulston provides a list of Loughner's behaviors that "may have contributed to his actions." According to Goulston, Loughner (1) was a "[p]risoner of his own imagination"; (2) suffered from "[r]eality-based persecutory fantasies"; (3) exhibited a "[l]oss of executive function"; and (4) acted out the "[r]evenge of the nobody." Furthermore, Goulston notes, "Worse than being a 'nobody' is feeling put down and pushed away, as Loughner may have experienced. . . . And when people with a disturbed mind . . . feel put down and pushed away, they often find a way to get back in and get even." So, it seems that "experienced multiple rejections" could be added to Goulston's list.

Goulston's stated purpose with his list, however, is to enumerate the "factors [that] may have contributed to [Loughner's] actions." *Time* takes the act of listing of qualities a step further. In "If You Think Someone Is Mentally Ill: Loughner's Six Warning Signs," Kate Pickert and John Cloud provide an early warning checklist for the sane to use to identify the insane. They begin by pointing out Loughner's unusual and unstable behavior, noting, "In retrospect, it's easy to see the evidence that Tucson, Ariz., shooter Jared Loughner was mentally unstable. In his community-college classes, he would laugh randomly and loudly at nonevents. He would clench his fists and regularly pose strange, nonsensical questions to teachers and fellow students." The authors wonder, "[C]ould anything have been done to prevent the violence? What signs that trouble lay ahead were missed? What signs were observed but ignored?" Then, they cap their rhetorical questioning with their main purpose: "In short, what can be done to prevent a potentially ill or unstable person from harming others?"

To assist readers in "prevent[ing] a potentially ill" person—note the word "potentially"—"from harming others," Pickert and Cloud provide a checklist to identify someone who is "potentially" mentally ill. The checklist includes six items: (1) "disorganized thoughts and speech," (2) "inability to function in social situations," (3) "paranoia," (4) "regularly smok[ing] marijuana," (5) scaring one's classmates, and (6) contacts with campus police. Pickert and Cloud seem to argue that these six signs indicate potential mental illness and the capacity to "harm others."

Pickert and Cloud point out, however, "Regardless of resources available . . . the problem with someone like Jared Loughner is that, without a court order, he would not have received treatment without a self-referral." They blame, in part, Loughner's college for not doing enough: "Similarly [to the shooting at Virginia Tech], it seems that Pima Community College (and Loughner's classmates and instructors) didn't do enough to recognize [the] six warning signs in Loughner." In other words, future tragedies would be preventable, were we all to just use these six warning signs and then call the authorities and seek a court order to restrain the potentially mentally ill person.

The articles of this set help allay anxiety in readers, providing them a way to discover who is mentally ill and enabling them to stay away or report behavior. Pickert and Cloud's list of symptoms intends to give readers the means to identify those persons with whom they come in contact who are potentially dangerous and mentally ill, ostensibly providing the tools to create a kind of citizens' patrol of the insane. These articles represent the ultimate Burkean division, drawing lines of demarcation between an in-group and an out-group, lines that are then—ideally—policed by the in-group.

Looking to the Future: Rhetoric of the Scapegoat

Once the signs of "potentially" dangerous mental illness are recognized, however, a third set of articles urges that action must be taken to prevent the mentally ill from committing crimes. Rather than suggesting expensive and politically unpopular changes to health-care services for the mentally ill, these articles scapegoat the "insane" to relieve the in-group's guilt over the lack of these services, services that arguably might have prevented a tragedy. Instead of expanded health-care treatment, for example, they argue almost exclusively for involuntary committal or criminal arrest.

In fact, the tone of these "action" articles sounds a lot like a discussion of terrorism rather than of health care. Indeed, Benedict Carey quotes Randy Borum, "an expert on threat assessment" in his article on Loughner. Borum states, "The whole thing speaks to the need for some coordinated way to detect such threats." Comparing Loughner to the shooter at Virginia Tech in 2007, Carey writes, "These institutions [colleges] typically have no single person or center that tracks the sorts of complaints that teachers and fellow students were making about Mr. Loughner. Nor do they have the legal authority to force people into treatment against their will." Forcing treatment and institutionalization becomes a common theme in the articles that look to the future and try to suggest a solution to the problem of spree killings.

In "Should Mentally Ill Be Locked up Against Their Will?" Katz and Freeman (writing for *CBS.com*) open their article with a question: "If Jared Loughner, the man accused of killing six and injuring 12 in Arizona last Saturday, turns out to be suffering from schizophrenia, as many doctors have surmised, why shouldn't the state have had the power to lock him in a mental ward BEFORE [emphasis in original] he went on a rampage?" They present the issue as one of individual rights versus the rights of society: "That might sound like common sense, but the law in most places is designed principally to protect individual rights. If you don't appear to be an immediate threat and you haven't broken the law, authorities are hard-pressed to commit you for more than a few days." The authors advocate the ability to lock up the mentally ill with less red tape, so to speak.

Dean Reynolds, too, asks whether the mentally ill should be locked up against their will, writing that "Loughner was deemed a problem at school by teachers," and "he could have been committed." Pickert and Cloud make a similar observation: "There was arguably enough evidence for Pima [Community College] authorities to go to a judge and have Loughner involuntarily committed to a mental hospital."

With this third set of articles, the circle of division and scapegoating is complete: from articles that look to the past with a tone of anxiety and regret, to articles that look to the present with checklists to allay anxiety, to articles that look to the future, seeking to implement those checklists and involuntarily institutionalize the mentally ill. This third set of articles allays the regret expressed by the first set by scapegoating the mentally ill, urging institutionalization—essentially "pre-crime" incarceration—without much nuance.

Talking Back: A More Nuanced Approach

The articles that provide the most nuanced critiques of the mental health system, and the most practicable solutions for preventing violence, are those that are produced by advocates for the mentally ill. These solutions almost always argue for more funding for mental health care. For example, Katz and Freeman cite a more nuanced voice, an important advocate for the mentally ill, Dr. Ken Duckworth, medical director of the National Alliance on Mental Illness (or NAMI, an advocacy group composed of the mentally ill and their allies): "[Duckworth] says there is another problem here—limited access to care. Arizona has the second lowest number of psychiatric beds in the country, just 5.9 per 100,000 people."

Indeed, NAMI has produced a post-Tucson report titled "State Mental Health Care Cuts: A National Crisis." They ask, "How did Jared Loughner fall through the cracks when the signs of a serious psychiatric crisis seemed so clear?" (1) They note that the problem is often one of money: "Even during the best of economic times, youth and adults living with mental illness struggle to access essential mental health services and supports. Services are often unavailable or inaccessible for those who need them the most." Between the stigma attached to mental illness (12), stigma increased by the types of news reports examined earlier in this article, and the lack of access to care (12), potentially violent people do fall through the cracks of care—care that could have prevented violence in the first place.

Psychologist John M. Grohol, writing on PsychCentral.com, asks whether Loughner is "An Example of Our Broken Mental Health System." Grohol specifically criticizes the *Time* article providing the six warning-signs checklist and writes, "Many are pointing out that Loughner suffered at the hands of the broken Arizona state mental health system. That's wrong, though. He would have had actually had to have *interacted* with that system in order for this argument to make sense." Rather than making a simplistic argument that our mental health system should be able to involuntarily commit people before they have committed a crime, as the scapegoating articles tend to do, Grohol argues that what "Jared Loughner . . . may be an example of is our lack of communication amongst numerous parties who are all involved with the same individual in different ways—a comprehensive social safety net." He criticizes the college for kicking Loughner out and then washing its hands of him, ignoring the fact that "students are a part of a larger community, a community that deserves to be treated with mutual respect and care." He advocates mandatory education on mental health issues in schools and greater communication among community groups that interact with people who might be mentally ill. He writes, "Let's de-stigmatize mental health concerns even more, so that other students feel free to question when one student seems to be acting in an erratic and concerning fashion in and outside of the classroom." He notes that his suggestions are probably a "pipe dream." By pointing out the stigma attached to mental illness, Grohol identifies the underlying problem: often, people with psychiatric disabilities do not seek care because they fear stigma. Articles such as the ones that call for easier involuntary committal only add to this fear.

Stephanie Mencimer, writing for *Mother Jones*, also criticizes the lack of funding for mental health care. in "Should Mental Health Be a Public Safety Issue?" She writes:

> In light of the Tucson tragedy, it would be nice to see the mental health system, or what's left of it, come up for real discussion, including serious consideration of vastly expanding mental health services so that people like Loughner's parents or his philosophy professor . . . could have actually gotten him the help he needed before he killed someone.

Mencimer's tone is fiery, chastising Arizona for cutting forty percent of its mental health-care budget in the year before the shooting. Like Grohol, she calls for real mental health reform, reform that costs money (although she also advocates for involuntary committal in a less-than-nuanced fashion).

Conclusion

As this study of articles on Jared Loughner shows, the public rhetoric after a spree killing committed by a mentally ill person tends towards division and scapegoating of the mentally ill as a group (rather than of the killer as an individual). The regret expressed by the articles that look toward the past is cleansed in the articles that provide checklists for identifying the mentally ill and the articles that argue for scapegoating the mentally ill—via involuntary committal—in order to prevent future violence.

Grohol points to the political and financial issues that are at play in mental health care: "[W]hen it comes right down to it, society cares *only so much* for the poor and indigent who have mental health concerns. We only care when a Congressperson or a bunch of people get shot at, and then, within weeks, the nation's attention turns elsewhere." The articles in this study demonstrate that publicly scapegoating the mentally ill assuages popular guilt over the lack of care our society provides to the mentally ill and the lack of money to provide it—care and money that could help prevent tragedies.

NOTES

[1] A note on methodology: I searched for articles using the LexisNexis service, using the ALL-NEWS database and the search terms Loughner AND Tucson AND Psychiatry. I limited the search to articles published in January of 2011. I conducted further searches of Internet resources, using search terms "psychiatry" and "Loughner" and limiting my search to January of 2011. With both searches, I discarded sources that dealt with the procedures of Loughner's trial (e.g., Loughner's fitness to stand trial, the forced medication of Loughner, and Loughner's insanity defense).

[2] Others have written extensively on the Burkean scapegoat, including Desilet and Appel. See also Carter, *Kenneth Burke and the Scapegoat Process*.

WORKS CITED

Borrowman, Shane, and Marcia Kmetz. "Divided We Stand: Beyond Burkean Identi-fication." *Rhetoric Review* 30.3 (2011): 275-92. Print.

Brummett, Barry. "Symbolic Form, Burkean Scapegoating, and Rhetorical Exigency in Alioto's Response to the 'Zebra' Murders." *Western Journal of Speech Communication* 44.1 (1980): 64-73. Print.

Burke, Kenneth. *Permanence and Change: an Anatomy of Purpose.* Berkeley: U of California, 1954. Print.

---. *The Philosophy of Literary Form: Studies in Symbolic Action.* Berkeley: U of California P, 1973. Print.

---. *A Rhetoric of Motives.* Berkeley: U of California P, 1969. Print.

Carey, Benedict. "Red Flags at a College, But Tied Hands." *NYTimes.com.* The New York Times, 11 Jan. 2011. Web. May 2012.

Carter, C. Allen. "Kenneth Burke and the Bicameral Power of Myth." *Poetics Today* 18.3 (1997): 343-73. Print.

---. *Kenneth Burke and the Scapegoat Process.* Norman: U of Oklahoma P, 1996. Print.

Chan, Megan H. "Ariz. Shooting Suspect's Teacher: I Felt He Was a 'Threat.'" *USAToday.com.* Gannett, 9 Jan. 2011. Web. May 2012.

Desilet, Gregory, and Edward C. Appel. "Choosing a Rhetoric of the Enemy: Kenneth Burke's Comic Frame, Warrantable Outrage, and the Problem of Scapegoating." *Rhetoric Society Quarterly* 41.4 (2011): 340-62. Print.

Goulston, Mark. "Jared Loughner: Understanding the Arizona Shooter from the Inside Out." *Huffington Post.* HuffPost News, 10 Jan. 2011. Web. May 2012.

Grohol, John M. "Jared Loughner: An Example of Our Broken Mental Health System?" *PsychCentral.* Psych Central, 13 Jan. 2011. Web. May 2012.

Jasinski, James. *Sourcebook on Rhetoric: Key Concepts in Contemporary Rhetorical Studies.* Thousand Oaks: Sage, 2001. Print.

Katz, Neil, and David W. Freeman. "Jared Loughner Case: Should Mentally Ill Be Locked Up against Their Will?" *CBS.com.* CBS, 11 Jan. 2011. Web. May 2012.

Klawonn, Adam. "What Motivated Giffords' Shooter?" *Time.com.* Time, 9 Jan. 2011. Web. May 2012.

Lewiecki-Wilson, Cynthia. "Rethinking Rhetoric through Mental Disabilities." *Rhetoric Review* 22.2 (2003): 156-67. Print.

Mencimer, Stephanie. "Should Mental Health Be a Public Safety Issue?" *MotherJones.org,* 11 Jan. 2011. Web. May 2012.

National Alliance on Mental Illness (NAMI)."State Mental Health Cuts: A National Crisis." March 2011. Web. May 2012.

Pickert, Kate, and John Cloud. "If You Think Someone Is Mentally Ill: Loughner's Six Warning Signs." *Time.com.* Time, 11 Jan. 2011. Web. May 2012.

Prendergast, Catherine. "On the Rhetorics of Mental Disability." *Towards a Rhetoric of Everyday Life: New Directions in Research on Writing, Text, and Discourse.* Ed. Martin Nystrand and John Duffy. Madison: U of Wisconsin P, 2003. 189-206. Print.

Pryal, Katie Rose Guest. "The Genre of the Mood Memoir and the Ethos of Psychiatric Disability." *Rhetoric Society Quarterly* 40.5 (2010): 479-501. Print.

---. "The Creativity Mystique and the Rhetoric of Mood Disorders." *Disability Studies Quarterly* 31.3 (2011): n. pag. Web. May 2012.

Reynolds, Dean. "Loughner Proves Need for Mental Health Awareness." *CBS.com.* CBS, 14 Jan. 2011. Web. May 2012.

Romero, Dennis. "Marijuana: Tucson Massacre Suspect Jared Loughner Was 'Habitual' Pot User." *LAWeekly.com.* LA Weekly LP, 11 Jan. 2011. Web. May 2012.

17

RHETORIC RE/FRAMED AS EXCHANGE

Baudrillard, Perlocutionary Performance, and 9/11 Ten Years Later

Brian Gogan

One year after the attacks of September 11, 2001, Verso Books published a three-book series called the 9/11 series. As its title suggests, the series analyzes the events of 9/11 through what Verso labels as "three highly original and readable accounts," each crafted by one of "Europe's most stimulating and provocative philosophers" ("9/11"). Paul Virilio offers the first contribution to the series, Jean Baudrillard provides the second, and Slavoj Žižek the third. Virilio, Baudrillard, and Žižek are, indeed, "provocative" thinkers—so much so that their contributions to the 9/11 series provoked Carlin Romano to name them the "Verso bad boys," refer to them as "intellectual junk merchants," and cite them as exemplars of what Romano calls "Eurotrash philosophy" ("An Oasis").

For those readers familiar with Carlin Romano's writing, his contemptuous remarks about the 9/11 series contributors are perhaps not that surprising. Romano writes regularly for *The Chronicle Review* as critic at large, and his columns often begin with a vitriolic *ad hominem* attack and end with a scathing one-liner. The column that reviews Verso's 9/11 series follows Romano's formula. The column begins by defining "Eurotrash philosophers" as "trendy" thinkers that "give European philosophy a bad name" ("An Oasis"). Then, the column moves from one book in the series to the next, labeling each author a "Eurotrash philosopher" and using this label as grounds to disparage their contribution to the series. In the end, as is Romano's habit, the column discredits the 9/11 series as "the disgraceful, slipshod exploitation of the event by meretricious Eurotrashians, eager to pop off" ("An Oasis").

Romano's use of a fallacious argument to denigrate the entire 9/11 series is troublesome in a myriad of ways, not the least of which is the way it ignores the rhetoric at work in the 9/11 series. Following Verso's description of the series, Romano frames the 9/11 series as a philosophical project, understands the series contributors as philosophers, and evaluates the series accordingly. However, I argue that the 9/11 series is best evaluated rhetorically, that the contributors to the 9/11 series work foremost as rhetors, and that their contributions must be understood as rhetoric. In brief, I want to reframe the 9/11 series as a fundamentally rhetorical project. But since my space here does not allow me to analyze the rhetoric of the entire 9/11 series, I will support my reframing of the series by analyzing the rhetoric of what is arguably the series' most controversial text: Jean Baudrillard's "Requiem for the Twin Towers."[1] My analysis aims to shows that a rhetorical study of "Requiem" allows us to judge the text, its author, and perhaps the entire 9/11 series much more favorably than did individuals one decade ago.

To a greater degree than the contributions from Virilio and Žižek, Baudrillard's "Requiem" seems to outrage series readers.[2] Romano, for one, addresses Baudrillard's "Requiem" before any of its serial counterparts. Citing a line from "Requiem," Romano passes over Virilio and Žižek and, instead, anoints Baudrillard as "the Eurotrash patron saint" ("An Oasis"). Likewise, Walter Kirn of the *New York Times* references the text of "Requiem" as he awards Baudrillard a "[f]irst prize for cerebral cold-bloodedness." Kirn makes no mention of the other two books in the Verso series.

The severity with which Romano and Kirn discuss "Requiem" and, subsequently, Baudrillard can, at least initially, be attributed to the way in which Baudrillard's "Requiem" departs from the conventional rhetoric of the requiem genre. The requiem is a composition crafted for the purpose of bringing about peaceful repose for the recently deceased, and it may take the form of a written composition (e.g., a dirge), a musical composition (e.g., a score), or even an ecclesiastical composition (e.g., a mass) ("Requiem," def. n.1). Regardless of the requiem's form, the composition works for peaceful repose and, as such, the requiem genre departs from pragmatic understandings of rhetoric. Most notably, the requiem does not attempt, as Lloyd F. Bitzer would have it, to "change the world" or alter "reality through the mediation of thought and action" (4). Instead, the requiem attempts to change the metaphysical world, and that metaphysical change cannot be situated in reality. To be clear, the requiem genre emerges from a social context or, put in Carolyn R. Miller's terms, the "recurrent situation" of death (151). The requiem genre does bridge, as Miller explains, "private intentions with social exigence" (163). But rather than adhering to Miller's notion of "Genre as Social Action," the requiem genre is most aptly described as spiritual action. The requiem genre works in good faith to favorably and peaceably condition that which cannot be known by the living—namely, the state of the nonliving.

The nonpragmatic nature of the requiem genre, including the uncertainty surrounding the composition's effects, makes Baudrillard's "Requiem" especially susceptible to harsh criticism. Baudrillard's readers cannot simply evaluate the text's impact upon the departed in the way that they might assess the impact of a political speech upon an electorate. Conventionally, then, requiems are judged in terms of the degree to which they appear to promote peaceful repose. Measured by conventional criteria, Baudrillard's composition is remiss; the often-quoted lines from Baudrillard's "Requiem" fail to produce the impression of peaceful repose. On the contrary, they challenge it. For instance, Baudrillard associates the collapse of the World Trade Center towers with a suicide, writing that "[s]eeing them collapse themselves, as if by implosion, one had the impression that they were committing suicide in response to the suicide of the suicide planes" ("Requiem" 43). This line is, in fact, the very line that Romano references to support his classification of Baudrillard as "Eurotrash." Kirn's review of "Requiem" draws its ire from the line stating "that the horror for the 4,000 victims dying in those towers was inseparable from the horror of living in them—the horror of living and working in sarcophagi of concrete and steel" ("Requiem" 41). Indeed, "Requiem" abounds with lines that break from the convention of the requiem genre. The line that is perhaps most egregious occurs towards the end of "Requiem," and it states: "The Twin Towers were worth destroying" ("Requiem" 46). These unconventionally violent and stirring lines are among the most controversial and most objectionable in the entire 9/11 series.

It should be further noted that, because of its contentious claims, Baudrillard's "Requiem" functioned—albeit ironically—as an unconventional requiem for Baudrillard himself. Upon Baudrillard's death on March 6, 2007, many obituaries invoked "Requiem" in ways that did not exactly promote Baudrillard's peaceful repose. *The National Post* declared that the Baudrillard's text "exhibited an extreme case of a self-induced intellectual high" (Fulford). Worse yet, the *Chronicle of Higher Education* referred to "Requiem" as Baudrillard's "greatest act of intellectual decadence" and noted that its lines were criticized on account "of their distinct moral stench" (Romano, "The Death"). Perhaps more tellingly, *The Economist* positioned "Requiem" as the text that convinced "[m]ost Americans . . . that they did not understand Mr. Baudrillard very well" ("Jean Baudrillard").

Indeed, as *The Economist* obituary suggests, the controversy surrounding "Requiem" is a problem of understanding and specifically a problem of understanding rhetoric. In order to evaluate the intellectual and ethical merit of "Requiem," the text's radical break with convention needs to be understood in terms of Baudrillard's theory of rhetoric.

Rhetoric, for Baudrillard, is the performance of symbolic exchange. As Sonja K. Foss, Karen A. Foss, and Robert Trapp explain in their *Contemporary Perspectives on Rhetoric*, symbolic exchange is a concept that is indispensable to Baudrillard's work, and at the same time, it is a concept that "places [Baudrillard] squarely in the field of rhetoric" (300). Baudrillard develops the concept of symbolic exchange throughout his oeuvre and discusses it using a number of different terms. In its most basic sense, symbolic exchange can be described as the movement of language between the real and the imaginary, between the pragmatic and the nonpragmatic, between appearance and disappearance, or, as Michelle Ballif reminds us, between production and seduction (10). Accordingly, the purpose of Baudrillardian rhetoric is to sustain the movement of language, and this purpose differs significantly from other rhetorical theories. Whereas as other rhetors working under other rhetorical theories might mobilize rhetoric when they seek persuasion, identification, representation, or association, Baudrillard finds recourse in rhetoric when he deems that exchange has slowed or, even worse, stopped.

By issuing certain unconventional statements, Baudrillardian rhetoric performs symbolic exchange, and as such, it could be classified as a perlocutionary performative. As J. L. Austin explains, the perlocutionary speech act is unconventional, and it achieves certain effects by way of issuing an utterance (121). Similarly, Baudrillardian rhetoric aims to achieve an effect—namely, symbolic exchange—by composing texts that deviate from convention. But it is precisely when a text such as "Requiem" deviates from convention that it becomes controversial, objectionable, and offensive. In other words, Baudrillard's offensiveness derives from the perlocutionary nature of his performative rhetoric. Thus, Baudrillard's ethics are bound to his rhetoric, and critical evaluations of the former must account for the latter. Before critics deride the "distinct moral stench" of "Requiem," they need to follow Judith Butler in recognizing that performative utterances are, at least in part, rhetorical (15).

When the 9/11 series is reframed as a rhetorical project, and when Baudrillardian rhetoric is reframed as the performance of exchange, "Requiem" can indeed be understood differently. As I will demonstrate in the analysis that follows, Baudrillard's theory of rhetoric positions "Requiem" as a strong perlocutionary performative, one that endorses symbolic exchange in a way that critics should recognize as emblematic of Baudrillard's work. On these grounds, and perhaps on these grounds only, we come to agree with William Merrin's assertion that "[m]ost of Baudrillard's analysis [in "Requiem"] is actually defensible" (106).

The essentially performative nature of "Requiem" becomes clear when critics trace the text's genesis. "Requiem" was, in fact, born as an oral performance with Baudrillard crafting "Requiem" in the months following September 11, 2001, and first delivering it orally at a 9/11 debate. The debate, entitled *"Recontres philosophiques outré-Atlantique,"* occurred in Washington Square, Manhattan, and was sponsored by New York University and France Culture radio (Turner, "Requiem" 36). As "Requiem" translator Chris Turner explains, the text that Baudrillard delivered at this debate was slightly more elaborate than the text published by Verso. Turner's translation notes four points at which the oral version of the text offered more details than the print version. Although Turner refers to the differences between the oral text and print text as "slight variations," two of these variations are rhetorically significant (36).

The first significant variation concerns the introduction of "Requiem." In the print text, "Requiem" opens abstractly, coldly proclaiming: "The September 11 attacks also concern architecture, since what was destroyed was one of the most prestigious buildings, together with a whole (Western) value-system and world order" (37). But, as Turner's footnote explains, the opening that Baudrillard provided during his debate performance has been excised from the printed text. The change is significant, since Baudrillard's oral introduction articulates the purpose of "Requiem." In this oral introduction, Baudrillard confesses that there is a difficulty speaking about 9/11. He acknowledges that there is no way anyone can possibly explain the events of 9/11, and then he offers "Requiem" to his audience as an analogy—that is, as "an analysis which might possibly be as unacceptable as the event" but which strikes "the symbolic imagination in more or less the same way" (37n 1).

The variation, here, positions "Requiem" as exemplary Baudrillardian rhetoric. The oral introduction confirms the text's status as a perlocutionary performative—that is, as a text that brings about an effect as a consequence of its utterance. As Baudrillard discloses, the text's goal is symbolic exchange. By working to effect the symbolic imagination through analysis, the text challenges the real explanations that dominated the discussions of 9/11. By playing the imaginary against the real, "Requiem" not only abdicates explanatory value, but it also sustains symbolic exchange. To be clear: the text is unacceptable, and it is designed to be so. Baudrillard tells us that "Requiem" is an analogy to an unacceptable event. He is, in other words, telling us that "Requiem" is a wholly figurative work that should not be understood literally.

The second significant variation concerns the conclusion of "Requiem." In the print text, Baudrillard concludes his composition with a bold declaration: "By the grace of terrorism, the World Trade Center has become the world's most beautiful building—the eighth wonder of the world" (48). However, according to Turner, Baudrillard adjusted his conclusion during the 9/11 debate. In the oral version of the text, Baudrillard closes with a remark concerning the requiem genre, stating: "So I set out to produce a Requiem, but it was also, in a way, a Te Deum" (48n 4).

The variation, here, shows that Baudrillard is aware of his text's unconventionality. Baudrillard admits "Requiem" deviates from the requiem genre and, specifically, that his text might more accurately be classified as a Te Deum, or a hymn of praise ("Te Deum"). Baudrillard's admission not only reinforces the classification of his text as a perlocutionary performative, but it also gestures towards the way the text plays the imaginary against the real. Producing a conventional requiem would have necessitated that Baudrillard's "Requiem" promote the appearance of peaceful repose. To the contrary, his text challenges peaceful repose to disappear. Disappearance, or the imaginary, plays against appearance, or the real. By challenging the real to disappear, Baudrillard preserves the movement of language.

To be sure, Baudrillard's Te Deum—his hymn of praise for the destruction of the Twin Towers—needs, as I have argued, to be understood rhetorically. This text is emblematic of Baudrillardian rhetoric, in that the destruction it champions is analogous to the disappearance, the seduction, and the imaginary that Baudrillard heralds in his other texts. In his writing, Baudrillard often endorses the imaginary over the real, since, according to Baudrillard, "[e]veryone prefers to lend credence to reality" (*Fragments* 7). Thus, Baudrillard's contribution to the 9/11 series can be understood as deploying the classic sophistic move of making the weaker side of exchange look the stronger.[3] As such, Baudrillard's cold and rather abstract interest in 9/11 as an architectural event needs to be understood as a gesture towards an exchange analogy. He invokes architecture figuratively and uses the terms "construction" and "destruction" as analogs to the real and the imaginary. His play on this architectural analogy provides new perspective on his most offensive statements in the text. When Baudrillard claims that "[t]he Twin Towers were worth destroying," he is not making a political claim or an ethical claim. His assertions are rhetorical, as is his entire text. In this statement, he is making the weaker side of exchange, figuratively known in this architectural analogy as destruction, look the stronger. Thus, his Te Deum uses an analogy to suggest that destruction has the potential to trump construction and that the imaginary can still usurp the real—that is, until the next exchange. Upon reevaluation, then, Baudrillard's Te Deum is, at worst, susceptible to the criticism that it is rhetorical tedium—that it conforms to Baudrillard's rhetorical theory in an almost monotonous fashion.

NOTES

[1] When it was first published in 2002 as part of the 9/11 series, "Requiem" was the second of two essays in Baudrillard's book *The Spirit of Terrorism*. In 2003, Verso published a new edition of Baudrillard's book that supplemented the original two essays with two additional essays.

[2] In *Baudrillard and the Media*, Merrin notes the Baudrillard's contribution to Verso's 9/11 series "has become one of [Baudrillard's] most successful and famous essays" (105). Writing in 2005, Merrin credits this book with "restoring [Baudrillard's] intellectual profile" (105). Nonetheless, Merrin summarizes a number of "hostile reactions" to the book, including those from Julliard of *Liberation* and Minc of *Le Monde* (105).

[3] Ballif and McComiskey each draw comparisons between Baudrillard and the prototypical sophist Gorgias.

WORKS CITED

"9/11." *versobooks.com*. Verso Books, n.d. Web. 18 Mar. 2012.

Austin, J. L. *How to Do Things with Words*. 2nd ed. Ed. J. O. Urmson and Marina Sbisà. Cambridge: Harvard UP, 1975. Print.

Ballif, Michelle. *Seduction, Sophistry, and the Woman with the Rhetorical Figure*. Carbondale: Southern Illinois UP, 2001. Print.

Baudrillard, Jean. *Fragments: Cool Memories III, 1990-1995*. 1995. Trans. Emily Agar. New York: Verso, 2007. Print.

---. "Requiem for the Twin Towers." *The Spirit of Terrorism and Other Essays*. 2002. New ed. Trans. Chris Turner. New York: Verso, 2003. Print.

Bitzer, Lloyd F. "The Rhetorical Situation." *Philosophy and Rhetoric* 1 (1968): 1-14. Print.

Butler, Judith. *Excitable Speech: A Politics of the Performative*. New York: Routledge, 1997. Print.

Foss, Sonja K., Karen A. Foss, and Robert Trapp. "Jean Baudrillard." *Contemporary Perspectives on Rhetoric*. 3rd ed. Long Grove: Waveland P, 2002. 299-338. Print.

Fulford, Robert. "A French Intellectual—In the Worst Sense of the Term." *nationalpost.com*. National Post, 10 Mar. 2007. Web. 19 Mar. 2012.

"Jean Baudrillard." *economist.com.* The Economist Newspaper Limited, 15 Mar. 2007. Web. 19 Mar. 2012.Kirn, Walter. "Notes on the Darkest Day." *nytimes.com.* New York Times, 8 Sep. 2002. Web. 18 Mar. 2012.

Kirn, Walter. "Notes on the Darkest Day." *nytimes.com.* New York Times, 8 Sept. 2002. Web. 20 Apr. 2012.

McComiskey, Bruce. *Gorgias and the New Sophistic Rhetoric.* Carbondale: Southern Illinois UP, 2002. Print.

Merrin, William. *Baudrillard and the Media: A Critical Introduction.* Malden: Polity P, 2005. Print.

Miller, Carolyn R. "Genre as Social Action." *Quarterly Journal of Speech* 70 (1984): 151-67. Print.

"Requiem." Def. n.1. *oed.com.* The Oxford English Dictionary. 3rd ed. 2010. Web. 20 Mar. 2012.

Romano, Carlin. "An Oasis in the Desert of Eurotrash Philosophy." *Chronicle of Higher Education* 49.20 (2003): n. pag. *Education Research Complete.* Web. 10 Mar. 2010.

---. "The Death of Jean Baudrillard Did Happen." *Chronicle of Higher Education* 53.29 (2007): n. pag. *Education Research Complete.* Web. 10 Mar. 2010.

"Te Deum." Def. *oed.com.* The Oxford English Dictionary. 3rd ed. 2010. Web. 20 Mar. 2012.

Turner, Chris, trans. "Requiem for the Twin Towers." *The Spirit of Terrorism and Other Essays.* By Jean Baudrillard. New York: Verso, 2003. 35-48. Print.

18

CULTURAL HISTORIC ACTIVITY THEORY

An Analytic Methodology for the History of Rhetoric

Shawn D. Ramsey

James J. Murphy has asserted that to understand the history of rhetoric requires more than a familiarity with the books produced in its history; that is, "knowing about its books is not a sufficient ground for the history of a subject" (187). Long before Murphy's assertion, Wilbur S. Howell wrote that "if we call dialectic and rhetoric the methods by which ideas may be made to prevail and to influence the course of cultural and political history, then the ideas themselves are by extension the very things which the study of the method ultimately imparts" (46). More recently, scholars in the history of rhetoric have framed critiques of the limiting narrative of rhetorical history as a problem of historiography; but historiography implicates underlying methodologies that reinforce flawed historical narratives. Thomas P. Miller has leveled a critique against methods in historicizing the rhetorical tradition that ignore the complex contextual elements at work in remote historical periods. Miller argued that in using such methods, "we have to ignore, or at least simplify, the complex differences between their political, intellectual, and educational contexts" (27). Richard Leo Enos has also critiqued a narrow and bookish methodological approach to the history of rhetoric, calling for an examination of the locales and artifacts associated with rhetorical practices in historical periods, places, and their respective traditions. Enos has called for a closer examination of the material and the archaeological, arguing that our field should "expand our history of rhetoric by including sources that are not only visible but tangible." (66). A similar iteration of this argument can be found in Takis Poulakos's call for historians of rhetoric to "produce alternative versions of our tradition, to admit the limitations and biases of our peculiar viewpoints, and to leave behind us various and divergent histories of rhetoric" (186). These statements are only a small sample of a vast body of scholarly literature in the field of the history of rhetoric, which critiques historiography and indicts traditional histories of rhetoric for marginalizing various cultures, figures, genders, and traditions. This paper's central assertion is that such critiques can be remedied with a methodological analytic, by modifying methods of scholarly investigation rather than re-theorizing the writing of history. To this end, I examine Paul Prior's cultural historic activity theory (hereinafter CHAT) as a methodological analytic to approach questions and problems in rhetorical history. The disparate arguments that implicate theory and historiography in the study of rhetoric implicitly call for methodological and analytic changes that can address neglected rhetorics situated in the past, in order to provide a more inclusive set of narratives in the history of rhetoric.

Prior's cultural historic activity theory, developed in *Writing/Disciplinarity*, was intended to create a framework that proposed to study the development of scholarly writing. Prior's work proceeds on the assumption that this rhetorical activity is a "situated, distributed, and mediated" activity (5). Rather than treating the history of rhetoric as "a unified anonymous structure of linguistic, rhetorical, and epistemic conventions," Prior's theory instead is promising as far as reflecting rhetorical history as embodied in "a very human world" (25). Prior's approach, which is grounded in the concept of discourse communities, grew out of the theory of distributed cognition, which links "things happening within and between artifacts, people, and the world" (29). It is ideally suited to an inquiry into the history of rhetoric as a temporally situated set of complex systems because, as Prior explains: "Activity implicates co-action with other people, artifacts, and elements of the social-material environment" (29). Prior identifies five kinds of media within functional systems: "persons, artifacts (semiotic and material), institutions, practices, and communities" (30).

> *Artifacts* refer to material objects fashioned by people (e.g., written texts, furniture, instruments, and built environments) or taken up by people (e.g., ocean currents for travel, the night sky as a navigational aid, animals as domesticated food stock, a stone as a weapon). Artifacts are also durable symbolic forms, like natural languages, mathematics, and specialized disciplinary discourses that may be inscribed in material objects, but that are also internalized by and distributed across persons. [*Practices*] refer to ways of acting with and interacting in worlds . . . . *Institutions* refer to stabilizations of activity around formal and informal social groupings. . . . *Communities* refer to potentials for alignment that emerge from any "common" experiences. (31; emphasis in original)

The fifth and final medium is that of *persons*, which Prior does not define for obvious reasons. Prior further explains that these media are not mutually exclusive, and he has visually represented his theory to suggest a constant weaving and reweaving of these media (31).

Prior's theory, implemented as an analytic research methodology, is promising on several counts. Its attention to the role of persons, particularly those excluded from traditional histories of rhetoric, potentially provides conceptual space and methodological attention to those same persons. The theory's attention to practices and artifacts, likewise, can permit the examination of rhetorical artifacts not necessarily confined to learned treatises. Likewise, communities and institutions as subjects of examination can reveal rhetorical traditions that are not confined to elite and patriarchal groups overemphasized in such traditional locales as courts, assemblies, or other venues exhaustively examined as the locus of rhetorical practice—to the exclusion of the far more varied locales and communities with distinct and unexplored rhetorical traditions. Prior's theory argues that, in the context of writing, we can better understand what writing does, and how it does it, by examining the systems of activity in which writing is historically embedded. But if we shift the central inquiry of Prior's analysis away from writing, which is a far narrower activity (and one that could arguably be a subdivision of rhetoric more broadly defined), to directly focus on rhetoric as a temporally embedded concept—whether spoken, written, verbal, visual, theoretical, or material—a rich and textured understanding of rhetorical activity in a given historical period might emerge.

However, Prior's model as a methodological analytic might contain a limitation that at once becomes very apparent. Where do complex meta-concepts such as rhetoric fit in this theory as a methodological analytic? Writing, which was the central subject of Prior's inquiry, is clearly a practice and an artifact, necessarily involving persons at work in institutions and communities. But consider what rhetoric is from a variety of perspectives in relation to the media at play in Prior's theory. Is rhetoric an artifact, that is, a durable symbolic form or a kind of specialized discourse? Certainly, the canonical "artifacts" and discourses that treat rhetoric can be called symbolic artifacts, and similarly, they can be called a specialized discourse, if we define rhetoric in its most traditional sense: a set of learned texts. Conversely, rhetoric may not be reduced to an artifact at all: it can be a traditional or wholly innovative set of ideas, shared by a community, an institution, a culture, or one individual. Moreover, a rhetoric may be an inchoate set of ideas that are in no way durable and change over time and across cultures. Indeed, the reason that rhetoric is historicized as an idea is precisely because of the development and change, both conceptually and practically, across and between historical periods, and even between rhetoricians in the same temporal space who formulate radically different articulations of its central tenets. Rhetorics can arguably be both theoretical and completely without practical application, embedded in ideologies, epistemologies, power relations, and assumptions underpinning other philosophical fields, from ontology, to theology, to semiotics and metaphysics. Likewise, reducing rhetoric to a "material object" taken up by people is very reductionist indeed.

In similarly obvious fashion, rhetorics are not persons; rhetoric may be practiced by persons, read by persons, and theorized by persons, but ideas that transform over time are not persons in any sense. Rhetoric, similarly, is not an institution; over several millennia of transformation as an idea, rhetoric has had relationships to institutions, or been authorized by them, but the study of rhetoric and the development of rhetoric as an inchoate concept has had a life separate from institutional actors, educational institutions, or social institutions. Rhetoric has arguably operated independently within, or without, or even in resistance to institutions, and it has contributed to both the stabilization and the destabilization of institutions. Likewise, rhetoric, as a set of concepts either with or without practical application, may not necessarily involve stabilization around, or even potentials for stabilization around, communities. Because of the limitations of space, I invite the reader to take Prior's model and apply other inchoate ideas that represent vast and complex intellectual phenomena across time—for example, the nature of dialectical disputation in the Middle Ages, peripatetic philosophy in ancient Greece, or metaphysics in theological culture in the fifteenth century. Possibly owing to activity theory's intellectual roots in Vygotskian dialectical materialism, it might be incompatible to nonmaterial, intangible, and highly internalized concepts underpinning intellectual and verbal activity systems.

This incompatibility is illustrated by the webtext of Prior and his colleagues, "Remediating the Canons." The text attempts to examine the traditional canons through the extremely complex media at work in Prior's theory in a contemporary context. Most of the contributions to the webtext devote minimal time and space to demonstrating a familiarity with the canons in their many formulations throughout the history of rhetoric and generally suggest that rather than "revising and reinterpreting the classical canons, it is time to begin remapping the territory of rhetorical activity." The central problem with "Remediating the Canons" is that few of the webtexts attempt anything other than a perfunctory approach to defining the canons or showing how they evolved over time. In so doing, the argument turns the canons into straw men, which the authors then proceed to tear down as inadequate when compared to the authors' proposed remediations. The webtext's limited historicization of the canons stand in contrast to the canons' very complex metamorphoses throughout rhetorical history, and their proposed "need" for remediation are a form of begging the question: we inadequately describe the canons and therefore they are inadequate. For example, in the "node" on the canon of memory, there is offered only a few sentences about the nature of the canon of memory, describing it as "largely ignored" (although citing both Yates and Carruthers). This leads one to ask: by whom was the canon of memory ignored? Paolo Rossi, in his excellent book *Logic and the Art of Memory*, historicizes the way the *ars meorativa* became a subdiscipline of extensive study throughout the Renaissance and Enlightenment.

But I do not critique the treatment of the Prior et al. argument for remediating the canons on the basis that it lacks historicization because, in all fairness, historicizing the canons was not their authorial intent. However, I do offer this example as evidence of how Prior's theory, unmodified, does not lend itself to the integration of meta-conceptual media at work in historical inquiry. The webtext reflects the incompatibility of cultural historic activity theory (CHAT) with extremely complex, historically situated ideas in rhetoric by simply characterizing them as antiquated and requiring remediation. Arguing that rhetoric or rhetorical concepts require remediation, without a comprehensive grasp of how they operated over time, does not seem to sufficiently warrant remediation. It is a bit like arguing that concepts in theology require remediation because the Bible is not ideally suited to effective multimodal interpretation on Twitter and, in turn, that a more viable theory of Twitter-based Biblical exegesis is required. I posit that the argument calling for remediating the canons is not sufficiently warranted without a more comprehensive understanding of their historical role. I emphasize, however, that I point to the webtext's inadequate historical treatment of the canons not as a critique of the text itself but as evidence that CHAT is not well suited to the accommodation of meta-theoretical concepts as part of its analysis. A seeming inability to historicize rhetoric attendant to the current trend of "remediating" rhetorical concepts is not the point of this argument; rather, it is that cultural historic activity theory is a viable analytic methodology to provide a nuanced and rich historicizing analytic of rhetoric, if it is modified to examine the idea of rhetoric as its own media of analysis.

This is the conundrum I examined when attempting to apply the very promising analytic provided by Prior's theory—in sum, moving from theory to methodological application for an inquiry into historical rhetoric. At first, perhaps, simply changing the focus of Prior's inquiry from writing to rhetoric seemed like a viable solution for its use as a methodology to intellectual history. But based on the foregoing issues, I set upon altering the model provided by Prior: when dealing with an idea such as rhetoric, which might be described as all (or none) of the other media represented in his theory, I added rhetoric itself as an additional medium to investigate the inchoate concept at the center of a historical inquiry, as a separate and interdependent element in the analytic. Adding an additional medium at work in Prior's analytic to investigate rhetoric in a given period produced interesting and encouraging results. In studying communicative activities that implicate rhetoric in the Middle Ages, I have privileged rhetoric, its own medium with dimensions affecting everything else in turn, since in Prior's model rhetoric cannot be subsumed into any one individual category. Like the other units of analysis in his model, rhetoric weaves and reweaves itself into the persons, artifacts, practices, communities, and institutions surrounding it. As a scholar of rhetoric in the Middle Ages, I have used Prior's theory-as-analytic to provide my work with insights into the rhetorical traditions of women in the twelfth century and used it to explain certain ambiguous qualities in the rhetoric of Alcuin of York. The limitations of this format prevent me from discussing these in detail, however, so I turn to a comparison of Prior's theory-as-methodology with other research methods in historical rhetoric to illustrate its utility.

In incorporating the idea of rhetoric as its own medium when researching historical rhetorics, CHAT as an analytic methodology can address Thomas Miller's critique of trends in rhetorical history by taking our attention away from "abstract continuities" and contextualizing the rhetorical tradition in the actors, times, artifacts, and other media in their own temporal and historical milieu (27). Likewise, it provides a methodology that accommodates Enos's call for a closer examination of the material and the archaeological by addressing the artifacts at play in rhetorical activity systems, answering the call that our field should "expand our history of rhetoric by including sources that are not only visible but tangible" (66). Because this methodological and theoretical framework permits the examination of the economic, social, and political networks of a given historical moment, it can similarly analyze historical periods by examining rhetorical activities in their respective contexts. Historiographic critiques of the rhetorical tradition's exclusion of certain marginalized groups are similarly served because the rhetorical activities of these groups and cultures can be actively analyzed with the contextualizing framework of CHAT to embrace lost traditions of communication and persuasion not found in conventional histories of rhetoric.

It is of note that this analytic framework is also compatible with more traditional approaches to methodology in rhetorical history. Consider this narrative by James Kinneavy, regarding when he began to unearth the concept of *kairos*. Kinneavy indicates that he had been reading theology for his own edification when he kept noticing a term—*kairos*—referred to in the text. He then began to examine the etymology and origin of the term in connection with Greek and Hellenistic rhetoric. As Kinneavy himself explains, "I ran across it in [Paul] Tillich, the theologian . . . . Then I read Levi and others who had historical articles on it going back to the pre-Aristotelian and pre-Platonic philosophies in Greece. . . . I reread the *Phaedrus*, and I was just amazed how important this word was" (qtd. in Thompson 76). In a sense, Kinneavy's methodology moved from the conceptual to the contextual, in reverse fashion from the present methodological inquiry. Kinneavy was investigating rhetorical concepts, artifacts, persons, and practices in his landmark study.

Consider a slightly different narrative. James J. Murphy began his professional career by studying Chaucer, and he began to systematically examine and catalogue all of the medieval rhetorics he could find, beginning with a search for primary sources. Twenty years later he produced *Rhetoric in the Middle Ages* (Murphy, personal correspondence). Thus, in a sense, he began with practices and persons and moved on to artifacts, as his search led him to comb library catalogues for primary sources. Finally patterns began to emerge, reflecting three distinct categories in the medieval theory of rhetoric, in an almost inverse relationship to Kinneavy's methods in recovering *kairos*. Murphy characterized these decades of research as a search "for any manuscript entries—not necessarily titles—even remotely connected to rhetoric" (personal correspondence). In the process of so doing, he began to learn exhaustive amounts of information about the persons who wrote those rhetorics and the practices for which those rhetorics were used.

Finally, consider CHAT as a methodological heuristic, and its compatibility with feminist methodologies of historicization and recovery. Jacqueline Jones Royster and Gesa F. Kirsch, in *Feminist Rhetorical Practices*, state:

> We look at *people* at whom we have not looked before . . . in *places* at
> which we have not looked at seriously or methodologically before . . . at
> *practices* and *conditions* at which we have not looked closely enough . . .
> and at *genres* that we have not considered closely enough . . . and we
> think again about what women's *patterns of action* seem to suggest about
> *rhetoric.* (72; emphases added)

I have emphasized certain terms to illustrate how the media of inquiry in
Royster and Kirsch's methodological summary closely mirror the media at
play in a CHAT analysis. Thus, it is apparent that CHAT analyses, when contrasted with traditional and feminist methodological approaches, is a compatible analytical method of inquiry whose utility has been shown.

All of the accounts discussed above are examples of the methodology
associated with work in rhetorical history, and they are selected by virtue of
being drawn from studies that remain of lasting importance to the transdisci-
pline of rhetoric. I offer them to illustrate how patterns in methods of inquiry
emerge that closely mirror the use of CHAT as a methodological framework.
But the limitations inherent in this analytic methodology for rhetorical history
must include this qualifier: if the necessary inclusion of rhetoric as an idea is
one medium that was omitted in the original model, there could very well be
others, and I do not argue that this analytic is a prescriptive "lockstep" of procedures and methods for investigating rhetorical traditions. Nevertheless, fully
contextualizing rhetorical traditions at a historical remove is not only served
by such an analytic examination, but it also might be greatly expanded by the
increasing availability of existing archival materials in the digital age. With the
proliferation of disciplines and resources converging on the subject of rhetoric
as a topic of historical inquiry, combined with the readily available and
increasing number of textual artifacts being digitized and made available to
everyone on the World Wide Web, one can only hope that the amount of
information and those processing it will advance the study of the history of
rhetoric light years ahead of its current state.

A more comprehensive methodological analytic, such as that suggested by
CHAT, can provide more nuanced contextual examinations of rhetoric as an
idea and a practice in the disparate times and places where it existed as a complex cultural edifice. If we accept the assumption that rhetoric is an activity system using technological and conceptual mediation to produce communicative
acts that either produce or arrest social change, then Paul Prior's theory might
have utility as an analytic and a system of methodological inquiry.

WORKS CITED

Carruthers, Mary. *The Book of Memory.* 2nd ed. Cambridge: Cambridge UP, 2008.
   Print.
Enos, Richard Leo. "The Archaeology of Women in Rhetoric: Rhetorical Sequencing
   as a Research Method for Historical Scholarship." *Rhetoric Society Quarterly* 32. 1
   (Winter 2002): 65-79. Print.

Howell, Wilbur Samuel. *The Rhetoric of Alcuin and Charlemagne.* New York: Russell & Russell, 1965. Print.

Miller, Thomas P. "Reinventing Rhetorical Traditions." *Learning From the Histories of Rhetoric, Essays in Honor of Winifred Bryan Horner.* Ed. Theresa Enos. Carbondale: Southern Illinois UP, 1993. 26-41. Print.

Murphy, James J. "Conducting Research in the History of Rhetoric: An Open Letter to a Future Historian of Rhetoric." *Publishing in Rhetoric and Composition.* Ed. Gary A. Olson and Todd Taylor. Albany: State U of New York P, 1997. 187-96. Print.

---. Personal correspondence. 2012.

Poulakos, Takis. "Historiographies of the Tradition of Rhetoric: A Brief History of Classical Funeral Orations." *Western Journal of Speech Communication* 54.2 (Spring 1990): 172-88. Print.

Prior, Paul A. *Writing/Disciplinarity.* New York: Routledge, 2009. Print.

Prior, Paul A., et al. "Remediating the Canons." *Kairos* 11.3 (2008): n. pag. Web. May 2012.

Rossi, Paolo. *Logic and the Art of Memory: the Quest for a Universal Language.* Trans. Stephen Clucas. New York: Continuum, 2000. Print.

Royster, Jacqueline Jones, and Gesa F. Kirsch. *Feminist Rhetorical Practices: New Horizons for Rhetoric, Composition, and Literary Studies.* Carbondale: Southern Illinois UP, 2012. Print.

Thompson, Roger. "*Kairos* Revisited: An Interview with James L. Kinneavy." *Rhetoric Review* 19 (2000): 73-88. Print.

Yates, Frances A. *The Art of Memory.* London: Pimlico, 1992. Print.

SECTION
IV

RE/FRAMING EMBODIMENT AND RHETORICAL AGENCY

19

BODIES UNDER CONSTRUCTION

Rhetorical Tactics for Rescripting Rape

Kaitlin Marks-Dubbs

[W]e must not imagine a world of discourse divided between accepted discourse and excluded discourse, or between the dominant discourse and the dominated one; but as a multiplicity of discursive elements that can come into play in various strategies. . . . [D]iscourse can be both an instrument and an effect of power, but also a hindrance, a stumbling-block, a point of resistance and a starting point for an opposing strategy. Discourse transmits and produces power; it reinforces it, but also undermines and exposes it, renders it fragile and makes it possible to thwart it.

— Michel Foucault

It is important to try to shift our critical optics (at least slightly) about street movement rhetoric so that we might see beyond how <bodies *plus* words> function, and begin seeing how <bodies-words-images> intersect to form (an)other rhetoric of resistance that is qualitatively different than a critic might have assumed.

— Darell Enck-Wanzer

Queer. Dyke. Fat. Slut. These slurs simultaneously identify and render legible certain bodily features or acts as nonnormative, flawed, and discursively policeable. Social movements reclaiming these terms illuminate such interpellations as a potential site for countering and rescripting such outwardly determined identities. This essay examines the rhetorical strategies of the SlutWalk movement's discursive efforts and tactics of exposing and undermining the power of interpellation through the reclamation of the term "slut."

While SlutWalk founders' most immediate instigation to organize appears in the form of a Toronto police officer advising York University students and staff about on-campus safety, this officer's words speak for a much larger set of long-standing cultural sentiments. On January 24, 2011, a representative of the Toronto Police Department advised staff and students that "women should avoid dressing like sluts in order not to be victimized."

Numerous media outlets have singled out this officer's words as inciting participants in cities worldwide to organize local "SlutWalks" in order to reappropriate the word "slut" and "make a unified statement about sexual assault and victims' rights." His story is certainly both the most immediate and publicly salient example of victim-blaming tied to the organization of the SlutWalk movement but one of only many rape scripts that frame rape as almost inevitable unless prevented by women themselves (Marcus).

The persistence of such scripts is precisely why the rhetorical act of walking is so significant to the SlutWalk movement's promotion of survivors' rights; many rape prevention strategies target women as the bearers of responsibility of either causing or preventing rape in decisions of how (or whether) to travel between their homes and a social locations. Police officers, universities, friends, and family members all warn women never to walk alone at night, especially if they have consumed alcohol, often by invoking notions of what constitutes not only a "safe" but a "smart" decision. Such advice assumes a raped-in-the-bushes/dark alleyway script that frames women as opening themselves up to rape by the mere decision to leave the house (particularly after dark). Furthermore, it dangerously obscures the possibility of rape by an acquaintance, friend, or family member in the home, on a date, or potentially while walking a woman home. While the act of walking in mass does not entirely operate to reclaim mobility and exposure as the right of women to safely walk alone, it does function to attract attention to the participants claiming the right to walk without being raped or being interpreted as "asking for it."[1]

In their organized Walks, SlutWalk participants write of, on, with, and through their bodies. Many write and carry signs with various slogans such as, "My Body Is Not an Invitation," "Clothes ≠ Consent," "Rape Is Not a Fashion Critique," and "Consent Is Not Something I Wear." Many march in bras, miniskirts, or other revealing clothing often imbued with sartorial significance relating to contemporary sex work or fetish gear. Some write messages on their bodies, such as "My Skin Does *Not* Cause Rape." Others are dressed in jeans and a sweater with signs indicating that they are wearing the clothes or style of clothes they wore when they were raped, and their signs ask readers if it was their fault. These multimodal arguments often perform their verbally written messages, as in the example of a woman who exposes her entire back on which is written the message that her skin does not cause rape. In this way, women use their bodies both to critique gender codes and to embody alternate codes (Sheridan 260). This paper asks how such uses of the body as writing space and mode of argument might call into question or better inform the boundaries of written, literate, and/or semiotic practice. My study of the contemporary SlutWalk movement examines how social activists use their bodies not only to critique cultural scripts that identify rape as the result of women "dressing like sluts" but further to perform and embody alternatives to such scripts. Joining conversations that have worked to unpack the deployment, intersection, and impacts of visual, material, and embodied rhetorics (Keane; Marback; Selzer and Crowley; Sheridan), this study specifically examines how verbal and nonverbal rhetorics of social activism tactics (DeLuca; Enck-Wanzer) may simultaneously work to collude and undermine one another in challenging and changing common cultural scripts.

Throughout the digital archives created by SlutWalk organizers, participants, and observers, however, traditional print consistently appears in the most widely circulated images to mediate the messages of the bodies portrayed. This paper proposes that the limitations of scholarship that Darrel Enck-Wanzer observes within the study of social movements[2] may be, at least in part, because those are the texts that are perceived as more easily legible and thus more commonly circulated and archived. International Facebook pages such as SlutWalk Toronto, SlutWalk Berlin, SlutWalk Morocco, and SlutWalk UK consistently post the same promotional materials and documentary images across their profile pages, decontextualizing artifacts of individual walks and blending them across international contexts. Such blending of archives makes the SlutWalk movement as an international phenomenon difficult to study without a great deal of travel to the various walks organized. Thus, the study of such a wide-scale social movement is likely to rely heavily on photo, video, and textually descriptive accounts of others' experiences at these movements more so than a scholar's physical participation at a series of events (or so, at least, my own limited resources of finance and time suggest such to me). This essay will examine digital representations of a series of international, embodied rhetorical events to examine what uses of text about the body, text on the body, and bodies as text are most commonly picked up and circulated.

As I analyze the SlutWalk movement's effort to rescript rape, I question the role of traditional print articles in mediating the semiotic messages of revealing clothing and exposed skin. Studies such as Judith Butler's theorization of bodies as simultaneously material and discursive (*Bodies That Matter, Gender Trouble*) highlight the performative aspects of embodied identity in sending messages of cultural identity through the space bodies take up, the gestures they make, the clothing they wear, etc. In SlutWalks worldwide, written signs are used to mediate bodily signs, such as gesture and body language, with messages such as, "This is **Not** My 'I Want You' Face." SlutWalk participants send the message that clothing does not equal consent and that consent is not something they wear, by wearing revealing clothing and by mediating their fashion statements with writing in the form of carried signs, promotional posters, digitally published mission statements, news stories, and other publicity.

My rhetorical analysis of such texts affiliated with the SlutWalk movement examines multiple modes of signification, including images of participating subjects and bodies and their performances, written and/or illustrated signs and promotional materials, and written mission statements. In this analysis, I ask how the SlutWalks' efforts to reclaim "slut" inform the roles expected of traditional writing in mediating the semiotic rescripting of social stigmas deemed legible on the body. What questions does the SlutWalk mission raise regarding intersections of not only written, literate, and semiotic practice (and our studies of them) but also intentional, unintentional, and reappropriated meanings in signs?

Visible Stigma and Coming Out as a Rendering of Legibility: A Theoretical Overview

As I examine the bodily legibility of interpellations of embodied deviance, such as "slut," I apply theoretical frameworks including the trope of the closet and the metaphor of coming out to examine the intersecting roles of various semiotic modes such as writing, clothing, and the body itself in rescripting rape and reclaiming "slut." My interest in coming-out theory lies particularly in how metaphors of coming out and the closet have been extrapolated from sexuality studies to social activism for specifically visible stigmas, such as the fat activist movement. While the concept of coming out was initially deployed with connotations of revealing a secret, recent theory and activism have framed coming out as a tactic of self-definition and even a declaration of refusal to compose one's embodied identity to fit common norms, such as thinness.

As Kenji Yoshino theorizes the role of visibility in American legal rights and protections, he argues that the closet is a trope that is applicable not just to invisible groups but to visible groups as well, a metaphor for passing and also for covering, defined as being allowed to retain and reveal a trait but not flaunt it (12).[3] Rape prevention strategies, such as those told to the students and staff at York University, often script rape as a consequence of women not properly covering—both literally and within the construct of Yoshino's theorization—their sexed and potentially sexual bodies. Directions to avoid dressing "like sluts" in order to avoid rape and sexual assault assume that the flaunting of the female body is 1) not a right to women and 2) a semiotic message that not only provokes but, to some extent, legitimizes acts of rape and sexual assault. Women are expected, culturally and through legal systems, such as the police department in Toronto, to literally cover their bodies in order to cover their sexuality. Women who do not do so are thus held accountable as the cause of rape or assault.

SlutWalk is, of course, only one of many such social movements to reclaim identificatory terms used to label social stigmas of body in its appearance (e.g., "fat") or in its relation to other bodies (e.g., "queer"). The movement's use of the term "pride" in its efforts to shrug off the stigma ascribed to "slut" certainly follows that of the LGBTQ movement. Adoption of similar tactics has previously been studied in relation to LGBTQ and fat activist movements. Building off Yoshino's work and Goffman's theorization of stigma, Abigail Saguy and Anna Ward examine what they observe as the understudied issues of how different (embodied) realities shape the diffusion of social movement narratives (4), through questions of why and how fat acceptance activists have come to use coming-out narratives and how they are using them differently than gays and lesbians have (2). Saguy and Ward observe that fat-rights activists are not disclosing, as much as affirming, their fatness, thus reclaiming the term "fat" (which is commonly used as an insult) as a neutral or positive descriptor, as they reject the terms "obese" and "overweight" as pathologizing normal human variation, and innovating on the concept of coming out as a *"destigmatization strategy"* (2; emphasis in original; see also Murray). While the SlutWalk movement does not explicitly use the metaphor of coming out, I argue—through a study of recent coming-out theory—that they deploy the strategy, nevertheless.

Yoshino observes that, at the surface level, Eve Sedgwick's claim that it is possible to come out of the closet as a fat woman appears "counterintuitive, as obesity is a visible characteristic. It would thus seem that the fat individual who declared that she was fat would not be divulging more information than was already in the public realm" (10). As Michael Moon observes, the stigma of size "could never be hidden because it simply *is* the stigma of visibility" (229). The notion of a woman coming out as fat thus requires a nuancing of coming-out theory that I identify as controlling the *intelligibility* rather than the visibility of embodied identities.

Moon posits that "in this society everyone who sees a fat woman feels they know something about her that she doesn't herself know" and elaborates that this feeling of insider knowledge results from the pathologization of fatness as a medical issue of obesity:

> it is medicine that lends this notionally self-evident (though, as recent research demonstrates, usually erroneous) reflection the excitement of inside information; it is medicine that, as with homosexuality, transforming difference into etiology, confers on this rudimentary *behavioral* hypothesis the prestige of a privileged narrative understanding of her *will* (she's addicted), her *history* (she's frustrated), her *perception* (she can't see herself as she really looks), her *prognosis* (she's killing herself). The desire to share this privileged information with the one person thought to lack it is more than many otherwise civilized people can withstand. (229-30; emphasis added)

For these reasons, Sedgwick responds, the process of coming out is "a way of staking one's claim to insist on, and participate actively in, a renegotiation of *the representational contract* between one's body and one's world" (230; emphasis in original). Similarly, constructions of "Slut Pride" and "Proud Sluts" do not necessarily disclose information, such as sexual practices, so much as refuse to take shame in the interpellation of "slut," so that it might not be used in future power plays that stigmatize, punish, or hold women accountable for their own rapes based on their appearance or their consensual sexual practices. In figuratively—and sometimes literally—uncovering, the participants of the SlutWalk movement acknowledge and thereby refute the projective fantasies that general culture has about sluts (Yoshino). I thus present coming out as both an implicit tactic of SlutWalks and as a rendering alternative legibility for those coming out—though rendering visibility, as this essay demonstrates, is often part of the process of rendering one's body legible.

The Semiotics of the Bodies and Words at Work at SlutWalks: A Data Analysis

The following section of this paper examines the SlutWalk movement's various semiotic tactics for articulating women's bodies as nonvictims, regardless of how they compose themselves with clothing or consensual sex acts. Part of this lies in making bodies and the cause visible, as its promoters circulate materials spreading the movement in chronicling various walks, promoting new walks, and simply proliferating the message that survivors are not to be blamed for being raped. Certain relationships between bodies, images, and traditional print texts circulate more frequently than others.

This data analysis specifically examines the SlutWalk movement as it has been digitally archived by its organizers and participants. While I began my study of the movement with the intent to examine it not merely in terms of, as Enck-Wanzer articulates, <bodies *plus* words>, I have come to suspect that a great deal of intentionally deployed rhetorics about bodies often operate with an approach that can easily steer scholars toward such a (perhaps overly simplified) analysis of bodies and words as purely additive.

Enck-Wanzer proposes that studying discourse with the assumption that different forms intersect with each other equally will help us, scholars, to see something differently than we would if we were to assume that the primary social work is being done by *either* verbal, visual, *or* embodied forms (181). He examines what rhetorical moves scholars study as they examine the rhetoric of social movement, observing that the majority of such scholarship frequently: exhibits a verbal bias that focuses specifically on protestors' written and spoken words; reduces nonverbal rhetoric to the role of instrument in enabling/facilitating verbal rhetorics; and reifies or fetishizes the metaphorical notion of "text" "in a way that misses the radical fragmentation of late-modern movement rhetorics" (180). In turn, he proposes the study of intersectional rhetoric, "a rhetoric that places multiple rhetorical forms (in this case, speech, embodiment, and image) on relatively equal footing" (177). Following Henry Jenkins et al.'s argument that in the choice to spread texts and their ideas, consumers appraise and ascribe value, this analysis sets out to analyze images of embodiment as they are circulated by SlutWalk organizers, participants, and allies through numerous international Facebook pages and mediated by traditionally printed text.

Of the SlutWalk movement's various semiotic methods of rescripting rape, two are the most visibly circulated among the multiple cities' and countries' SlutWalk pages: 1) images of text only, either in photos of handmade signs or in circulation of Facebook "photos" that are not photos at all, but written texts, and 2) indexical relations between traditionally printed language and tactically composed bodies that proliferate throughout the images of various international SlutWalks.[4] That is to say, a great many of the photos of bodies are specifically of individuals holding signs that reference their clothing.

Tactics of articulating their message by pairing the composition of one's wardrobe with traditional print include:

- pairing revealing garments with messages such as "NOT ASKING FOR IT!"—a basic articulation of the message that clothes do not correlate to consent;
- survivors and allies working to counter the stereotype of the victim as visibly a slut, often through indexing the covering clothing worn when raped;
- at least one frequently circulated image of a survivor who pairs either a short skirt or shorts with a sign narrating her rape, referencing the shortness of her shorts, and voicing her condemnation that rapists do not realize that they are rapists because of cultural scripts blaming women for their clothing. Such an example works to narrate the experience and elucidate the systematic script of victim-blaming, as the survivor articulates that 1) her rapist is a rapist; 2) he does not know that he is a rapist because she had initially flirted with him, and her shorts were too short, and our rape culture has suggested that she is to blame; 3) she suffered from the blame placed on her when she was afterward called a slut and a whore and was spat on by her boyfriend and given dirty looks by her friends.

The prominent circulation of images of participants with traditional print writing among the various SlutWalks suggests that organizers and participants from numerous cities and countries have judged this method of activism particularly productive in representing and potentially furthering the movement's cause. While women (and men) in underwear or stilettos work to physically claim space for visually "slutty" bodies to walk safely, the agents circulating images of SlutWalks that have been held and promoting SlutWalks that are being organized do not tend to proliferate images of such bodies without text to mediate their message.

SlutWalk, New York City, October 2011. (Photograph by David Shankbone)

At a Walk, individuals or groups without signs or writing on their bodies would be immediately contextualized by other participants with signs by promotional flyers, by public speaking, and by chanting. In archiving these events and promoting future events, these simultaneous meaning-making signals are absent. Once online, a writer could contextualize images of these individuals with narratives of the SlutWalk experience or links to the Slut-Walk main page on Facebook, but readers can also consume the images without unpacking narratives or following links. Within the SlutWalk movement, traditional print repeatedly functions to counter potential misunderstandings or misrepresentations of the movement, perhaps best exemplified in one image of a sign that reads, "Don't be so distracted by the underwear that you forget THIS MARCH IS ABOUT RAPE." Concerns of readers/viewers misunderstanding the message (or writers misrepresenting it) appear to inform the proliferating circulation of both physical signs from various Walks and poignant or catchy digital print texts within the "photos" of SlutWalk Facebook pages.

In many ways, circulating images of handmade signs can also function to invoke bodies as the viewer composes them in his or her imagination. Images of signs prepared for the initial SlutWalk (Toronto) have circulated widely beyond SlutWalk Toronto's Facebook page, illustrating both the large number of signs created en masse before the Walk and the embodied act of sign making. These stacks of handmade signs invoke bodies to the extent that they are hand drawn for the purpose of being carried by and with numerous bodies. Though they do not entirely work to compose the specific bodies that might have produced them or might show up to carry them, the mass-organized signs suggest a mass of bodies, and bodies in numbers are themselves, of course, a rhetorical tactic of signifying solidarity, citizens taking a stance, voting blocks, and movement.

Concluding Thoughts

As Foucault observes in this essay's beginning epigraph, "discourse can be both an instrument and an effect of power" (as in the initial interpellation of "slut"), "but also a hindrance, a stumbling-block, a point of resistance, and a starting point for an opposing strategy" (as demonstrated by the SlutWalk movement's reveling in the term "slut" in an effort to lessen its stigmatizing power). As others have done before them with terms such as "queer" and "fat," SlutWalk organizers, participants, and promoters instantiate Foucault's work in ascribing pride rather than shame to the interpellation of "slut," insisting that it not be used to blame survivors for their rape.

SlutWalk participants work to rescript cultural narratives of victim-blaming through the composed deployment of bodies, images, and traditional print, but do so unevenly, ultimately favoring compositions that include the latter. The resulting digital archive presents an impression that, despite all of the interest and effort devoted to organizing physical performances of bodies, promoters of the SlutWalk movement fear that the rhetoric of organized bodies is inadequate in articulating the movement's cause. However, I posit that to focus on traditional print does not entirely erase participating bodies. In promoting events such as organized walks, these circulated texts call bodies together, explicitly in inviting participants to attend and support the cause, and implicitly in calling for bodies to physically support them throughout the Walk.

The favoring of these print texts does, however, call attention to a more general belief held—beyond SlutWalk—that images are more subject to interpretation than words, and thus that the bodies of SlutWalk are intrinsically more ambiguous than the print accompanying the body, either as a material text in the Walk or as promotional material online. Such ambiguity could be particularly crippling to this movement, as images of bodies without context can easily appear as pandering to the male gaze—the very privilege they actually seek to challenge. Because viewers bring with them the cultural assumption of a "slut," as (potentially) rendered legible by clothing, clarifying that the Walks are not performing bodies for the male gaze but rather are claiming the right to safely perform any identity without fear of or blame for sexual violence is important to furthering the purpose of the movement.

It is worth noting that SlutWalk participants walk a tightrope when deploying revealing clothing as a semiotic message arguing that revealing clothing is not a semiotic message to men. I in no way mean to suggest that in wearing a short skirt, low neckline, or stilettos a woman is signaling sexual availability, sexual interest, promiscuity, or consent, and yet I acknowledge that identifying clothing as carrying meaning to SlutWalk observers in an effort to frame clothing as not signifying meaning outside of the Walk is seemingly contradictory. While this tactic succeeds in claiming a safe space for bodies regardless of their attire (at least during the time of the Walk), its clarity to the general public learning of the movement through news coverage, social networks, and the blogosphere is often tenuous (especially in the case of conservative Web forums and blogs).

As I noted earlier, studying such an international phenomenon as a participant or observer is difficult given the scale of the movement. Because this movement frequently reaches audiences through digital mediation, I have been interested in studying how the physical, embodied, and ephemeral Walks have been documented and circulated beyond their sites of physical practices. I hope, however, as cities such as starting-point Toronto are now holding their second annual SlutWalk, that future researchers (myself ideally included) can work on location and, perhaps through using an ethnographic approach, can take into consideration the role of affect in the physical participation of the Walks. Some participants reveal their bodies to the public with little fear of sexual violence in the relative safety of like-minded antirape activists, while others march fully covered, in outfits like those they wore at the time of their rapes to show that they were not safe when covered by clothing, as many other survivors have not been and will not be in the future.

What are the effects and experiences of the Walk that cannot be captured and may ultimately be lost through digital archiving, even if filmed or narrated by participants and observers?

NOTES

[1] Participating men generally appear to operate as allies bolstering support for the movement but not necessarily with the same rhetorical functions as the women. That is, men frequently participate either in Walks themselves or in related media, circulating the message that men should avoid rape and sexual assault by stopping when their partners don't want to engage in sexual activity. Others support the movement by stating that men should try to "walk in her shoes" to see beyond male privilege, but even so, men do not seem to be able to identify as potentially raped or blamed for being raped the way women can (as Marcus critiques, cultural scripts consistently see women as rape-able).

[2] Such as focusing on appeals deployed through traditional writing.

[3] Yoshino explains, as an example, that a Catholic might be allowed to be a Catholic (without converting) and reveal that she is a Catholic (without passing) but not be allowed to wear religious paraphernalia (thus covering).

[4] In fact, it is often difficult to track images with any degree of certainty to a particular Walk unless signs with the city's name are included in the photo or promotional material circulated, though some images are tagged with the name of a particular city or country's Walk.

WORKS CITED

Butler, Judith. *Bodies That Matter: On the Discursive Limits of "Sex."* New York: Routledge, 1993. Print.

---. *Gender Trouble: Feminism and the Subversion of Identity.* New York: Routledge, 1990. Print.

DeLuca, Kevin. *Image Politics: The New Rhetoric of Environmental Activism.* New York: Guilford, 1999. Print.

Enck-Wanzer, Darrel. "Trashing the System: Social Movement, Intersectional Rhetoric, and Collective Agency in the Young Lords Organization's Garbage Offensive." *Quarterly Journal of Speech* 92.2 (2006): 174-201. Print.

Foucault, Michel. *The History of Sexuality.* Trans. Robert Hurley. London: Routledge, 1990. Print.

Jenkins, Henry, Sam Ford, and Joshua Green. *Spreadable Media.* New York: New York UP, 2013. Print.

Keane, Webb. "Semiotics and the Social Analysis of Material Things." *Language & Communication* 23 (2003): 409-25. Print.

Marback, Richard. "Unclenching the Fist: Embodying Rhetoric and Giving Objects Their Due." *Rhetoric Society Quarterly* 38.1 (2008): 46-65. Print.

Marcus, Sharon. "Fighting Bodies, Fighting Words." *Feminists Theorize the Political.* Ed. Judith Butler and J.W. Scott. New York: Routledge, 1992. 385-403. Print.

Moon, Michael, with Eve Sedgwick. "Divinity." *Tendencies.* Durham: Duke UP, 1993. 215-51. Print.

Murray, Samantha. "(Un/Be)Coming Out? Rethinking Fat Politics." *Social Semiotics* 15:2 (2005): 153-63. Print.

Saguy, Abigail, and Anna Ward. "Coming Out as Fat: Rethinking Stigma." *Social Psychology Quarterly* 74.1 (2011): 53-74. Print.

Sedgwick, Eve. *Epistemology of the Closet.* Berkeley: U of California P, 1992. Print.

Selzer, Jack, and Sharon Crowley, eds. *Rhetorical Bodies*. Madison: U of Wisconsin P, 1999. Print.

Sheridan, David Michael. "Fabricating Consent: Three-dimensional Objects as Rhetorical Composition." *Computers and Composition* 27 (2010): 249-65. Print.

SlutWalk. *Facebook*. n.d. Web. 7 May 2012.

Slutwalk Berlin. *Facebook*. n.d. Web. 7 May 2012.

SlutWalk Morroco. *Facebook*. n.d. Web. 7 May 2012.

SlutWalk Toronto. *Facebook*. n.d. Web. 7 May 2012.

Slutwalk UK. *Facebook*. n.d. Web. 7 May 2012.

Yoshino, Kenji. *Covering: The Hidden Assault on Our Civil Rights*. New York: Random House, 2006. Print.

20

(Re)Framing the Interests of English Speakers

"We Are All Khaled Said"

Katherine Bridgman

Located on the eastern side of Egypt's second largest city, Sidi Gaber has for centuries been a neighborhood that welcomed travelers from the east to Alexandria. In June of 2010, however, Sidi Gaber became known for something other than its warm tourist welcome. On June 6, this area witnessed a threshold event in the mobilization of Egyptians for the revolution that would come the following year: the brutal death of 28-year-old Khaled Said. In addition to a handful of well-organized silent protests, this event sparked the creation of two Facebook pages that memorialized Said's death. The first page to appear was in Arabic and administrated by Wael Ghomin, the now famed political activist and Google executive. While this page was geared toward Egyptians living in Egypt, the second Facebook page to appear was in English and directed toward an international audience of supporters and allies. Two years later, to date, the English Facebook page has more than 215,000 followers.

This presentation employs the framework of Kenneth Burke's identification to look at how the English language Facebook page, "We are all Khaled Said," participated in the creation of a global movement for national change—a movement marked by protests around the world that have transcended the local/global demarcation and lent meaningful support to Egypt's national revolution. In particular, I ask how the anonymous administrator of this page persuades his international audience to transition from observers to participants in the revolution. How, in other words, can we begin to critically understand the use of social media as a tool for social protest, as more than a conduit of information, and as a tool for engagement and mobilization? I argue that the administrator of "We are all Khaled Said" persuades his audience by creating an identification with page followers that hinges on the mutually embodied experiences of the revolution, embodied experiences that protestors and supporters come to share through the affordances of Facebook's design.

I examine the page's facilitation of this mutually embodied experience in three steps. First, I investigate Facebook's newsfeed that, according to Kristin

Arola, "encourages us to understand ourselves in relation to the action of others" (8). Second, I analyze the ways in which the images posted to this Facebook page testify to the embodied experiences of social protestors in Egypt and around the world while simultaneously eliciting parallel embodied responses and actions from page followers. Finally, I track the unique ways that the administrator of the "We are all Khaled Said" Facebook page employs the "events" feature to solidify his identification with page followers. These "events" underscore the implications of digitally facilitated embodied experiences within a platform such as Facebook and draw our attention to the ways in which these experiences have contributed to a revolution that successfully removed a dictator after more than a quarter century of being in power.

Identification and Embodiment

Following his historical overview of the variety of definitions that have been given to rhetoric, in *A Rhetoric of Motives* Kenneth Burke suggests that "persuasion" is the "Edenic" term from which these definitions have "Babylonically" split (586). What has remained—regardless of how one defines rhetoric—is the role of identification as the root of persuasion. Burke writes that a speaker can only persuade his audience insofar as he can "talk his language by speech, gesture, tonality, order, image, attitude, idea, *identifying* your ways with his" (579). It is in this way that identification creates consubstantiality between the speaker and her audience. Without this consubstantiality with the audience, there is no identification with and thus no persuasion of the audience.

As Burke explains, the ability of the rhetor to identify her ways with those of her audience is shaped by both intrinsic and extrinsic elements of the rhetorical scene. While the primary intrinsic elements that the rhetor must consider are the opinions held by the audience, extrinsic elements include what Burke simply describes as "non-verbal factors" (588). He writes: "Hence, the rhetorician's exploiting of opinion leads into the analysis of non-verbal factors wholly extrinsic to the rhetorical expression considered purely as a verbal structure" (586). Here, I suggest that one of these extrinsic factors is the embodiment of both the speaker and the audience.

For Burke, the bodies of both the speaker and her audience are at the root of the speaker's need to create identification. Identification is the necessary response to the division between these two parties—a division that originates in their corporeal bodies. In *A Rhetoric of Motives*, Burke writes: "Identification is compensatory to division. If men were not apart from one another, there would be no need for the rhetorician to proclaim their unity. If men were wholly and truly of one substance, absolute communication would be of man's very essence" (546). This division of substance that is at the root of rhetoric begins with the flesh, with what Burke refers to in *A Grammar of Motives* as the "first 'biological revolution,'" the "'birth trauma' due to the bursting of the body that has been made necessary by the growth of the fetus to the point where the benign circle of protection, the 'enclosed garden,' had threatened to become a malign circle of confinement" (405). Thus, it is the flesh of our bodies that instigates the very need for us, as "symbol-using animals," to achieve consubstantiation and identification with our audiences through the use of rhetoric. Here, I suggest that a key means of this identification is the facilitation of a rhetorical exchange that is mutually embodied by both speaker and audience.

To this end, Katherine Hayles pushes Burke's observations about the body one step further when she addresses the situatedness of the corporeal body. Using the term "embodiment," Hayles describes the ways that speakers are not only divided from one another by the corporeal limits of their bodies but are also brought together as bodies are "always situated by the spatiotemporal coordinates of particular cultural practices, climates and physical circumstances" (qtd. in Munster 62). When speakers identify their ways with those of their audience, they are entering the spatiotemporal coordinates of their audience; they are facilitating a mutually embodied experience of rhetorical exchange. In the context of Burkean identification, the term embodiment illuminates the ways in which the "extrinsic" factors of persuasion become the building blocks of identification and enter into meaningful arrangements in the creation of a mutually embodied rhetorical experience such as I suggest we see occurring on Facebook pages like "We are all Khaled Said."

Who Was Khaled Said?

On June 6, 2010, Khaled Said entered an Internet café in Sidi Gaber that was owned by Hassan Mosbah. Reportedly, Said had with him a video that showed police corruption—members of the Egyptian police force standing over a desktop covered with illegal drugs that they had supposedly confiscated—which he was planning to post online. As Said went to upload this video online, members of the police entered the Internet café and dragged him into the street, where they proceeded to beat him to death. In an interview after the incident, the café owner remarked: "We thought they would just interrogate him or ask him questions. But they took him as he struggled with his hands behind his back and banged his head against the marble table inside here" ("Egypt Café"). The official State report of his death was that Khaled Said was a known drug user, and his cause of death was suffocation from a "cigarette containing drugs."

Said's death is only one example of the abuses occurring as a result of the "emergency law" that was a central tool of oppression used by Hosni Mubarak's regime for more than thirty years. As onlookers witnessed Said's beating in a doorway on the side of the street and images of his battered body were uploaded to the Web, Egyptians immediately took to the streets in protest. The night of his death, protestors gathered in Cairo to demand the resignation of the interior minister—many carrying before-and-after images of Said's face with text reading, "Why did he die?"

Within days, the English "We are all Khaled Said" page appeared on Facebook. The first post to this page by the administrator is an explicit call to the international community to support what would grow into the Egyptian Revolution that reached a pinnacle on January 25 of the following year. From its inception, the page's anonymous administrator has sought identification with his audience by evoking a mutually embodied experience of social protest. In what follows, I will trace how he draws on Facebook's design to create this form of identification on multiple levels within the page.

The News Feed

One way that "We are all Khaled Said" facilitates a mutually embodied experience that allows the administrator to identify with his audience is through updates that appear on followers' news feeds. "Facebooking," we must remember, is itself an embodied cultural practice. Jason Farman illuminates the powerful connection that Facebook is able to make between cultural practice and embodied experience when he writes that interfaces such as Facebook are produced through their interactions with the embodied user. In this way, "The interface is deeply connected to our experiences of embodiment and how embodied practices get inscribed through cultural forces and habits" (63). When users sit at their computers or pull out their mobile devices and scroll through news feeds, the brief pieces of text from friends and pages such as "We are all Khaled Said" enter into new relationships with one another through the interface that brings Facebook writ large into contact with the corporal body of the user—a body that is scrolling, clicking, and commenting. The resulting mutually embodied experiences of the page "We are all Khaled Said" occur as a result of both the universality of Facebook's design (i.e., all users experience a single Facebook design) *and* the spatiotemporally embodied practice of the user. Creating packets of information that can enter these "spatiotemporal coordinates" (Hayles; qtd. in Munster), the administrator of "We are all Khaled Said" creates an identification with users by "talking [their] language by speech, gesture, tonality" and embedding his messages within the familiar and immediate design of this social networking platform.

In "The Design of Web 2.0: The Rise of the Template, The Fall of Design," Kristin Arola writes that "if we are to critically engage with the rhetoric of the interface and with Web 2.0, we must pay attention to how Web 2.0 interfaces are shaping our interactions and ourselves" (7). Facebook's news feed is a key example of this. Although the news feed has gone through several iterations over recent years, the observation can be made that this feed "encourages us to understand ourselves in relation to the actions of others" (8). The news feed brings the voices and interests of a variety of friends and groups chosen by the Facebook user into the same visual field. This visual proximity shapes the meaning acquired by these brief pieces of text that are aggregated by Facebook in the news feed. So, for example, many see the updates from "We are all Khaled Said" alongside updates from friends and family about where they've eaten dinner or gone on vacation. As these users scroll through their news feeds, they are making meaning of these small pieces of text as they exist in relation to each other and to themselves at that time.

"We are all Khaled Said" capitalizes on the design of the Facebook news feed as a way of bringing the experience of one protestor into a mutually embodied experience with Facebook followers. Insofar as this makes that which is distant to the subscriber more immediate, users are moved to see the social protest of "We are all Khaled Said" as part of the day-to-day interests of their lives. As updates from pages such as the "We are all Khaled Said" page appear in the same visual field as updates about where friends ate dinner and what their children have been up to over the holiday, subscribers begin to act in an embodied context influenced by these protests.

Testimonies of Embodied Experience

A second way that "We are all Khaled Said" creates mutually embodied experiences that contribute to the audience's identification with the administrator and his message is through the posting of images that both testify to the embodied experiences of social protestors in Egypt and elicit similar embodied responses from page followers. As I mentioned earlier, the first post on the page is an invitation to the page's international followers to participate in one of several silent protests that followed Khaled Said's death. These "silent stands" occurred mostly in Alexandria and Cairo. However, protest organizers such as this page's administrator helped spread these protests around the globe.

The administrator of "We are all Khaled Said" persuaded followers to participate in these protests in two ways. First, the administrator identified his sense of social justice with that of followers by posting an album titled "Systematic Torture and Mistreatment of Egyptian Citizens by Police Officers." The graphic and firsthand images in this album are testimonies to the embodied realities of these protestors and the mistreatment of Egyptians. As these images identify with followers' values of social justice, they also create a mutually embodied experience as followers view the images within Facebook, clicking and responding to them there. As such, the images elicit responses from viewers such as that of Jackie Anderson who commented: "oh. that is so painful to even look at. Bless him." This response is an example of what becomes a mutually embodied exchange between the page's administrator and his English-speaking audience within the design of Facebook. The second step in the page's persuasion of followers to participate in these protests occurs in a follow-up post that includes an album of international protestors around the world standing silently in black, holding pictures of Khaled Said. These images attest to the mutually embodied experiences of followers, as they post and participate on the Facebook page, engage with their lives beyond the screen, and spread the revolution as they do so.

An Invitation to Protest

A final means by which the "We are all Khaled Said" Facebook page employs embodiment in the creation of identification with page followers is through its creation of "events." These "events" reiterate the identification of the page's administrator with followers as peers in a global protest movement. Events offer a more focused and direct way to single out members and elicit their cooperative action. For example, when people are invited to an event they are asked either to "join" or to choose a "maybe" option. In the context of this Facebook page, events are a way of pushing followers to explicitly declare their supportive actions in ways that extend beyond simply "liking" posts or commenting on images.

More recent events that we see on the page are those inviting subscribers to participate in the January 25 protests of 2011—what are perhaps the most famous of the Egyptian Revolution. Although the "events" hosted by this page rarely occur in one physical location, the explicit suggestion is that they can be attended by the page's administrator and all of the page's followers. They will act together; they will be consubstantial. Suggesting as it does that all supporters of the revolution can attend these protests, these events solidify the mutually embodied experience of a global movement that the Facebook page "We are all Khaled Said" is participating in.

Conclusion

As we consider the ways in which the administrator of "We are all Khaled Said" persuades English-speaking followers of this page, we ask ourselves: What difference does this make for those who are fighting for the revolution in the streets? Here, I have offered a response to this question using a framework that extends our understanding of Burkean identification to include embodiment. When we begin to understand embodiment as a means of identification, we can begin to understand the ways in which identification has been a critical means of persuading a global audience to support this national revolution. We can begin to see the ways in which this revolution has been enacted globally in the living rooms, yards, and town centers of pro-testor-followers of this Facebook page. Here, we have been able to see that as individual followers of the page are persuaded to protest in these and other locations, they enter into a mutually embodied experience with the page's administrator—an experience of social protest that extends beyond their computer screens, their living rooms, or their town centers and reaches a global audience.

WORKS CITED

Arola, Kristin. "The Design of Web 2.0: The Rise of the Template, The Fall of Design." *Computers and Composition* 27 (2010): 4-14. Print.

Burke, Kenneth. *A Grammar of Motives and A Rhetoric of Motives.* Cleveland: Meridian, 1962. Print.

"Egypt Café Owner Describes Police Beating Death." *Asharq Alawsat.* H.H. Saudi and Research, LTD, 16 June 2010. Web. May 2012.

Farman, Jason. *Mobile Interface Theory.* New York: Routledge, 2012. Print.

Munster, Anna. *Materializing New Media: Embodiment in Information Aesthetics.* Lebanon: UP of New England, 2006. Print.

"We are All Khaled Said." *Facebook.com.* Facebook, 19 July 2010. Web. May 2012.

21

BEFORE GARRICK

Elizabeth Barry, Mistress of Emotion on the Restoration Stage

Elizabeth Tasker Davis

Theater and rhetoric have shared in practices and methods of delivery for thousands of years. Dating back to ancient Rome, Cicero and Quintilian frequently compared orators with actors—stressing the importance of the voice, eyes, face, and bodily gestures in the art of persuasion. The classical connection between drama and rhetoric persisted for centuries and strongly influenced neoclassical elocutionary theory in seventeenth- and eighteenth-century France and England.[1] Like Cicero, eighteenth-century British proponents of elocution embraced the canon of delivery as the main pursuit of rhetoric and advised that, to achieve the most persuasive and effective oratory, rhetoricians should be trained as actors in voice and body control. Yet, even though both acting and public speaking were male-only occupations that shared similar delivery methods, the acting profession in the classical and neoclassical Western traditions held a lower social status and carried a negative, feminized connotation in contrast to the masculine practice of oratory. Acting remained a marginalized profession through the early modern period, a situation further instantiated during the golden age of Shakespearean drama by the fact that all female parts in public playhouses were played only by men or boys.

After the Restoration of the Stuart monarchy in England, however, when London playhouses (which had been shut down during England's Commonwealth period) reopened, actresses, by kingly decree, took over the portrayal of female roles. The sight of women on the London stage aroused tremendous attention. Actresses enjoyed instant popularity with the public and quickly became a major rhetorical influence on British culture, but in an era dominated by patriarchy and libertinism, they were also doubly devalued in respectability—by gender and profession—as females and as actors. Public performance by females was both an attraction and a source of anxiety for British society. Publications of the period show increasing concern about morality and the negative influence that risqué and sexually exaggerated performances might have on audiences. By mid-century, England had taken a socially conservative turn toward propriety, modesty, and a feminized model of didactic benevolence. In this increasingly strict moral climate, actresses remained popular, but behavioral models continued to shift, and the neoclassical acting style, as Paul Goring argues, began to seem ostentatious as "the body [became] an important (and problematic) textual space for the symbolic inscription of politeness" (6). Along with these ideological transformations, public preferences in plays and actors mirrored a new taste for sensibility and discernment.

With England's evolving notions of decorum, it is no surprise that Elizabeth Barry, the Restoration actress who had received the highest critical acclaim and who had become a model for theatrical technique from the 1680s through the early 1700s, quickly faded from the pages of elocution theory. In the subsequent era of polite theater, the great mid-eighteenth-century actor David Garrick became a textbook example of elocutionary practice, and his legacy influenced acting theory all the way to the twentieth century. Differing in eras and genders, Barry and Garrick share somewhat in theatrical accomplishments: both enjoyed stage careers that spanned more than thirty years; both were viewed as the greatest actors of their sex in their own times; both became theater managers and amassed fortunes from the theater business; and both were recognized for their naturalistic portrayals of memorable characters. In the late seventeenth century, Barry was renowned for her natural expression of emotion and her realistic pathetic appeal in tragedy. Several decades later, Garrick was credited with transforming acting from an overly mannered declamatory style to a more multifaceted and natural style of delivery (Goring 121-25; Stone and Kahrl 23-51). Ironically, critics praised both Barry and Garrick as revolutionary in their "natural" styles. Clearly what constituted "natural" style in the late seventeenth century had changed by the mid-eighteenth century. Barry's innovations in naturalistic elocution made a strong impression on the audiences and theatrical delivery techniques of her period, but her name fell out of elocutionary theory in the latter half of the eighteenth century when the delivery style of acting diverged from that of oratory, and with it Barry's feminist impact on the history of Western rhetoric also was lost. The disparate longevity of Barry's and Garrick's legacies, then, is due to timing as well as gender.

Clearly, audiences' tastes will and do shift across generations, but it is also noteworthy that the female gender traditionally carried negative connotations in relation to delivery within the classical, neoclassical, and modern eras of Western rhetoric and drama, all of which privileged masculine delivery and its associated techniques. In ancient Rome, rhetorical theorists gendered delivery style as either Attic or Asiatic (also known as Atticist or Asianist). As Amy Richlin explains, Attic style was masculine, authoritative, and objective while Asiatic was feminine, flamboyant, and emotional; Atticist was the prescribed, clean, and trusted style; Asianist was the decried, sexy, and distrusted style; signs of femininity, such as high or faltering voice, uneven use of literary figures, erratic gesturing, and immodest or flamboyant dress were associated with acting, a profession that was considered effeminate and "suffered a diminished civil status" (100). Classical Asiatic delivery style, with its tendency toward a feminized flamboyance, was also common in the neoclassical London theaters of the Restoration and early eighteenth century where both male and female roles took on exaggerated tones in heroic tragedy and satiric comedies of manners. Nevertheless, masculinity still connoted power, as well as wit, while femininity tended to connote either empty coquetry or naïve virginity.

The combination of sexually provocative femininity and male superiority produced a complex rhetorical situation in the Restoration theater. Even though Charles II decreed that it was more fitting and natural for women to play female parts in the public theater, on the Restoration stage, as Cynthia Lowenthal states, "bodies were valorized when they were aristocratic, male, and Protestant, while the most intensely performative, aggressively veiled, and oft 'discovered' bodies were always those of women" (19). The sight of female actors performing in public, although they were wildly popular, was an intrusion into the ideologically male public sphere. Restoration actresses were emblematic of the public female, to many an aberrant and repugnant image. The authenticity of actresses disturbed the status quo; as Judith Butler argues, the performing human body is "a surface whose permeability is politically regulated" (177), and "the various acts of gender create the idea of gender" (140), but gender is an act that "[a]s in other ritual social dramas . . . requires a performance that is repeated" (178). The actresses' public performances destabilized received notions of gender and constituted an act of subversion by speaker upon audience. As Paul Goring notes, however, "flesh can bestow authority through the persuasive rhetoric of 'nature'" (19). Actresses were real female individuals who, with their unique appearances and personalities, helped introduce a more complex understanding of female roles, restrictions, and capabilities.

Outstanding actresses, such as Elizabeth Barry, influenced playwrights, genres, and audiences of their time. A supreme tragedienne, a deft comedienne, and a skilled business woman, Barry's theatrical contributions have been subject to thorough analysis from the perspective of theater history by Elizabeth Howe who notes that, for more than thirty-six years, "from 1673 to 1709 the brilliant Elizabeth Barry is known to have played 142 named parts" (9). While Barry was initially known as a comedienne, she helped establish the genre of "she-tragedy" in the 1680s and '90s, perfecting its hallmark character type: the suffering female. As multiple sources indicate, Barry acted as a conduit of emotion: she could feel as her character would and make the audience feel that way too. Barry's affectively powerful delivery was a neoclassical skill common to both acting and oratory and served as a textbook example of Restoration elocutionary standards for movement, gesture, expression, and speech.

In fact, Charles Gildon uses Barry's acting to illustrate many of his points on elocution in *The Life of Mr. Thomas Betterton* (1710), an extensive work that, despite its title, is not a biography of Betterton but rather a lively and engaging study "devoted to rules for the stage that can also be applied to the bar and pulpit" (Glen 101). Gildon's manual describes the various movements, gestures, facial expressions, and speech styles that a speaker would use to deliver persuasive performances and portray human passion. He stresses that actors must convey movement and gesture appropriate to each passion, and these motions must be visible to the spectators and also must appear natural (51-53). Likewise, Gildon describes the virtues of effective speech, whether for the stage, bar, or pulpit, as Purity, Perspicuity, Ornament, and Hability (or Aptitude) (93). Gildon also underlines that, to be convincing, an actor "must vary with his Argument, that is, carry the Person in all his Manners and Qualities . . . in every Action and Passion . . . that his Eyes, his Looks or Countenance, Motions of the Body, Hands and Feet, be all of a Piece" (34). Praising the naturalness of Barry's acting as outstanding among her peers (both male and female), Gildon states: "Among those Players, who seem always to be in earnest, I must not omit the Principal, the incomparable Mrs. Barry; her Action is always just, and produc'd naturally by the Sentiments of the part, which she acts" (39).

Barry's acting style apparently was not untaught genius but rather a skill that she cultivated through training. Very early in her career, it is rumored, John Wilmot, Earl of Rochester, saw Barry perform, pronounced that she had no ear for line-reading, and made a bet that he could transform her into a successful actress. Although the circumstances of how and why Rochester decided to train Barry are speculation, sometime during 1675 and 1676 he did train her in acting, and she became his mistress and protégé. As eighteenth-century writer Edmund Curll tells it, Rochester taught Barry to "enter into the Nature of each Sentiment; perfectly changing herself . . . into the Person, not merely by the proper Stress or Sounding of the Voice, but feeling really, and being in the Humour, the Person represented, was supposed to be in" (Highfill et al. 314; Howe 114). Comments from colleague later in Barry's career support that she maintained this method approach. For example, fellow actress, Mrs. Bradshaw, states that "Mrs. Barry" taught her to "make herself Mistress of her Part, and leave the Figure and Action to Nature" (Highfill et al. 324).

These descriptions of Barry's method for developing her characters and portraying naturalistic emotion sound similar to the "naturalized" style of acting that theater historians credit actor David Garrick with introducing to English theater in the 1740s. Garrick biographers, George Stone and George Kahrl, explain that he "studied the individual characteristics of the role he played and became the person personated" (31). Garrick's techniques are well documented in many mid-century works on acting and elocutionary theory, including Aaron Hill's *The Art of Acting*, John Hill's *The Actor: A Treatise on the Art of Playing*, and Denis Diderot's *Le paradoxe sur le comédien*. As Diderot saw, Garrick was "able to make the audience believe he was the character he was portraying" (Stone and Kahrl 41). Although we have no live recordings of Barry or Garrick acting, numerous sources support that they both achieved an astonishing level of realism in their performances; these sources also describe the delivery techniques each actor used.

Through the multiple modes of expression, carriage, gestures, and voice, Barry became the mistress of emotion. Cibber describes how Barry used her body and voice to convey pathos:

> A Presence of elevated Dignity, her Mein and Motion superb and grace-fully majestick; her Voice full, clear, and strong, so that no Violence of Passion could be too much for her; And when Distress or Tenderness possess'd her, she subsided into the most affecting Melody and Softness. In the Art of exciting Pity she had a Power beyond all the Actresses I have yet seen. (95)

As Cibber explains, Barry captivated audiences with her fluidity in depicting changing emotions. Comedian Anthony Aston said that Barry's face "some-what preceded her Action, as the latter did her Words, her Face ever express-ing the Passions" (Highfill et al. 324). Her technique, then, included a pattern of succession in which her facial expression spoke first, before gestures and words. In its overall effect, as Jocelyn Powell notes, Barry was the creator of "a new acting style designed to 'stir rather than penetrate human nature' and . . . tragic actors like Betterton then followed her lead" (Howe 108). By today's standards, Barry's acting might seem extremely melodramatic, calling to mind the great actress of early cinema, Greta Garbo, master of expression and gesture in silent film, who successfully broke into "talkies." But Barry's acting style was also frequently described as "just or judicious," suggesting that she maintained "a high degree of control" in her delivery (Highfill et al. 324). Gerard Langbaine comments that she "did the poet all the *Justice* so admirable an actress, when she most exerts herself, could do" when acting in Thomas Southerne's *The Innocent Adultery* (136). Barry conveyed feminine emotion through facial expression, movement, gesture, and speech, but she also demonstrated a level of control and nuance typically associated, ironi-cally, with masculine neoclassical elocution.

By Garrick's time, however, the formality and restraint associated with the neoclassical delivery style began to seem stiff and archaic to audiences. Goring suggests that mid-century acting may have evolved into this state of artificial mannerisms, not so much from the influence of Restoration actors, but more from the influence of Charles Gildon's widely read publications on elocution and oratory, which may have exaggerated the similarities of style between Restoration stage elocution and classical oratory and declamation (121-25). From her reading of Gildon, Howe conjectures that the neoclassical naturalistic style of acting was not based on naturalness itself but rather guidelines on ingrained habitudes from "a vast array of seventeenth-century books describing correct social behavior" (Howe 13). Whether we accept Goring's or Howe's explanations of neoclassical acting, its high melodra-matic style was still prevalent on the stage when Garrick introduced an alter-native elocutionary style through which he strove to convey emotional complexity and subtlety rather than purity. As Stone and Kahrl explain, "conventional (rhetorical) theory . . . conceives of the universal nature of the emotions in mankind, and seeks ways to communicate them in stylized and often symbolic fashion" (30). Yet, Garrick's style differed from Restoration declamation in that he gave greater "attention to detail in the idiosyncrasy of characterization, the particularization . . . rather than the generalized universal appearance" that in effect "wrought a change significant to all acting" (28). Since Garrick's time, the delivery methods of acting and oratory diverged and have followed mostly separate trajectories to the present day.

During the Restoration, however, acting and oratory shared the canon of delivery—even though they differed in their prescribed delivery styles—but Barry's delivery style was not her only contribution to rhetoric. Beginning in the 1680s, Barry transcended her early image of witty Restoration comic heroine, and she developed her specialty in tragedy, the genre that she helped to feminize into she-tragedy. She-tragedy constitutes an important eighteenth-century site for feminist rhetoric by exposing dysfunctions in patriarchy, which were not only affecting women at that time but the entire British culture. At the forefront of this dramatic genre, Barry created a new model of female psychological realism on the stage and thereby broke the patriarchal mold of the female as fitting neatly into one of three categories: virgin, wife, or whore. As August Staub explains, dramatic tragedy functions as enthymeme, building group consensus and linking myths together in an enacted, "public and entirely visual event" (9). Barry's tragic heroines were enthymematic in illustrating the dehumanizing aspects of early modern patriarchy, particularly as it impacted females.

In her roles, Barry posed an argument for noticing and sympathizing with females, particularly suffering females, in a male-dominated society. With her pathetic style established, Barry became renowned for playing fallen women as sympathetic characters often thrust into unjust situations in both comedy and tragedy. As pointed out by Howe, Barry's work gave focus to the sexual double standard in English society:

> It was only when Barry's mesmeric talents were employed in the portrayal of prostitutes and mistresses that their problematic situation was given detailed consideration and their sufferings vividly realized. . . . Thanks to Barry, the prostitute and the mistress became a source of conflict and debate in the theater and so contributed to the fresh upsurge of interest in women and women's problems at the end of the [seventeenth] century. (130)

Barry's portrayals of women outside the margins of respectability showed them as victims of social circumstance. Her dramatic rhetoric in its depiction of social injustice was persuasive in an indirect and artistic context, different from the direct persuasive appeals of the classical orator, the fundamentalist preacher, or the even the nineteenth-century female suffragette, but persuasive nonetheless.

Barry's first noted tragic performance was in the role of Monimia in Thomas Otway's *The Orphan* in 1680, followed in 1682 by her creation of Belvidera, the suffering wife, in Otway's greatest tragedy, *Venice Preserved*. Although Belvidera was not the lead character in the play, her role as a helpless female victim caught in the machinations of a deadly political plot was, perhaps, the most pathetic. Critics and biographers have noted how Otway's real-life, unrequited love for Barry formed her as his tragic muse[2] (Highfill et al. 315-16). Howe goes as far to say that Barry's influence on Otway is what caused the focus of tragedy to shift from the hero to the heroine (113). Inspired by Barry's incredible gift for arousing pathos in the audience, other playwrights began writing plays for her tragic acting skills. Thomas Southerne, for example, designed his most successful tragedy, *The Fatal Marriage*, specifically for the talents of Barry. In his dedication, Southerne writes of Mrs. Barry, "I made the play for her part, and her part has made the play for me; . . . by her power, and spirit of playing, she has breath'd a soul into it" (Jordan and Love 10-11). High praise from critics and the public further make clear Barry's contribution to the successful initial run of *The Fatal Marriage*. Jordan and Love cite a number of contemporary reviews of the play, including a letter from a member of the Windham family of Felbrigg, which states, "I never saw Mrs. Barry act with so much passion as she does in it; I could not forbear being moved even to tears to see her act" (5). Southerne's remarks and the high praise that Barry received from critics and the public make clear the extent of the actress's influence on tragedy, which went far beyond her initial connection with Otway to encompass a wide audience of fans who were captivated and moved by her performances.

Barry inspired and created provocative and memorable female characters whose existence challenged simplistic female stereotypes by arousing public interest in what a woman could actually do or how she might truly feel. Howe notes that no other actress of her era played near the variety of character types that Barry portrayed, which included comic ingénues, adulterous wives, female libertines, prostitutes and fallen women, mothers, and, her specialty, the tragic heroine (81). In addition to her innovatively emotional acting style, Barry garnered a level of public acclaim unprecedented for a stage performer during the Restoration. In the 1680s, she became the first actor (male or female) to be granted a benefit performance in which she alone received all of the night's profits, a perk that no other performer received before 1695 and one that made her annual salary exceed even the top-paid actor, Thomas Betterton. She also had responsibilities for collecting the acting company's pay from the Lord Chamberlain and distributing it to players. In 1695 Barry, Thomas Betterton, and Ann Bracegirdle successfully petitioned the king to be able to form their own theater company in which they were the principal owners (Howe 28-30).

The career of Elizabeth Barry, from the 1670s until her retirement in 1710, is one of the greatest professional female success stories of the late seventeenth- and early eighteenth centuries. Not only did her popularity continue to rise over the course of her career, but she increased her income through theater business management and ownership. Like many actresses, however, Barry's personal reputation was one of sexual promiscuity, and critics and satirists in her own time often disparaged her financial success as another indication of insatiability. But, in posterity, Barry's many professional achievements outweigh her notoriety. To those accomplishments already mentioned, I would add her prefiguring David Garrick in developing a naturalistic acting style and the significance of her protofeminist performances in transforming the female image in Western society. One wonders, then, with her considerable public-speaking and business skills, and her audience rapport, what Elizabeth Barry might have done if the venues of podium and pulpit had been available to her during her lifetime.

NOTES

[1] In the eighteenth century, the classical term *elecutio* was transformed into the modern English term *elocution*, and its meaning changed from the classic meaning of style to its modern meaning of delivery.

[2] Otway's feelings for Barry are proven beyond a doubt by the expression of his tortured passions in five letters written to her sometime in the early 1680s. Otway's letters to Barry were first published anonymously in 1697 and later attributed to Otway in 1713.

WORKS CITED

Butler, Judith. *Gender Trouble.* New York: Routledge, 1999. Print.

Cibber, Colley. *An Apology for the Life of Colley Cibber, Comedian.* 1740. Ed. John Maurice Evans. New York: Garland, 1987. Print.

Diderot, Denis. *Le paradoxe sur le comédien.* Paris, 1770. Print.

Gildon, Charles. *The Life of Mr. Thomas Betterton.* London: Frank Cass and Company, 1969. Print.

Glen, Rochelle. "Charles Gildon." *Eighteenth-Century British and American Rhetorics and Rhetoricians.* Ed. Michael Moran. Wesport: Greenwood, 1994. 99-103. Print.

Goring, Paul. *The Rhetoric of Sensibility.* Cambridge: Cambridge UP, 2005. Print.

Highfill, Philip H. Jr., Kalman A. Burnim, and Edward A. Langhans. *A Biographical Dictionary of Actors, Actresses, Musicians, Dancers, Managers and Other Stage Personnel in London, 1660-1800.* Vol. 2. Carbondale: Southern Illinois UP, 1987.

Hill, Aaron. *The Art of Acting.* London, 1753. Print.

Hill, John. *The Actor: A Treatise on the Art of Playing.* London, 1750. Print.

Howe, Elizabeth. *The First English Actresses.* Cambridge: Cambridge UP, 1992. Print.

Jordan, Robert, and Harold Love, eds. *The Works of Thomas Southerne.* Vol. 2. Oxford: Clarendon, 1988. Print.

Langbaine, Gerard. *An Account of the English Dramatic Poets,* 1691. Print.

Lowenthal, Cynthia. *Performing Identities on the Restoration Stage.* Carbondale: Southern Illinois UP, 2003. Print.

Richlin, Amy. "Gender and Rhetoric: Producing Manhood in the Schools." *Roman Eloquence: Rhetoric in Society and Literature.* Ed. William J. Dominik. London: Routledge, 1997. Print.

Staub, August."The Enthymeme and the Invention of Troping in Greek Drama." *Drama As Rhetoric/Rhetoric As Drama: Theatre Symposium.* Ed. Stanley Vincent Longman. Tuscaloosa: U of Alabama P, 1998. 7-13. Print.

Stone, George Winchester Jr., and George M. Kahrl. *David Garrick: A Critical Biography.* Carbondale: Southern Illinois UP, 1979. Print.

22

"WE THE PEOPLE"—OF COLOR

Environmental Justice Activists, the US Constitution, and the Public Work of Rhetoric

M. Karen Powers

> The tension between inclusive and restrictive definitions of the national community has a long history. There has never been a single answer to the question "Who is an American?"
>
> — Eric Foner

Since the US Constitution was written more than two hundred years ago, rhetorical reframings of this canonical document have repeatedly redefined fundamental principles such as liberty, justice, and equality at the center of idealized American democracy. The most striking reinterpretations in the course of this lengthy and controversial history, including the abrupt mid- to late-1800s' shift from constitutionally sanctioned slavery to some measure of constitutionally endorsed protections from racial discrimination, have hinged on the question: "Who is an American?" (Foner 150). Invoking ideologies of race to reinterpret the nation's foundational document in the interest of social progress continues in the present era, with more recent engagements in this profoundly rhetorical process tending to animate a politics of difference that resists rather than reifies a monolithic and hegemonic national identity. In one such instance, the Environmental Justice Movement, a loose alliance of church, labor, civil rights, and community groups that emerged in the 1980s in opposition to mainstream environmentalism, explicitly challenged the meaning of national identity in the contemporary United States by revising the Preamble to the Constitution in their "Principles of Environmental Justice" (Lee xiii-xiv). A major purpose for writing this countertext—to contest deceptively inclusive notions of "We the People"—situates the movement among "counterpublic spheres," sites that Gerard Hauser designates as "rich source[s] for studying how marginalized groups constitute arenas of discourse in which they can address issues of identity, establish action agendas, forge group solidarity, and challenge authority" (xi). Citing ongoing racism, classism, and poverty as pivotal circumstances that motivate their participation in current environmental debates, activists rely largely on disidentification with "We the People" to accomplish precisely the goals Hauser delineates as they "call attention to the ways the disparate distribution of wealth and power often leads to correlative social upheaval and the unequal distribution of environmental degradation and toxicity" (Adamson et al. 5).

Collaboratively drafted in 1991 at the First National People of Color Environmental Leadership Summit in Washington, DC, "Principles" dismantles the bifurcation of natural and human worlds that authorizes the traditional focus on wilderness protection. Such a rhetorical reframing fashioned by a historically disenfranchised group broadens the scope of what might be considered environmental issues and affects what can be thought, spoken, written, and imagined about threats to the natural environment, particularly as those threats disproportionately affect people of color. "Principles" writers embody Hauser's "effective change agents" when they illuminate this artificial division that has long fostered environmental racism, although such a concept was unnamed until 1982 when it entered into the debate in rural, predominantly African-American Warren County, North Carolina (xii). Attending a demonstration protesting a municipal solid waste landfill for PCB-tainted soil, Benjamin Chavis invented the phrase "environmental racism" to describe and denounce "racial discrimination in environmental policy-making, enforcement of regulations and laws, and targeting of communities of color for toxic waste disposal and siting of polluting industries" (qtd. in Bullard 32). As a rhetorical practice that interjects and complicates identity politics coalescing around designations of "American," "Principles" both reshapes environmentalism and reconstitutes the Constitution by reframing the historical text in ways that reveal how a putative homogeneous national identity sanctions injustices affecting the contemporary US's multiracial constituency.

Disrupting commonplace language that cloaks disproportionate access to liberty, justice, and equality with a rhetoric of social unity, "Principles" draws attention to repercussions of persistent racial injustices by juxtaposing "We the People" with "We, the people of color." This text alludes to past deliberations about citizenship to refocus the current debate on long-standing conflicts that Donna Chavis resurrects with her incisive question: "Aren't we protected by the Constitution?" (qtd. in Lee 209). Chavis, a member of the Summit's National Planning Committee, critiques history's standard formulation of American identity that glosses the "many forms of genocide"—"cultural genocide," "spiritual genocide," and "physical genocide"—that continue to threaten minority peoples (qtd. in Lee 209). This lingering divide between democratic ideals and material realities for people of color even in the late-twentieth century drove the movement's agenda to disidentify with the community constructed by the Constitution, a manifest document the US audience would likely immediately recognize, if not recite from memory.

As a detailed comparison of the two preambles illustrates, "Principles" closely imitates the language and themes of the original document to challenge the authority and authenticity of its basic tenets rather than to affirm them. The US Constitution's Preamble reads:

> We the People of the United States, in Order to form a more perfect
> Union, establish Justice, insure domestic tranquility, provide for the com-
> mon defence, promote the general Welfare, and secure the Blessings of
> Liberty to ourselves and our posterity, do ordain and establish this Con-
> stitution for the United States of America.

The "Principles" preamble resonates with the dominant document in terms of
lexicon, syntax, style, structure, and cadence but, rather than signal allegiance
to a revered historical discourse, explicitly rejects this official rhetoric of social
unity by publicly declaring a dramatically different notion of shared identity:

> We, the people of color, gathered together at this multinational People of
> Color Environmental Leadership Summit, to begin to build a national
> and international movement of all peoples of color to fight the destruc-
> tion and taking of our lands and communities, do hereby re-establish our
> spiritual interdependence to the sacredness of our Mother Earth; to
> respect and celebrate each of our cultures, languages and beliefs about
> the natural world and our roles in healing ourselves; to insure environ-
> mental justice; to promote economic alternatives which would contribute
> to the development of environmentally safe livelihoods; and, to secure
> our political, economic and cultural liberation that has been denied for
> over 500 years of colonization and oppression, resulting in the poisoning
> of our communities and land and the genocide of our peoples, do affirm
> and adopt these Principles of Environmental Justice. (Lee xiii)

Although the "Principles" preamble is significantly longer, a characteristic stemming from the countertext's strategy to both imitate and elaborate the
original language, the two texts are essentially one-sentence position statements announcing citizens' presumed rights and privileges in participatory
democracy. Two central concepts are named with identical or similar nouns:
"Justice"/"environmental justice" and "Liberty"/"liberation." The "Principles" preamble appropriates (and once modifies) several of the Constitution's
version's verbs: "establish"/"re-establish," "insure," "promote," and
"secure." In one sense, the preambles are similar prefatory statements in that
they assemble their constituencies around shared identities, establish their
basic premises and promises, and prepare their audiences for the respective
texts that follow.

In another sense, the two documents' dissimilarities are most telling,
given the Environmental Justice Movement's articulated differences that
build multicultural group solidarity to renounce the Constitution's authority
to establish a single identity. The constitutional preamble uses the phrase
"We the People of the United States" to construct community largely in
terms of geographic and national boundaries. These few words have historically sufficed to inscribe a melting pot notion of American citizenship that
continues to prevail. These few words have traditionally intimated one people, unified not just by physical demarcations but ostensibly by common ideological, sociocultural, economic, and political mores. "Principles" changes
the historical document's venerated pronouncement of national community

to counter this official and widely circulated text that assumes and authorizes a complex of Eurocentric ideologies defining race, class, nation, culture, history, and democracy. Revising "We the People" to read "We, the people of color" not only signals a striking disidentification with essentialist expectations tied to established ideas of US identity, but it also reconstructs community to contravene the standard story, to refuse the implicit invitation to assimilation.

The environmental justice text alters the opening phrase of the Constitution's Preamble to create an idea of community that coalesces around race. Signaling resistance to subjugation under "We the People," "We, the people of color" disrupts an undifferentiated identity that renders invisible diverse peoples, as well as lends credence to traditional we-are-all-in-this-together environmentalism. The revision of the Constitution's powerful three-word phrase weights the dominant language with the racist and exploitative views it sustains to expose mainstream environmentalism's dubious egalitarianism. The point turns on this logic: If environmental degradation equally affects "We the People," the reality that only some people, typically people of color and poor people, live intimately with the life-threatening consequences while others grapple with such problems from a relatively safe distance defies explanation. Kristin Shrader-Frechette notes that the dilemma is the result of a "tilted playing field," and she argues that this asymmetry that environmental justice activists deem untenable is "created by the unequal power of vested interests," a repercussion unacknowledged in "We the People" but emphasized in "We, the people of color" (186). The Constitution's Preamble and mainstream environmentalism share a dependence on universalized humanism, a stance deeply embedded in a disingenuous rhetoric of inclusion. As a consequence, unequal access to power is disregarded and legitimate conflicts of race embedded in environmental debates are suppressed, subsumed under the ostensibly common goal of human well-being.

Although both preambles appear to privilege unity over difference, the dissimilar articulations of community announced in their very brief opening phrases are significant. Unlike the Constitution's Preamble, the "Principles" equivalent recognizes that different social and geographic locations, histories, worldviews, and material conditions shape the terms of national citizenship. Three times, "Principles" writers counter a rhetoric of social wholeness, which typically works either to wholly exclude or to wholly assimilate, with a rhetoric of diversity. First, they proclaim that "We, the people of color" defy definition in terms of geographic/ national boundaries since they comprise a "multinational" community. This explicit resistance to the conflation of nation-state and community is again underscored when they pledge to build a "national and international movement of all peoples of color." Finally, they construct community with boundaries elastic enough "to respect and celebrate each of [their] cultures, languages, and beliefs about the natural world." Adopting race as a political category that disrupts boundaries of nation, geography, culture, language, and belief system allows the Environmental

Justice Movement to take steps toward what Iris Marion Young calls an "openness to unassimilated otherness" (320).

"Principles" writers challenge the constitutional Preamble's homogeneous idea of community, not by replacing it with an analogous vision but by interjecting a "politics of difference [that] lays down institutional and ideological means of recognizing and affirming differently identifying groups in two basic senses: giving political representation to group interests and celebrating the distinctive cultures and characteristics of different groups" (Young 319). "Principles" writers do not dismiss the idea of community but reconfigure it as a cultural formation that attends to the tensions between unity and difference embedded in the question, "Who is an American?" (Foner 150). As they express their intention to join in a common struggle against "500 years of colonization and oppression," they vow, in the same breath, "to respect and celebrate each of [their] cultures, languages, and beliefs." It is not surprising then that the word "community" does not appear in their preamble, while "communities," the plural form, appears twice. In the first phrase of the text, "Principles" writers claim the right to self-definition, describing themselves in ways that resist assimilation into standard interpretations of "We the People." Writing their own preamble serves as a rhetorical means of critiquing the unity-in-sameness ideology recognizable not only in historical discourses of nation such as the Constitution's Preamble but also in more recent articulations of intersections between human and natural worlds such as late twentieth-century environmentalism.

If the environmental justice preamble departs from the Constitution's model by constructing a different rhetoric of community, that strategy is reinforced by offering an alternative treatment of history. Despite the fact that the Constitution's Preamble registers a singularly symbolic moment in American history, the official reorganization of the former colonies into the United States, the text is largely disconnected from the past. In fact, except for one allusion to the future in which the framers hope to "secure the blessings of Liberty" not only for themselves but for their "Posterity," the Constitution's preamble is fixed in a timeless present. This separation of culture from history lends an aura of objectivity and universality, supporting the illusion that the United States is, has always been, and will always be a cohesive nation of one people. Conversely, although the "Principles" preamble is also written in the present tense, multiple references to the past situate the Environmental Justice Movement and the multicultural peoples for whom it speaks within particular sociocultural, economic, political, and historical contexts.

Moreover, "Principles" writers speak explicitly of beginnings, not to break with the past but to claim it. They have gathered "to begin to build a national and international movement of all peoples of color to fight the destruction and taking of [their] lands and communities." The preamble thus works as a rhetorical overture for a text that does not just acknowledge history but turns on the belief that the past and the present are woven together to create the very material realities that have necessitated declarations like

"Principles." In fact, one of the preamble's primary purposes is to mark the commencement of a collective endeavor to expose, interrogate, and transform current oppressive politics and practices that are authorized by particular versions of history. While the Constitution's preamble tacitly disavows a legacy of atrocities marring American history such as the enslavement of Africans and the attempted extermination of Native Americans, ironically in full swing at the time of its writing, the "Principles" preamble emphasizes how this past works in the present. The writers use passive voice, never overtly naming those responsible for the "destruction and taking of [their] lands and communities," "over 500 years of colonization and oppression," and "the genocide of [their] peoples," but implicit references to the devastating impact of European expansionism on the Americas are unmistakable.

Perhaps equally clear is the presentation of the Constitution's Preamble as a representative imperial narrative that supports ideologies authorizing neocolonial conditions that have shaped the lives of multiple minority groups even in the early decades of the twenty-first century. The Preamble to the Constitution functions as a scaffold on which "Principles" writers stand as they invoke, embellish, rewrite, and ultimately dismantle dominant ideologies established by past interpretations of the canonical text. The Constitution was adopted in 1787 to "form a more perfect Union, establish Justice, insure domestic Tranquility, provide for the common defence, promote the general Welfare, and secure the Blessings of Liberty." In response, the "Principles" preamble invokes those same tenets to declare a similar commitment to vital social reconstruction. Yet, opening with language that promises to echo ideologies embedded in one of the most well-known artifacts of American public life and political culture, only to openly flout those expectations by radically altering the document, suggests that the environmental justice preamble operates, in large part, not merely to resist but to reconstitute this text. Out of this written retort emerges a rhetoric of social justice that redefines environmentalism by means of a dramatic reframing of the Constitution, particularly as that document mis/understands and mis/represents "We the People" at this moment in history.

Appropriating and modifying the Constitution's preamble, a particularly powerful idiom of nation, provides "Principles" writers a rhetorical strategy for highlighting the failure of "We the People" to achieve the aims stated in one of the nation's most hallowed cultural texts. At least for significant numbers of people of color, those promised ideals are yet to be realized. More than two centuries after the ratification of the Constitution's Preamble, the environmental justice equivalent works to discredit key American cultural myths embedded in the historical document. For people of color, there is no "Tranquility" when "colonization and oppression" result in "the poisoning of [their] communities and land and the genocide of [their] peoples." There is no "common defence" when people of color must continue to "fight the destruction and taking of [their] lands and communities." There is no "general Welfare" when "environmentally safe livelihoods" are scarce for people of color. There are no "Blessings of Liberty" when people of color continue to struggle "to secure [their] political, cultural, and economic liberation." In short, for people of color facing environmental hazards, there is no "Justice." The juxtaposition of the historical Preamble to the US Constitution with the daringly different preamble to the "Principles of Environmental Justice" is a deliberate and courageous rhetorical move, one that makes a pointed political statement about how environmental problems might be more broadly demarcated and more fairly adjudicated if "We the People" is defined in ways that would genuinely acknowledge and truly value a multicultural democracy. To further that agenda, "Principles" writers exemplify Hauser's "capacitated citizens": devising efficacious rhetorical processes of disidentification, reinterpretation, and persuasion, they revise the mainstream definition of environmentalism to foreground inextricable links among social, economic, and environmental problems (xii). At the same time these activists challenge racist ideologies embedded in environmental politics and policies, they also bring to the fore sociocultural differences that have historically been expunged in uncritical interpretations of "We the People."

Such powerful rhetorics of resistance temper sobering observations like one recently voiced by political scholar Chris Hedges who maintains that "the civic, patriotic, and political language we use to describe ourselves remains unchanged. We pay fealty to the same national symbols and iconography. We find our collective identity in the same national myths. We continue to deify the founding fathers" (27). While the activists who organized The First National People of Color Environmental Leadership Summit and wrote the "Principles of Environmental Justice" would likely concede Hedges's concluding point—"[T]he America we celebrate is an illusion. It does not exist"—they would just as likely take exception to their inclusion in his collective "we" for the same reasons that motivate their staunch resistance to assimilation into "We the People" (27). Mindful of rhetoric's "performative power" to serve "liberatory ends" (Hauser xii), these activists reanimate the question perennially, provoking endeavors to reframe the US Constitution: "What of those within the 'circle of we?'" (Foner 153). In answer, the "Principles of Environmental Justice" posits the "fundamental moral view that all life is sacred and that justice is an inescapable imperative in human society," a principle at the center of the public work of rhetoric, a principle at the heart of radical social transformation, a principle essential to achieving a more perfect union for us all (Madison et al. 53).

WORKS CITED

Adamson, Joni, Mei Mei Evans, and Rachel Stein, eds. *The Environmental Justice Reader: Politics, Poetics and Pedagogy.* Tucson: U of Arizona P, 2002. Print.

Bullard, Robert D. *Confronting Environmental Racism: Voices from the Grassroots.* Boston: South End P, 1993. Print.

Foner, Eric. *Who Owns History? Rethinking the Past in a Changing World.* New York: Hill and Wang, 2002. Print.

Hauser, Gerard. Foreword. *The Public Work of Rhetoric: Citizen-Scholars and Civic Engagement.* Ed. John M. Ackerman and David J. Coogan. Columbia: U of South Carolina P, 2010. ix-xii. Print.

Hedges, Chris. *Death of the Liberal Class.* New York: Nation Books, 2010. Print.

Lee, Charles, ed. *Proceedings: The First National People of Color Environmental Leadership Summit.* Washington, DC: United Church of Christ Commission for Racial Justice, 1991. Print.

Madison, Isaiah, Vernice Miller, and Charles Lee. "The Principles of Environmental Justice: Formation and Meaning." *Proceedings: The First National People of Color Environmental Leadership Summit.* Ed. Charles Lee. Washington, DC: United Church of Christ Commission for Racial Justice, 1991. 49-55. Print.

Shrader-Frechette, Kristin. *Environmental Justice: Creating Equality, Reclaiming Democracy.* Oxford: Oxford UP, 2002. Print.

Young, Iris Marion. "The Ideal of Community and the Politics of Difference." *Feminism/Postmodernism.* Ed. Linda J. Nicholson. New York: Routledge, 1990. 300-23. Print.

23

HIDING AND SEEKING RHETORICAL VISIBILITY OF LGBTQ PEOPLE AT THE SMITHSONIAN

A Theory of Postmortem Rhetorical Agency[1]

Jessica L. Shumake

"FINISH THE FUCKING COMIC!" is the message Marguerite Van Cook, co-illustrator of David Wojnarowicz's then, still unfinished graphic memoir *Seven Miles a Second*, received—from the dead Wojnarowicz—while reading her own Tarot cards (Beronä). Scholars in various disciplines tend to relegate after-death communication to Gothic literature written to entertain, to "the non-Western or premodern" or to "the neurotic or infantile mind" (Mitchell 7-8). However, the prospect of completing the unfinished work of the deceased is fraught with the same risks as the enactment of rhetorical agency in any context because all communicative transactions require writers and speakers to conjure an imagined, ideal, or actual interlocutor.[2] Despite the fact that mediumistic devices, such as the Tarot, tend to be disqualified as mere poetic whimsy, folk superstition, or childish ideation, the Tarot has been used as a vehicle for the livings' projections of agency to precipitate a project's completion, as it was for Van Cook.

I contend that through the paradox of censorship at the Smithsonian in 2010 Wojnarowicz's postmortem rhetorical agency increased by propelling him to national public recognition and visibility. My focus here is rhetorical agency—a rhetor's ability to effect change—under circumstances where he or she is constrained by a range of discursive, sociopolitical, and ideological forces.[3] Moreover, I acknowledge that death is a serious material barrier to an embodied rhetor carrying out world in the world.

My interest is in reframing individual longings for communication or communion with Wojnarowicz alongside a collective need to revivify his life world, dream world, and the density of his struggle. I also aim to work through the process of imaging what shape collective loci of encounters with the artist might take. These encounters may include consideration of armed collective resistance given that in *Close to the Knives* there are numerous instances where Wojnarowicz contemplates armed resistance against agents of the state who sought to entrap gay men, enforce bigoted laws against same-sex acts, and/or to quarantine those affected and infected by AIDS. I mention the latter because in the process of giving new life to Wojnarowicz's legacy—through public protest, social commentary, and archival methods—one is likely to be surprised by how radical and untamable Wojnarowicz is as a rhetor. Only once have I embraced the freedom to assign his writing to students, specifically the essay "Postcards from America X Rays from Hell" in *Close to the Knives* (111-23). Herein I asked students in a course that serves as a survey of the rhetorical tradition how, in Wojnarowicz's own words, "[m]aking the private into something public has terrific repercussions . . . and [in so doing] the term 'general public' disintegrates" (*Close* 121). The refusal to engage the world in an impersonal or general way, in part, issues from Wojnarowicz's commitment to bringing attention to his everyday life.

Rhetoric then, for the artist, is a series of practical interventions that arise in response to material needs and intersect with the rough ground of civic action based on ideals about what constitutes a livable life. As a rhetor, Wojn-arowicz is concerned with the enactment of gathering places for reflection and action or the dialectical relationship between *vita contemplative* and *vita activa*. For Wojnarowicz, *vita contemplative* (a social action agenda) and *vita active* (the cultivation of a rich inner intellectual and imaginative life) cannot and should not be separated. Thus, Wojnarowicz's postmortem rhetorical agency helps scholars and activists to understand how the context of massive cultural loss, as a result of the AIDS epidemic, the homophobia that frames it, and a whole host of intersecting oppressions, propels the deceased's rhetoric to national attention. Dominant interpretations of the Smithsonian's censorship of Wojn-arowicz's artwork, ostensibly justified on the basis of his depiction of Christian iconography and queer sexuality, suggest that censorship limited the artist-and-activist's rhetorical agency. I argue, however, that communal responses to Wojnarowicz's embodied legacy enabled the living to wrest control from dismissive audiences after his death, a process I call "postmortem agency."

In the essay that follows, I start by giving specific consideration to Wojn-arowicz's unfinished film *A Fire in My Belly*; however, in an extended analysis I consider the circumstances surrounding the publication of his unfinished comic memoir *Seven Miles a Second*, which space does not permit me to explore here. Because fleshing out the role of postmortem agency is a necessary task for reshaping the social and political imagination, an analysis of the unfinished work of the dead, specifically the rhetorical force and resonance of the embodied experiences the dead left behind and unfinished, impels the living to act and thus conditions the possibility for the deceased's continued participation in public life.

Wojnarowicz's postmortem agency—he died in 1992 at age thirty-seven—materialized most recently through a controversy surrounding the

Hide/Seek: Difference and Desire in American Portraiture exhibition at the National Portrait Gallery in Washington, DC (Smithsonian; Katz et al. *Hide/Seek*). The exhibition opened October 30, 2010, and ran until February 13, 2011. To summarize briefly, the Smithsonian received complaints from a small, albeit vocal group of conservative activists regarding purportedly anti-Christian, blasphemous, and homoerotic imagery. Secretary of the Smithsonian G. Wayne Clough then removed a film installation by Wojnarowicz with the aim of fortifying the institution against threats from prominent Republicans to decrease federal support and increase federal scrutiny. Clough's stated goal was to "sustain the long-term strength of an institution" he "cares deeply about [so as] to allow it to serve" its "educational mission" ("Statement").

Unlike the resuscitation of the lost memoir *Seven Miles a Second* by way of Van Cook's engagement with the Tarot, the curators of Hide/Seek: Difference and Desire in American Portraiture did not engage in "spiritualist discourse" about their decision to feature the film in the exhibition.[4] With orthodox humdrumness, curators Jonathan D. Katz and David C. Ward (Wojnarowicz, *Fire*), with the permission of the Wojnarowicz estate, worked with a video editor to shorten Wojnarowicz's unfinished film, *A Fire in My Belly,* from seven to four minutes, to remove scenes of overt sexuality, and to add a soundtrack from an ACT UP (the AIDS Coalition to Unleash Power) demonstration to the silent original. Arguably, the fact that a bowdlerized version of *A Fire in My Belly* was not permitted to play quietly on a monitor during the exhibition is a testament to the potency of Wojnarowicz's unfinished original. Elizabeth Freeman, in *Time Binds,* terms this kind of potentiality "undetonated energy" from the queer past (xvii). As an artifact of queer rage from the culture wars in the late 1980s and early 1990s, the film retained much of its power to offend religious conservatives. The offense conservatives expressed regarding the Smithsonian exhibition led to Wojnarowicz's censorship. Thus, these very objections became the condition of his public visibility. Furthermore, digital media implicated in the circulation of Wojnarowicz's *A Fire in My Belly* in online form, which made it possible for more people to see multiple versions of the film, to challenge its removal from the Smithsonian, to stage deliberate social action in protest, and to circulate public declarations of dissent.

In a handwritten note in his 1988 diary, Wojnarowicz presages considerations of postmortem rhetorical agency with regard to the difficulty of taking direct action to overcome constraints on speaking as a PWA (person with AIDS) and the collective process through which to do so: "Don't give me a memorial if I die—give me a demonstration" ("Spain/Paris/USA").[5] A demonstration, as a visible manifestation of resistance to an established order, furthers Wojnarowicz's memory in a way that expressions of personal grief at a memorial service may not be able to accomplish because they are less public.[6] Notably, Wojnarowicz's request for a demonstration has been granted at least twice since his death. On July 29, 1992, ACT UP celebrated his life and mourned his passing by way of a march through the East Village (Wojnarowicz, "Announcement"). Demonstrators also convened in protest at the Smithsonian after *A Fire in My Belly* was removed on the eve of World AIDS Day, November 30, 2010, from the National Portrait Gallery.[7] Further, two activists were banned from the Smithsonian for life when one activist stood outside the Hide/Seek: Difference and Desire in American Portraiture exhibition to film a fellow activist, who wore an iPad around his neck, on which Wojnarowicz's censored film played, as he distributed fliers about its censorship (Mead). The significance of these brief though visible and politicized interventions is that while censorship limits the democratic potential public museums represent, censorship can simultaneously create new opportunities for dissident speech, rhetorical identification, and collective action. The public attention that ensued from the Smithsonian's censorship resulted in centralizing Wojnarowicz's work. The fact Wojnarowicz's artwork regained prominence after his death mobilized his postmortem rhetorical agency in the sense that critics who labeled and dismissed his artwork as "anti-Christian" and a form of "hate speech" opened a space to reengage with the substance of his ideas (Donohue). For example, curator Wendy Olsoff articulates that the cross in *A Fire in My Belly* is an expression of the persecution and suffering of both Christ and PWAs (qtd. in Judkis). In sum, the import of Wojnarowicz's agentic power here, in the film he left unfinished, is that it becomes a wounded thing in need of protection by the living and summons them to it as if from the grave.

There are several implications that follow from the fact that Wojnarowicz's film installation was the only item removed from the Hide/Seek exhibit. First, through the paradox of censorship, Wojnarowicz moved from the periphery to the center of a group of LGBTQ artists who, through hard-won social and political engagement during the AIDS crisis, brought attention to the inaction of the American Medical Association, the federal government, and the Catholic Church at the beginning of the AIDS epidemic. In this way, Wojnarowicz's censorship could render him a kind of martyr to the cause of opposing homophobia and other forms of dehumanization and discrimination.[8] Wojnarowicz's iconography certainly considers martyrdom in social and political terms, while rejecting its overt theological baggage. Wojnarowicz's use of iconography from the Catholic faith has resulted in him posthumously being referred to as "St David Wojnarowicz" by Richard Maguire who suggests that much of Wojnarowicz's work manages to outline his mortal predicament and to enlist empathy from others, thus creating an opportunity for both identification and disidentification through the conscious involvement of audiences in his own dying, compelling us to witness and even defend him postmortem (251).

Secondly, the inclusion of Wojnarowicz's *A Fire in My Belly* in the Hide/Seek exhibit was consistent with curators David C. Ward and Jonathan D. Katz's aim to include testimony from witnesses and artists who experienced intense pain and trauma during the AIDS crisis without succumbing to a simplistic "Yay, gay people!" take-home message. As Emily Colucci affirms, Wojnarowicz "made a career out of depicting moments that were silenced by hegemonic and heteronormative society, such as his queer sexuality and childhood abuse." Indeed, Wojnarowicz's advocacy on behalf of the disenfranchised during his lifetime is extraordinary when considering the difficult circumstances against which he struggled from silence to "full accusatory voice" (Jellerson 60). Moreover, Wojnarowicz's experience as a "professional pallbearer" connects the AIDS epidemic to his life history (*Close* 120). Through Wojnarowicz's testimony and witness, as a multiply oppressed person, one can see the terrific potential of his voice to reverberate and thus draw people with similar subjectivities out of silence and invisibility, which is precisely what happened after his censorship at the Smithsonian. In other words, attempts by religious conservatives to threaten and create moral panic can simultaneously carve space for Wojnarowicz's message and legacy to achieve greater public visibility.

Claims that Wojnarowicz's censored film is a response to the AIDS crisis become complex because Katz and Ward added a soundtrack to *A Fire in My Belly* that included the protest chants: "Black, white, gay, straight: AIDS does not discriminate," "One, two, three, four: civil rights or civil war," "Hey, hey, ho, ho. Homophobia's got to go," and "ACT UP! We're pissed. We want a cure and not a list" (Wojnarowicz, *Fire*). In consultation with Tom Rauffenbart, the executor of Wojnarowicz's estate, Brent Phillips, New York University's Fales Library and Special Collections media archivist, issued a fact sheet. Phillips's fact sheet states that the question of whether *A Fire in My Belly* is a direct response to the AIDS crisis is open for discussion. However, the original film "predates Wojnarowicz's finding out he was HIV positive and the change in his work that reflects his status" (Phillips). Phillips also refutes claims made by journalists that Wojnarowicz made *A Fire in My Belly* as a tribute to his friend, mentor, and lover, Peter Hujar, after Hujar's death from AIDS-related complications on November 26, 1987.[9] Moreover, Phillips affirms that the original film was never finished, although the reason Wojnarowicz left it incomplete is unknown. Since Wojnarowicz has not spoken from beyond the grave to clarify whether he intended *A Fire in My Belly* as a response to homophobia and the dehumanization of PWAs, all one can reasonably do is attempt to decipher the film *in situ*, as I demonstrate.

In a grant application to the Pollack-Krasner Foundation, Wojnarowicz explains the film as follows: "I have been making a series of small films; one based on travels to Mexico deals with ancient and modern culture there as well as the effects of modern religion and economics on ancient customs" ("Business").[10] Though it would have been rhetorically ineffective for Wojnarowicz to describe *A Fire in My Belly* as a polemic against the Catholic Church, the state, and the medical establishment, that interpretation is at least as plausible as the one Wojnarowicz offers to the Pollack-Krasner Foundation as he endeavors to garner financial support to complete the film. Much like Van Cook's appeal to Tom Rauffenbart to resume labor on the unfinished graphic memoir (Rauffenbart), Wojnarowicz's grant proposal sought to convince readers not only that he was doing important artistic work on the relationship between economics, culture, and religion but also that he could deliver on the promise of completing that work and getting it into the public sphere.

Despite the fact that Wojnarowicz did receive a Pollack-Krasner Foundation grant—that is, his rhetorical framing of the grant application was successful—one can say with certainty that during this period of his life he faced obstacles that contributed to *A Fire in My Belly* never being completed.[11] These include Peter Hujar's diagnosis and then caring for Hujar each day while he bore the brunt of Hujar's mercurial temperament, rage, and despair (Carr 254). Fran Lebowitz describes Hujar's illness as "an intensely emotional, arduous situation" for Wojnarowicz and the small number of people who took care of Hujar because he "had no money, no insurance, no anything" (70). Wojnarowicz's labor as a caregiver during this time was difficult, though his own diagnosis, near eviction, and intense depression offer crucial insight into why *A Fire in My Belly* was postponed indefinitely.

Nonetheless, during this time period Wojnarowicz did write with as much intensity and focus as his waning and waxing health would allow. Dennis Cooper asserts that the artist's commitment to writing and documenting his experience throughout his life has resulted in the following outcome: "Whereas Wojnarowicz's art is probably doomed to an eternity spent in gay-and/or AIDS-themed group shows, his writing is far more likely to be remembered" (186). As Cooper observes, Wojnarowicz chronicled his private experiences as a dedicated diary writer from his teens until his death. His surviving thirty-one journals stand as evidence that for him the act of writing was a habit not unlike brushing one's teeth. Wojnarowicz documented his daily experiences, recorded his dreams, collected narratives from street people, and wrote poetry that challenged all forms of oppression. Thus, Wojnarowicz's agency is manifested rhetorically in poetic and prose form.

The field of rhetoric has long privileged the agency of the living to enact change or to do things in the world. However, the "old ghosts" that materialize through Wojnarowicz's multimedia artwork and writing possess rhetorical force insofar as they concretize the prospect of holding open space and time for minoritarian intervention in the present and future (*Waterfront* 117). I understand Joshua Gunn's suggestion that "[t]alking to the dead is simply a more conspicuous elaboration of the underlying fantasy that is central to rhetoric: the mediation of Self and Other across a terrible, yawning gap" as compatible with my theory of postmortem rhetorical agency (2). A reach back to engage with the substance of Wojnarowicz's archive seeks not to bury, forget, or ontologize, but to explore how communities come into being through conjuring the world he imagined, documented, and inhabited—a world that drifts in and out of linear time and is not fixed on the aesthetic plane but gestures toward the ethical. The imagination is a radical space where the dead can speak through loosening the stitches that have silenced meaningful engagement with their embodied experience. I am suggesting that we, the not yet dead, follow and remember Wojnarowicz to enact that lasting change he envisioned.

NOTES

[1] When I use the term LGBTQ I refer to Lesbian, Gay, Bisexual, Transgender, and Queer.

[2] Fleshing out a working definition for postmortem agency, let alone rhetorical agency in general, is an important task, given that in the last few years rhetorical agency has become a central topic at scholarly meetings and in journals in the field of rhetoric. See, for example, Geisler's description, in *Rhetoric Society Quarterly*, of the 2003 Alliance of Rhetoric Societies (ARS) conference wherein the future of rhetorical studies garnered divergent responses to the question: "How ought we to understand the concept of rhetorical agency?" (9). Further, see Gunn and Lundberg's critical response to Geisler "Ouija Board, Are There Any Communications" and Geisler's reply to Gunn and Lundberg in "Teaching the Post-Modern Rhetor."

[3] Campbell proposes that agency is (1) "constituted and constrained by externals that are material and symbolic; (2) is 'invented' by authors who are points of articulation; (3) emerges in artistry or craft; (4) is effected through form; (5) is perverse, that is inherently protean ambiguous, open to reversal" (2).

[4] I borrow this phrase from Gunn who uses it to argue that "[t]alking to the dead is simply a more conspicuous elaboration of the underlying fantasy that is central to the ways we think about rhetoric: the mediation or reconciliation of Self and Other across a terrible, yawning gap" (2).

[5] I use PWAs to refer to people with AIDS throughout.

[6] The NAMES Project AIDS Memorial Quilt is an important counterargument to the claim that memorials have less potential for rhetorical agency than demonstrations. However, Rand argues that the AIDS "Quilt conserves a limiting form of social recognition that severely constrains its potential as a site for activating social change" (655). The capacity of a demonstration to reach into the future rhetorically and to extend a community of PWAs in the late '80s and early '90s suggests the prospect for being remembered not only as squares on a quilt but also, and more disturbingly, as outraged spirit presences, challenging established authority.

[7] *Washington Post* reporter Dawson described the protestors as mostly artists. There were approximately one hundred demonstrators in attendance.

[8] The term "martyr" is complicated because of the residue of religiosity attached to it. The *Oxford English Dictionary* describes the word "martyr" as emerging from the Latin with the meaning "to witness." The first definition is imbued with religious overtones: "A person who chooses to suffer death rather than renounce faith in Christ or obedience to his teachings; a Christian way of life, or adherence to a law or tenet of the Church." See the *OED* online for the full entry.

[9] A text panel at the end of the film reads "Film In Progress, David Wojnarowicz 1986-87" (Phillips).

[10] Notably, Wojnarowicz's censored film is a surrealist montage that includes Day of the Dead iconography and related practices of what one might consider postmortem agency: *memento mori* objects; an actor playing a suffering Christ with a crown of thorns; ants crawling on a crucifix; a Catholic holy card of St. Bernadette with broken chains, gazing upward while being consumed by fire in purgatory. The ants on the crucifix became the focus of critics' attention.

[11] After the Smithsonian's censorship, *The New York Observer* reporter Peers interviewed the current chair of the Pollock-Krasner Foundation, Charles Bergman. Bergman offered vehement criticism of the censorship of *A Fire in My Belly*, noting that Wojnarowicz received a grant from the foundation to complete the film in 1989. Bergman further insists that the film was entirely "appropriate to the [*Hide/Seek*] exhibition" (qtd. in Peers).

WORKS CITED

Beronä, David A. "A Renegade of Expression: David Wojnarowicz's Autofiction in Comics." *Image [&] Narrative* 22 (May 2008): n. pag. Web. Feb. 2013.

Campbell, Karlyn Kohrs. "Agency: Promiscuous and Protean." *Communication and Critical/Cultural Studies* 2.1 (2005): 1-19. Print.

Carr, Cynthia, ed. *On Edge: Performance at the End of the Twentieth Century.* Hanover: UP of New England, 1993. Print.

Clough, Wayne. "Statement: Wayne, Clough, Secretary, Smithsonian Institution." *Newsdesk.si.edu.* Newsroom of the Smithsonian Institute, 20 Jan. 2011. Web. 15 Feb. 2011.

Colucci, Emily. "Some Sort of Grace: David Wojnarowicz's Archive of the Death of Peter Hujar." *Anamesa: An Interdisciplinary Journal* 8.1 (2010): n. pag. Web. 10 January 2011.

Cooper, Dennis. "Odd Man Out: David Wojnarowicz." *Smothered in Hugs: Essays, Interviews, Feedback, and Obituaries.* New York: Harper Perennial, 2010. 182-87. Print.

Dawson, Jessica. "Demonstrators Gather to Protest Removal of Wojnarowicz Art from National Portrait Gallery." *The Washington Post.com.* Washington Post, 3 Dec. 2010. Web. 28 Dec. 2010.

Donohue, William. "Smithsonian Hosts Anti-Christian Exhibit." *The Catholic League.org.* Catholic League for Religious and Civil Rights, 30 Nov. 2010. Web. 1 Dec. 2010.

Freeman, Elizabeth. *Time Binds: Queer Temporalities, Queer Histories.* Durham: Duke UP, 2010. Print.

Geisler, Cheryl. "How Ought We to Understand the Concept of Rhetorical Agency? Report from the ARS." *Rhetoric Society Quarterly* 34.3 (2004): 9-18. Print.

---. "Teaching the Post-Modern Rhetor: Continuing the Conversation on Rhetorical Agency." *Rhetoric Society Quarterly* 35.4 (2005): 107-14. Print.

Gunn, Joshua. "Refitting Fantasy: Psychoanalysis, Subjectivity, and Talking to the Dead." *Quarterly Journal of Speech* 90.1 (2004): 1-23. Print.

Gunn, Joshua, and Christian Lundberg. "'Ouija Board, Are There Any Communications?' Agency, Ontotheology, and the Death of the Humanist Subject, Or, Continuing the ARS Conversation." *Rhetoric Society Quarterly* 35.4 (2005): 83-106. Print.

Jellerson, Donald. "Haunted History and the Birth of the Republic in Middleton's Ghost of Lucrece." *Criticism: A Quarterly for Arts and Literature* 53.1 (2011): 53-82. Print.

Judkis, Maura. "National Portrait Gallery Censorship Controversy: Who Was David Wojnarowicz." *TBD.com.* TBD Arts, 2 Dec. 2010. Web. 22 Dec. 2010.

Katz, Jonathan D., David C. Ward, and Jennifer Sichel. *Hide/Seek: Difference and Desire in American Portraiture.* Washington, DC: Smithsonian Books, 2010. Print.

Lebowitz, Fran. "An Intimate Portrait." *Brushfires in the Social Landscape.* New York: Aperture, 1995. 70-82. Print.

Maguire, Richard. "The Relics of St David Wojnarowicz: The Autobiography of a Mythmaker." *Life Writing: Essays on Autobiography, Biography, and Literature.* Ed. Richard Bradford. New York: Palgrave Macmillan, 2009: 247-68. Print.

Mead, Stephen. "Activist Banned for Life from Smithsonian for iPad Protest of Censored Gay David Wojnarowicz Art Piece." *Art Review.com.* Art Review, 9 Dec. 2010. Web. 10 Mar. 2011.

Mitchell, W. J. T. *What Do Pictures Want?: The Lives and Loves of Images.* Chicago: U of Chicago P, 2005. Print.

Peers, Alexandra. "Whitewashing the Art World: What's Behind the Climate of Censorship." *Observer.com.* The New York Observer, 12 Jan. 2011. Web. 24 Nov. 2011.

Phillips, Brent W. "Fact Sheet." Message to Jessica L. Shumake. 21 July 2011. E-mail.

Rand, Erin J. "Repeated Remembrance: Commemorating the Aids Quilt and Resuscitating the Mourned Subject." *Rhetoric & Public Affairs* 10.4 (2008): 655-79. Print.

Rauffenbart, Tom. Introduction. *Seven Miles a Second*. By David Wojnarowicz. Art by James Romberger and Marguerite Van Cook. New York: DC Comics, 1996. 1-3. Print.

Smithsonian Institution. Hide/Seek: Difference and Desire in American Portraiture. National Portrait Gallery, Washington, DC, 30 Oct. 2010—13 Feb. 2011. Public Exhibition.

Wojnarowicz, David. "Announcement of Memorial" in Series IV, Box 9, Folder 17, David Wojnarowicz Papers, Letters at Fales Lib., New York University. TS.

---. "Business Correspondence" in Series II, Box 2, Folder 15, David Wojnarowicz Papers, Letters at Fales Lib., New York University, 1988. TS.

---. *Close to the Knives: A Memoir of Disintegration*. New York: Vintage Books, 1991. Print.

---. *A Fire in My Belly*. 1986-87. Ed. Jonathan D. Katz and Bart Everly. The Estate of David Wojnarowicz and the P.P.O.W Gallery, New York and the Fales Library and Special Collections, NYU. 2010. Digital file with additional audio added from ACT UP demonstration.

---. *Seven Miles a Second*. Art by James Romberger and Marguerite Van Cook. New York: DC Comics, 1996. Print.

---. "Spain/Paris/USA" in Series I, Box 1, Folder 20, David Wojnarowicz Papers, Letters at Fales Lib., New York University, 1988. Print.

---. *The Waterfront Journals*. New York: Grove P, 1996. Print.

24

FEMININE *ETHOS,* AFFECT, AND INTERSUBJECTIVITY IN *THE SHOWINGS OF JULIAN OF NORWICH*

Heather Palmer

Contemporary efforts to expand the field of rhetorical study have encouraged scholars to look at material typically considered outside the canon of rhetorical history. As many scholars of the history and theory of rhetoric have noted, particularly those concerned with women's rhetoric or rhetoric of the body, the canon has excluded the rhetorical activities of women, since rhetoric is typically limited to public speech, an area dominated by men. Robert Gaines, among others, has argued for the "de-canonizing of ancient rhetoric" and, in order to move away from the limits of the normative and constitutive influences of the Western Rhetorical Tradition,[1] offers us what he calls a corpus, rather than a canon.[2] The rhetorical corpus, then, is a counter to the exclusive rhetorical canon and, according to Gaines, would contain "known texts, artifacts, and discourse venues that represent the theory, pedagogy, practice, criticism, and cultural apprehension of rhetoric in the ancient European discourse community" (65). The emphasis on a rhetorical corpus thusly conceived rather than a canon opens the field up to the diverse modes of participation by women in rhetorical discourse. Since rhetoric is traditionally associated with reason and the intellect,[3] a particularly fruitful area of study in the corpus is the rhetorical dimension of activities considered to be decisively nonrhetorical, such as the practices of the early modern female Christian medieval mystics.

One such mystic whose rich textual practices leave behind perplexing yet incredibly generative questions for rhetorical analysis is Julian of Norwich. Julian of Norwich (circa 1342-1420 CE) was considered one of the greatest of English mystics—and, as far as we can tell, the first female author of a book extant in English. We know her as a historical figure only by the text, *Revelations of Divine Love Showed to a Devout Ankress by Name Julian of Norwich,* and Margery Kempe's account of a conversation with her noted in the *Book of*

Margery Kempe. We do not know her family name, because the name comes from the name of the Church and the city in which she was an anchoress, a contemplative who lived in an enclosure in the churchyard to better apprehend the divine. Her *Book of Showings*[4] documents her sixteen revelations or showings, which began around age thirty with the onset of an illness (May 13, 1373), during which she saw intensely corporeal visions of the Passion of Christ and the sorrow of his Mother. She first recounted these visions in the Short Text (ST), consisting of twenty-five chapters, and twenty years later, with the benefit of the wisdom of contemplation the anchoritic life afforded her, she wrote the Long Text (LT), consisting of eighty-six chapters.

Scholarship on Julian has typically focused on her institutional role as an elder anchoress in the affairs of the Church. The introduction to Edmund Colledge and James Walsh's edition of *The Book of Showings* contextualizes her work by explaining that throughout history women exercised various church ministries: as deaconesses, the women who converted their husbands in the first centuries or in the new barbarian kingdoms of the sixth-eighth centuries, the nuns who have deserved the title of missionaries among the Anglo-Saxon and Germanic people of the same period. Some women, from the twelfth century CE on, had a real teaching role in the Church: for example Hildegard of Bingen was called a prophetess—and during the last century, St. Catherine of Siena and St. Teresa of Avila were granted official title of Doctor of the Church. The teaching roles for women during this time were varied: St. Catherine of Siena and St. Bridget of Sweden were involved in politics; St. Hildegard was said to possess encyclopedic learning; and St. Teresa made contributions to constitutional law. What these women had in common was a spiritual experience out of which emerged practical and doctrinal implications. They all had revelations of some kind, which complemented the official teachings of an active church. As Jean Leclercq tells us in "La vie spirituelle," a new dimension was made possible because these teachers were women; "they opened new horizons to the teaching authority of a Church which, if it remained exclusively a masculine stronghold, would have been limited and partial" (4). So, it would have missed the characteristic genius of the feminine with its intuitive approach to reality—and it is in this context that Julian acquires her more comprehensive significance as a mystic.

Liz Herbert McAvoy's *Authority and the Female Body in the Writings of Julian of Norwich and Margery Kempe* illuminates the strategies both Julian and Margery Kempe used to assert what she calls a "gynaecentic authority available to female mystics and writers in their attempts to validate the public, sometimes prophetic female utterance" (207). And yet, what has remained largely unarticulated is how they use specific rhetorical strategies (such as their bodily visions and corporeal sights) to offer us an ethics of the body in the representational practices of their visions of the divine, specifically the vivid corporeal dimension of the relationship with Christ's Passion. And yet, the devaluation of the body in the Western Rhetorical Tradition often forecloses the possibilities of embodied *affect*, the lived intensity of textual becoming, an ethics of the body. It is now commonplace for feminist scholars of patristic traditions in Christianity to note this marginalization of the body—the association of the flesh with materiality and sin, the spirit with reason and the ascension to the spiritual. Margaret Miles puts it most bluntly, "In Christianity, the body scorned, the naked body, is a female body" (185). To move conceptually beyond such reductive polarizations of experience, I rely on Brian Massumi's conception of affect[5] in *Parables for the Virtual*, which defines this modality as movement, sensation, indeterminacy, exteriority, and becoming, as distinguished from stasis, concreteness, and being. This dimension of affect, as we'll see, finds an anchor in Julian's rhetorical practices and gives us viable alternatives to patristic traditions of establishing *ethos* through self-effacement—the effacement of the body—by *reviving* Greco-Roman rhetorical practices of self-cultivation, in which the lived reality of the self is affirmed through discourse and intersubjective relations with the other.

Intersubjectivity is a mutual co-arising of interdependent subjects that *creates* their respective experiences. It is ontological and yet relies on a cocreative nonphysical presence, and it brings distinct subjects into a type of being—or becoming-other—that is rhetorical. The concept of intersubjectivity holds the promise of cocreativity, where relationship is ontologically primary. All individuated subjects coemerge, or co-arise, as a result of a holistic "field" of relationships. The being of any one subject is thoroughly dependent on the being of all other subjects, with which it is in relationship. As Maurice Merleau-Ponty explains, "I live in the facial expressions of the other, and as I feel him living in mine" (218). Here, intersubjectivity precedes subjectivity—and refers to an "interpenetrating," a cocreation of *loci* of subjectivity—an *ethos* based on affective relations between nonessentialized *ethos*, a dynamic that Julian embodies in her relationship with the divine.

Ethos is the place from which we speak, the locus of our identity-experience, and provides a space to reconsider the relationship between the body and language.[6] Since the category of "woman" has typically been cast structurally as "extradiscursive," outside the language of reason and logic, the concept of a feminine *ethos* helps us to consider the intersections of the text and the body in Julian's textual practices, the ways that "bodies and words [might] couple and struggle," in Massumi's words (*Shock* xxiii). As I intend to show in the more extended version of this work, tracing the contours of a "feminine *ethos*" through the text of Julian's *Showings* shows us how her affective piety complicates the primary oppositions on which epistemological considerations of *ethos* and character are based: knowledge as absolute, impersonal, and objective, versus knowledge as experiential, personal, and relative; the self as unitary, self-conscious essence, versus the self as divided and fragmented, radically constructed by historical and material contingencies that it cannot transcend. We find in both Julian's textual and material practices a common goal: to intensify affective experience in order to more fully instantiate an epistemology of substance and sensuality. This study of Julian therefore situates itself in the interstices between the literary study of the visions of early Christian mystics and rhetorical studies in order to help elaborate how an *ethos* of affect is articulated through and by the body, even one in confinement.

I'd like to first address the methodology of doing rhetorical histories such as this and the issue of anachronism, the historian's temptation to project, either consciously or unconsciously, the values of her time onto the past. In her 2009 essay, "Medieval and Renaissance Rhetorical Studies of Women," Christine Mason Sutherland pointedly claims that this anachronism "is a particular temptation for feminist historians of rhetoric" (61).[7] Along with Sutherland, I believe that one way to compensate for this tendency is to use a holistic approach to our subjects and to immerse ourselves, as much as possible, into the material contingencies of their lives—to include both *ethos* and *pathos* in our scholarly concerns. Sutherland emphasizes the necessity of starting from one's own experience, to focus on "the connection between researcher and researched" (62). The question is how, through what methodologies, can we connect medieval Christian mystics such as Margery Kempe or Julian of Norwich and twenty-first-century scholars of rhetoric in order to amplify "experiential meaning," meaning immanent in experience and time, made through shared experiences of affect, converging at the hinge of both *ethos* and *pathos*? This approach is generative, in the sense that an emphasis on experience as epistemology challenges us to rethink the field of rhetorical history. Or, as James Murphy tells us, a generative approach to rhetorical history will "identify the known and to go beyond that to the as-yet unknown," by acknowledging that the history of rhetoric is not just the history of its books (194, 187).

In framing a methodology of rhetorical history in this way, the historian-critic is an active agent in the creation of meaning, but such a study isn't arbitrary: it is fully based in the text, and the text is fully based in the context, and the context is fully based in the text, according to Michael Leff and Fred Kauffield. Such an experiential/affective rhetorical approach to history opens us to the ontological depths of others and lends itself to the study of rhetorical practices, not given prime placement in the "prestige hierarchy" of our discipline, which has focused on public discourse, a space from which women have been excluded, as Carol Poster[8] and others have noted. On one hand, Julian, as an anchoress, willfully forgoes the public space of discourse by excluding herself literally from it, and on the other, she reaches out to us from within the confines of the anchorhold across the threshold of more than six hundred years. Several groups of interrelated questions serve as our points of entry into the text rather than analysis based on the chronological development of Julian's thought: 1) What exactly are the rhetorical strategies Julian uses to position herself in the text—how does she construct an *ethos* within the kairotic constraints of religious orthodoxy to assert the truth of her visions and intersubjective relationship with the divine? 2) What are the alternatives to patristic traditions of establishing *ethos* through self-effacement—the effacement of the body—that Julian offers us? And, finally, 3) How does

Julian's rhetorical self-positioning overspill the constraints imposed on her, culturally and discursively, into the affective and ethical dimensions of a relationship of intersubjectivity?

Julian wrote when the Catholic Church was concerned with the Lollards' push for popularizing the English vernacular and making the entire Bible available to all people. This was considered heretical and, as Cheryl Glenn notes, so was their leniency to women preachers (102). There are debates as to the extent of Julian's rhetorical training and awareness: for example, some claim that she undoubtedly had rhetorical and philosophical training, as an early member of the convent and then the anchorage, and find proof of her philosophical and rhetorical literacy in her prose style, her syllogistic argument structures, and her method of ratiocination to build a system of knowledge; Colledge and Walsh, the translators of the version I'm using, claim that "Julian became such a master of rhetorical art as to merit comparison with Geoffrey Chaucer" (Norwich 401).

Her mastery of rhetoric perhaps explains how Julian carefully crafts a feminine *ethos* in language determined by myths of filial paternity and presence, careful not to violate orthodoxy through her self-construction as an emissary or vehicle for revelations from God. And yet, in order to reach her mostly uneducated audience she uses the vernacular to communicate her visions, and, as Cheryl Glenn also notes, she takes care not to alienate any of her audience, "particularly the males, for any reason" (102). Glenn goes on to point out that Julian uses humility as a strategy of ethos "to her advantage, the better to secure goodwill and then moralize" (102)—and I agree, of course, that she uses an *ethos* of humility, a commonplace among many mystics of the time, to reassure us of her piety and secure goodwill, but I don't think she makes these gestures just to moralize to us—her discourse substantively accomplishes much more than mere moralizing, as we'll see.

Probably convent educated from an early age, Julian was aware of the labyrinthine structures of ecclesiastical power and authority (McAvoy 3) and the ways that rhetoric was imbricated in them—an awareness emblematic of much anxiety of the time over who was sanctioned to wield the power of Church doctrine. Julian repeats her accord with the Church's teachings in order to show that she values them—and, in line with the practices of female Christian mystics of the time, she wishes to imitate Mary's humble attitude. Consider how she negotiates such concerns in the rhetorical self-fashioning of the following: "I pray you all for God's sake, and I counsel you for your own profit, that you disregard the *wretched worm*, the *sinful creature* to whom it [intense visions of the Passion] was shown" (ST 133; emphasis added).

It is also worth noting that specific characteristics of her projected *ethos* change from the ST to the LT, as Jean Leclercq notes in the introduction to both: "the whole tone and temper have changed . . . . Previously she conveyed a certain apprehension about her humility, as though her readers might not believe her when she proclaimed her unworthiness" (33). By the time she wrote the LT, however, she could assert her humility simply, and she could plainly ally herself with her audience, "you who are simple, to give you comfort and strength; for we are all one in love" (LT 191). She thus attenuates the intensity of the rhetorical gestures of self-deprecation in the LT, written twenty years after the first visions. Julian's narrative voice changes from a "naïve desire to gain experience through imitation of Christ's suffering . . . towards a far more mature wisdom and insight than is evidenced in the ST" (McAvoy 206). She crafts a new *ethos* based on the transformation of her first understanding of the original "mystical utterance" in order to craft an *ethos* that fits her new knowledge of the divine (McAvoy 207). We could call her awareness of this transformation, and rhetorical attention to its representation, evidence of *metanoia*. Let me clarify the senses in which I use the term: in theology, it means repentance, but Julian uses *metanoia* to rewrite herself into the LT rhetorically, to rework the statements of the ST in order to strengthen their efficacy through the force of the evolution of her wisdom and understanding. *Metanoia* is used in recalling a statement in two ways—to weaken the prior declaration or to strengthen it. So, although she attenuates some of the language of the ST in the LT, her use of *metanoia* strengthens her original claims by more carefully qualifying them.

Somewhere between the ST and the LT, written some twenty years later, she has a transformation for which she must recraft a new *ethos*. Her *ethos* seems neither distinctly Platonic nor sophistic, but retains traces of both, almost dialectically in the Hegelian sense of *aufheben*, which preserves and destroys. In an abbreviated and thus necessarily reductive summation, the Platonic *ethos* transcends materiality, its own body, and the presence of others as part of the sensory, phenomenal world. Unlike the sophistic *ethos*, which is constructed in collaboration with the community (the *kairos* of the rhetorical situation), such subjectivity happens in a radically interiorized space. Being is separate from materiality, out of the reach of "otherness," of one's own body, or even of the beings of others' physicalities. The Platonic *ethos* asserts its own existence through the metaphysics of self-presence, and I'm interested in how Julian's self-presentation unsettles a logic of identity intersubjectively in terms of the enfolding of two modes of being—the interior and exterior, the material or bodily and the ghostly, and in the maternal body of Christ, the male and the female, as we will briefly explore in the final section of this study.

The structures of Julian's thinking are quite rhetorically remarkable in their depth and ambition: she uses the unusual, disturbing, and uncanny sensibility of her visions as a way of engendering a text—with herself as an author—of both an experiential and a metaphysical knowledge. Thus, she is not merely a passive receptacle of mystical experience; instead, she actively mediates the experience in discourse, and she uses ratiocination to parse her revelations in a nuanced and critically sophisticated manner. Jean Leclercq defends her as a highly literate and rhetorically sophisticated presence, explaining that she used a rhetorical ratiocination to explain her visions:

> She gets "suggestions" and "sharings"; she then has "doubts." She even asks questions; finally, she accepts. She "consents" and she "chooses." "Bodily visions" and "corporeal sights" stimulate her search for understanding. The revelation is never sufficient; it is a grace and God takes all the initiative, but there must be human effort. (5)

We find markers of rhetorical agency in Julian's human effort to make sense, to desire the extra-sensory through bodily sight:

> I *desired* the three graces by the gift of God. The first was to have recollection of Christ's Passion. The second was a bodily sickness, and the third was to have, of God's gift, three wounds . . . . But despite my all my true faith I *desired a bodily sight*, through which I might have more knowledge of our Lord and savior's bodily pains, and of the compassion of our Lady and all his true lovers . . . . That I would know them and suffer with them. (ST 125)

Here her affective apprehension of the immanence of God has epistemic weight—to desire to know the bodily experience of the divine.

We also find in the text Julian's integration of philosophical concepts into the analysis of her supranormal, mystical experience. For example, Julian offers us the alternatives to patristic traditions of establishing *ethos* through the effacement of the body by reviving certain strands of self-cultivation from Greco-Roman arts of character. After all, it would be superficial, as Simon Goldhill points out, "to try to understand Christianity without appreciating its long and passionate involvement with Greek and Latin language and society" (98). Common knowledge often obscured is that Christianity came into existence in the culture of classical antiquity—and the first four centuries of its foundational developmental years occurred during the Roman Empire (Goldhill 98). The background I'm most concerned with here is the development of *ethos*, or character, and its practices of self-formation. Around 50 CE, Seneca the Stoic instructs us on the refined art of self-examination to shape character; and by 397 CE, Augustine advises confession as a self-regulating technology of character that helps bring the body into subjection. The major conception of character with which I am concerned is as an art of self-composition through frank/free speech, in which, for much of the Greco-Roman rhetorical tradition, truth resides not within the interior of self, but in the practices of self-examination through discourse. Specific disciplinary exercises called *askesis* were designed to cultivate an exemplary *ethos* through the practice of *parrhesia* and the discipline of the body's appetites.

The other key conception of character from the early Christian practices of *ethos* emphasizes foundational knowledge of the self as a pre-existent substantive essence and the discovery of truths hidden deep within oneself. This discovery takes place within the rhetorical genre of the confessional, which emphasizes asceticism and detachment from the world, a foundational disembodiment; whereas the Greco-Roman arts of character were designed to fully engage the (male) individuality in the world, both materially and ethically. Both practices have radically different conceptions of truth-telling, which inscribe a particular relationship to textuality, the body, and the spirit. The nun and scholar Prudence Allen calls Julian's acts of will in unflinchingly exploring the Passion a rhetorical self-fashioning (411). And I would also argue that in this rhetorical will, she chooses a specific relationship to herself, that of a *parrhesiast*, as Michel Foucault (*Fearless Speech*) conceives it: she prefers herself as a truth-teller of the affective force of her revelations rather than as a living being who is false to herself. In Julian's life-long earnest self-cultivation, she provides affective proof of her claims to a direct relationship with the divine. Her contemplation of the physical sufferings of the Passion is through the vehicle of what she calls bodily sight and brings her rhetorical will closer to God's will: "It is God's will, as I understand it, that we contemplate his blessed Passion [by contemplating the] cruel pain he suffered with contrition and compassion; and our Lord revealed that at this time, and gave me the strength and grace to see it" (214). And further, Julian distinguishes between a bodily sight and an imaginative vision when recounting the revelations: "and I saw it so plentiful that it seemed to me that if it had in fact and in substance been happening there, the bed and everything all around it would have been soaked in blood" (LT 199-200).

Julian affirms her lived reality of the divine through discourse—and engages us with an ethics or *ethos* of affectivity in what I call, in a willfully anachronistic gesture, Julian's "logic of sense," following from Gilles Deleuze's affective epistemology as explored in the text *The Logic of Sense*. Julian uses a logic of sense to prove the validity of her claims to know God— and we see her rely on this as a rhetorical proof throughout the text. Consider the following examples of affect as a rhetorical force: she has "ghostly sight" when she begins to feel Christ's suffering with her own passion, an intersubjective experience of pain that all creatures are capable of experiencing because of the "great unity between Christ and us . . . for when he was in pain we were in pain, and all creatures able to suffer pain suffered with him" (LT 210). Furthermore, she outlines her metaphysics of substance and sensuality in her sixteenth revelation:

> And when our soul is breathed into our body, at which time we are made sensual, at once mercy and grace begin to work, having care of us and protecting us with pity and love, in which operation the Holy Spirit forms in our faith the hope that we shall return up above to our substance, into the power of Christ, increased and fulfilled through the Holy Spirit. So I understood that *our sensuality is founded in nature, in mercy and grace,* and this foundation enables us to receive gifts that lead us to endless life. For I saw very surely that our substance is in God, and I also saw that God is in our sensuality, for in the same instant and place in which our soul is made sensual. (287 LT; emphasis in original)

In this logic, she asserts the validity of an *episteme* of the ethical, in the sense Foucault uses the term, a way of knowing things that is coextensive with the discourse it generates. As Foucault argues in *The Order of Things,* every new *episteme* establishes a new relation between words and things (385-87). Julian's discursive strategy in the *Showings* establishes a consubstantial relation between her own suffering and Christ's through affect as rhetorical force. Interestingly, Julian, while removing her bodily presence from the public sphere, underscores its centrality to her epistemology throughout the texts and the rather graphic renderings of the Passion.

Consider the affective force of the following, the manner in which the language breaks under the strain of her experience:

> Christ showed me part of his Passion, close to his death. I saw his sweet face as it were dry and bloodless with the pallor of dying, and then deadly pale, languishing, and then the pallor turning blue and then the blue turning brown, as death took more and more hold upon his flesh . . . . This was a painful change to watch, this deep dying, and his nose shrivelled and dried up as I saw; and the sweet body turned brown and black, completely changed and transformed from his naturally beautiful, fresh and vivid complexion into a shrivelled image of death. (206)

Here Julian is under dual constraints: to become the conduit of God's voice, a pure vessel, she must erase her body as vehicle for voice while simultaneously insisting on the reality of her ghostly and bodily sight of the Passion. Julian's *ethos*, then, is constitutive of the boundary of both presence and absence in a metaphysical and a material sense: the flesh and the spirit. She insists on affective presence as a vital hermeneutic that is ultimately nondualistic. Julian's discursive relationship with herself and the other (the divine) refigures the presence of identity through an ethics of intersubjectivity—one that manages to move beyond a representation or reduction of the other. The identity of Julian is for the other in the "silent" (in quotes because she gives the divine the cloak of language) interlocutor who speaks through her affect. The divine remains, ultimately, incommensurable with any language of presence or being, and yet the text retains traces of it/him, the saying of the other that overflows linguistic categories that demarcate identity.

The point is: Julian makes rhetoric matter, performing the radically ethical work of unsettling repressive identity categories through a sustained engagement with the realm of affect, defined not as emotion, but as the intensity of textual becoming. Truth resides at the level of sensation and in the intersubjective relation of self to the divine, a being that is described as simultaneously a being of affect and spirit. What we are left with is a subject of sensation and its representation in a discourse that does not separate the experience of its life from its expression. Despite Julian's concern with orthodoxy and her own sinful and fallen nature, she opens the door to the possibility of overthrowing a metaphysics of dualisms such as presence/absence, bodily/ghostly and affords us the opportunity to consider, as Brian Massumi does, as previously cited, "how bodies and words couple and struggle; whether or in what circumstances they might pass into each other, as in expression's performative passing into content; how their mutual immanence must be lived, and experienced most directly and intensely" (*Shock* xxiii). The injunction to live the mutual immanence of bodies and words is both poetic and ethical—and one that Julian offers to give us opportunities for response, extension, and departure. It seems via a rhetoric of affect and intersubjectivity, the anchorhold's walls within which Julian was physically enclosed were permeable, and her rhetorical gestures extend outside its walls, much in the way she brings about the reciprocity of body and soul.

NOTES

[1] Gaines offers a pointed challenge to the "fiction" of the rhetorical tradition; see also Miller who notably argues, "The rhetorical tradition is a fiction that has just about outlived its usefulness" (26). I am "strategically essentializing" (to use Gayatri Spivak's language) the concept of the Western Rhetorical Tradition here to provide a backdrop for Julian's distinctive rhetorical practices.

[2] Gaines traces the word *canon* to its ecclesiastical roots—as a list of books divinely inspired—before distinguishing the normative force of the ecclesiastical canon from the constitutive force of the disciplinary canon, however conceived: The former gives us a list of texts that must somehow be obeyed; the latter gives us "an institutional sphere of authorized instruction and investigation" (62).

[3] See Sutherland's summation of the related scholarship in "Medieval and Renaissance Rhetorical Studies of Women."

[4] In this paper, in the Works Cited, *Showings* is listed under Norwich; this version was edited and translated by Edmund Colledge and James Walsh. It is this volume that is the source for citations of ST, LT, and Norwich's words.

[5] A good place to look for a meditation on the relationship among aesthetics, affect, and ontology is the essay "Percept, Affect, and Concept" in Deleuze and Guattari's *What is Philosophy?*, and in Emmanuel Levinas's mediations on the "sensuous lived experience" in *Otherwise than Being*. I also like Smith's explanation:

> via affects, the subject is connected to and affected by what Deleuze and Guattari call intensities—forces "outside" of and *other* than the self-form (or any other form of social organization and determination, for that matter), which have the potential to expose subjects to the disorganizing and disordering forces of desire. (886)

In Julian's case, the desire is, of course, the desire for/to be consubstantial with the Holy Ghost and its trinitarian (or otherwise) manifestations.

[6] *Ethos*, the calling of self into being through language, is a fundamental part of the rhetorical situation, although I do not mean that this "situation" stands apart or precedes the rhetoric through which it is articulated, as Bitzer seems to. *Ethos* is a *relationship* between selves, texts, and bodies, not a linguistic accident or foundational entity. Many interpretations tend to value an *ethos* that is stable and credible, a subject *of* knowledge without considering how it is subject *to* bodies of knowledge. On one hand, this approach is understandable since it sidesteps the metaphysical minefields of morality and ethics, yet it substitutes another system of valuation that replaces good as a moral category with good as a category of coherent, unitary, rational being. This view of *ethos* makes an ontological demand: to represent a subject of knowledge in language that is self-identical, constitutive of the "author." In this economy of representation, signifiers and their signifieds must match up, the subject of discourse must be coterminous with the conscious rational author in a transparent language, in which we mean what we say and say what we mean, with no excess or play. The abject, the unconscious, the excess, the innumerable, and ungraspable traces of signification have no place in this model.

[7] This "temptation," as Sutherland puts it, is also characteristic of classic transference as defined in psychoanalytic thought: as Lacan wrote, "As soon as the subject supposed to know exists somewhere, there is transference" (qtd. in Evans 199).

[8] See Poster.

WORKS CITED

Allen, Prudence R.S.M. *The Concept of Woman Volume II: The Early Humanist Reformation, 1250-1500.* Grand Rapids: Eerdmans, 2002. Print.

Bitzer, Lloyd. "The Rhetorical Situation." *Philosophy and Rhetoric* 1.1 (Jan. 1968): 1-14. Print.

Deleuze, Gilles. *The Logic of Sense.* New York: Columbia UP, 1990. Print.

Deleuze, Gilles, and Felix Guattari. *What is Philosophy?* New York: Columbia UP, 1996. Print.

Evans, Dylan. *An Introductory Dictionary of Lacanian Psychoanalysis.* New York: Routledge, 1996.

Foucault, Michel. *Fearless Speech.* Ed. Joseph Pearson. Los Angeles: Semiotext(e), 2001. Print.

---. *The Order of Things.* New York: Vintage, 1994. Print.

Gaines, Robert. "De-canonizing Ancient Rhetoric." *The Viability of the Rhetorical Tradition.* Ed. R. Graff et al. Albany: State U of New York P, 2005. 61-73. Print.

Glenn, Cheryl. *Rhetoric Retold.* Carbondale: Southern Illinois UP, 1997.

Goldhill, Simon. *Love, Sex, and Tragedy: How the Ancient World Shapes Our Lives.* Chicago: U of Chicago P, 2004. Print.

Leclercq, Jean. "La vie spirituelle." *Julian of Norwich: Showings.* Ed. and Trans. Edmund Colledge and James Walsh. New York: Paulist, 1978. Print.

Leff, Michael, and Fred Kauffeld, eds. *Texts in Context.* Davis: Hermagoras P, 1989.

Levinas, Emmanuel. *Otherwise Than Being or Beyond Essence.* Trans. Alphonso Lingis. Boston: Martinus Nijhoff, 1981. Print.

Massumi, Brian. *A Shock to Thought: Expression after Deleuze and Guattari.* New York: Routledge, 2002. Print.

---. *Parables of the Virtual: Movemet, Affect, Sensation.* London: Duke UP, 2002. Print.

McAvoy, Liz Herbert. *Authority and the Female Body.* New York: Boydell and Brewer, 2004.

Merleau-Ponty, Maurice. *Phenomenology of Perception.* Trans. C. Smith. London: Routledge, 1962. Print.

Miles, Margaret R. *Carnal Knowing: Female Nakedness and Religious Meaning in the Christian West.* New York: Vintage, 1989. Print.

Miller, Thomas. "Reinventing Rhetorical Traditions." *Learning from the Histories of Rhetoric.* Ed. Theresa Enos. Carbondale: Southern Illinois UP, 1993. 26-41. Print.

Murphy, James. "Conducting Research in the History of Rhetoric." *Publishing in Rhetoric and Composition.* Ed. Gary A. Olson and Todd Taylor. Albany: State U of New York P, 1997. 187-95. Print.

Norwich, Julian. *Julian of Norwich: Showings.* Ed. and Trans. Edmund Colledge and James Walsh. New York: Paulist, 1978. Print.

Poster, Carol. "(Re)Positioning Pedagogy: A Feminist Historiography of Aristotle's *Rhetorica.*" *Feminist Interpretations of Aristotle.* Ed. Cynthia Freeland. University Park: Pennsylvania State UP, 1998. 327-50. Print.

Smith, Daniel. "Desire and Immanence." *JAC* 23.4 (2005): 884-900. Print.

Spivak, Gayatri. *In Other Worlds.* New York: Routledge, 2006. Print.

Sutherland, Christine Mason. "Medieval and Renaissance Rhetorical Studies of Women." *The SAGE Handbook of Rhetorical Studies.* Ed. Andrea Lunsford. Thousand Oaks: SAGE, 2009. 53-65. Print.

25

IDENTIFICATION, CONSUBSTANTIALITY, INTERVAL, AND TEMPORALITY

Luce Irigaray and the Possibilities for Rhetoric

Janice Odom

Rhetorical studies prefer not to think too much about the fact that Aristotle's *On Rhetoric* forms a very small part of his intellectual output or that his rejection of Platonic philosophy signals no rejection of philosophy as such. It is easy to forget that when he fled Athens to escape prosecution following the death of Alexander, Aristotle did so not in the name of rhetoric but in the name of philosophy, declaring that his departure was motivated so that, as the story goes, "the Athenians might not twice sin against philosophy" by killing him as they had Socrates ("Aristotle").[1] And so, when the French feminist Luce Irigaray takes on Aristotle, she does so as a philosopher, and he fares poorly under her analysis, his vituperations against women being both vicious and libelous. She cites Aristotle's philosophical characterizations of women as similar to boys in physique (and, of course, the boy is just a poor carbon copy of a man), as "infertile male[s]," as "foul," as taking no pleasure in coitus or if taking pleasure being unable to conceive, as possessing "prime matter" (that is, boundlessness, formlessness) in their menstrual blood, and as being frozen in place like plants, unable to move on their own (*Speculum* 160, 163).

Now I think it puts not too fine a point on it to say that in addition to being a philosopher, Aristotle has been something like rhetoric's grand patriarch for 2,500 years, and so given Irigaray's own extraordinary sensitivities to the power of rhetoric, it is curious that nowhere does she address Aristotle as a rhetorical theorist or what the implications his notions about women might have for the status of that theorizing. I take this refusal, a blind spot even, to be a consequence of Irigaray's commitments to philosophy (despite her quarrel with its history and theorizing), where ethics' central question has always been *"how to live?"* and metaphysics' *"what is there?"* (Walton 147-48). This is not to say, however, that Irigaray has no theory of rhetoric. To be sure, her theorizing of sexed language alone has *significant* implications for the discipline's theory and practices.

In distinct contrast to philosophy, however, the common thread running throughout rhetoric's checkered history has been the quest to arrive at a satisfactory theory and practice of political, judicial, and social change. We have never concerned ourselves with big "T" truth, leaving that to philosophy and religion, instead contenting ourselves with the possibility that we might be able to arrive at little "t" truth, our accommodation to what we believe to be the inevitability of the universe, that what counts as truth is *neither* constant nor eternal. I want to suggest, however, that putting Luce Irigaray's philosophical project in contact with the rhetorical enterprise makes visible one of our most serious ethical dilemmas.

Having said as much, I want to be bold enough also to say that despite Aristotle's initial hateful characterizations of women, Irigarayan scholars also need rhetoric, and it is in this intersection that we will find how her work enriches ours. As one of the two oldest continuous intellectual traditions in the West, the field of rhetoric has amassed an enormous body of theory *about* and set of practices *aimed at* how audiences might be moved to think, know, feel, or do something. In fact, nothing is more central to the rhetorical enterprise than change, and we, as rhetorical scholars, spend most of our time thinking about how it happens and how it might be brought about, and in this sense, I am convinced that *our* project is profoundly important to that of Irigaray.

This is to say that a theory of how change might be brought about has never been more urgent for Irigarayan scholars, as she has turned in her later, much more political work, to a complete rejection of a separatist politics and to the desire to bring men into women's struggles, saying: "women's liberation should come about through a dialectic with the other gender and its liberation" (*Democracy* 14). Hence, Irigaray *needs* rhetoric to bring its enormous potential to bear on the question of how men might be brought into the struggle for how sexual difference might be realized as a social positivity and not a violence.

Now, having said that, I want to say that rhetoric needs Irigaray no less than she needs rhetoric, and so I have a quite humble aim here: to grapple in a very speculative, and very limited, fashion with the way in which rhetoric might be put in contact with Irigaray in the interest of moving beyond Aristotle's misogynist legacy and, I argue, that of his twentieth-century successor, Kenneth Burke, in order to suggest our affinities.

As is well-known, until the mid-point of the twentieth century, Aristotle's definition of rhetoric as "the discovery of the available means of persuasion," and *persuasion* as our master term, stood without challenge. However, despite a strong feminist presence in rhetorical studies, the question of the extent to which the entire rhetorical enterprise might be problematized in respect to its hostility to the feminine has remained undertheorized. In my view, that condition is only worsened by the intervention of the literary theorist, Kenneth Burke, who is perhaps most (in)famous in rhetorical studies for declaring that "Man is the symbol-using animal" (*Language* 3). In 1950, he accomplished, with the publication of *A Rhetoric of Motives*, what no one else had: he revised the master term of rhetoric from Aristotle's *persuasion* to his own term, *identi-*

fication. He writes, in a now quaint sexism, in a very famous passage, which I quote at length in hopes of ultimately making my point here:

> A is not identical with his colleague, B. But insofar as their interests are joined, A is *identified* with B. Or he may *identify himself* with B even when their interests are not joined, if he assumes that they are, or is persuaded to believe so. Here are ambiguities of substance. In being identified with B, A is "substantially one" with a person other than himself. Yet at the same time he remains unique, an individual locus of motives. Thus he is both joined and separate, at once a distinct substance and consubstantial with another. . . .

> For substance, in the old philosophies, was an *act*; and a way of life is an *acting-together*; and in acting together, men have common sensations, concepts, images, ideas, attitudes that make them *consubstantial*. (20-21; emphasis in original)

In other words, speakers do not "persuade" audiences: they *create identifications* that move audiences to an action or an attitude by crafting arguments that apparently join the interests of the speaker and the audience. In this way, audiences come to have an interest in acting together in common, for a common purpose.

Crucially, he fails to problematize identification here within the context of a sexed language, despite his well-known theorizing elsewhere of the way language shapes social reality. Moreover, he easily passes over the certainty that speakers will convince audiences that their interests are joined, *even when they are not*, in point of fact, showing his hand by relying on the masculine pronoun and by reverting to the "old philosophies" to ground his notion of consubstantiality. Indeed, Irigaray's appraisal of the "old philosophies" as profoundly committed to treating substance as a solid, as a property of the masculine, discloses just how, in relying on them, Burke could arrive at an equally interested, sexually indifferent notion of substance based on commonalities among *Mankind*.

Notwithstanding the influence of Burke's formulation of rhetoric, for Irigarayan scholars, his enthusiastic embrace of a Freudian identification must be put over and against Irigaray's relentless critique of Sigmund Freud/Jacques Lacan and the Oedipal complex where identifications create the sexed subject. For Freud/Lacan, the little girl can never identify with the mother *as* a woman and especially not with those (crazy) females who do not accept their castration and who therefore, in Freud/Lacan's view, *act like* men. Because her mother is castrated (mutilated, incomplete, without a penis, and so undesirable for identification), her own mother's body can never be "the body," which the "woman" takes to have "the same interest" as her own. She may temporarily identify with her mother, but she is obliged to give up that identification so that she may move into the Symbolic order with its Law of the Father where her function is to be The Body and The Phallus *for* man. To be truly "feminine," then, a woman is consigned to identification with the father, and she must give up all hope of identifying with the woman who is her mother; indeed she must be jealous of, even hate, her. *But perhaps of even more significance, because she is castrated, there is no chance that man will want to identify with her either.* Hence, the question of identification in rhetoric is not merely vexed for women, but profoundly cathected.

Now Burke would have less trouble with this critique than one might imagine, as his explanation of his project in his *Rhetoric* begins to make visible as he

> considers the ways in which individuals are at odds with one another or become identified with groups more or less at odds with one another. . . . "[I]dentification" is . . . to confront the implications of *division.* . . . If men were not apart from one another, there would be no need for the rhetorician to proclaim their unity. (22)

He later goes on to spell out that rhetoric is fundamentally an adversarial process in which opponents take up battle on

> a mediatory ground that makes their communication possible, thus providing the first condition necessary for their interchange of blows. [When you] put identification and division ambiguously together, so that you cannot know for certain just where one ends and the other begins, . . . you have the characteristic invitation to rhetoric. (25)

In other words, men's and women's differences are an invitation to "good" rhetoric that will produce "common" ground through verbal combat. Irigaray, however, would surely find this scenario devastating for women and in it what is most objectionable about Man: a preoccupation with conflict, war even, when talking about communication, and the drive to consolidate the other into self-sameness and the One. Whereas, as Cecilia Sjoholm makes painstakingly clear, Irigaray is all too aware of the rhetoricity of the language of identification and conflict; when it comes to the implications for women of his theorizing, Burke does not know what he is saying.

What Burke cannot hear is that his theory of consubstantiality requires that it be in the instant that the gap between identification and division *closes* that agency occurs, as it becomes possible to act collectively only in the moment that one shares substance with another or, as Irigaray would have it, in the moment one shares solids, which for her is the domain of the masculine. Thus, in the process of constituting audiences, "good" rhetoric will necessarily exclude from that scene the feminine, which is identified with fluids. Even worse for rhetoric, in relying on a notion of substance to shore up his theory of identification, Burke guarantees a certain kind of misfire; for as Damien Casey points out, substance that concerns itself with "identity," not "alterity," *does not open itself to reception.* As he puts it: "The nature of love, Irigaray argues, is not just to give love, but to create a space for its reception" (54; see also Irigaray, *Ethics* 55). A jealous rhetoric, I think Irigaray might say, made *for* the One, cannot speak *to* the Two.

Irigaray, however, opens the possibility that something like agency and action can take place elsewhere and without the foreclosure of woman's fluidity. This, then, is her gift to rhetoric: the interval, that is, the "nearness or distance between subject and object" (Olkowski 82), the spacing that would pry open what Irigaray describes as "the freedom of questioning between two" (*Ethics* 183). As Dorothea Olkowski notes, Irigaray's turn to the interval points to a "change in the foundations of language" and, therefore, is of the essence to rhetoric's capacity for acting within and through the interval to effect social and political change (77). However, there is a caution here for rhetoric, for Olkowski writes that this change in foundations "requires more than a strategy, a tactic, although it may well require that too" (77). In other words, while strategy and tactics may be *necessary* for change, as rhetoric has always claimed, they are not *sufficient*. Irigaray writes: "Language would be more of the order of a temporal bridge between retroaction and anticipation" (*Ethics* 176), which as Olkowski notes, "constitut[e] the interval," and they are the "something more" than strategy and tactic (77).

Irigaray thinks this "temporal bridge" that stretches between reaction to the past and a future yet to come as the intertwining of the one and the other. Her famous two lips—the labia—remind us that the gap is constantly opening and closing, rubbing, touching, never becoming one, yet never fully breached. Moreover, Sjoholm characterizes the intertwining as *rhetorical* and "creat[ing] an imbalance" (105). Now rhetoric has always relied on the unbalancing of the way things are now for its action, the something that is produced in the seizing of the opportune moment when stasis is disturbed and something otherwise might take place. Rhetoric, then, might have quite another potential than merely producing identifications through strategy and tactics, and that is to produce the *limit* for sexed beings. This is to say that rhetoric has the potential for making visible the Two.

What is striking about one of Olkowski's alternative descriptions of the interval is its uncanny resemblance to rhetoric's potentials when it is not thought instrumentally, that is: "articulated as that moment in which reality is created as unforeseen and absolutely new, such that one can never speak of the actualization of possibilities but only of the actualization through differentiation of the virtual, that is, the real but unactualized (in space) multiplicity" (82). What this suggests to me is that rhetoric, as a rich source of production of realities "unforseen and absolutely new," has the potential to inhabit the excessive surplus of the interval.

Olkowski takes us further with this possibility by turning to Henri Bergson's notion of the interval and affectivity that she finds in Irigaray, that is, "the interval lies between affective excitation and reaction[,] . . . [a moment] at the intersection of matter and memory" (82). Significantly for rhetoric, a notion of interest also emerges in Bergson's theory that finds its way into Irigaray's conception of the interval. Olkowski contends that within the interval there are two lines of becoming, one oriented toward affect, one toward perception. On one line,

> affective temporality (the subject) . . . pays attention only to what inter-
> ests it in the moment of the interval. . . . [On the other,] the subject
> becomes conscious of an affective recollection that nonetheless corre-
> sponds to its perception and that is adopted by that subject according to
> its interests. Each recollection is actualized . . . not as the past of its own
> present, but as freedom, as a new present, a moment of creation, and this
> takes place precisely in the interval. Thus, the interval is the moment, the
> gap, the abyss, between affective temporality and active extensionality
> between time and space. (83)

Moreover, as Olkowski points out, "woman's own affective temporality . . .
makes everything possible: speech, promises, alliances" (83). The interval,
then, would be decisive insofar as rhetoric is concerned, as it puts interest and
the passion of the lived body together in a way that does not consume either
A or B, as Burke would have it, and yet keeps a notion of interest alive that
would provide an excitation for change that now becomes possible through
woman's affective temporality.

For this reason, a failure to account for woman's affective temporality is
not only lethal for her but for rhetoric as well. Without a doubt, when
Olkowski continues, she makes this clear:

> [T]he body of perception is directed by and toward its interests in the
> world, and it perceives those interests as solid objects to be acted on,
> while the body of affection is fluid ontological memory. . . . Without the
> interval, that gap between what is perceived and felt and what is acted,
> no new memory images will ever arise to join perception, and no new
> acts will ever occur. (84)

If Olkowski is correct in her reading of Irigaray, there really will be nothing
new under the sun until sexual difference is taken seriously by rhetoric, and
temporality may be the key.

It is my sense that at the end of Barbara Biesecker's rigorous book on
Burke (where, not incidentally, she saves Burke from himself) that her gift to
rhetoric intersects with Irigaray's and, consequently, between them holds out
great promise for our future. Biesecker imagines "temporality . . . as radical
undecidability, potential discontinuity, and rupture and, thus . . . a resource
of social change" (101). Her characterization bears a strong resemblance to
Olkowski's description of the interval and its potentials: "temporality is the
haphazard and unruly force that constitutes a spatiotemporal breach that
makes possible a human intervention that may interrupt or divert what
appears to be destined" (Biesecker 101). This "rupture" or "spatiotemporal
breach" marks the critical moment as a decision not to *close* the interval but
as the effort to hold it *open*. The key term of rhetoric, then, would not be
thought as "identification" where A and B are joined, irrespective of real
interests, but as "interval" where interest excites affective temporality, joining
perception with memory, in a space where two intertwine without joining,
where the *friction* of sexuate being produces "the unforeseen and absolutely
new" (Olkowski 82).

Where Burke's theory of identification takes difference and division to *precede* rhetoric's operation, Irigaray's thinking of the interval would teach us that difference and division are an *effect* of rhetoric when we take seriously the notion that we are in the grip of a determining sexual indifference of the One. That is, as Irigaray puts it so poignantly, "If we are to be as one, isn't it necessary for us first to be *two?*" ("Three Genres" 150).

Irigaray's critique of identification and sexual difference lays out the dilemma to which an ethical rhetoric must address itself. Irigaray concurs that identification involves a surrender, but where Burke sees this only as an opportunity for persuasion, Irigaray foregrounds the ethical bind that occurs when surrender takes place within the economy of one sex, where there is only one language available to both sexes, and where that language already represents only masculine desire. That is, she asks the hard questions that Burke evades: can there be anything like "choice," when the conditions of representation preclude genuine alternatives? When one sex *must* take its interests to be consubstantial, the same, with those of the other sex? What can it mean for rhetoricians to go on talking about agency in the same old way in the face of her critique of sexual indifference?

It is my profoundest hope that by putting Irigarayan scholars and rhetorical studies in contact with one another that the something new Irigaray aches for might take place, that there might be an intertwining such that sexual difference might become social and political reality and that rhetoric might become the force for the real, radical change that it has always yearned for.

NOTE

[1] This story may very well be apocryphal but has been widely disseminated about Aristotle's sudden departure from Athens.

WORKS CITED

"Aristotle (384-322 B.C.)." *The Classical Library.* The Classical Library, 2000. Web. 18 May 2012.

Biesecker, Barbara. *Addressing Postmodernity: Kenneth Burke, Rhetoric, and a Theory of Social Change.* Tuscaloosa: U of Alabama P, 1997. Print.

Burke, Kenneth. *Language as Symbolic Action.* Berkeley: U of California P, 1968. Print.

---. *A Rhetoric of Motives.* Berkeley: U of California P, 1969. Print.

Casey, Damien. "Luce Irigaray and the Advent of the Divine." *Pacifica* 12.1 (Feb. 1999): 27-54. Print.

Irigaray, Luce. *An Ethics of Sexual Difference.* Trans. Carolyn Burke and Gillian C. Gill. Ithaca: Cornell UP, 1993. Print.

---. *Democracy Begins Between Two.* Trans. Kirsteen Anderson. New York: Routledge, 2001. Print.

---. *Speculum of the Other Woman.* Trans. Gillian C. Gill. Ithaca: Cornell UP, 1985. Print.

---. "The Three Genres." *The Irigaray Reader.* Ed. Margaret Whitford. Cambridge: Basil Blackwell, 1991.140-53. Print.

Olkowski, Dorothea E. "The End of Phenomenology: Bergson's Interval in Irigaray." *Hypatia* 15.3 (2000): 73-91. Print.

Sjoholm, Cecelia. "Crossing Lovers: Luce Irigaray's *Elemental Passions.*" *Hypatia* 15.3 (2000): 92-112. Print.

Walton, Kendall. "Aesthetics—What? Why? And Wherefore?" *The Journal of Aesthetics and Art Criticism* 65:2 (2007): 147-61. Print.

26

THE EMERGENCE AND SHAPING OF WELLS'S VOICE IN HER EARLY PUBLIC RHETORIC

Sue Carter Wood

> Thou knowest I hunger & thirst after righteousness & knowledge. O, give me the steadiness of purpose, the will to acquire both. Twenty-five years old today? May another 10 years find me increased in honesty & purity of purpose & motive!
>
> — Ida B. Wells
> July 16, 1887
> Memphis Diary

The incendiary nature of Ida B. Wells's rhetoric is evident not just in the pamphlets of her antilynching campaign but also in the newspaper editorials following the lynchings of three young African American businessmen, one a close family friend. Her writings in her newspaper, the Memphis *Free Speech,* following the March lynchings propelled her to a national spotlight, with black newspapers and some white newspapers across the country following the evolving situation (Giddings 183-95). This period of intense and passionate reporting culminated with Wells's editorial of May 21, 1892, where she claimed that the real motive for lynchings had nothing to do with black men raping white women. In her own words:

> Eight Negroes lynched since last issue of the "Free Speech" one at Little Rock, Ark., last Saturday morning where the citizens broke into the penitentiary and got their man; three near Anniston, Ala., one near New Orleans; and three at Clarksville, Ga., the last three for killing a white man, and five on the same old racket—the new alarm about raping white women. The same programme of hanging, then shooting bullets into the lifeless bodies was carried out to the letter. Nobody in this section of the country believes the old threadbare lie that Negro men rape white women. If Southern white men are not careful, they will over-reach themselves and public sentiment will have a reaction; a conclusion will then be reached which will be very damaging to the moral reputation of their women. (qtd. in Royster 79)

Following publication of this editorial, as biographer Paula J. Giddings notes, "the Memphis dailies . . . stirred up the city with provocative words of their own" (210). Wells's editorial was discussed in the *Memphis Commercial* and republished in *The Evening Scimitar*, the editors of both making it clear, in detail, what should happen to its unnamed author. Almost immediately, a white mob destroyed the offices of the *Free Speech*; Wells's partner narrowly escaped the city with his life; and Wells's life was threatened. Given the extreme responses to the editorial, one must wonder about Wells's intent, her reading of the rhetorical situation, and her choice of strategies. Did she anticipate the strong reactions her editorials would provoke? Or did she underestimate the response of white readers? Did she compose her editorial impulsively, even carelessly, rushing before leaving on a long-planned trip? Or did she intentionally violate taboos about what subjects should not be uttered publicly?

A study of Wells's early career is insightful in understanding the rhetorical sensibilities and acumen she had developed by the point she crafted her inflammatory editorials in Memphis. Shirley Wilson Logan discusses Wells's rhetorical education in *Liberating Language: Sites of Rhetorical Education in Nineteenth-Century Black America*. Discussing Wells in the context of her newspaper work in the 1880s, Logan argues that Wells, along with Frederick Douglass, "understood their editorial roles as an engagement with rhetorical education" (101). Logan summarizes Wells's journalistic work between 1884 and 1887 as "a period during which she edited the Memphis literary society's *Evening Star*, read widely, kept a notebook of ideas, wrote to the local and national press, participated in organizations of journalists and worked as a correspondent" (103).[1] Indeed, my reading of Wells's Memphis diary from 1885-1887 reveals a young woman whose rhetorical education involved reflection on the rhetorical situations in which she found herself, strong feelings of regret, acceptance, or resolve and often decisive, impassioned action. Further, in reading the diary alongside the autobiography, it is clear that in the years leading up to 1892, Wells had become astute at reading rhetorical situations and reframing them so as to bring power to those who had been construed as powerless.

My reading of the development of Wells's rhetoric is guided by Kelly Myers's 2011 *Rhetoric Society Quarterly* article "*Metanoia* and the Transformation of Opportunity," this year's recipient of the Charles Kneupper award. Myers's discussion of the relationship between *kairos*, or opportunity, and *metanoia*, or regret, offers insight into the processes by which Wells developed her characteristic and strident rhetoric and shaped the impassioned voice of her antilynching campaign. Following a brief discussion of *kairos* and *metanoia*, I use Wells's Memphis diary and her autobiography to chart her developing rhetorical prowess. In this way, I argue, it is possible to better appreciate the rhetorical strategies and calculated risks Wells took in publishing the inflammatory editorial of May 21, 1892.[2]

Kairos and Metanoia

As Myers demonstrates, *kairos,* or opportunity, was linked in both ancient writings and European paintings with *metanoia,* or regret. The two concepts are linked closely, even intimately so, with *metanoia* indicating a "powerful internal activity, movement on the level of the soul" (7). Opportunities, both those seized and those missed, have the potential to affect the souls of rhetors, prompting "repentance, regret, reflection, and transformation" (7). Myers continues that "metanoia is a reflective act in which a person returns to a past event in order to see it anew" (8). *Metanoia* carries with it powerful emotions that come with the potential to spur change. As Myers explains, "[T]he emotional response that comes with reflection is often a motivating force that leads to a transformation" (8). Such transformation is enabled through the insight or knowledge gained in such opportunities: "In *metanoia,* mind and body, feeling and intellect, collaborate in creating new knowledge and perspective" (9).

Of direct relevance to understanding the rhetorical situation in which Wells found herself in 1892 is the relationship of *kairos* and *metanoia* to the context of a situation and the agency of a rhetor. As Myers explains:

> [A]fter the opportunity is revealed, action must be taken, and after the initial action, subsequent actions will follow that then confirm or deny *metanoia.* Thus *kairos* and *metanoia* can be re-imagined in a way that returns agency to the individual and in fact makes action crucial to the revelation of *metanoia.* (10)

That is, with opportunity and the new knowledge it brings, comes the responsibility to act. While Myers's discussion of *metanoia* is deeper and richer than this brief sketch allows, the key concepts explained here lend themselves to analyzing Wells's development as a rhetor.

Wells's Reflections

It is evident that Wells was transformed by the March 1892 lynchings in Memphis. But how did Wells come to both the strong voice, with which she spoke out against injustice, and the rhetorical acumen, with which she read and responded to rhetorical situations? Considering the diary she kept in Memphis in 1885-1887, along with her recollections of the years leading up to the lynchings, provides insight in this regard.[3] In the discussion that follows, I identify three patterns of rhetorical behavior Wells developed in the years leading up to 1892, patterns that informed Wells's rhetorical strategies and influenced the shaping of her public voice.[4] Most pertinent are her feelings about her outspoken nature, her ability to reframe situations so as to speak out, and her ability to move beyond the opinions of others to investigate matters for herself.

Speaking Out

First there is the matter of her self-described "sharp tongue." In the diary, several times Wells acknowledges her outspokenness, coupled with regret at the result, ending with a petition to God to help her change her behavior. The December 29, 1885, entry illustrates this pattern. Wells had been dismissed from Rust College without completing a secondary school degree because of something harsh she had said (50).[5] She records her thoughts on visiting the campus four years later: "[T]he day has been a trying one to me; seeing old enemies, visiting old scenes, recalling the most painful memories of my life, talking them over with those who were prominent actors during my darkest days" (24). She petitions God for forgiveness for what she said: "O My Father, forgive me, forgive me & take away the remembrance of those hateful words, uttered for the satisfaction of self. Humble the pride exhibited and make me Thy child" (24). The yearning for forgiveness displays simple regret for what was said and the pride that motivated her words.

Six years later, Wells shows a more sophisticated understanding of her duty to utter what should be brought to the attention of the public. In fact, she displays considerable rhetorical savvy about the situation, determining to speak up, anticipating the likely consequences of doing so, and strategizing to minimize them. In 1891, Wells published an editorial in the *Free Speech* about the inferior conditions in Memphis schools for African Americans, and afterward the city school board chose not to rehire her, thus ending her only steady income. Wells acknowledges she was aware she might lose her job and chose to publish her critique anyway: "I was still teaching and I wanted to hold my position. Yet I felt that some protest should be made over conditions in the colored schools" (*Crusade* 35-36). Tellingly, before she ran the editorial, Wells appealed to Reverend Nightingale, a partner in the newspaper, to sign it himself. When he refused, Wells opted to run the editorial anyway, unsigned but easily attributable to her. Wells recounts that "I had taken a chance in the interest of the children of our race and had lost out. . . . I thought it was right to strike a blow against a glaring evil and I did not regret it" (*Crusade* 37). Wells's recollection of these events in her autobiography brings to mind Myers's point that "the practical application of *kairos* and *metanoia* insists upon strategic navigation, an approach in which the kairotic moment and the repercussions that follow are met with a balance of skill and intuition" (12).

Clearly Wells had moved from simple repentance over her words she regretted to claiming her outspokenness, to channeling it so as to change the shape of her life and the work she could do. Against Myers's discussion of the transformative potential of *metanoia*, what is most striking about this incident is its role in propelling Wells full-time into the work of journalism—and into the race work she pursued for the rest of her life. Wells seized the opportunity to speak her mind about a matter of race and lost her teaching job as a result—but she also gained the opportunity to devote her energies to journalism, that is, to the activist work she felt drawn to do.

Turning the Tables

In the Memphis diary, Wells records instances of gossip about her, the entries revealing her rage and at times desire for vengeance, along with harsh criticism of those who should know her better. In one entry, Wells records the rumor, circulated through a series of letters, that she had had an affair with a fellow teacher (113). She hears another rumor that her youngest sister, Lily, is actually her own illegitimate child (115). And she confronts rumors that when she was a sixteen-year-old orphan supporting her younger siblings in Holly Springs, she had an affair with a much older doctor who was white (*Crusade* 17). Such rumors angered Wells and caused her to reflect on her own behavior and, at times, to investigate, to find the source of misimpressions and misinformation. Wells's actions stop there, with her being angry, vengeful—and silent.

An incident in 1891 shows Wells responding in a strikingly different matter. A trusted family friend revealed that a minister with whom she had stayed while travelling for the *Free Speech* had warned several young men to stay away from Wells and accused her of immoral behavior (*Crusade* 43). Wells asked to meet the minister to discuss his comments, and unknown to him, she also brought the five friends to whom he had told his tale, along with her family friend. Wells ingeniously engineered a situation entirely to her advantage, confronting the gossiper with not only character witnesses but also an apology she had written that she expected the minister to read to his congregation (43-45).

The Wells of 1891 was capable of analyzing a difficult rhetorical situation and reframing it to her advantage, displaying the cunning intelligence that Myers links to *metis* (12). Wells effectively silenced the rumor at its source, transforming herself from a woman accused to a woman fiercely protecting her own good name: "I told him that my good name was all that I had in the world, that I was bound to protect it from attack by those who felt that they could do so with impunity because I had no brother or father to protect it for me" (*Crusade* 44). Wells's speech goes one step further, for she delivered it to an all-male audience of black men used to monitoring the behavior of black women. With them, she shares a history of all women in slavery who "fought and died rather than yield to the pressure and temptations" of sexual activity. With them, she shares a vision of herself, and of all young black women in the South, as "one southern girl, born and bred, who had tried to keep herself spotless and morally clean as my slave mother had taught me" (*Crusade* 44). Myers, citing Dale L. Sullivan, discusses how "the *kairos* and *metanoia* dynamic can be utilized to move an audience" (12), by providing audience members with a vision that they can believe in. Whether or not Wells's male audience that day accepted her vision of the purity of black women is beside the point, for Wells had created a situation in which she silenced the minister, substituted her words for his, and spoke aloud her own vision of herself.

Becoming Informed

Wells was at times both impulsive and stubbornly decisive.[6] More relevant to this discussion are instances where Wells truly wrestled with a difficult situation and struggled to know what course to take, bringing to mind rhetoric's traditional concern with those aspects of human affairs about which it is impossible to know what is right. During the summer of 1886, Wells was troubled about her future. She would not know until the end of the summer whether she would be rehired by the Memphis schools, and she was torn about whether to join her widowed aunt and younger sisters, who had recently relocated to Visalia, California.[7] Deeply conflicted yet compelled by her aunt's letters, she went to Visalia, sold her return ticket, and was hired in the black school. She taught for four days before resigning, then left for the promise of a job in Kansas City, where she taught for a single day before resigning and returning to teach in the Memphis schools (*Diary* 112).

In the diary entries from July through September of 1886, the word "regret" figures heavily, from selling her return ticket (93) to going into debt to purchase tickets "home" to Memphis (99). It is easier to appreciate that for weeks and weeks Wells was unsure of where her duties should lie, wrestling deep in her soul with the decision she ultimately made, praying for guidance, and, living away from Memphis, growing to value the life she had begun there. Thirty years later, Wells explains her seeming indecisiveness as the result of her finding each situation to be very different than what had been presented to her (*Crusade* 24-27). From the diary, it is easy to see that Wells was dependent on the opinions of others, on information she could glean from letters she received or from conversations with chance acquaintances. Lacking other means of informing herself about her future prospects in California or Missouri, she tested each out, however briefly, before returning to Memphis.

If Wells was deeply conflicted about her duties in 1886, she was torn about life in Memphis for African Americans in the months leading up to, and the weeks following, the 1892 lynchings—but she was not without resources to understand the developing situation there. In her autobiography, Wells notes that she was in Natchez on newspaper business when she heard about the lynchings, and that in her absence the *Free Speech* advised African Americans to leave Memphis:

> The city of Memphis has demonstrated that neither character nor standing avails the Negro if he dares to protect himself against the white man or become his rival. There is nothing we can do about the lynching now, as we are out-numbered and without arms. The white mob could help itself to ammunition without pay, but the order was rigidly enforced against the selling of guns to Negroes. There is therefore only one thing left that we can do; save our money and leave a town which will neither protect our lives and property, not give us a fair trial in the courts, but takes us out and murders us in cold blood when accused by white persons. (*Crusade* 52)

The black community of Memphis responded, with hundreds leaving right away, thousands saving to do so in the coming weeks, and community leaders organizing information meetings and aid efforts (*Crusade* 53-57; Bay 89-95). Facing this volatile situation, Wells responded by gathering information. Wells questioned the promises of advertising from land companies in Kansas and Oklahoma. She investigated the matter herself, spending three weeks in the Oklahoma Territory in communities where black migrants had settled. She reported her findings, positive and negative, so that readers might give the matter of leaving informed consideration (Giddings 195-200). She investigated her personal situation, to see what options might be possible. Wells came to advocate emigration to Africa, a hotly debated issue among the African American elite at the time (Giddings 199). It would take Wells until well into May to decide whether she would leave Memphis herself, and even whether she herself would advise others to do so, querying her partner, J. L. Fleming, about relocating the paper to Oklahoma and writing her long-time supporters about possibilities in New York and Philadelphia (*Crusade* 58).

In the weeks and months following the March lynchings, Wells also began investigating lynchings, and it was through this investigation that she was truly transformed, gaining the new perspective and knowledge Myers references in discussing *metanoia*. In an oft-quoted passage from her autobiography, Wells recounts how she had always accepted claims that lynchings were motivated by black men raping white women. But when three men known to her of unimpeachable character were lynched, Wells came to a new perspective: "This is what opened my eyes to what lynching really was. An excuse to get rid of Negroes who were acquiring wealth and property and thus keep the race terrorized" (64). Myers explains:

> [m]etanoia offers an important form of reflection in which the emotional impact of a missed opportunity motivates a transformation of thought, advancing a rhetor's understanding of the situation. Thus through such a learning process, painful as it may be, a rhetor becomes better prepared for the next moment of opportunity. (11)

It is easy to see that Wells was prepared with facts about the real reasons behind lynchings in the next several years, as she lectured and as she published her antilynching pamphlets "Southern Horrors: Lynch Law in All Its Phases," "A Red Record," and "Mob Rule in New Orleans." It is worth noting as well that even before publishing her May 21 editorial, Wells had personally investigated the lynchings on which she had reported (*Crusade* 64-65; Giddings 207-08). Indeed, at the point that she penned that editorial, Wells was writing about both the new vision she had and the knowledge she had sought out to confirm it.

Conclusion

Given the rhetorical education Wells had acquired by the spring of 1892, I agree with Bay's assessment that Wells brought to the May 21 editorial considerable rhetorical acumen, as well as direct knowledge of likely consequences for black journalists who questioned the traditional justification for lynching (104). I have used Myers's discussion of *metanoia* and *kairos* to highlight ways that Wells developed the rhetorical sensitivities she brought to bear on the Memphis lynchings in the spring of 1892, illustrating particularly that Wells learned to reframe rhetorical situations so as to open up a space in which to speak her mind. I have also indicated that the investigations into lynchings for which Wells is so well known had their roots in the transformational moment that Wells wrote about in her autobiography, a moment that can be better appreciated against the images Myers shares of opportunity coupled with regret.

It is perhaps fitting that I end with an image Wells recorded in her Memphis diary some five years before that editorial, on the occasion of her birthday, where her earnest plea seems almost ironic in comparison to what the years would soon bring: "Thou knowest I hunger & thirst after righteousness & knowledge. O, give me the steadiness of purpose, the will to acquire both. Twenty-five years old today? May another 10 years find me increased in honesty & purity of purpose & motive!" (151). The voice of the twenty-five year-old could not have possibly foreseen the effects that racial violence would have on her, or the power her voice would gain.

NOTES

[1] On top of that I add maintaining correspondence with family, friends, and acquaintances and teaching school to support herself, at times, while her eleven-year-old sister was living with her. In addition to discussing Wells's rhetorical education through her newspaper work, Logan discusses Wells's self-education through such efforts as elocution lessons and participation in a literary society (42-45).

[2] Following the March lynchings, Wells published other writings in the *Free Speech* that are available only through their republication in other black newspapers of the era. Giddings helpfully uses many of these in her discussion of the atmosphere in Memphis from March to June of 1892.

[3] Wells's writings go only so far, however. Her autobiography, like any of that genre, was shaped for a public audience and as such may not reflect Wells's thinking leading up to her 1892 editorial. Further, many of Wells's diaries and papers, including those from 1892, were lost in a house fire. The published diary recounts her life from the end of December 1885 to May 1887, years before the editorial was published, and more briefly two periods of her life later on.

[4] In applying these concepts to understand Wells's rhetorical situation in Memphis in 1892, I take as given the many opportunities, both those seized and those lost, in Wells's early life: the good fortune to live in a small town where a freedman's school, Rust College, provided formal education; the misfortune of losing her parents and one brother to Yellow Fever, along with the fortune to be visiting her grandmother out of town when the epidemic hit; the misfortune of the altercation on the railroad in 1884, the good fortune in the initial ruling in her lawsuit against the railroad; the misfortune in having that ruling overturned in an opinion that insulted her; and the good fortune in the career in journalism that resulted from writing about that lawsuit.

[5] During her lifetime, Wells neither detailed what happened nor identified the key actors.

[6] Her impulsiveness is amply documented in diary entries, for example resolving to follow greater economy one week and the next spending $3.50 for a new hat (*Diary* 138). There are as well examples of her speaking decisively, most notably when, at sixteen years old, she decides, against the wishes of adults in her community, to keep her siblings together in the family home following the death of their parents.

[7] The aunt's household included her own three young children as well as Wells's two younger sisters, Annie and Lily. On her way to visit California, Wells stopped in Topeka to attend a meeting of the National Education Association and to visit in Kansas City, Missouri.

WORKS CITED

Bay, Mia. *To Tell the Truth Freely: The Life of Ida B. Wells*. New York: Hill and Wang, 2009. Print.

Giddings, Paula J. *Ida: A Sword among Lions*. New York: HarperCollins, 2008. Print.

Logan, Shirley Wilson. *Liberating Language: Sites of Rhetorical Education in Nineteenth-Century Black America*. Carbondale: Southern Illinois UP, 2008. Print.

Myers, Kelly A. "Metanoia and the Transformation of Opportunity." *Rhetoric Society Quarterly* 41.1 (2011): 1-18. Print.

Royster, Jacqueline Jones. *Southern Horrors and Other Writings: The Anti-Lynching Campaign of Ida B. Wells, 1892-1900*. Boston: Bedford/St. Martin's, 1997. Print.

Wells, Ida B. *Crusade for Justice: The Autobiography of Ida B. Wells*. Ed. Alfreda M. Duster. Chicago: U of Chicago P, 1970. Print.

---. *The Memphis Diary of Ida B. Wells: An Intimate Portrait of the Activist as a Young Woman*. Ed. Miriam DeCosta-Willis. Boston: Beacon, 1995. Print.

SECTION

V

RE/FRAMING RACIAL, ETHNIC, AND CLASS IDENTIFICATIONS

27

"HISPANIC AND WHITE ONLY"

Rhetoric and the Changing Notion(s) of Race in the United States

Malinda Williams

Beginning in 2000, the US Census Bureau made a significant change to the way it inquired about questions of race and Hispanic origin. First, the bureau placed the question asking respondents if they were Spanish/Hispanic/Latino directly before the question on race, whereas in 1990 this order was reversed—the question on race appeared a full three questions before the one on Spanish/Hispanic origin (Grieco and Cassidy 2; "Appendix E"). More significantly, however, in the 2000 questionnaire respondents were given the option of selecting one or more racial categories to indicate their racial identity, including white, black, American Indian, and several categories of Asian origin (Grieco and Cassidy 2). This format for the question on race was used again in the 2010 census, but additional changes were made to the question identifying Hispanic, Latino, or Spanish origin: first, respondents were advised that "For this census, Hispanic origins are not races," and they were also given particular options for identifying their national origins beyond the previously included categories of Mexican, Puerto Rican, and Cuban, including "Argentinean, Colombian, Dominican, Nicaraguan, Salvadoran, Spaniard, and so on" (Humes et al. 1). Both censuses used the terms "Hispanic" and "Latino" interchangeably, and both also made clear that Hispanic persons could be of any race.

Interestingly, in both the 2000 and 2010 censuses, the Hispanic population overwhelmingly identified as either "white" alone or "some other race" alone. The 2010 figures show, first, that the Hispanic population overall has grown by 43 percent since 2000, and that 53 percent of this population self-identifies as "white only," up from 48 percent in 2000. Also in 2010, nearly 37 percent of Hispanic individuals identified themselves as "some other race," a designator that is most often used to signify national origin. Another compelling statistic from the 2010 report is that only 6 percent of Hispanic respondents claimed two or more races, and even more compelling, only 2.5 percent self-identified as black or African American; these figures are despite the fact that throughout Latin America there is a considerable population with a racially mixed heritage that includes a significant African component.

I begin with this rather lengthy account of census results not merely because I find them interesting, but more importantly because this data raises complicated questions about our conceptions of race in this country, which on the one hand are perpetually fluid and, on the other, remain entirely static. For instance, although the US Office of Management and Budget (OMB) revised their standards for classifying race and ethnicity back in 1997 to consider "Hispanic or Latino" to be an ethnic and not a racial category ("Revisions"), common parlance still conceives of "Hispanic" as a racial term. And, although both the 2000 and 2010 censuses make clear that an individual of Hispanic origin may be of any race, in this country the terms "Hispanic" and "Latino/a" are most often used as racial designations to define someone as *not* white. So, given these common and widespread (mis)understandings of official ethnic and racial standards, what is the significance of a growing population that rejects these notions and asserts its whiteness more than half of the time? And, in a nation where historically "one drop" of African blood has defined an individual as black, what does it mean to have a significant portion of society reject this notion? In short, what do these and other statistics that have emerged from the Hispanic community in the United States say about the contemporary rhetorics of race in this country? Because race is a social (and often rhetorical) construction, it is crucial that we pay attention to the way(s) that prevailing conversations about race in the United States are being influenced and "reframed" by this growing population.

One of the most compelling current conversations on race and the Hispanic community surrounds the case of George Zimmerman, the man (at the time of this writing) on trial for fatally shooting teenager Trayvon Martin in Florida. As I'm sure we're all aware, initial reports of the incident described Zimmerman as a white man who shot and killed an unarmed black teenager. As the story unfolded further, it was revealed that Zimmerman's father is white but his mother is Peruvian, so news outlets began to describe him first as "Latino" or "Hispanic" and eventually as a "white Latino" or "white Hispanic." It is this second set of terms that seems to be causing confusion or even anger amongst many members of the general public. On the more benign end of the spectrum of reactions, listener Richard Fishman writes in to NPR's Scott Simon that he

> was confused by a reference to Mr. Zimmerman . . . as a white Latino. I've never heard that term. Has it been used before? Seems to me that many in the media are trying at all costs to disassociate Mr. Zimmerman from his minority status, and make sure he is characterized at least partially as white. ("Your Letters")

For Fishman, then, the term "white Latino" seems like a ploy invented by the media to exploit and sensationalize the "white man kills black teen" elements of the story.

Fishman certainly is skeptical, but his response is tame compared to the more vehement reactions reported by NPR's "Tell Me More" host Michel

Martin. In an e-mail complaining about the show's coverage of the case, listener Harlan McKenna begs Martin to

> please stop saying that George Zimmerman is white. Today you said he's white of Hispanic descent. He's mixed race, just like Obama. When did you ever refer to Obama as white of African descent? This is infuriating and irresponsible. I can only conclude that you think the story of white man murders black teen is more volatile than Latino man kills black teen. ("In Trayvon Martin Case")

Again, this listener imagines the term describing Zimmerman as both white *and* Latino or Hispanic is some part of a media conspiracy meant to boost ratings, but in this case he makes the bold claim that its use is "irresponsible." I find this word compelling and curious—what exactly does McKenna deem irresponsible? The media exploiting the racial elements of the story, or the fact that a man can be both Latino *and* white? I lean more toward the latter interpretation, especially considering his reference to Obama's racial makeup. It is true that you would never hear Obama referred to as a white man of African descent, despite the fact that one of his parents is white and the other is African. In this country at least, it takes only "one drop" of black blood to make someone black, and it is rarely, if ever, the choice of an individual with both black and white ancestry to claim a white identity, at least not without suffering allegations of "passing" for white.

McKenna's comment, among others, prompted an episode of "Tell Me More" devoted to discussions of who is considered white in this country, and Martin's guest was sociologist Jean Halley from Wagner College in New York. Halley's intention on the show was obviously to educate the public on issues of race and racial construction, and she shared her belief that race "is not a biological reality. It's a social reality" ("In Trayvon Martin Case"). Most, if not all, credible contemporary scholars and academics agree with Halley. Ian Haney López, a leader in the field of race and law, defines race as "a vast group of people loosely bound together by historically contingent, socially significant elements of their morphology and/or ancestry" ("The Social Construction" 193); similarly, critical race theory pioneers Michael Omi and Howard Winant define it as *"a concept which signifies and symbolizes social conflicts and interests by referring to different types of human bodies"* (55; emphasis in original). What is central to these various definitions of race is the consensus that it is *socially* constructed.

As expected, the public comments responding to the transcript of this story on NPR's website run the gamut from support for Halley's and Martin's views to Rodney King-esque reactions of "can't we all just get along" to out-and-out challenges to the notion that race is not biological. One particularly heated response that is worth quoting here comes from Christopher Longest; he emphatically declares that "Halley's statement about race not being a 'biological reality' is fodder for the uninformed and racially/politically [sic] biased. Race is determined by genetics" ("In Trayvon Martin Case"). Given the scholarly consensus that race is indeed a social construction, however, it seems that Longest is the one who is uninformed. In her book *Skin: A Natural History*, Nina Jablonski traces the evolutionary reasons for the spectrum of skin colors across the human population, claiming that skin shade can indeed tell us about "the nature of the past environments in which people lived" (95), but she rejects the notion that skin color can be used effectively as a marker of racial identity. She argues that despite the belief that there is a connection between skin color and inherited differences that distinguish humans from each other, there is less genetic difference among geographically dispersed humans than in other similar animal species (95). Skin color difference is just the most obvious way that people vary from one another, and as such it is a convenient way to categorize people into distinct groups, as if that categorization were somehow natural.

Despite this and similar evidence to the contrary, however, Longest is unfortunately not alone in his thinking on what race is, which either means those of us who research and write about issues of race and culture need to do a better job of translating our work for the general public, or the general public is just not that interested. In the latter part of his comment, Longest did make one cogent claim I agree with: "Race and culture are obviously connected but there are cultural distinctions within races" ("In Trayvon Martin Case"). Indeed, in addition to defining race as a social construction, Omi and Winant claim that racial formation, which they define as "the sociohistorical process by which racial categories are created, inhabited, transformed, and destroyed" (55), occurs not only because of the influence of various social structures but also because of cultural factors that attribute to the "origins, patterning, and transformation of racial difference" (56). What this means, then, is that any particular understanding of race must take into account not only the *social* customs, relationships, and institutions that form racial categories but also the *cultural* ideas, beliefs, and behaviors that give those categories meaning.

Let's turn our attention, then, to both the social and cultural customs that have shaped our understandings of race here, in the United States; in this country, a person is defined as black if he or she has "one drop" of blood from an African ancestor. This is not, of course, a natural category, but rather one that was developed through the social need of early Americans to create some concept of racial purity (and support that concept through the law) and through the continued cultural need to maintain definitive racial categories and differences. In her book *Notes of a White Black Woman*, Judy Scales-Trent maintains that the need to formulate racial norms in the United States began as early as 1662 with antimiscegenation laws in Virginia, and that by the 1700s, white Southerners operated under the social rule that anyone with any kind of African ancestry would officially be considered black; it did not take long for this social rule to be codified into law (3-4). Even though today these racial purity and antimiscegenation laws either no longer exist or, if they do, are not necessarily enforced or given credence, their impact on United States' conceptions of race still strongly remain. The "one-drop" rule, then, continues to define who is black in the United States, and, according to Scales-Trent, this perception is generally accepted by both blacks and whites alike (4).

It is important to note that the "one-drop" rule defines not only who is black in the United States but also who is *not* white, despite any skin-color-evidence to the contrary. Scales-Trent claims that at the genesis of the United States' "one-drop" rule, its developers had other options, including considering those of mixed descent to be white; creating a new, third category; or eliminating the concept of race altogether (4). It is no great stretch to claim that these early Americans did not opt for one of these alternatives because they had a vested interest in preserving whiteness and all the privileges it affords. The benefits of this privilege are still felt today; Omi and Winant claim that "Our ability to interpret racial meanings depends on preconceived notions of a racialized social structure" (59), and indeed without the "clear" definitions of who is white and who is black within the United States, one could not rely on skin color alone to determine racial difference. Haney López argues that "White identity is just as much a racial fabrication [as any other racial identity], and Whites are equally, or even more highly, implicated in preserving the racially constructed status-quo" ("The Social Construction" 192). The primary reason for this, of course, is that any change to the definition of who is white in the United States would mean, in part, that white privilege would begin to lose its meaning, a daunting and terrifying prospect for many.

In his seminal text *Who Is Black?*, scholar F. James Davis points out that the United States' one-drop rule "is unique in that it is found only in the United States and not in any other nation in the world" (13). Indeed, the construction of race and understanding of who is black and white is much different throughout Latin America. While in general our understanding of race in the United States boils down to a black/white dichotomy, most countries in Latin America conceive of race as a color-continuum, with the extreme poles of black and white and many shades in between. Members of the same immediate family, in fact, can be considered different races if there is enough difference in their skin tones. These shades are not merely inconsequential descriptions either but are often official and legally recognized categories.

Take the Dominican Republic, for instance: while to North American eyes the vast majority of the Dominican population would appear to be black, in the Dominican Republic itself only Haitians are black. Dark-skinned Dominicans are more commonly called "Indios," and again, this is not merely a casual term but is an official racial designation that appears on drivers' licenses and other state documents. And, of course, Indio is just one in a panoply of terms used to describe race and shades of skin tone in the Dominican Republic. There are complex social and historical events that have shaped the Dominican understanding of racial categorization but most notable among them is the relationship between the two nations that share the island of Hispaniola: the Dominican Republic and Haiti. Unlike their neighbors to the west, Dominicans conceive of themselves as the proud descendents of both the conquistadors from Spain and the Taíno Indians who were the island's pre-Colombian inhabitants, but the undeniable African element of their heritage has, for the most part, been rhetorically erased. This myth of a Hispanic and indigenous heritage was created in part to distinguish Dominicans from Haitians and has coalesced into a complex anti-Haitian sentiment known as *antihaitianismo* ideology. Scholar David Howard describes *antihaitianismo* in this way: "The Other [i.e., the Haitian] is invariably perceived as black, heathen and alien to white, Spanish *dominicanidad* or 'Dominicanness.' Haiti in popular prejudice, stands for all that is allegedly not Dominican: *négritude*, Africa and non-Christian beliefs" (5). Even those Dominicans who are clearly of African descent participate in this reframing of their history by emphasizing not only their European Spanish roots but their professed indigenous roots as well, hence the term "Indio."

In his excellent book *Black in Latin America*, Henry Louis Gates, Jr. explores the often unseen (at least to North American eyes) presence of blacks and blackness in six Latin American countries, and I am especially moved by his chapter on the Dominican Republic. Gates's surprise and incredulity at this nation that "proudly declare[s] that its heritage [is] primarily 'Spanish, Catholic, and white'" (122) but either ignores or outright denies the African component of its heritage is certainly what many North Americans experience on learning about the Dominican construction of race and its historical roots. Ironically, however, it is often not until confronting North American conceptions of race that many Dominicans recognize, either willingly or unwillingly, their own blackness. Anthropologist Juan Rodríguez, whom Gates interviewed for his book, articulates the experience this way: "I had to discover that I was black. And I discovered that I was black in America, when I first went to New York. Most Dominicans don't discover that they are black until they go to New York" (qtd. in Gates 131). Just as many North Americans have been confused and unsettled by the media's use of the term "white Latino" in the Zimmerman case, many Dominicans would be equally confused and puzzled by the term Afro-Dominican; in their minds, it is a condition that just cannot exist.

But what, if anything, can the Dominican case in particular and/or the Latin American case in general tell us about the racial future of the United States? In his extremely influential book *White By Law*, Haney López does not imagine a future where the Latin American color-continuum model is adopted in the United States, but rather he sees an expanded definition of who is white that will include "those whose physical characteristics most closely resemble the morphology associated with Whites" (155). This could certainly broadly include members of the Hispanic community, and in many ways it already does. But Haney López is also quick to point out that an expanded understanding of who is white would do little, if anything, to ameliorate the lived experiences of discrimination and injustice by members of the Hispanic community at large and in fact could work to make injustices invisible, much in the way that colorblind ideology makes institutional forms of racial discrimination invisible (*White By Law* 162). Indeed, although Latin American constructions of race may recognize categories beyond the dichotomy of black and white, they also operate as "pigmentocracies," or racial hierarchies that privilege the shades of skin on the lighter end of the racial spectrum and denigrate those on the darker end. It seems, then, that although it may take a different form, racial discrimination still exists within both racial systems.

I would like to conclude here with a brief allusion to a news story that dominated the airwaves: that of the "minority baby boom." According to most reports, so-called minority births edged out white births in the United States by 50.4 percent vs. 49.6 percent. However, as Matthew Yglesias points out in his *Slate* article "The Myth of Majority-Minority America," "'A minority,' the census release clarified, 'is anyone who is not single-race white and not Hispanic.' It's not that the census is counting the wrong thing. Rather, I suspect an awful lot of these 'minority' babies are going to be white when they grow up." He continues to relate his own experience as someone who culturally and phenotypically identifies as white but who happens to have a Cuban-American grandfather and a Spanish surname. It is what Yglesias pointedly refers to as the government's "odd one-drop-of-blood conception of Latino identity" that accounts for the majority figure. But, similar to Haney López, Yglesias believes that rather than becoming a genuine "majority-minority" state, the "future of American whiteness will likely evolve to include a larger share of ancestry from Asia and Latin America, just as in the past it's expanded to include people from eastern and Southern Europe." If another prediction that Haney López relates comes true—that by the year 2100 one in three Americans will be Latino (*White By Law* 144)—then this certainly is likely to be the case, given the problematic history of racial formation both in this country and across Latin America.

WORKS CITED

"Appendix E: Facsimiles of Respondent Instructions and Questionnaire Pages." *United States Census 1990*. U.S. Census Bureau, 21 Sept. 1992. Web. 21 May 2012. PDF file.

Davis, F. James. *Who Is Black? One Nation's Definition*. University Park: Pennsylvania State UP, 1991. Print.

Gates, Jr., Henry Louis. *Black in Latin America*. New York: New York UP, 2011. Print.

Grieco, Elizabeth M., and Rachel C. Cassidy. "Overview of Race and Hispanic Origin: Census 2000 Brief." *United States Census 2000*. U.S. Census Bureau, March 2001. Web. 21 May 2012. PDF file.

Haney López, Ian F. "The Social Construction of Race." *Critical Race Theory: The Cutting Edge*. Ed. Richard Delgado. Philadelphia: Temple UP, 1995. 191-203. Print.

---. *White By Law: The Legal Construction of Race*. Rev. ed. New York: New York UP, 2006. Print.

Howard, David. *Coloring the Nation: Race and Ethnicity in the Dominican Republic*. Oxford: Signal Books, 2001. Print.

Humes, Karen R., Nicholas A. Jones, and Roberto R. Ramirez. "Overview of Race and Hispanic Origin: 2010." *United States Census 2010.* U.S. Census Bureau, March 2011. Web. 28 March 2011. PDF file.

"In Trayvon Martin Case, Who's Considered White?" *Tell Me More.* NPR, 5 April 2012. Web. 22 May 2012.

Jablonski, Nina G. *Skin: A Natural History.* Berkeley: U of California P: 2006. Print.

Omi, Michael, and Howard Winant. *Racial Formation in the United States: From the 1960s to the 1990s.* 2nd ed. New York: Routledge, 1994. Print.

"Revisions to the Standards for the Classification of Federal Data on Race and Ethnicity." *Office of Management and Budget.* The Whitehouse, 30 Oct. 1997. Web. 21 May 2012.

Scales-Trent, Judy. *Notes of a White Black Woman.* University Park: Pennsylvania State UP, 1995. Print.

Yglesias, Matthew. "The Myth of Majority-Minority America." *Slate.* The Slate Group, 22 May 2012. Web. 25 May 2012.

"Your Letters: Racial Terms and Baseball Legends." *Weekend Edition.* NPR, 7 April 2012. Web. 22 May 2012.

28

REFRAMING THE SECRET IDENTITY OF WHITENESS

The Rhetorics of White Privilege in Superhero Media

Bryan Carr

The success of the Marvel Studios film *The Avengers* shows that, if nothing else, the superhero continues to resonate across different groups of people. The film broke the US box office record on the first weekend of its release with more than $200 million in box office receipts and has already crossed the $1 billion mark in worldwide box office sales ("'The Avengers' Smashes Records"; Cunningham). While the film has been well received by critics and fans, the relative lack of minority cast members in the film (of the major characters, only one—superspy Nick Fury—is played by a minority actor, Samuel L. Jackson) illustrates a broader issue present in much of superhero media: the overrepresentation of white characters and actors. Indeed, most characters in superhero media are white, leading to the bemused question of whether there is something innate about whiteness that attracts superpowers (Sims). Whiteness in superhero media is, as it is in other outlets of society, often viewed as the default or most common ethnic configuration.

The rhetorical implications of such a statement bear further inquiry. Is the omnipresence of white characters and white actors in superhero media a coincidence of the times in which many characters were created? Or is there evidence of a larger undercurrent of white privilege found across the various forms of superhero media? Such questions could provide insight into how these forms of media reflect and shape American popular culture. Moreover, a rhetorical analysis of these forms of media could provide insight into the consequences that the infusion of white privilege throughout the genre has for society as a whole. To that end, this essay will propose a rhetorical analysis of several different aspects of superhero media and the rhetorical implications they represent. Through this analysis, the essay will propose that rhetorics of white privilege are present throughout superhero media.

Conceptual Definitions and Rhetorical Analysis

White privilege is perhaps most easily understood as a set of special advantages and guarantees that individuals possess solely as a function of a white ethnic identity (McIntosh). The white privilege paradigm suggests that society is arranged to benefit those who possess a white ethnic identity via a system of "hegemonic structures, practices, and ideologies that reproduce whites' privileged status" (Pulido 15). Through the influence of various social structures such as the government and the media, such arrangements are portrayed not only as "universal and natural," but also as "common sense" (Litowitz 519). White privilege, then, is best considered as an ideology through which people consciously or unconsciously view the world; whites themselves often do not realize the role that white privilege plays in their position in society because they often do not view themselves as part of an ethnic group (Doane; Eagleton; Ferguson). This conceptual definition provides fertile ground for rhetorical analysis because white privilege often informs the positions and worldviews taken by individuals and as such can also influence their rhetoric.

To understand how white privilege manifests in the superhero media, a modified version of Kenneth Burke's cluster criticism approach will be used (Foss). The analysis in this essay is somewhat complex in nature because it attempts to analyze not just one artifact but also the output of a multimedia industry. The cluster criticism approach requires the identification of specific concepts and ideas, or clusters, around which other key terms and words can be found to give insight to the rhetor's actual worldview and perspective (Foss). Because the unit of analysis is so large and multifaceted, these concepts will be identified through a grounded approach in which recurring themes found throughout superhero media will act as the clusters for this essay.

To that end, this essay proposes three main rhetorical themes. The first is that of whiteness as a "default," or as the natural, state of being. The second is the definition of nonwhite characters by their race. The third and final rhetorical theme is the labeling of whiteness as "classic" and desirable. These rhetorical clusters come from two different sources: the content creators (the producers of comics, television, cartoons, and other superhero media) and the fans (those who consume the aforementioned content). These rhetorical clusters and sources comprise the rhetorical landscape in which this analysis will be conducted.

Whiteness as "Default" Ethnicity

The white privilege paradigm suggests that those who identify as white do not see themselves through an ethnic lens but do identify others through the characteristics of their ethnicity (Doane). In effect, white individuals see themselves in a sort of normal or default state and view those who belong to other ethnic groups as being unique in accordance with their ethnic identity (Doane). Whiteness, in this paradigm, is considered the normal or natural state, and any other ethnicity is unusual. Superman, one of the prototypical superheroes, is an alien from the planet Krypton. Yet, rather than appearing as "alien," he is viewed as the ultimate ideal of humanity; rather than possessing identifiably extraterrestrial physical characteristics, Superman has the dark hair, human features, and white complexion that would identify him as the Midwestern farm boy he was raised by his adoptive Earth parents to be. Certainly this background does not match that of creators Jerry Siegel and Joe Schuster, both of whom were the sons of Jewish immigrants who fled Nazi Germany (Iverson). While Superman has been identified at least as non-Aryan, he also does not possess any identifiably Jewish characteristics, likely due at least in part to an attempt by the creators to avoid the sense of anti-Semitism present at the time of the character's creation (Iverson). Still, since that time, the character has been portrayed primarily as a Protestant Midwesterner, belonging to America and the world at large as the ultimate paragon of virtue and humanity. That the character also happens to be unmistakably portrayed as white suggests a deeper sense of white privilege at work.

Similarly, even when content creators attempt to introduce new minority characters to take over the identities of white superheroes, such changes are seldom permanent if they happen at all. These so-called "legacy characters," which use the power sets, costumes, and superhero identities of their predecessors to battle crime, not only do not forge their own unique identity but also are often sacrificed in the name of returning to a marketable status quo (Sims). In 2010, DC Comics killed off Ryan Choi, a character of Asian descent who took over the identity of The Atom, in order to bring back Ray Palmer, a white character who had been popular during the 1960s and 1970s (Carr; Sims). Choi's death, combined with the general lack of representation of minority characters in several of the best-selling comics that year, suggested that minority characters were seen as subordinate to white characters, who were generally portrayed as lead characters (Carr). Such situations are not limited to the page. In 2008, rapper and actor Common was slated to take up the role of the superhero Green Lantern in a motion-captured adaptation of the *Justice League* comics, the project was canceled and actor Ryan Reynolds was cast as a white Green Lantern in a big-budget film shortly thereafter (Harling).

Whether intentional or not, the rhetorical message from content creators was that the white characters are the default version of the character and the one most suitable for mass audience consumption. The implication of this scenario is that white versions of superhero characters are the most marketable, suggesting that there is significant influence from white privilege present in the media marketplace. When combined with the rhetorical example of Superman as a white character, a clear rhetorical message of whiteness as a default and accepted mainstream norm is sent. Therefore, the actors and characters chosen to represent superheroic identities in these forms of media represent a rhetorical cluster that supports the idea of white privilege in superhero media.

Definition of Nonwhite Characters by Ethnic Stereotypes and Characteristics

In his essay "'Black Skins' and White Masks," Marc Singer suggests that superhero comics have a long tradition of relying on "visually codified representations in which characters are continually reduced to their appearances" and on characters that are "externalized into their heroic costumes and aliases" (107). Such a notion is wholly in keeping with the notions of white privilege, as those who belong to the white ethnic group often identify others primarily by their ethnicity and classify individuals into monolithic groups based on those characteristics (Bonilla-Silva; Doane). Often, the out-groups (minority groups) are classified and organized according to stereotypes that the in-groups (whites) assign universally to all individuals who share a certain set of characteristics (Allport). These phenomena carry over into the world of superhero media as well.

Singer suggests that while the rhetoric of the "secret identity" is useful for exploring the duality of identity that minorities experience in contemporary society, it is seldom used for that purpose (Singer). Indeed, the secret identities given to minority superheroes are often innately tied to their ethnic identity. DC's Black Lightning character, a young man capable of wielding electricity as a weapon, is named in part because of his powers but also because of the color of his skin; in his superhero code name his ethnicity is first and foremost. Effectively, even in the negotiated space of superheroes and secret identities, Black Lightning is still identified by his race first. Similarly, the Marvel hero Black Goliath, a man capable of growing to phenomenal sizes, is identified again by the color of his skin first and the nature of his powers second (it is worth noting, however, that the character's name was eventually changed to simply Goliath). Fellow Marvel superhero Luke Cage, a man with super strength and impenetrable skin, was relegated to stereotypical jive talking in his earliest 1970s appearances and frequently appears shirtless and exuding a sort of hyper-masculinity similar to other portrayals of black men in the media in his most recent appearances (Ward). This is to say nothing of Asian superhero characters, who are often either defined by their proficiency with martial arts or stereotyped through other means, such as the case of the *X-Men* character Jubilee, a Chinese-American woman who can generate miniature explosions and flashes of light akin to fireworks from her fingertips (Carr; Narcisse). By comparison, white superheroes have a much broader range of potential names and identities, generally based on their powers or other nonracially defined characteristics. Names like Iron Man, Batman, and Spider-Man speak of the characters' powers and origins, not their ethnic identity.

Again, the rhetorics of white privilege once again rear their head. This essay has already shown that in a paradigm of white privilege, whiteness is viewed as a default or natural state. This extends to the understanding of the "other" as a group that is identical or at least similar across individuals. Such an understanding often is reflected, either consciously or unconsciously, in the media that is created by members of a society. In the case of superhero media, a clear distinction between the multifaceted and nonstereotyped white characters and their more monolithically represented counterparts has developed. White characters are given substantially more variety in their power sets, names, and identities than are minority characters, suggesting again that being a white superhero has its privileges, at least in terms of persona design.

The Labeling of Whiteness as "Classic" and "Desirable"

The previous two clusters in this rhetorical analysis have focused primarily on the examples of white privilege that can be seen in rhetoric from the content creator level. However, an equally prolific source of rhetoric comes from the fans that consume such media, as well. Often, fans of superhero media are resistant to change and innately distrust any liberties taken with their artifacts of interest. The literature suggests that this resistance is in part due to the fact that consumers of comics use them as a means of escape and catharsis and may resent the encroachment of big media into their space of fandom (Brown; Smith). However, when the issue of change turns to the introduction of new minority characters or the casting of nonwhite actors in traditionally white roles, it is possible that the rhetoric is not simply a question of defending one's chosen form of escapism. One must look only to the minor controversy over the casting of black actor Idris Elba as the character Heimdall in the recent *Thor* film for proof; the white nationalist organization Council of Conservative Citizens attempted to boycott the film simply because Heimdall had been traditionally portrayed in Marvel comics and mythology as a white character (Calhoun). While this is perhaps an extreme case from a heavily ideological organization, milder forms of this same phenomenon can be found in other instances of superhero media.

In the summer of 2011, Marvel Comics made news by replacing the freshly dead *Ultimate* version of Peter Parker (the alter ego of Spider-Man) with the biracial character Miles Morales.[1] Morales, a character of both African-American and Hispanic descent, made major news headlines for taking on the heroic identity and drew predominantly positive opinions from fans and the press (Truitt). However, not all fans were happy. Several of the letters written in to the first issue of the new *Ultimate Spider-Man* comic took issue with the introduction of the character. One fan wrote that they were "extremely disappointed and offended" that the company would kill off one of its characters "for the sole reason of diversity," claiming that the introduction of Morales was an "insult" to the character of Peter Parker (Bendis and Pichelli 23). Another claimed that Morales had "stolen Peter Parker's identity" and that the character was "too iconic" to be replaced," while other fans claimed they would stop reading not only the comic under question but also all Marvel comics (Bendis and Pichelli 23). One fan summed up the sentiment clearly by stating not only that the introduction of Morales "betrayed" Spider-Man and fans of the character but also that the new character "will never be able to be Peter Parker" (Bendis and Pichelli 23). This last statement perhaps sums up this rhetorical cluster best by implying that there is something inherently desirable or preferable about the original white character that a new biracial character cannot hope to emulate or replace.

When a minority character takes over a role traditionally fulfilled by a white character, superhero fans often become defensive and protective of their preferred version of the character. While nostalgia and emotional attachment are likely a factor in this situation, it is impossible to divorce completely the implications of race and ethnicity from such sentiments, particularly when they are implicitly stated within the text of fan complaints. Moreover, the rhetoric appears astonishingly similar to the rhetorics of "we" and "them" and a perceived feeling of violation and encroachment that Aimee Rowe identified in the rhetoric of US nationalists with regard to the immigrant population (122). Indeed, just as Rowe identified the spatial aspect of such rhetors' attempt to create a distinction between "Americans" and "Immigrants," it could be argued that many fans have created spatial separation between an idealized fiction and the introduction of new material (Rowe). Just as the US nationalists argued that an unwelcome invader was encroaching on their way of life, many fans may feel that their idealized version of a character and the connection they feel to that character are threatened by the winds of change. This rhetorical cluster once more reflects the influence of white privilege in all forms of society. There is a clear preference and greater value assigned to the trait of whiteness as a classic, natural, and definitive component of identity among some consumers of identity.

Conclusions and Implications

Through analysis of these three clusters, recurring themes of white privilege and whiteness as a default, shared, and desirable characteristic permeate superhero media both at the levels of content creation and content consumption. Both creators and fans are complicit, though arguably to different levels and toward different ends, in maintaining a system of white privilege and valorization. Potential changes or challenges to the white-centric status quo are often mitigated or criticized through fan rhetoric or simply eliminated via editorial edict. Therefore, the interests of white fans and creators are generally upheld, suggesting that the system of white privilege permeates this form of culture just as it does other forms of culture and life.

It is to this end that the essay suggests a reframing of the power of whiteness and white privilege by placing it not just in the realm of the sociological but also into the realm of communication and rhetoric. McIntosh's understanding of white privilege as the metaphorical "invisible knapsack" is useful to understanding how white privilege permeates society but spends comparatively little time exploring how white privilege can influence rhetoric and communication, much less media (McIntosh). However, the conclusions of this analysis are not incompatible with that definition. Certainly one of the tools in the invisible knapsack could be a generally greater ease of acceptance of white characters and actors in media. Thomas Nakayama and Robert Krizek suggest that mapping the dimensions and domain of whiteness in discourse as well as the power relationships it represents is necessary for the proper development of communication studies (305). Therefore, this essay suggests that white privilege be examined as a significant source of influence on various forms of rhetoric, communication, and media as it can often drive and lend a system of meaning to the specific choices of rhetoric and language used in these forms. While superhero media may be subject to specific concerns and issues that are not present in other forms of media, they nonetheless make the case that white privilege can be significantly influential in the way we communicate with each other and entertain ourselves.

NOTE

[1] The *Ultimate* universe of Marvel comics is considered to be a separate dimension of stories from that of the normal Marvel Comics universe; as such the "classic" Peter Parker is still very much alive in the original Marvel Universe.

WORKS CITED

Allport, Gordon. *The Nature of Prejudice.* Reading: Addison-Wesley, 1954. Print.

The Avengers. Dir. Joss Whedon. Perf. Robert Downey, Jr., Chris Evans, Mark Ruffalo, Chris Hemsworth, Scarlett Johansson, Jeremy Renner, Tom Hiddleston, Clark Gregg, Cobie Smulders, Stellan Skarsgard, and Samuel L. Jackson. Walt Disney Studios, 2012. Film.

"'The Avengers' Smashes Records." *CNN.com.* Turner Broadcasting System, 7 May 2012. Web. 7 May 2012.

Bendis, Brian Michael, writer; Sara Pichelli, illustrator. *Ultimate Comics All-New Spider-Man* #1. New York: Marvel Comics, 2011. Print.

Bonilla-Silva, Eduardo. *Racism Without Racists: Color-blind Racism and the Persistence of Racial Inequality in the United States.* 3rd ed. Lanham: Rowman & Littlefield, 2010. Print.

Brown, Jeffrey A. "Comic Book Fandom and Cultural Capital." *Journal of Popular Culture* 30.4 (1997): 375-97. Print.

Calhoun, Bob. "The Misguided *Thor* Race Controversy." *Salon.com.* Salon Media Group, 20 April 2011. Web. May 2012.

Carr, Bryan. "Ryan Choi Is Dead: Ideological Representations of Asians and Asian Americans in American Superhero Comics." Association for Education in Journalism and Mass Communication Convention. St. Louis. 12 Aug. 2011. Address.

Cunningham, Todd. "'The Avengers' Bashes Way to Billion Dollars at Worldwide Box Office." *Yahoo! Movies.* Yahoo! Inc., 13 May 2012. Web. 13 May 2012.

Doane, Ashley W. "Dominant Group Ethnic Identity in the United States: The Role of 'Hidden' Ethnicity in Intergroup Relations." *The Sociological Quarterly* 38.3 (1997): 375-97. Print.

Eagleton, Terry. *Ideology: An Introduction.* London: Verso, 1991. Print.

Ferguson, Robert. *Representing Race: Ideology, Identity, and the Media.* New York: Oxford UP, 1998. Print.

Foss, Sonja K. *Rhetorical Criticism: Exploration and Practice.* 4th ed. Long Grove: Waveland P, 2009. Print.

Harling, Danielle. "Common Out as Green Lantern in Justice League Movie." *HipHopDX.* ComplexMusic. 3 Apr. 2009. Web. May 2012.

Iverson, Jeffrey. "In Search of Superman's Inner Jew." *Time.com.* Time Inc., 2 Nov. 2007. Web. May 2012.

Litowitz, Douglas. "Gramsci, Hegemony, and the Law." *Brigham Young University Law Review* 2 (2000): 515-51. Print.

McIntosh, Peggy. "White Privilege and Male Privilege: A Personal Account of Coming to See Correspondences through Work in Women's Studies." TS. Wellsley College Center for Research on Women. 1988. Print.

Nakayama, Thomas K., and Robert L. Krizek. "Whiteness: A Strategic Rhetoric." *Quarterly Journal of Speech* 81 (1995): 291-309. Print.

Narcisse, Evan. "The Ryan Choi Memorial Day Asian Superhero Roll Call." *Time.com.* Time Inc., 31 May 2010. Web. May 2012.

Pulido, Laura. "Rethinking Environmental Racism: White Privilege and Urban Development in Southern California." *Annals of the Association of American Geographers* 9.1 (2000): 12-40. Print.

Rowe, Aimee Carrillo. "Whose 'America'? Rhetoric and Space in the Formation of U.S. Nationalism." *Radical History Review* 89 (2004): 115-34. Print.

Sims, Chris. "The Racial Politics of Regressive Storytelling." *Comics Alliance.* AOL Inc., 6 May 2010. Web. May 2012.

Singer, Marc. "'Black Skins' and White Masks: Comic Books and the Secret of Race." *African American Review* 36.1 (2002): 107-19. Print.

Smith, Greg M. "Conference Report: Comic Arts Conference at the San Diego Comic-Con." *Cinema Journal* 49.3 (2010): 88-92. Print.

Truitt, Brian. "Miles Morales Begins Reign as Star of 'Ultimate Spider-Man.'" *USA Today.* Gannett Co. Inc., 14 Sept. 2011. Web. May 2012.

Ward, Elijah G. "Homophobia, Hypermasculinity, and the U.S. Black Church." *Culture, Health, & Sexuality* 7.5 (2005): 493-504. Print.

29

PUBLIC SPHERE, THEATER, AND THE RHETORIC OF REIMAGINING AN IDENTITY

Oriental to Asian American

Karen Ching Carter

This paper explores a key moment in time in which the theater, as a public sphere, acted as a space that changed social perceptions of Asian Americans in the twentieth century. In this paper, I look at the transformation of how Asian Americans went from being perceived as "Oriental" to Asian American. But first, I need to define what I mean by Oriental. Oriental is a term used by the West to mean people and cultures from the Orient—the East, referred to as Asia. Orientalism, as specifically defined by Edward Said, is the discursive mode through which the East is constructed as distinct from the West (see also Abu-Lughod 466). Orientalism provides a view of the West as rational and progressive while the East is viewed as backward—inferior to the West. Oriental people, as hailed by Orientalism, encompassed many cultures that spanned Asia. However, included in one monolithic group were the Chinese, Japanese, Filipino, South Asians, and Central Asians.

Although Orientals were made up of differing cultures within Asia, they were described and perceived as if they were all the same. As immigrants into the Americas, Oriental people were viewed as inassimilable aliens who brought economic competition, disease, and immorality (Lee 537). So, I discuss the process of changed perceptions of "Oriental" not as a phenomenon from the point of view of one Asian ethnic group; instead, I use the term Oriental and the term Asian American in a broad sense to include several groups from Asia, because legal and social policies affected persons of Asian descent equally.

The question becomes: how does the public space of theater invite cross-cultural inquiry to counter mainstream ideologies? And a further question: what makes everyday people take rhetorical agency to counter embedded ideologies that dominate society? In response, I suggest that the public space of theater performance is a counterpublic site that invites cross-cultural inquiry—that is, which promotes public and private dialogue between performer and audience through rhetorical displays of gesture to persuade others of the validity of certain cultural and linguistic identities. To further this claim, I suggest that an investigation of the Forbidden City, a San Francisco Chinese-themed night club,[1] can contribute to our understanding of the relationship between theater as a local public sphere and as a site for social reconstitution. Specifically, such an investigation can help us understand how Asian Americans were transformed from being viewed as the "Oriental yellow plague"[2] to being seen as a "model minority." When Oriental Americans took their place on a theater stage, they exemplified the uniqueness of cross-cultural inquiry as a process of extricating Orientals from Orientalism.

Before continuing, I need to discuss the notion of *kairos,* which is a central theme of this paper. In classical rhetoric, *kairos* is intrinsically related to time and space. It is a qualitative measure of an opportunity that could occur if action is taken. With this in mind, we can think of it as something that can happen but not just at any time. James Kinneavy and Catherine Eskin analyze the concept of *kairos* in Aristotle's *Rhetoric* as the right time to do something (132). The *kairotic* opportunity I discuss here is World War II. In terms of time, it was a war across the Asian Pacific, and in terms of space, it was San Francisco. World War II was the driving force that created the opportune environment to foster change for second-generation Asian Americans in the United States. World War II kairotically acted as a change agent in Caucasian American attitudes about Orientals, because prior to the war many Caucasian Americans only knew Orientals described to them through the lens of Orientalism. In addition, legal structures that regulated Chinese immigration, segregation, and denial of US citizenship contributed to the isolation of not just the Chinese, but other Asian groups socially, politically, and physically.[3]

The war created a unique opportunity. The Forbidden City's opening in 1938 was timely in that this innovative type of entertainment took advantage of social location and the structural forces surrounding World War II. The West Coast of the United States, and San Francisco in particular, was the major departure point for servicing the war in Asia (at the time the club opened, the US had not officially entered the war but lent its support to countries that the Japanese had invaded), as well as a port of entry for civilian, diplomatic, and military personnel returning from Asia. Non-Asian Americans had spent time experiencing Asia and its people. For returning Americans, the Chinese-themed night club not only served as a place for food and entertainment, but it also served as a place to view Asians as Americans. Furthermore, going to the Forbidden City was the first time many Caucasian Americans came in contact with Asians and Asian Americans. Thus, combined with the political forces prior to and during World War II, Forbidden City performances by second-generation Americans of Japanese, Chinese, Filipino, and South Asian descent provided other Americans a new view of Orientals.

The rhetoric of Orientalism was one thing. The rhetoric of second-generation Asian Americans was another. The path from being seen as an Oriental caricature (as the "yellow plague") to being viewed as an Asian American (as a human being) is the path this paper explores. Beginning with Jürgen Habermas's concept of the public sphere and drawing from Nancy Fraser, Michael Warner, and Miriam Hansen, I discuss the theoretical foundations of the alternative public sphere and its overlapping relationship to theater. I then argue that the alternative public sphere can be expanded to a night club and that theater performance acts as a counterpublic. Finally, I expand and illustrate how the Forbidden City dancers, themselves, participated in this rhetorical process of reimagining an identity.

Alternative Public Sphere and Theater

If the public sphere is a discursive space, which creates and invents counterdiscourses, then such a space can exist in a night club. The Habermasian public space is not absent.[4] Technically speaking, we could see the bourgeois, white public sphere in attendance at the Forbidden City, and the Asian Americans, an alternative public, as performers. The time was mid-twentieth-century America in San Francisco. World War II brought the country out of depression and into prosperity. The war created jobs. With people working, there was money to spend on entertainment. The bourgeois, white public is not only present but financially able to afford the entertainment culture, provided here by second- and third-generation Asian Americans as singers, dancers, musicians, strippers, and chorus-line performers (for Asian American performers, this was the only possible place to perform).

In response to Habermas's theorization of the public sphere, Nancy Fraser examines how he failed to examine other nonbourgeois, competing public spheres. She calls these "alternative publics." One of her main points in "Rethinking the Public Sphere" is to challenge the idea that political participation happens through talk and that citizens in this medium will deliberate their common affairs. She states that this space of citizen talk is "separate from the state apparatuses, economic markets and democratic association" (57). Communication between citizens is within a space that occurs between Habermas's bourgeois public and alternative publics. She states that this space creates "parallel discursive arenas," which "invent and circulate counter discourses" (57). For Habermas, the public sphere is defined as having boundaries between public and private. Fraser implies that in this political space, there are no boundaries between private and public (71), because a dialogue would emerge between the counterdiscourse and the dominant, bourgeois public sphere.

In the case of entertainment theater, such as a night club, it is often assumed that there are boundaries between private and public because the audience is viewed as passive spectators not as a deliberative public. However, in live theater performance there is always the superficial fictive performance and the performers' private bodies, which are displayed in public space. There is a dialogue between audience and actors, even if it is not obvious to the outside observer. In cinema, the audience can also be seen in interaction with the action on the screen. For example, Nicholas Balaisis discusses the role of cinema in a Cuban public sphere. In a socialist ideologically charged environment, in which political criticism is prohibited, popular Cuban films gave "publicness" with bodily signs and cues to the spectators (Balaisis 28). Balaisis notes that "the bourgeois public sphere . . . is rooted in an act of abstraction where individuals must transcend" (29), according to Michael Warner, the "given realities of their body" to be a "social body" (qtd. in Balaisis 29). Warner implies that for performer and spectator, the interaction is a social one in which the experience of viewer identification is transferred from performer to spectator. From this process of transfer, the spectator can imagine a new realm of identification or be led into the ideology of the performance. This kind of rhetorical force allows the spectator to believe that he or she is actually creating a new text—particularly, if the display of texts on the screen is unlike what the spectator believes to be the norm.

So I now ask, can theater performers be a counterpublic? Fraser defines counterpublics as publics that formulate oppositional interpretations of their identities, interests, and needs. However, Warner points out that the main difference between Fraser's definition of "counter" and Habermas's public sphere is the word "opposition" (118). Warner extends the definition of counterpublic in his book *Publics and Counterpublics* to include that the counterpublic maintains on some level, conscious or not, an awareness of its subordinate status (119). Thus, what brings a marginalized group of people to be counter is the idea that they know they are marginalized, and it is through their public association that they are transformed into a counterpublic. Awareness of subordinate status is intertwined with societal notions of language and body. Warner notes that "in Western culture masculinity has traditionally been thought to occupy a public space and femininity to occupy a private one" (24). For example, ratification of the Nineteenth Amendment to the US Constitution in 1920 granted the right to vote to women. Prior to that only men could assert a public voice in voting for a representative in public office. Warner is insightful in pointing out that "being public is a privilege that requires filtering or repressing something that is seen as private" (23).

Like Warner, Miriam Hansen has expanded the notion of alternative publics in her book *Babel and Babylon* in which she examines early twentieth-century cinema. Hansen argues that cinema offers two spaces that intersect the public sphere. First is the physical space constituted by the structure and location of the cinema and second is the text of the film itself (108). Her interest is in the notion that spectatorship is a social experience "[that] is articulated, interpreted, negotiated and contested in an inter-subjective, potentially collective and oppositional form" (108). Hansen expands the notion of the alternative public sphere in cinema spectatorship by grounding her argument not from the idea of film as passive reception, but rather from the notion that, in the early part of the twentieth century, cinema/theater was a site of social interaction. Her main point is that cinema at the time included lecturers and live performers in music and dance. Passive reception was not the norm, and audience participation was active even with the screen-spectator dualism. Hansen's exploration of early twentieth-century cinema/theater has proven quite fruitful for purposes of analysis of theater as a counterpublic. What I find insightful is her framework for clarifying the alternative public sphere in asking, "for whom is the sphere an alternative?" From her perspective social groups left out of dominant discourse, such as immigrants and women, had no other access to institutions of public life. They were not considered an audience in view of rising industrialization, urbanization, and migration. Cinema emerged in this context of widespread displacement of older societal structures that divided the ethnic, the working class, and women from dominant discourse. Hansen argues that "cinema allowed [these oppressed groups] the public recognition of concrete needs, conflicts, anxieties, memories and fantasies" (92). Alternative public spheres, such as cinema/theater, developed because of, and in spite of, the forces to standardize cinema for mass production. While Hansen speaks of the spectator as the alternative public, she also discusses the many theaters that catered to ethnic spectators. Ethnic theaters provided ethnic performers an alternative space to perform as well. The ethnic theater was and still is an accepted form of entertainment within the ethnic community; performers perform who they are, liberated from the stigma of performing a stereotype imposed by the dominant culture.

In theater performance, there are no boundaries between private and public. Actor and spectator create the "discursive arena" that Fraser described. Just as Hansen and Balaisis point out in cinema, the conversation between the spectator and the actor is a social interaction in which meaning is being conveyed. In the case of a fictive program outside a social norm, actors and spectators can become counterpublics in that they are performing against a norm.

Expanding the Public Sphere and the Forbidden City Night Club

Ralph Cintron attempts to answer the question: how does one create respect within conditions of little or no respect? In his book *Angels' Town*, Cintron talks about a condition of in-betweenness, which he says is an unlocatable place. In analyzing a Mexican American community, Cintron discusses that for Latino/a Americans the in-between life is more than the Anglo versus Mexican duality. In-betweenness is layered with socioeconomic levels, a mix of urban and rural backgrounds, ethnicities, varied styles of language, levels of education, and varied amount of time spent in the United States. Like Mexican Americans, even with all the layers of in-betweenness, white America saw Orientals as only one monolithic group.

In her book *Intersecting Voices*, Iris Marion Young talks about the breadth of communicative democracy. In the area of preserving listening across difference, she discusses the idea of how to confront difference and thus to create a bridge to understanding. She sets forth three elements that act together to preserve listening: the act of greeting, the rhetorical act of persuasion, and the action in narrative storytelling. While Young directs her elements toward rational deliberation, her elements that encourage listening are seen quite normatively in theater performance. This notion of expanding the public sphere into theater is much broader than that of Habermas in which social experience is articulated, negotiated, interpreted, and contested. Within the context of mass society, there are not only privileged single sites for public appearance but also multiple sites in which power materializes and is negotiated by a viewing audience. From this angle, theater can be seen as a space in which a viewing audience can negotiate the sometimes contradictory nature of social relations. Theater would seem to be an innocuous space of cultural engagement, yet crucial ideas concerning public life can be constituted and negotiated. The Forbidden City night club, for example, offers all of the elements of communicating with the "other," as articulated by Young: the Chinese-themed theater had hospitality (friendly greeting), a full Chinese or American dinner and late-night dancing (persuasive listening), and a floor show (narrative storytelling).

With regard to in-betweenness, I apply Hansen's notion of theater as an alternate sphere and space of social exchange for ethnic audiences and performers. The Forbidden City night club offered a stage: an open cultural space for second-generation Asian American performers. In dance, music, comedy, and food, the Forbidden City night club expanded the public sphere for Asian Americans while countering, at the same time, their image as Orientals. Forbidden City performers were in communication with the "other." The "other" in this case was Caucasian Americans. It literally brought Asian Americans together with the white, middle-class public sphere. The in-betweenness of Asian diversity could be seen in the Asian Americans as performers and in Asian Americans as patrons to the club. While night club attendance was popular across the nation, the Chinese-themed club changed "Oriental"—a matter of race—into "Chinese"—a matter of culture. From a political standpoint, "Chinese" ceased to be a reason for exclusion from American society.

In addition, I use Young's definition of communicative democracy to expand the public sphere in a night club because it fits better than Habermas's notion in terms of constituting social action. For example, critics had opposed Chinese integration into Hollywood, yet the Chinese-themed club corrected the historical cultural discrepancy that existed between the Orient and the Occident by actually providing a space for talented Asian Americans to perform in public. While the roles continued to depict Chinese Americans in stereotypical roles such as houseboys or laundrymen, at least they were roles played by Chinese Americans, not by white Americans made up to look Chinese. This represented an act of basic justice for previously marginalized Asian Americans, as the Forbidden City brought global awareness to a largely ignorant non-Asian American population.

Reimagining an Identity

The best example of looking at how the Forbidden City night club performers acted as a counterpublic is by looking at some of the dance acts. Dance acts served as spectacles of cultural transformation in reworking the ideology of Orientalism. When examining these acts, one could see that Asian American identity straddled somewhere between self-understanding as ethnic Asians and images portrayed through Orientalism. Orientalism taught Asian Americans lessons about who they should be, but in the context of business and entertainment, they then could use Orientalism to their advantage.

Noel Toy was billed as the Chinese Sally Rand, a burlesque dancer. As we might know, performance, particularly the burlesque, is not passive. Her fan dance, called "The Chinese Joy Dance," was performed seminude with soft, large-feather fans. The large feathers signified sensuality and gentleness, while her interaction with the soft material evoked the familiar discourse of Orientalism as exoticism; yet, the dance itself was on Caucasian Western terms. The act was an embodied performance in combination with a material quality. Toy embodied a preconceived notion that Oriental women are naturally sexually alluring. While adopting the burlesque, she evoked the allure of Orientalism as exoticism. This is evident in a conversation she had with a patron, which was relayed to Arthur Dong in his 1989 video, *Forbidden City, U.S.A.*:

> *Patron would say*: Is it true what they say about Chinese girls, that sex is different than White girls?
>
> *Noel Toy comments*: They would look at me to see if I was really different.
>
> *Patron would say*: Is it true?
>
> *Noel Toy*: Sure, didn't you know? [laughs] (*Forbidden City*)

The audience could accept Toy because her dress was related to the Caucasian culture, yet her Asian face made the audience see her perform something exotic with the overtone of "Orientalism." She became the Oriental object they expected.

Frances Chun, a chorus dancer at the club, sometimes dressed as an Arabian genie. She said she felt at home at the Forbidden City dressed in a harem costume (*Forbidden City*). Her colorful portrayal of a harem girl reflects the extent to which even Asian Americans adopted stereotypes and replayed the image back, as naturally as it might have been expected by a Caucasian American performer. As the actor, she was being expressive with her performance. For the audience, she met their expectation of something decidedly Oriental but could act as a connection to understanding Asian Americans.

Paul Wing and Dorothy Toy did not dance the narrative of Orientalism. Instead they were compared to icons Fred Astaire and Ginger Rogers. Wing—in a top hat and tuxedo—and Toy—in a long, flowing satin dress—shared with the audience a common imagery of Astaire and Rogers. But inside this Chinese-themed club, Wing and Toy expanded the cultural space for themselves while gaining acceptance as dancers, particularly for Wing, for an Asian man was often depicted in Hollywood as weak and feminine. Their dancing allowed an Oriental culture to be understood and accepted among Caucasian Americans. For all the performers, the stage was a symbol of a source of strength from which one could assert a voice. Just as Noel Toy accepted her show name as the Chinese Sally Rand, Paul Wing and Dorothy Toy also accepted their show billing as the Chinese Fred Astaire and Ginger Rogers. Accepting subordinate status to popular white American celebrities was both a business ploy and a conscious awareness of subordinate status in American society. But these performers became markers that incorporated elements of Orientalism that defied a norm. Notable were their Asian faces in Western dress that disrupted the codes of Orientalism.

At the start of World War II, American fascination with Orientals became more important in that the Forbidden City was more than a theater: it was a night club, a theater with hospitality. Entertainment at the Forbidden City club included a full Chinese or American dinner, a floor show, and late-night dancing. It played a vicarious role in the public sphere. With the hospitality of a night club atmosphere that included dinner and dancing, the club was not speaking at people, it was speaking with people and in the voice of the audience. Asian Americans had been in America, yet many white Americans had never encountered a person of Asian descent. Moreover, popularly, Asians were depicted in Hollywood films as poor English speakers dressed in strange clothes. It was "shocking" to the white audience to see an Asian man dancing like Fred Astaire and an Asian woman who could dance as well as Ginger Rogers. It was novel for non-Asian Americans to be eating and dancing among the Asian American performers and Asian American patrons in the audience. In the state of in-betweenness, displays of Oriental ethnicity were balanced by displays of Americanization. Consciousness and behaviors of the performers were transformed along American lines in order to create respect where little respect previously existed for ethnic "Orientals." So when Mary Mammon, a chorus girl, said that performing was "a way to show our stuff," she evoked the idea that rhetorical action is influenced by certain ideologies, but we "everyday" people can transform those ideologies.

Discussion

Without the external, political exigencies of World War II, there would be no sense as to why the Forbidden City was successful as a Chinese-themed club and so popular with Caucasian American audiences. Most importantly here, however, is that through the external forces of history we can see why the Forbidden City performers could take rhetorical agency and successfully contribute to changing views of Orientals in the American mind. In interviews in the video *Forbidden City, U.S.A.,* the performers remembered how "we performed" at the Forbidden City night club. The "we" refers to a collective action and particular social formation of Asian American performers. They existed without a larger connective network of Caucasian performers.

Their performances were a symbol of Asian American continuity and unity within San Francisco. Toy Yat Mar (the Chinese Sophie Tucker) was asked about some of the effects of the war on Japanese American performers, and she replied, "during the war, some [Japanese American performers] were taken [to concentration camps;] others [Japanese] had to flee. I don't like looking back, it was very sad" (*Forbidden City*). The internment of Japanese Americans made concrete the awareness among Asian Americans of their subordinated status in America. From this angle, the Forbidden City night club theater acts can be seen as a counterpublic.

Through the use of Orientalism, performers combined their American-ized selves to harmonize Oriental and Occidental cultures, rather than to oppose them. Theater performance was a way to respond to the growing ethnic curiosity and to provide Asian Americans a venue to perform, as well as a venue to be spectators of American entertainment. The significance of "Orientalists" acts could be seen as a way for Asian Americans to take back the definition of who they were as Orientals, as ethnic people, and as Americans. While the definition of "Orientals" was once controlled by the "other" (white West), it was now controlled by the insider Asian Americans. Asian Americans could be recognized as "Oriental" on their terms, through their connections, and through their creativity. When owner Charlie Low opened the Forbidden City in 1938, he not only proved it to be a commercial success, he took rhetorical agency to use the Forbidden City as an alternative counterpublic space to integrate people from two, distinct, racially defined categories. This rhetorical move was unheard of at a time of pending war in the Asian Pacific and during Chinese exclusion within the United States.

While the Caucasian American audience could read this alternative theater space as a fundamental cultural change, the Asian American performers saw themselves on stage, effecting a manifestation of their identity in an ongoing and active process socially situated in relation to time and context. As Noel Toy (the Chinese Sally Rand) said: "Our traditions were not [old]. [We were] modern Chinese in a modern American way" (*Forbidden City*).

Conclusion

While the purpose of this paper is to show how the Forbidden City night club operated as a counterpublic space for Asian American performers, the question of how Asian Americans went from being depicted as the "yellow plague" to the "model minority" needs to be further researched. This was only one moment in time in which the *kairos* of war allowed for Asian American performers to perform for the public and, in turn, through discursive cultural engagement, for them to be accepted by the public. The history of Asian American acceptance into American society speaks to broader contemporary issues of ethnic groups with diverse cultural and religious backgrounds. The changing image of any specific group of people within a society is a process that can only happen over time in context to and in conjunction with a changing society. As social actors, people act and react within complex political and economic contexts. These contexts carry different stakes and kinds of power that influence the way people think about the world around them. This implies that human cultures cannot be boiled down to a list of characteristics. Human cultures and the rhetoric that surrounds them are naturally contradictory and convoluted. As such, the boundaries between private and public coalesce naturally to create a discursive space for an alternative public sphere.

NOTES

[1] While the club was marketed as a Chinese-themed club, its performers were not only of Chinese descent, but included those of Japanese, South Asian, and Filipino descent.

[2] See Lee. Anti-Asian sentiment was prevalent throughout North and South America in the nineteenth and early twentieth centuries. Chinese immigration, later extended to other Asian cultures, was described negatively in terms such as the "yellow plague," "yellow wave," and "Mongol invasion."

[3] See Lau. In addition to exclusion and denial of US citizenship, other laws impacted Asians. Twenty-eight states had antimiscegenation statutes, prohibiting intermarriage between whites and Asians, and the "California Alien Land Law of 1913" prohibited all Asians not eligible for citizenship from owning property.

[4] See Habermas's *The Structural Transformation* in which he discusses the evolution of the bourgeois public sphere in eighteenth-century Britain. The bourgeois public sphere is a sphere of private people who join together to form a public in order to reason in rational, critical debate.

WORKS CITED

Abu-Lughod, Lila. "Writing Against Culture." *Anthropology in Theory*. Ed. Henrietta Moore and Todd Sanders. Malden: Blackwell, 2006. 466-79. Print.

Balaisis, Nicholas. "Cuba, Cinema and the Post-Revolutionary Public Sphere." *Canadian Journal of Film Studies* 19.2 (2010): 26-42. Print.

Cintron, Ralph. *Angels' Town: Chero Ways, Gang Life, and Rhetorics of the Everyday*. Boston: Beacon, 1997. Print.

Forbidden City, USA. Dir. Arthur E. Dong. Deep Focus Productions and PBS Video, 1989.

Fraser, Nancy. "Rethinking the Public Sphere: A Contribution to the Critique of Actually Existing Democracy." *Social Text* 25/26 (1990): 56-80. Print.

Habermas, Jürgen. *The Structural Transformation of the Public Sphere*. 1962. Cambridge: Massachusetts Institute of Technology P, 1991. Print.

Hansen, Miriam. *Babel and Babylon: Spectatorship in American Silent Film*. Cambridge: Harvard UP, 1991. Print.

Kinneavy, James L., and Catherine R. Eskin. "Kairos in Aristotle's *Rhetoric.*" *Written Communication* 11.1 (Jan. 1994): 131-42. Print.

Lau, Estelle T. *Paper Families: Identity, Immigration Administration, and Chinese Exclusion*. Durham: Duke UP, 2006. Print.

Lee, Erika. "The Yellow Peril and Asian Exclusion in the Americas." *Pacific Historical Review* 76.4 (2007): 537-62. Print.

Said, Edward. *Orientalism*. New York: Random House, 1978. Print.

Warner, Michael. *Publics and Counterpublics*. New York: Zone, 2002. Print.

Young, Iris Marion. *Intersecting Voices*. Princeton: Princeton UP, 1997. Print.

30

9/11/11

The Visual and Rhetorical (Re)Constitution of Muslim American Identity Politics

Nicholas S. Paliewicz

September 11, 2001, initiated a narrow orientation of the world predicated on the exclusion of Muslims and Arab Americans. The event established a Western narrative grounded in a framed rhetoric of security that religiously views Muslims as the enemy of freedom and democracy. I argue that this rhetoric demonstrates Kenneth Burke's second stage of rebirth in his pollution-purification-redemption cycle: purification. Following the original sin of the 9/11 terrorist attacks, American authorities scapegoated Muslims and Arab Americans to preserve an American religious orientation. Muslims and Arab Americans continue to carry the guilt from the 9/11 sin. This paper argues that post-9/11 rhetoric is driven by religious motives that defend capitalism as the Western orientation in need of protection. Potentially, as represented by the September 11, 2011, issue of the *New York Times*, the 9/11 memorial and museum may represent Kenneth Burke's stage of redemption.

To help us understand the symbolic constructions of post-9/11 discourse, this paper initiates a dramaturgy of the 9/11/11 scene. This essay is composed of three primary sections: the rhetoric of rebirth, post-9/11 religious orientation, and 9/11/11. The first section reviews Kenneth Burke's rhetoric of rebirth. Next, to argue the relevance of religious orientation to post-9/11 rhetoric, I describe America's framed orientation of the world following the 9/11 tragedy: security. Here, I also review other scholars focused on President George W. Bush's rhetoric of securitization to argue that national rhetoric was centered on purifying itself from the contaminations of the Muslim Other. Finally, the third section analyzes the *New York Times'* special edition of 9/11/11: "The Reckoning: America and the World a Decade After 9/11." I argue that this text reframes post-9/11 discourse with a terministic screen of cost. The cost of protecting our religious orientation has been significant. Yet, the *New York Times* (*NYT*) visually describes the 9/11 memorial and museum as potential symbols of redemption.

The Rhetoric of Rebirth

In *Permanence and Change*, Burke identifies three orders of rationalization: magic, religion, and science. Each order maintains particular constructs of rationalization. The order of magic features the control of natural forces; the order of religion features the control of human forces; and the order of science features the control of technological order. Applying Burke's anatomy of purpose to post-9/11 discourse, I argue that post-9/11 rhetoric is centered on a very vivid order of religious orientation. This argument assumes that motives associated with capitalism have replaced motives traditionally driving religion, specifically Christianity. It is important to remember that Burke's religious process of rebirth is ultimately a secular view on the Christian process of the soul's progress. Following Burke's three-cycle dramatistic process of pollution-purification-redemption, we can see the religious order of capitalism as the driving factor of rhetorical motives in post-9/11 rhetoric. Let us begin this review.

Pollution is the state of guilt that is "intrinsic to the social order" and "'inherited' by all mankind, being 'prior' to any individual lapse into 'actual sin'" (Burke, *Language* 144). Guilt is an innate consequence of hierarchical order since disobedience of its commandments is inevitable as we do our best to reach the top. Purification, the second stage of the rhetoric of rebirth is the cleansing of guilt to achieve redemption. Purification typically involves victimage or mortification. Victimage is the process of scapegoating, where guilt is transferred to a designated victim. This allows individuals to "battle an external enemy instead of battling an enemy within" (Burke, *Philosophy* 203; see Burke, "Rhetoric of Hitler's Battle"). Consequently, consubstantiality occurs between those purified by the process of victimage because they are able to share a common enemy that represents the guilt from original sin. Mortification, on the other hand, is self-inflicted punishment, where the individual rather than a scapegoat burdens the guilt. Finally, the third stage of this dramatistic cycle is redemption. This is the symbolic rebirth where guilt has been cleansed, and the individual achieves a new state of "physical, spiritual, or psychological" redemption (Foss, Foss, and Trapp 178).

As we will see, post-9/11 discourse constituted a framing of security suited to protect its religious orientation. A decade following the event, the *NYT* reframed identifications according to cost. Following Burke's rhetoric of rebirth, post-9/11 rhetoric follows a cycle of pollution and purification. At this point, it is unclear whether we have achieved redemption. In order to arrive at this question, the next section reviews literature on the topic of post-9/11 securitization. This section demonstrates the significance of America's rhetorical stage of purification following original sin. I argue that the rhetorical frame of security was used to defend our religious orientation of capitalism.

Post-9/11 Religious Orientation

Post-9/11 religious orientation is driven by neoliberal attitudes. Primarily, terrorists attacked the symbolic epicenter of capitalistic faith: the World Trade Center. The Twin Towers simply represented the pinnacle of capitalism. Although the towers themselves were not aesthetically glorified, other than their sheer size, their symbolic value was unique to Western capitalism. It was from these towers that globalization was orchestrated. According to Slavoj Žižek, "The only way to conceive what happened on September 11 is to locate it in the context of antagonisms of global capitalism" (49). Terrorists attacked our hierarchical order of the world. The attacks represent the first stage of rebirth: pollution. All rhetorical events following this initial stage are considered post-9/11 discourse.

America was immediately burdened with a traumatic sin that disobeyed the hierarchical order of capitalism. This sin had to be purified. And as the post-9/11 story unfolded, the spirit of capitalism (belief in our hierarchical order) outweighed logical premises that opposed decisions for war (see Gershkoff and Kushner; Zarefksy, "Making the Case"). Somebody, other than American capitalists, had to carry the burden of guilt. A self-imposed process of mortification would have been too damaging to our religious orientation. Our Western ways of life had to prevail. If the logic of capitalism were to be questioned or denied by its very followers, then the process of mortification would deteriorate its own hierarchical order. Perhaps for this reason, President Bush repeatedly told Americans to go shopping immediately following the attacks (Skocpol). Also, so began the alternative process of victimage: scapegoating. As we know, the United States went to war and heightened domestic politics of securitization and racialization. Muslims and Arab Americans were scapegoated in order to purify our nation from the ethnic Other that was responsible for attacking our religious order.

Through political rhetoric, national imagery, and popular culture, Muslim Americans have been scapegoated, identified as enemies of the state (Merskin; Naber; Oswald). Americans interpellated by this rhetoric were invited to join a collective consciousness predicated on the elimination of the Muslim orientation. This increased prejudice and violence against Muslims and Arab Americans (May and Modood; Jamal and Naber; Merskin; Volpp). Political leadership of the United States imposed feelings of insecurity to wage war. President Bush's war metaphor, for instance, was used to "[construct] an enemy unworthy of internal deliberation" (Zarefsky, "George W. Bush" 153). Through epideictic rhetoric, visual imagery, and creation of self and audience, Bush established clear authority over public interpretation of the 9/11 events (Murphy). Consequently, America united under Bush's "medicine-man" tactics (Thompson 366) "in the greater interest of God" (Bell 154). The president successfully identified a common enemy and "a geographic center in order to realign post-9/11 attitudes sufficient to identify the non-Western other as the common enemy" (Thompson 350). This rhetoric initiated a religious orientation centered on the dissociation of Muslim and Arab Americans, justifying redemptive violence under the War on Terror to transform the scapegoat (Ivie). The racial evils of the Muslim Other had to be purged (Gunn) and potentially transformed.

Muslim and Arab Americans have gone from "invisible citizens" to "visible subjects" since the 9/11 terrorist attacks (Naber), allowing most Americans to transcend division by identifying against the visible dissociation of Muslim subjects. This racialization is unique to US global policies (Jamal and Naber). In particular, the marginalization of Arabs and Muslims is a strategy used to "manufacture public consent needed to support, finance, and defend these policies" (Cainkar 49). Consequently, this racial disenfranchisement has allowed national discourse to prioritize a new symbolic hierarchy that rationalized national unity at the expense of Muslim orientations.

In sum, the 9/11 attacks were symbolic acts that disobeyed America's global order of capitalism. This religious orientation is how America viewed the world, protecting its subjects from the mysteries of the unknown. For this reason, the attacks were simply incomprehensible, as their relative orientation was beyond our logology. To preserve the integrity of our Western order, governmental institutions created a very narrow terministic screen that framed post 9/11 through the lens of security. This was designed to protect our religion of capitalism and garner rhetorical consubstantiation amid a political world of division. Identification not only belied political consensus but prompted new symbolic labor. This labor was affective, and it included sympathy, remorse, and patriotism, all of which remain pious in kind. The symbolic order belonging to the realm of capitalism remains an orientation that is dependent on fixed analogous and verbal associations linked to the War on Terror. As a metaphor for purification, this is used to exclude the image of those believed to represent orientations beyond a post-9/11 schema.

To speculate on the third stage of our national rhetoric of rebirth, we now turn to the *New York Times*. This text is an important indicator of this rhetoric because it projects the vernacular tonalities of post-9/11 discourse from both the city of New York (NYC) and the nation. Potentially, the third stage of rebirth manifested on the tenth anniversary of the terrorist attacks. This day is important because NYC opened the 9/11 memorial to friends and families of those who lost their lives on 9/11. This was socially constructed as a heightened day of remembrance. As indicated by the *NYT*, Ground Zero reconstruction efforts may represent redemption.

Therefore, the following section analyzes the *NYT*'s special edition newspaper released on 9/11/11. The text reveals three points. First, the *NYT* reframes post-9/11 religious orientation according to cost. Second, Muslim orientation is not prominently featured. And third, the visual qualities of remembrance and reflection, offered by the memorial and museum, may symbolically represent redemption from 9/11 guilt. Yet, since textual silences can manipulate ideology (Huckin), the presence/absence of Muslim and Arab American orientation in the text of study is important to note. Following Burke, "even if any given terminology is a *reflection* of reality, by its very nature as a terminology it must be a *selection* of reality; and to this extent it must function also as a *deflection* of reality" (*Language* 45).

9/11/11

The *NYT's* cover page displays both mystery and reflection. With a close-up image of a World Trade Center footprint pool, half of the image shows calm, reflecting water. The other half, focusing on the inside of the footprint itself, shows an abyss of darkness. Entitled "The Reckoning: America and the World a Decade After 9/11," the newspaper is dedicated to "the decade's costs and consequences, measured in thousands of lives, trillions of dollars and countless challenges to the human spirit." The special issue features ten sections: "The Decade," "That Day," "War Abroad," "War at Home," "Remembrance," "Rebuilding," "Muslims Now," "9/11 State of Mind," "Portraits Redrawn," and "Endpaper."

The *NYT* reconstitutes a religious orientation of capitalism within a ter-ministic screen of cost. I argue that this text reframes the rhetorical process of rebirth that was unique to post-9/11 discourse. Already, the title of the special edition of the newspaper defines the situation: "The Reckoning." We have here, emerging on page one, and resonating throughout the remainder of the text, a terministic screen of costliness. The hierarchy of religious orientation has reframed the past decade as a situation measurable by calculation. This symbolic theme belongs to the logology of our religious universe since cost is a primary unit for measuring success. Indeed, the following ten years worked to make sense of the original sin and once again regain confidence in the hier-archical mysteries of economic order. And in doing so, as illustrated by the *NYT,* the United States reinitiated the dramaturgic process of rebirth. This began with the pollution of 9/11/01.

Pollution

The pollution of 9/11 is very clearly articulated throughout the text. Beginning in section one, "The Decade," the *NYT* depicts guilt associated with wreckage. The original sin was cast by the terrorists who hijacked the three destructive airplanes. The event immediately changed lives. "People repeated the same thing: My life will be changed forever. . . . [I]t was called the worst day in American history" (2). The shadows from this traumatic day weighed on American subjects. The attacks were incomprehensible, beyond words of our symbolic order. The numerical cost of this event is made clear on the bottom of the first page: "2,977 total victims of the attacks"; "3 victims added to the official toll who died because of dust exposure"; "343 fire department of New York personnel killed" (1). This was a day that people would not forget. "The memories remain fresh and overwhelming. The trem-bling ground, the wall of smoke that shut off the sun, the choking dust, the ghastliness of the jumping people" (2). The act of terrorism could not be immediately rationalized. Instead, people "needed the quiet," "joined the military," and even "stopped believing in God" (3). The narratives of these people demonstrate a national cry for help after the day's "witness to apocalypse" (4). Since no American was willing to bear the guilt associated with the motives behind the terrorist acts, the country needed a scapegoat.

Purification

Sections three and four of the *NYT* articulate the impact of war that followed 9/11. War abroad and war at home characterized the cost that Americans were willing to pay in order to rationalize the 9/11 sins and protect religious order. The United States identified Iraq and Afghanistan as the primary agents responsible for the terrorist attacks. Both countries overwhelmingly identify with the Nation of Islam. They were scapegoated and punished as the enemy. Military and domestic security efforts were taken to purify the world from terror. Meanwhile, the nation consubstantially united. "Looking back, the effectiveness of these efforts is also characterized by cost. The last decade redefined our understanding of what modern warfare is, and our notion of shadowy enemies and inconstant allies" (6). Again, cost is an important theme. Critics can note the use of cost to measure the success of post-9/11 efforts. Should the costs of victimage be greater or less than the costs of 9/11 in order to successfully purify sins? What is the limit? We are not yet given an answer, but the numerical costs of war abroad and at home are made clear. Abroad: "6,204 American military personnel killed in Iraq and Afghanistan operations"; "141 Military women killed"; "2,300 American contractors killed" (6). At home: "38,144 green cards issued to [most Middle Eastern] immigrants . . . in 2001"; "63,290 . . . issued in . . . 2010" (14). Readers are made to know that the costs have been significant. Articles regarding costs of this purification stage range from current military affairs in Afghanistan and Pakistan, personal war stories, the $3.3 trillion spent since 9/11 for purification efforts, civil liberties today, and contemporary attitudes of safety. These articles discuss efforts taken to redress the 9/11 grievances and evaluate their consequential weight in comparison to the original sin.

Readers are informed of the excessively high costs of domestic and foreign warfare. Although measures have been drastic, "polls describe a city and nation not fully recovered emotionally from the attacks, and do not want to forget" (15). What does this mean? Perhaps this implies that the stage of purification is not yet over. If this is the case, what additional acts must be taken to purify the nation from guilt? And to what extent? This rhetorical stage of rebirth can reveal frightening consequences (see Burke, "Rhetoric of Hitler's Battle"). Muslims and Arab Americans have paid the price of the scapegoat, and they continue to carry the burden of guilt.

Interestingly, the *NYT* does not discuss post-9/11 effects on Muslim life until section seven, "Muslims Now." This section follows previous topics dedicated to "Remembrance" and "Rebuilding." Perhaps this sequence indicates that Muslim victimage will not stop until we either stop remembering or complete the process of rebuilding the new World Trade Center. An article by Adam Liptak, entitled "Civil Liberties Today," focuses on changes made in criminal enforcement since 9/11, including a trend of arresting "early," and charging "broadly," of assuming one is "guilty until proven innocent," and of enacting a "seriously diluted" range of individual protections.

"Muslims Now" does not focus on racialized politics since 9/11. Instead, the section is dedicated to the turbulence of Muslim faith. *NYT* delivers various narratives revealing testaments of faith and changes in religious attitudes. "American Muslims who came of age in the last decade have had to navigate uncharted waters. For some, that has meant embracing the faith; for others, forsaking it" (25). The Arab Spring, for instance, is used to demonstrate a transformation among Muslims, "[showing] hard-line Islamists who had embraced violence a peaceful path to change" (24). According to one Egyptian, "now it is a different story. We are living up to the challenges and paying the price" (24). Interestingly, this section reveals a sense of self-transformation, even mortification, among Muslims:

> The Arab Spring has . . . [negated] premises fundamental to a world that bore and nurtured Osama bin Laden. Arab majorities, still harboring resentment toward Western policies, are first looking inward to promote change, blaming their own leaders for decades of political, economic and cultural decline. (24)

In sum, the process of purification has been costly. The *NYT* recasts the imagery of war as a questionable tool of purification. War remains an ongoing process of this second stage and begs the question: Have we been reborn?

Redemption

Although it is unclear whether we have arrived at the stage of redemption, the *NYT* visually offers a potential rebirth with the memorial and museum. In the section "Rebuilding," the *NYT* features a full page dedicated to visual images of Ground Zero efforts, including the four buildings of the new World Trade Center. We are told that this is "a place for the past and future" as "the World Trade Center site comes together, above and below ground" (22). The architecture of the new World Trade Center is stunning. As depicted, all buildings are made of glass. As they reach for the sky, spectators will likely be encouraged to reflect on the events that have made this space significant. The skyscrapers surround the plaza, the memorial, and the pools. Here, "more than 400 swamp white oak trees, each about 30 feet tall" fill in all remaining space (22). Readers are told that the trees should double in size over the years. This site depicts an image of solace and personal reflection. It is the home of post-9/11 rhetoric. Two reflecting pools occupy the footprints of the former Twin Towers. Here, as "water flows over small, serrated dams and cascades," "bronze parapets, inscribed with the names of the victims, are lighted from inside" (22). The memorial opened on 9/12/11, and as of this writing, the museum has not yet opened. Once complete, the visual qualities of this location will likely move the nation closer to rebirth. Its qualities of peace, reflection, and remembrance are beautifully etched by the *NYT*, indicating the significance of spatial, and potentially national, transformation. This point is demonstrated in a narrative by one of the construction workers, quoted by the *NYT*, alongside eighteen photographs of Ground Zero workers: "I have been [a] witness to the rebuilding of the World Trade Center from the beginning. . . . The builders inspire me. [They] have transformed a pile of despair into a teeming complex and a new and wonderful skyline" (23).

This process of rebirth is "transformative" and is visually represented by Ground Zero. The final article of this special edition is entitled "In love with death: Years of grieving and war. But recall, too, the hour of human decency" (36). Here, author Jim Dwyer puts our current situation in perspective: "Today, no one in a desert tent, or anywhere, would wonder about protests against the Iraq war. That is the way of things with anniversaries" (36).

Although the cost of purification has been significant, readers are told the memory of 9/11 lives on. "It lives in the truths the size of atoms, nearly invisible and—one hopes—indestructible" (36). Thus, the pollution of 9/11 is permanently engrained in all of us, forever. In the center of this final page, there is a dark image illuminated by two bright strands of light beaming from the footprints of the former World Trade Center.

Yet, the final cycle of rebirth should be met with scrutiny. Primarily, the permanent symbols attached to these buildings continue to enrich the Western orientation of religion that is forever tied to the symbology of what the Twin Towers stood for: unfettered accumulation of wealth. The reflective arousal offered by this location can equally be regarded as superficial. What is it that we are reflecting on and what are we remembering? Potentially, the visual cues of this location invite only a remembrance of rationalized cost that justified oppressive policies of purification. We should remember that capitalism wrought sin, and our nation's way of dealing with its trauma inspired consubstantiality through scapegoating. The entire visual scene, in its remembrance of original sin, could potentially justify the racial retribution taken on Muslims and Arab Americans, both domestically and internationally. So although the rhetoric of rebirth may come full circle, it is likely that this end process will not be critically reflective or recursive in any way. If anything, the scene glorifies the triumph of neoliberalism and reifies the pious spirit that kept it alive. Since the spirit of capitalism was attacked, we were obligated to respond in pious fashion. It is important not to forget this day because this was a day of testament: our nation could fall to the guiles of the Muslim Other and allow our spirit of capitalism to recede, or we could stand up and fight back. Clearly, we chose the latter.

Meanwhile, the rhetorical features of the *NYT*'s special issue indicate that attitudes are ambivalent toward the post-9/11 history. The numerical and rhetorical costs reveal that the post-9/11 consequences are higher than 9/11 consequences. Time has yet to determine the rebirth of the post-9/11 dramaturgy. Yet, released on the tenth anniversary of the attacks, this special edition demonstrates a temporary rest, or stasis, from the process of purification. The rhetoric of religion, (re)framed from security to cost, symbolically reconstructs the significance of original sin. Although terministic screens have changed, our religious orientation has not. The spirit of capitalism has, thus far, prevailed.

Concluding Remarks

In conclusion, analysis of the *NYT*'s special issue revealed that post-9/11 discourse has been reframed by a terministic screen of cost. This frame reifies a religious orientation of capitalism because it demonstrates that there is a price to our symbolic order. This order, since 9/11, had to be protected with policies designed to punish the scapegoat. The authority of this religious orientation remains predicated on belief. This means that the value of our logology is dependent on the number of those adhering to the spirit of post-9/11 symbology. National consubstantiation remains centered on the dissociation of our constructed scapegoat: Muslims and Arab Americans. The only rhetorical features that differ on 9/11/11, as revealed by the *NYT*, is that Muslim and Arab American identity politics has been reconstituted to fit the frame of cost. This frame is used to evaluate the cost-benefit of purification efforts. Although Muslim and Arab American racialization is not prevalent (see Huckin), it remains an important feature of the ongoing process of rebirth. Potentially, the 9/11 museum and memorial, as illustrated by the *NYT*, may indicate the final stage of redemption. Yet, redemption is likely only accessible to those who have identified with post-9/11 religious order, since the site appears to be visually etched with a rhetoric of purification. Consequently, the identity politics of Muslims and Arab Americans remain permanently tied to an oppositional orientation under the auspices of post-9/11 discourse.

WORKS CITED

Bell, Catherine. *Ritual Perspectives and Dimensions*. Oxford: Oxford UP, 1997. Print.

Burke, Kenneth. *Language as Symbolic Action: Essays on Life, Literature, and Method*. Berkeley: U of California P, 1966. Print.

---. *Permanence and Change: An Anatomy of Purpose*. Berkeley: U of California P, 1964. Print.

---. *The Philosophy of Literary Form: Studies in Symbolic Action*. Berkeley: U of California P, 1973. Print.

---. "The Rhetoric of Hitler's Battle." *The Philosophy of Literary Form*. By Kenneth Burke. Berkeley: U of California P, 1973. 191-220. Print.

Cainkar, Louise. "Thinking Outside the Box." *Race and Arab Americans Before and After 9/11*. Ed. Amaney Jamal and Nadine Naber. Syracuse: Syracuse UP, 2008. 46-80. Print.

Foss, Sonja, Karen Foss, Robert Trapp. *Contemporary Perspectives on Rhetoric*. Long Grove: Waveland, 1985. Print.

Gershkoff, Amy, and Shana Kushner. "Shaping Public Opinion: The 9/11-Iraq Connection in the Bush Administration's Rhetoric." *Perspectives on Politics* 3.3 (2005): 525-53. Print.

Gunn, Joshua. "The Rhetoric of Exorcism." *Western Journal of Communication* 68 (Winter 2004): 1-33. Print.

Huckin, Thomas. "Textual Silence and the Discourse of Homelessness." *Discourse Society* 13.3 (2002): 347-72. Print.

Ivie, Robert. "Fighting Terror by Rite of Redemption and Reconciliation." *Rhetoric & Public Affairs* 10.2 (2007): 221-48. Print.

Jamal, Amaney, and Nadine Naber, eds. *Race and Arab Americans Before and After 9/11.* Syracuse: Syracuse UP, 2008. Print.

May, Stephen, and Tariq Modood. "Editorial." *Ethnicities* 1.3 (2001): 291-94. Print.

Merskin, Debra. "The Construction of Arabs as Enemies: Post-September 11 Discourse of George W. Bush." *Mass Communication and Society* 7.2 (2004): 157-75. Print.

Murphy, John "'Our Mission and our Moment': George W. Bush and September 11th." *Rhetoric & Public Affairs* 6.4 (2003): 607-32. Print.

Naber, Nadine. Introduction. *Race and Arab Americans Before and After 9/11.* Ed. Amaney Jamal and Nadine Naber. Syracuse: Syracuse UP, 2008. 1-45. Print.

Oswald, D. L. "Understanding Anti-Arab Reactions Post-9/11: The Role of Threats, Social Categories, and Personal Ideologies." *Journal of Applied Psychology* 35.9 (2005): 1775-799. Print.

"The Reckoning: America and the World a Decade After 9/11." *The New York Times* 11 Sept. 2011: 1-38. Print.

Skocpol, Theda. "Will 9/11 and the War on Terror Revitalize American Civic Democracy?" *PS: Political Science and Politics* (Sept. 2002): 537-40. Print.

Thompson, Jason. "Magic for a People Trained in Pragmatism: Kenneth Burke, *Mein Kampf,* and the Early 9/11 Oratory of George W. Bush." *Rhetoric Review* 30.4 (2011): 350-71. Print.

Volpp, Leti. "The Citizen and the Terrorist." *UCLA Law Review* 49.5 (2002): 1575-600. Print.

Zarefsky, David. "George W. Bush Discovers Rhetoric: September 20, 2001, and the U.S. Response to Terrorism." *The Ethos of Rhetoric.* Ed Michael Hyde. Columbia: U of South Carolina P, 2004. 136-55. Print.

---. "Making the Case for War: Colin Powell at the United Nations." *Rhetoric & Public Affairs* 10.2 (Summer 2007): 275-302. Print.

Žižek, Slavoj. *Welcome to the Desert of the Real! Five Essays on September 11 and Related Dates.* New York: Verso, 2002. Print.

31

AFONG MOY

Reframing Gentility in the Early Nineteenth Century

K. Hyoejin Yoon

Scholars of American history and culture, like Richard Bushman, Karen Halttunen, David Scobey, and Christine Stansell, describe American society in the early nineteenth century as one preoccupied with class status. Gentility had been, in the eighteenth century, the "proper style" of the gentry class, but in the beginning of the nineteenth century, the middle classes, raised up by the Industrial Revolution, acquired the means to express what Bushman calls a "vernacular gentility" through their persons, manners, homes, and other accoutrements of respectability (xii-xiii). The democratic forces that enabled social mobility ironically created the desire for the rising classes to signal their own distinction from the lower classes. The performance of gentility drew from notions of European, Old World autocracies. Bushman sums up the oft-noted irony that "[a]t a time when the Revolution had ended the principles of monarchy and aristocracy and the forces of capitalist enterprise were leading Americans into industrialization, Americans modeled their lives after the aristocrats of a society that was supposedly repudiated at the founding of the nation" (xix). The desire for respectability created a mass market for consumers of genteel goods, and Chinese goods, in particular, were sought after as Americans appropriated the aristocratic manners associated with tea service and other refined habits. The artifacts of gentility, tea, silk, porcelain, and lacquerware, copied by prestigious European artists like Wedgewood, became more affordable so that everyday domestic life included tea sets, Nankins, patterned plates, and snuff boxes—the stuff that, according to historian John Haddad, shaped romantic images of China as an idyllic faraway land in the minds of average Americans (Greenberg 4; Haddad "Imagined"; Tchen 7, 21; Hung; Valenze).

It is within this context that, in 1834, a young Chinese woman named Afong Moy was brought to New York. According to Haddad, Nathaniel and Frederick Carne, brothers in the China trade, trafficked in affordable Chinese goods to meet the rising demand among middle-class consumers. Moy was exhibited as the "Chinese Lady" in November 1834 in a well-appointed apartment in New York City. Haddad argues that Moy was a living advertisement for the Carnes' business. Thereafter, she performed at the American Museum and other venues in New York (Odell).

The newspapers played a significant role in promoting Moy's exhibit as "the Chinese Lady." The *New York Commercial Advertiser, Daily Advertiser, Gazette,* and the *Star* carried numerous stories about Afong Moy in the late fall of 1834. Unlike the proliferating three-penny popular presses that were emerging in the 1830s and '40s, these were largely commercial papers, designed primarily for the "mercantile reader" (Crouthamel 91). During a time when there was only a fine line between news and advertisement, these papers greased the wheels of commerce (Henkin 116). The newspaper descriptions of Afong Moy were tied to the commercial enterprises they were paid to promote and advertise.

The newspapers forward a rhetoric of gentility that functions like Burke's rhetoric of identification through the way it paradoxically coheres a group through "communicative norms" and by illuminating the division or difference inherent in identification (Burke 1030). This paradox figures Moy as an ideal to which the American middle class should aspire. The newspapers sent a message about how the reading public ought to style themselves in the conventional performance of genteel manners. At the same time, that identification is founded on a desire to create distinction—to factionalize and further separate the "good society" from the rest. Furthermore, the identification is created in relation to a gendered and raced "other"—Moy serving as a synecdoche of foreign wealth and high culture. This paper considers the ways that the rhetoric of gentility coheres and divides the reading public and how a figure like Afong Moy became the medium for that social cohesion and division. Using categories of genteel performance identified by Bushman and Halttunen, I examine the newspapers' aggrandizing representations of Moy's exhibit, particularly the setting of the exhibit in a parlor, her genteel manners, and the associations made between Moy and European aristocracy.

Popular Representations of China and the Chinese

Popular representations of Chinese were most numerous and influential in mid- to late-nineteenth century when the Gold Rush and westward expansion brought thousands of Chinese laborers to the Midwest and West Coast. Populist concerns about labor displacement resulted in xenophobic propaganda that cast Chinese workers as hordes of degenerate "coolies," rat-eaters, or prostitutes (Lee). However, in the early nineteenth century, before its defeat in the Opium Wars, China was the wealthiest, most cosmopolitan nation of the time, viewed by many to be technologically and culturally advanced, and its status in the American imagination was influenced by Enlightenment and Romantic orientalism (Goldstein et al.; Hung; Miller; Ruskola; Sánchez-Eppler).

Newspaper representations of China and Chinese people in the early nineteenth century reflect mostly a benign curiosity into manners and customs, often in reprints of excerpts from travel writings of missionaries and entrepreneurs (Barrow; *Sketches*; Tiffany) or from English-language newspapers like the *Chinese Repository* in Canton. These excerpts describe marriage rituals, social customs, particularly the binding of women's feet, and often the luxurious homes of both Chinese merchants and European and American traders in port cities like Canton.

After Afong Moy's arrival, the New York newspapers printed articles about her first exhibit in November 1834. An article in the *New York Commercial Advertiser* and two others in the *New York Star* focused significantly on features of gentility that align with the characteristics addressed in Bushman's study: Moy's domestic setting, her dress and manners, and her social rank. The *Commercial Advertiser* set up an overview of these concerns:

> Miss Afong Moy[,] . . . safely arrived in New York, has taken the spacious and fashionable mansion, No. 8, Park-place, as her residence, which she has furnished in a style becoming a princess of the "celestial empire," and, indeed, presents in the decorations of her person, as well as her apartments, a specimen of oriental magnificence. We paid our devoirs to her ladyship a day or two since, and found a number of ladies and gentlemen were already occupying her drawing rooms, of which she "did the honors," with ease, grace and propriety. . . . She is seated on a throne of rich and costly materials and exhibits her little feet on a cushion sufficiently elevated to show them off to the best advantage. . . . Her costume is that of ladies of her rank, in the emporium of China, and indicated some four or five hours employment at her toilette, in which she no doubt excels. ("From the *N. York Commercial Advertiser*")

The "Lady" in the Parlor

Moy's exhibit took place in a parlor, a genteel, domestic space, rather than a theater stage, though no less designed for performance. The parlor, a nonutilitarian space reserved to receive and entertain company, was a hallmark of a refined house. In this setting, families could present their most decorative possessions to their guests (Bushman 251). Anne McClintock and Karen Halttunen describe the parlor as a performative space: a gendered, domestic "theater" for the display of commodities and femininity (McClintock 219); a "stage setting for genteel performance" (Halttunen 101-11). In the apartments at No. 8 Park Place, Afong Moy received her guests in the parlor, amidst furniture and decorations "*a la Chinois,*" according to the reporter from the *Star,* who found all of which to "form a perfect Chinese museum" ("Visit"). The reporter describes

> rich dazzling colors and elaborate workmanship of Chinese furniture and ornaments . . . —lamps of the most gorgeous construction hanging down from the ceiling, and the heat of which when lighted set in motion a number of curious images—porcelain vases filled with beautiful flowers—lacquered tables, covered with gold ornaments in relief—ottomans—cushioned chairs, models of junks and pagodas, screens at the

window spread over with figures of birds and flowers, and paintings that
might vie with the colors of Titian, steel mirrors[,] guitars and workboxes
in profusion. ("Visit")

It appears an intentional design by the proprietors to situate Moy in the
space of the parlor, with Chinese furnishings and decorations. The Carnes
capitalized on the currency that "'things' Chinese" had acquired and their
power to signal "cultural 'distinction'" (Tchen 13). Like a museum, the parlor
orders and mediates the viewer's experience and shapes the experience for
Moy's guests (paying customers) as a chance to exhibit their own "worthiness
and credibility" through the "social practic[e] of paying [a] call to a private
residenc[e]" (Tchen 10; see also Scobey). The newspapers played an important role in representing such genteel "instruments of power" (Bushman 404)
around which the reading public can cohere. The newspaper rhetoric com-
pels the emulation of others, and stirs their desire, according to Bushman, "to
partake of power, . . . glory, strength and beauty" (406).

The rhetoric of gentility articulates what Burke describes as the socializ-
ing element of rhetoric, which calls an individual to "form himself in accordance with the communicative norms that match the cooperative ways of his
society" (1030). Gentility is communicated through norms of decorations,
social spaces, and practices, cohering a middle-class Anglo-American identity around/through Chinese commodities, and thus "[t]eas, porcelains, and
other such luxury goods"—symbols of the patrician classes—are appropriated to communicate bourgeois respectability (Tchen 15).

Burke notes that, at the same time, "identification implies division" and
that it is involved in both "socialization and faction" (1033). The rhetoric of
gentility highlights the difference that undergirds the desire for identification, in this case, the difference between the middle classes and the patrician
aristocracy to which they aspire. There are additional factions implied here
as well. The first are the symbols, the communicative ways that further signify Moy's distinction, like the large gilt Chinese letters by the entrance to
her apartment that set it apart from the rest of the bourgeois neighbors.
("Miss Afong Moy—Second Visit"; emphasis in original). According to
Tchen, "the tasteful display of passionately coveted things from the 'orient' . . . distinguished one moneyed space from the other" (8). Second, the
significations of race, gender, and culture embodied by Afong Moy herself
establish a further difference that creates the need for points of contact. Jeffrey Murray argues that identification is achieved "through a symbolic overcoming of difference" (34).

Amidst the Barbarians

The ethos of the genteel subject is as important as the domestic space and
decorations in the rhetoric of gentility. The "telling mark of genteel aspira-
tion" (Bushman) is embodied in behaviors and attitudes that evince self-control, courtesy, and one's belonging in "polite society" (Halttunen). The *New*

York Evening Star attests to Afong Moy's "ease, grace and propriety"—displays of the appropriate behaviors and rituals of genteel society. Moy's exhibit is a total experience of such rituals. The reporter received a "polite card of invitation, written in Chinese characters, from Miss Afong Moy" ("Miss Afong Moy—Second Visit"). He reports on Moy's sumptuous silk costume and notes her fashionable delay due to her long and laborious toilette. His language is deferential, in the extreme, in describing her gracious manners and compares hers to the coarse and awkward gestures of the visitors.

He goes on to position himself as a supplicant: It was his "honor at last to be recognized by her ladyship," as she sat on "her cushioned throne." When she smiled and spoke a few words in Chinese, he "made due homage, as an honor that we deeply appreciate and shall long cherish." When she revealed her little feet to him, the reporter describes this as a coveted "mark of favor," which drew the attention of all in the room, and that might have compelled him to "fall prostrate" and kowtow. He notes that "it is not every barbarian, however *distingue*, that can hope from a daughter of the celestial empire, such distinguished courtesies" ("Miss Afong Moy—Second Visit").

This interaction is circumscribed by codes of gendered and classed social etiquette (Scobey) and described in a rhetoric that casts Afong Moy as a dignitary, in comparison to whom the reporter and the other American visitors appear as barbarians. The reporter for the *Star* expresses his eagerness "to show [Afong Moy] that we are not so uncivilized and such barbarous vandals as she perhaps had been taught to believe by the great patriarch of her country, *Con-fu-chee* [Confucius]" ("Visit"). Yet, he is chagrined by his own company, finding their "multiple bows, and attitudes, and gesticulations" of excessive politeness "ludicrous" ("Miss Afong Moy—Second Visit") in comparison to Moy's taciturn grace and "imperturbable composure" ("Visit").

Moy becomes a mirror for her American audience. The reflection invites the visitors to identify with her and associate themselves with the high-status Chinese commodities that add to her appeal and the demand she creates for the commodities. At the same time, she reflects back an image of them as subordinate and uncivilized. The *Star* article expresses a certain anxiety, self-consciousness, and deference to Moy's authority, looking to her for recognition of their achievement of respectability and distinction. According to Halttunen, the genteel hostess and her guests are locked into a reciprocating performance. Both host and guest are called on to "assist, encourage and honor the genteel performer's claim to gentility" (107). Moy's visitors affirm, legitimize, and recognize Moy's genteel performance, which is codified and communicated widely by the newspapers. The visitors also look to her for verification of their own performance. Implicit in this pact is the threat of judgment, which the reporters themselves voice in anticipation. Gentility is a social pact that depends on others for its recognition. For Americans who were easily influenced by European fads and especially vulnerable to critiques of American provinciality (Bushman), these communicative norms were crucial.

Aristocratic Nostalgia

Lastly, the rhetoric of gentility is asserted through allusions to the practices of European aristocratic court culture (Bushman; Halttunen; Lewis; Loeb; Tchen). The *Commercial Advertiser* presents Afong Moy as a "princess of the 'Celestial Empire,'" seated on a "throne" ("Miss Afong Moy—Second Visit"). The persistent construction of Moy as a "lady" bespeaks a design on the part of the proprietors and newspaper reporters to appeal to consumers' nostalgia for the trappings of European aristocracy.

The *Star* revives aristocratic codes by comparing Afong Moy to Napoleon's second wife, Marie Louise, the former Archduchess of Austria, and the parlor to "the compliment which Napoleon so delicately paid to Maria Louisa, when on her arrival at Paris on her marriage, she found the identical furniture, down to the very bird-cage, she had left at her boudoir in her palace of Schoenbrunn at Vienna" ("Visit"). Readers are invited to imagine Afong Moy as Marie Louise and her exhibit as an imperial gesture of affection and welcome for the foreign bride. The reference is fitting and suggestive in a number of ways. First, the historical context: Napoleon I defeated Austria in 1809 and sought to ally himself with the Imperial House of Habsburg by marrying Marie Louise to further legitimate his own imperial ambitions. As the great-niece of Marie Antoinette, Marie Louise embodied a lineage of European nobility. By association, Moy is lionized as a symbol of noble lineage and sanctifies the occasion of the parlor visit. Second, the reference to Schönbrunn Palace traces the genealogy of the symbols and artifacts of European aristocracy to the influence of Chinese culture and expensive and rare Chinese goods. Indeed, Marie Louise's great-grandmother, Maria Therese, the Austrian empress, was noted for her interest in Asian art objects and for decorating the palace in the Chinese taste (Yonan).

The Carne brothers capitalized on New Yorkers' emulation of the "European elite's craze for Chinese export items and European chinoserie" (Tchen 13). The less costly domestic goods aimed at the middle-class consumer were imbued with the value of the once rare and expensive Chinese goods that informed the "material expression of European orientalism" (Tchen 6).

Conclusion

The parlor setting, the niceties of formal invitations, emphasis on distinction, and the Chinese goods imbued with European, aristocratic values reveal a deep paradox in the American psyche that many describe as the tension between democracy and empire (Gustafson; Lewis; Loeb). Lori Anne Loeb argues that democracy in fact enabled empire and capitalism and that the flow of genteel commodities

> was most profitable in an open social and political structure; the product
> with snobbish appeal that connoted the taste and affluence of its pur-
> chaser could find a market much broader than the aristocracy once

democracy assumed a material as well as a political dimension. Status and luxury goods associated with status were potentially available to all in a democratic society. One of the pleasures, a fantasy dangled before the consumer, was the fulfillment of the democratic dream, at first politically and now materially. Luxury goods were not so much a reflection of hardened class lines as the ultimate, even if illusory, pleasure of an increasingly democratized society. (5)

Democracy came to mean one's ability to purchase and display luxury goods. Unconstrained by old class and gender boundaries, Americans were free to purchase and perform their way up the social ladder.

The rhetoric of gentility functions as a form of identification and is articulated through its attendant symbols: the parlor, genteel manners, and aristocratic associations. Newspapers construct what Kenneth Burke refers to as a "specialized activity [that] makes one a participant in some social or economic class." Performing genteel rituals, like visiting Afong Moy, becomes a means for readers and visitors to flaunt a "social insignia" of belonging to a particular social class. This demonstrates Burke's point that belonging is rhetorical (1023).

However, undergirding the class identifications enabled by Moy's exhibit and the newspapers' rhetoric is the specter of Moy's racial, gender, and cultural difference. Moy is a portal through which the middle class can experience refinement. Her construction as a personage of cultural superiority pushes against contemporaneous discourses of race. Racial theories of the time placed "Mongolians" in the middle of a racial hierarchy with Caucasians at the top and blacks at the bottom (Horsman). Moy is constructed as an icon of "oriental magnificence" that sets her apart from freaks and others who were put on exhibit, such as Sarah Bartmann, one of the Hottentot Venuses; Joice Heth, claimed to be the nursing mammy of George Washington; and Chang and Eng Bunker, the Siamese Twins (Bogdan; Miranda; Ponzanesi; Riess; Tchen). In these aggrandized representations, she is not simply an inferior other but a symbol of national and consumer economic aspirations, reflecting the tensions in national discourses that would tout both her racial inferiority and cultural superiority.

In this period, China exerted enormous international economic power as a primary source of export goods around the world, while limiting Anglo-American trade by closing its markets to foreign commodities. China was both admired for its venerable history and, not surprisingly, vilified by Europeans and Americans as a tyrannical society. Moy is described in various accounts as having escaped the jealousy of the Chinese, and her bound feet became the object of American curiosity and the symbol of her oppression. Americans denounced the backwards tyranny of Chinese culture while embracing its cosmopolitanism and refined wares. Afong Moy is the perfect figure as a victim saved from tyranny and thereby transformed into a model of idealized, aggrandized gentility.

According to Burke, rhetoric "considers the ways in which individuals . . . become identified with groups more or less at odds with one another"

(1020). This analysis enables a reframing of gentility—not as simply a claim to a monolithic, normative identity, but as a construct that is revealed for its instability and performative nature. This further reveals the transnational flow of ideas and commodities that helped to create American identity and also created the basis of the anxieties of how Americans shape up in comparison to Chinese and European cultures.

The rhetoric of gentility further reframes a commonsense and overly simplified assumption that the Chinese were always vilified and denigrated in the US imagination and its narratives. This brings me to my final point. In this analysis, the focus has been on the rhetoric of gentility expressed by the newspapers, genteel performances, and the significations of objects and spaces. I am conscious of how the voices of the newspaper men and the designs of the Carnes frame Afong Moy as a prop and that my analysis may reiterate that discursive violence that Asian American feminists and historiographers have warned against (Kang; Ling; Hune; Yung). My goal is not to simply minimize Afong Moy's agency in order to explore the rhetoric of gentility. While Afong Moy's own voice is yet to be recovered from the archives, my larger goal is to explore the possibility of the power of a person, even as a figure represented through the gaze of the dominant subject, to interrupt, complicate, and decenter traditional notions about the significance of race, class, gender, and nation. In order to achieve this, the reframing of gentility has to be done alongside a reframed view of the transnational, global economy of the eighteenth and early nineteenth centuries in which China was arguably the economic and cultural center (Frank; Greenberg; Pomeranz).

WORKS CITED

Barrow, John. *Travels in China.* Philadelphia: W. F. McLaughlin, 1805. Print.

Bogdan, Robert. *Freak Show: Presenting Human Oddities for Amusement and Profit.* Chicago: U of Chicago P, 1990. Print.

Burke, Kenneth. "From *A Rhetoric of Motives.*" *The Rhetorical Tradition.* Ed. Patricia Bizzell and Bruce Herzberg. Boston: Bedford St./Martin's, 1990. 1018-34. Print.

Bushman, Richard L. *The Refinement of America: Persons, Houses, Cities.* New York: Vintage, 1993. Print.

Crouthamel, James L. "The Newspaper Revolution in New York 1830-1860." *New York History* 45 (April 1964): 91-114. Print.

Frank, Andre Gunder. *ReOrient: Global Economy in the Asian Age.* Berkeley: U of California P, 1998. Print.

"From the *N. York Commercial Advertiser.* The Chinese Lady." Rpt. in *Connecticut Courant* 24 Nov. 1834. Print.

Goldstein, Jonathan, Jerry Israel, and Hilary Conroy. *America Views China: American Images of China Then and Now.* Bethlehem: Lehigh UP, 1991. Print.

Greenberg, Michael. *British Trade and the Opening of China 1800-42.* 1951. Cambridge: Cambridge UP, 1991. Print.

Gustafson, Sandra M. "Histories of Democracies and Empire." *American Quarterly* 59.1 (2007): 107-33. Print.

Haddad, John R. "Imagined Journeys to Distant Cathay: Constructing China with Ceramics," 1780-1920. *Winterthur Portfolio* 41.1 (2007): 53-80. Print.

Halttunen, Karen. *Confidence Men and Painted Women: A Study of Middle-class Culture in America, 1830-1870.* New Haven: Yale UP, 1982. Print.

Henkin, David M. *City Reading: Written Words and Public Spaces in Antebellum New York.* New York: Columbia UP, 1998. Print.

Horsman, Reginald. *Race and Manifest Destiny: The Origins of American Racial Anglo-saxonism.* Cambridge: Harvard UP, 1981. Print.

Hune, Shirley. "Chinese American Women in U.S. History." *The Practice of U.S. Women's History: Narratives, Intersections, and Dialogues.* Ed. S. Jay Kleinberg, et al. New Brunswick: Rutgers UP, 2007. 161-84. Print.

Hung, Ho-Fung. "Orientalist Knowledge and Social Theories: China and the European Conceptions of East-West Differences from 1600 to 1900." *Sociological Theory* 21.3 (Sept. 2003): 254-80. Print.

Kang, Laura Hyun Yi. "Conjuring 'Comfort Women': Mediated Affiliations and Disciplined Subjects in Korean/American Transnationality." *Journal of Asian American Studies* 6.1 (2003): 25-55. Print.

Lee, Robert G. *Orientals: Asian Americans in Popular Culture.* Philadelphia: Temple UP, 1999. Print.

Lewis, Charlene M. Boyer. "Elizabeth Patterson Bonaparte: 'Ill Suited for the Life of a Columbians Modest Wife.'" *Journal of Women's History* 18.2 (Summer 2006): 33-62. Print.

Ling, Huping. *Surviving on the Gold Mountain: A History of Chinese American Women and Their Lives.* Albany: State U of New York P, 1998. Print.

Loeb, Lori Anne. *Consuming Angels: Advertising and Victorian Women.* New York: Oxford UP, 1994. Print.

McClintock, Anne. *Imperial Leather: Race, Gender, and Sexuality in the Colonial Contest.* New York: Routledge, 1995. Print.

Miller, Stuart C. "The American Trader's Image of China, 1785-1840." *The Pacific Historical Review* 36.4 (Nov. 1967): 375-95. Print.

Miranda, Carlos A., and Suzette A. Spencer. "Omnipresent Negation: *Hottentot Venus* and *Africa Rising.*" *Callaloo* 32.2 (2009): 910-33. Print.

"Miss Afong Moy—Second Visit." *New York Star.* Rpt. in *Baltimore Gazette* 22 Nov. 1834. Print.

Murray, Jeffrey W. "Kenneth Burke: A Dialogue of Motives." *Philosophy & Rhetoric* 35.1 (2002): 22-49. Print.

Odell, George C. D. *Annals of the New York Stage.* Vol. 4. New York: Columbia UP, 1928. Print.

Pomeranz, Kenneth. *The Great Divergence: China, Europe, and the Making of the Modern World Economy.* Princeton: Princeton UP, 2000. Print.

Ponzanesi, Sandra. "Beyond the Black Venus: Colonial Sexual Politics and Contemporary Visual Practices." *Italian Colonialism. Legacies and Memories.* Ed. Jacqueline Andall and Derek Duncan. Oxford: Peter Lang, 2005. 165-89. Print.

Riess, Benjamin. *The Showman and the Slave: Race, Death, and Memory in Barnum's America.* Cambridge: Harvard UP, 2010. Print.

Ruskola, Teemu. "Canton Is Not Boston: The Invention of American Imperial Sovereignty." *American Quarterly* 57.3 (2005): 859-84. Print.

Sánchez-Eppler, Karen. "Copying and Conversion: An 1824 Friendship Album 'from a Chinese Youth.'" *American Quarterly* 59.2 (2007): 301-39. Print.

Scobey, David. "Anatomy of the Promenade: The Politics of Bourgeois Sociability in Nineteenth-century New York." *Social History* 17.2 (May 1992): 203-27. Print.

Sketches by a Traveller. Boston: Carter and Hendee, 1830. Print.

Stansell, Christine. *City of Women: Sex and Class in New York, 1789-1860.* New York: Knopf, 1986. Print.

Tchen, John Kuo Wei. *New York before Chinatown.* Baltimore: Johns Hopkins UP, 1999.

Tiffany, Osmond, Jr. *The Canton Chinese.* Boston and Cambridge: James Munro, 1849. Print.

Valenze, Deborah. Rev. of *Consuming Splendor: Society and Culture in Seventeenth-Century England*, by Linda Levy Peck, and *Luxury and Pleasure in Eighteenth-Century Britain*, by Maxine Berg, and *The Far East and the English Imagination, 1600-1730*, by Robert Markley. *American Historical Review* 113. 1 (2008): 119-22. Print.

"Visit to Miss Afong Moy, The Chinese Lady." *New York Star.* Rpt. in *Norfolk Advertiser* 15 Nov. 1834. Print.

Yonan, Michael E. "Veneers of Authority: Chinese Lacquers in Maria Theresa's Vienna" *Eighteenth-Century Studies* 37.4 (Summer 2004): 652-72. Print.

Yung, Judy. *Unbound Feet: A Social History of Chinese Women in San Francisco.* Berkeley: U of California P, 1995. Print.

SECTION
VI

RE/FRAMING DISCIPLINARY IDENTIFICATIONS AND ASSUMPTIONS

32

BOTH INSIDERS AND OUTSIDERS

Re/Framing Identification via Japanese Rhetoric

Dominic J. Ashby

This year's RSA conference theme calls for a reconsideration of Kenneth Burke's identification "as a place of perpetual reframing that affects who, how, and what can be thought, spoken, written, and imagined." My presentation engages this call by exploring how the Japanese rhetorical tradition involves ongoing cycles of identification and disidentification. I present the dynamic between *uchi* and *soto*, often translated as "inside" and "outside," as an alternative to Burke's identification. Where Burke's theory supposes a relatively static self and has been criticized as not supportive of difference (Ratcliffe), *uchi/soto* presents a fluid and contingent notion of self that potentially allows for greater heterogeneity. While the process of reframing self and social relations that makes up the *uchi/soto* dynamic is perhaps more immediately apparent within Japanese rhetoric, as anthropologist Jane Bachnik observes, the concept is not unique to Japan, and I see the dynamic as a useful analytical framework for work in other, including Euro-American, rhetorical traditions.

Before moving on to a comparison with Burke's identification, I will give an abbreviated explanation of the *uchi/soto* dynamic as rhetoric. I base my use of the concept on earlier works in the fields of linguistics and anthropology but with significant reinterpretation. *Uchi* and *soto*, like the English inside and outside, can refer to both physical location and interpersonal or social status. Earlier works[1] present the *uchi/soto* dynamic as a model to explain social interactions, focusing on the shifting between insider and outsider status. Grounded in the idea of indexing, in this model words and other behaviors "point" to one's situation within a social context to construct and maintain a social, relational self (Bachnik, "Introduction" 5). The indexical model of *uchi/soto* draws attention to shifting notions and portrayals of self that anthropologists observe among Japanese. The model allows for a fluid, contextual self and presents self and social order as mutually constitutive. The social order shapes what is proper behavior—what the role of each person is—while the relationship between members of the group shapes or deter-

309

mines the social order. The two reflect and respond to each other. As an infinitely recursive loop, one or the other could shift at any time, causing a corresponding shift in the other.

However, the indexical model of *uchi/soto* that Bachnik and others use envisions a sort of perfect reflection of preexisting social relations.[2] An explanation based on indexing gives no room for new meanings or relations, only for the perfect repetition or reflection of preexistent meanings, relations, and associations. I extend *uchi/soto* into the realm of rhetoric by rethinking the dynamic as also based in *reiteration*, from Judith Butler's explanation of performativity, rather than only in indexing (see *Bodies that Matter* and *Excitable Speech*). This move still accounts for the shifting and mutual constitution found in Bachnik's indexical model but opens more theoretical space for generating new meaning. Reiteration, ongoing repetition of norms but always with failure, allows the generation of new meaning along with the (always imperfect) continuation of traditional patterns.

It is important to remember that while the shifting of *uchi/soto* is more "importantly present" (Hall and Ames) in Japan, the spatial metaphor of inside and outside that grounds the dynamic is much more widespread. Bachnik writes, "the *universally defined* orientations for inside/outside are linked with *culturally defined* perspectives for self, society, and language in Japan" ("Introduction" 7; emphasis in original). This cultural importance of *uchi/soto* in Japan makes it worthy of study specifically as a key feature of Japanese rhetoric; however, what Bachnik describes as its more universal presence as various iterations of what in English we call inside and outside means the concept also has a conceptual foothold globally. For this reason, a rhetorical theory drawing from the culturally specific *uchi/soto* can easily be applied more broadly. For the remainder of this presentation, I focus on this latter, broader application of *uchi/soto*, putting it in comparison with Burke's identification.

Looked at comparatively, *uchi/soto* and Burke's identification are similar in that they both explain interactions between individuals, groups, and the divisions and connections between them. While commonalities certainly exist, as theories, *uchi/soto* and identification emphasize and support very different understandings of self and society, unity and diversity. These distinctions allow *uchi/soto* to produce meaningfully different readings of rhetorical action.

A Rhetoric of Motives contains Burke's best-known explanation of identification, although he discusses it elsewhere as well. In the *Rhetoric*, he introduces identification as such, linking it to the idea of consubstantiality (substance, having been a focus of *A Grammar of Motives*, acts as a bridge between the two):

> A is not identical with his colleague, B. But insofar as their interests are joined, A is *identified* with B. Or he may *identify himself* with B even when their interests are not joined, if he assumes that they are, or is persuaded to believe so.

> Here are ambiguities of substance. In being identified with B, A is "substantially one" with a person other than himself. Yet at the same time he remains unique, an individual locus of motives. Thus he is both joined and separate, at once a distinct substance and consubstantial with another. (20-21)

This focus on the individual and a consubstantial other, on the personal as "both joined and separate," has similarities to the *uchi/soto* model of self, which characterizes the individual in relation to a group, where the self is constituted by relationships with others. As Burke further explains, identification is always accompanied by division: "one need not scrutinize the concept of 'identification' very sharply to see, implied in it at every turn, its ironic counterpart: division" (*Rhetoric* 23). By identifying with one group, one may divide oneself from another. Similarly, the *uchi/soto* dynamic involves constant shifting between insider and outsider status, of belonging and not belonging. While these similarities draw identification and *uchi/soto* together, important distinctions abound.

A vitally important distinction between the *uchi/soto* dynamic and identification involves notions of the self. The self that underlies the *uchi/soto* dynamic constantly shifts in response to context. Bachnik observes that "Japanese terms for *self* and *person* . . . are unstable over time, constantly shifting and contextually dependent in use," and she argues "that the distinctions between self and social context are not drawn as sharply for Japanese[,] . . . that self is not viewed as 'fixed'" ("Introduction" 15). At first blush, the Burkean self seems equally dynamic. Burke writes, "the so-called 'I' is merely a unique combination of partially conflicting 'corporate we's'" (*Attitudes* 264). His definition posits a social self, an "I" formed by various relationships. However, though the Burkean self might be composed of "a unique combination of . . . 'corporate we's,'" the overall result is conceptualized as fairly constant. In the *Rhetoric*, when looking forward to the subject of the never-completed *Symbolic of Motives*,[3] Burke characterizes the individual self, separated from other people, as "at peace" and "outside the realm of conflict" (22). Here, "the individual is treated merely as a self-subsistent unit proclaiming its peculiar nature. It is 'at peace,' in that its terms *cooperate* in modifying one another" (23).[4] That is, once formed, the Burkean notion of self can "be" or "proclaim" its self on its own. Once put in contact with other selves, the potential for conflict, and therefore rhetoric, arises; however, this realm of contact Burke describes is an arena of individual selves *interacting* not *constituting* one another through that interaction, as in *uchi/soto*. The Burkean self may engage in discourse without itself being wholly discursive.

Uchi/soto and Burke's identification further differ in their sense of the frequency and ease or difficulty with which individuals shift affiliations. If we look across several of Burke's works, it quickly becomes apparent that while individuals certainly can shift their identifications, such shifting tends to be drastic or even traumatic, at least in the examples Burke presents. In *Attitudes Toward History*, Burke acknowledges that "changes of identity occur in everyone," while some changes are more "acute" than others (269)—that is, some changes might escape notice while others are more apparent and/or traumatic. However, these latter "acute" instances take up much more of Burke's attention, suggesting he sees them as more meaningful or somehow more deserving of analysis. Further, the language Burke uses to describe even the nonacute instances suggests disruption and trauma, involving "rebirth" and occurring as a result of "conflicts among our 'corporate we's'" (268-9).

Krista Ratcliffe's reading of Burkean identification also finds a self that resists change. Focusing on Burke's statement in *The Philosophy of Literary Form* that "a change of identity . . . would require a change of substance" (qtd. in Ratcliffe 57), Ratcliffe finds that "malleability [of identity] fosters fear and resistance of itself[;] . . . despite the malleability of identity, the fear and resistance of this malleability render identity not easily changed" (57). The Burkean self can shift through changes in identification but does so by moving completely from one state to another. Changes in identification involve replacement, with little chance for a return to previous identifications without equally drastic measures. Rather, Burke casts the process of reidentification in rather violent—and final—terms:

> We should also note that a change of identity . . . would require nothing less drastic than the *obliteration of one's whole past lineage*. . . . A thorough job of symbolic rebirth would require the revision of one's ancestral past itself. . . . We might interpret symbolic parricide as simply an extension of symbolic suicide, a more thorough-going way of obliterating the substance of one's old identity. . . . [T]his symbolic suicide itself would be but *one* step in a process which was not completed until the substance of the abandoned identity had been replaced by the new substance of a new identity. (*Philosophy* 41-2; emphases in original)

Here, Burke envisions a *total* change in identity—a drastic disavowal of the old self and allegiances, not the more incremental and strategic shifts that Ratcliffe is talking about as the point of rhetorical listening as a strategy, or the ongoing, situational shifting characterized by *uchi/soto*. Burke's identification aims toward an end point, a state of connection or consubstantiality that remains relatively permanent once established, barring violent disavowals.

Identifications tend toward stasis in Burke's model because they are more of a means to an end, the end being the establishment of common ground and the "compensation" for division. Each identification clears a space of common ground. Conflicting identifications might obscure or destroy other common ground, hence the resistance to major changes in identity and the drastic nature of the changes in identification Burke describes. *Uchi/soto*, by contrast, emphasizes an ongoing process of becoming, a state of flux involving porous boundaries between states of being. While identification yearns for an unattainable universality, *uchi/soto* deals in contingency and shifting focal points. Solidarity remains an important goal within Japanese rhetoric of *uchi/soto*, but it is a solidarity of shifting memberships and boundaries, and one without a universal, static ideal. Where for

Burke division stands as the obstacle to and tragic byproduct of identification, in *uchi/soto* difference might help form in-group solidarity through the exclusion and/or simultaneous incorporation of the outsider. One example of shifting exclusion and incorporation is found in mainstream Japanese attitudes toward *otaku*, dedicated or even obsessive fans. *Otaku* are sometimes derided, treated, and portrayed as outside of, even antithetical to, healthy social norms and structures, othered as everything wrong with Japanese society. At other times, *otaku* are celebrated as uniquely Japanese, one of many elements supposedly setting Japan apart from other cultures. Depending on context, *otaku* can be insider, outsider, or both.

An explication and rereading of one of Burke's examples of identification may help to crystallize the distinctions between identification and *uchi/soto*. In the introduction to *A Rhetoric of Motives*, Burke offers the brief example of "the politician who, addressing an audience of farmers, says, 'I was a farm boy myself'" as a case of identification (xiv). Burke's politician, by evoking a shared past as a farm boy, claims a measure of consubstantiality with his audience. Though he may no longer be a farmer, he lays claim to a substance, an assumedly formative set of experiences that cannot be taken away—short of through complete disavowal and an identificatory "death" and "rebirth"—which links him at a deep level to his audience. The politician may need to present his credentials, so to speak, through sharing stories or using specific terms or other shibboleths that the audience may or may not accept, but the act of identification is conducted via a supposedly stable part of his self.

From a perspective of *uchi/soto*, by claiming a shared past as a farm boy, the politician establishes a point of commonality which, when measured against points of difference, help establish how much of an insider or outsider he is. Moving beyond mere indexing, the politician might also use the intersection of historical meanings and associations of being a farm boy—the shared cultural experience or tradition he claims with his audience—with the current context of his speaking to build a new sense of what it means "to be a farm boy." Or, drawing from the narrative of farm-boy-ness and other experiences "outside" of that narrative (say, of being a state-house politician), he might build a new sense of what it means to be a politician, or of what it means to be a representative of the particular audience he is addressing. Of course, in a good speech all these possible approaches likely overlap. My point is not that using identification as a lens disallows such readings, but that it focuses on relatively stable states—either their creation or their revelation—while an *uchi/soto* perspective foregrounds process and flux.[5]

Comparison of *uchi/soto* and identification reveals how the two systems favor different readings of rhetorical action and make different assumptions about the self and interactions between selves and society. As Euro-American notions of self evolve, we need to adjust our rhetorical theories to account for those new perspectives. I see the *uchi/soto* dynamic as a valuable new lens for rhetorical inquiry. While the foundational work on *uchi/soto* comes out of studies of Japanese society, the principles can apply more broadly. Rather than applying only Euro-American rhetorical terminology to the rest of the world, here is an opportunity to respectfully borrow from another tradition. Greater attention to the *uchi/soto* dynamic as rhetoric is an opportunity not only to learn more about Japanese rhetoric but also to expand our range of tools and theories for understanding rhetoric in any number of contexts, global and local.

NOTES

[1] Bachnik and Quinn's edited collection *Situated Meaning: Inside and Outside in Japanese Self, Society, and Language* offers the most thorough examination of the indexical model of *uchi/soto*. See also Rosenberger's "Dialectic Balance in the Polar Model of Self," Bachnik's "The Two 'Faces' of Self and Society in Japan" and "*Kejime*: Defining a Shifting Self in Multiple Organizational Modes," which represent the early stages of what became Bachnik's *uchi/soto* dynamic.

[2] The very concept of indexing coming from Peirce supposes a sort of natural or irresistible connection between indexed pairs—Peirce himself used examples like smoke being an index of fire. Bachnik explains indexing in terms of "gauging," describing a process almost mathematical in precision:

> Indexes work by gauging points along a scale. . . . The logic involved in indexing relates the terms at each end of the scale inversely to one another. Being hot is inversely related to being cold, so that being hot means being not cold. Moreover, hot is defined according to degrees along the temperature scale, so that each degree of being hotter varies inversely (and precisely) with the corresponding degree of not being colder. ("Two Faces" 10)

[3] The third piece of Burke's planned trilogy beginning with *A Grammar of Motives* and *A Rhetoric of Motives*.

[4] This same section (*Rhetoric* 22 and 23) may suggest that identity and identification should be considered separately, in that *identity*, which (for Burke) exists in the individual, can exist in the "symbolic," whereas *identification* occurs in the realm of rhetoric, where multiple identities interact. Also see *Rhetoric* 27, where identification is shown to apply to principles and activities, not just to groups (though, of course, principles and activities have to be held and performed by people to exist). Again, Burke seems to indicate that identification only exists in the realm of rhetoric, while identity can exist in the Symbolic. We might, then, argue that *uchi/soto* is combining identity and identification in an inseparable form, where Burke seems to allow for their separation, at least analytically—*uchi/soto*, on the other hand, always insists we consider them together.

[5] Burke's example of a politician speaking to farmers and self-identifying as having been a farm boy also demonstrates that identification can serve both as an interpretive theory and as rhetorical praxis. That is, we can "read" the actions of the politician using the terms and questions of identification (we assume he is identifying in some way and look for how); we can also apply identification actively, as the politician does in his speech. The same holds true for the *uchi/soto* dynamic, which we might also think of as an interpretive and practical model.

WORKS CITED

Bachnik, Jane. "*Kejime*: Defining a Shifting Self in Multiple Organizational Modes." *Japanese Sense of Self.* Ed. Nancy Rosenberger. Cambridge: Cambridge UP, 1992. 152-72. Print.

---. "Introduction: *uchi/soto*: Challenging Our Conceptualizations of Self, Social Order, and Language." *Situated Meaning: Inside and Outside in Japanese Self, Society, and Language.* Ed. Jane Bachnik and Charles Quinn, Jr. Princeton: Princeton UP, 1994. 3-37. Print.

---. "The Two 'Faces' of Self and Society in Japan." *Ethos* 20.1 (1992): 3-32. Print.

Bachnik, Jane, and Charles Quinn, Jr., eds. *Situated Meaning: Inside and Outside in Japanese Self, Society, and Language.* Princeton: Princeton UP, 1994. Print.

Burke, Kenneth. *Attitudes Toward History.* 2nd ed. Los Altos: Hermes, 1959. Print.

---. *A Grammar of Motives.* New York: Prentice-Hall, 1945. Print.

---. *The Philosophy of Literary Form.* 2nd ed. Baton Rouge: Louisiana State UP, 1967. Print.

---. *A Rhetoric of Motives.* Berkeley: U of California P, 1969. Print.

Butler, Judith. *Bodies that Matter: On the Discursive Limits of "Sex."* New York: Routledge, 1993. Print.

---. *Excitable Speech: A Politics of the Performative.* New York: Routledge, 1997. Print.

Hall, David, and Roger Ames. *Anticipating China: Thinking Through the Narratives of Chinese and Western Culture."* Albany: State U of New York P, 1995. Print.

Ratcliffe, Krista. *Rhetorical Listening: Identification, Gender, Whiteness.* Carbondale: Southern Illinois UP, 2005. Print.

Rosenberger, Nancy. "Dialectic Balance in the Polar Model of Self: The Japan Case." *Ethos* 17.1 (1989): 88-113. Print.

33

THINKING AND SPEAKING THE CIRCLE

Symbolic Action in Navajo Rhetoric

Edward Karshner

There are many reasons to research the rhetorical systems of other cultures. Gerry Philipsen articulates one very important motivation as being: "Inquiry into the cultural variation in the patterns and uses of rhetoric may increase awareness of traditional presuppositions about rhetoric and may suggest new ways of viewing traditional patterns" (132). All too often, ideas about rhetoric become so accepted that these assumptions about rhetoric come to be taken as rhetoric itself. Only by looking at our rhetoric through the lens of another rhetoric, that great dramatistic exercise of identification advocated by Kenneth Burke, can we begin to see where traditional presuppositions have become problematic in their application.

I began to research Navajo rhetoric in the summer of 2008, while traveling with Bowling Green State University's summer Navajo experience trip. As I struggled to make sense of Navajo discourse patterns by applying them to what I considered Aristotelian rhetoric, I began to learn more about the misconceptions I had regarding my rhetoric than I was learning about *their* rhetoric. When I returned and began to research academic perspectives on comparative rhetoric, it became obvious that there was a struggle to understand what rhetoric was to us rather than what rhetoric was to others.

In one of the few texts to explore comparative rhetoric, George Kennedy devotes two sentences of two hundred and thirty-eight pages to *Diné* (Navajo) rhetoric. His assessment is worth quoting in full: "Explicit logical argument was almost nonexistent except for analogies to the natural world to explain a point, another feature that continued in modern Navajo oratory. Speakers usually set out a series of facts about themselves and the issue and left members of the audience to draw their own conclusions" (97). In considering this view, I am reminded of Burke's terministic screens and the implication that utterances reveal more about the speaker than the topic. In this case, a Western definition of rhetoric becomes one where information about the speaker and facts related to the topic are of little importance, and audiences should never be allowed to draw their own conclusions. This same limited definition of rhetoric is one held by many of my undergraduates and some of my graduate students. The discerning art of Aristotle has been reduced to Edward Bernays's cynical "engineering of the consent." Our discipline has been reduced to little more than a Jedi mind trick.

Rhetoric devoid of process, but obsessed with outcomes, emerges from a misunderstanding of Aristotle's primary definition of rhetoric. The classic definition of rhetoric we all share with our students is "the faculty [ability] of observing in any given case [situation] the available means of persuasion [*pistis*]" (105). This definition of rhetoric has become so accepted and standard that its complexity is often underappreciated. To begin, rhetoric requires an individual to have the ability to observe. We all possess multiple ways to observe through one or all of the five senses; however, Aristotle states that rhetorical observation requires a specific mind-set, faculty, or ability. This caveat can be taken to mean that the rhetor has a particular reason for and manner of observing.

Next, Aristotle stresses that this particular method of observation be applied to the particular situation at hand using the available means in that situation. The reason for this close but fluid observation of situations is to "persuade," that is to produce "*pistis*," meaning "belief" or "opinion." It is the ability to formulate, recognize, and act on belief that makes human beings able to actively participate in the epistemic process that Robert L. Scott believes rhetoric truly is. For Scott, the goal of rhetoric is not "truth" but *pistis*, which can be considered a "set of generally accepted social norms, experiences, or even matters of faith as references points in working out the contingencies in which men find themselves" (311). *Pistis* is both *a priori* and *a posteriori*, present in both problem and solution, and rhetoric collapses both into the "particular situation."

Taking into consideration rhetoric's messy pursuit of exigency, expectation, and goal, it is no wonder that a limited definition of rhetoric led Kennedy to not recognize a functioning rhetoric at work in *Diné* discourse. The *Diné* utilize a rhetoric that reflects an epistemology based on experience and expressed as a symbolic practice validated by a ceremonial system. Thought, symbol, and action are synthesized through participation in these ceremonies that alter an individual's perception of reality, thus maintaining the balance between the individual and the metaphysical system. This onto-cosmological compression into semiotic saturation will be explained as a rhetorical system, offering positive modifications to the characteristics and practices of contemporary, Western rhetoric.

For the *Diné*, rhetoric is the primary operating mechanism of their complex ceremonial system. Rhetoric is understood as a ritual that mediates an exigence by collapsing the space that exists between the beauty at the beginning and a return to that beauty at the end. Ritual rhetoric is a specific kind of ritual that is to be understood as a "technique of transformation. Desire is transformed into satisfaction: 'we act in this way and then feel satisfied.' There is change, of however subjective a kind" (Driver 173). According to

Gerry Philipsen, ritual rhetoric is a means of "maintaining or restoring order in the universe" (137). However, ritual rhetoric stresses a particular kind of maintenance—one based on an agent creating discourse and an audience participating in that discourse.

It is worth noting that ritual rhetoric, as with all rhetoric, is pragmatic in that it "comes into existence for the sake of something beyond itself . . . . [I]t performs some task" (Bitzer 3-4). The transformative rhetoric of the *Diné* should be understood as being in accord with Lloyd Bitzer's definition of rhetoric as: "A mode of altering reality, not by the direct application of energy to objects, but by the creation of discourse which changes reality through the mediation of thought and action" (4). The objective world is not transformed through the application of thoughts and words. Rather, subjective reality is altered through the mediation of thought and action. To be out of balance or feel the urgency of an exigence is to have one's thoughts in conflict with the demands of the current situation. To move forward, one must be willing to change that belief to fit whatever rhetorical situation presents itself. So, ritual rhetoric does not so much restore harmony to the universe, as it restores the individual to harmony with the universe and with others at work to understand their place in their own personal exigence. However, rhetorical exigence does not just place an individual outside personal, universal balance. As the individual seeks social invention, he/she may find him/herself at odds with others who also seek harmony. Scott writes: "In human affairs, ours is a world of conflicting claims. Not only may one person contradict another, but a single person may find himself called upon to believe or act when his knowledge gives rise to directives which are dissonant" (315). Ritual or ceremony becomes a way to restore order by quieting the noise. Ceremony takes us back to the foundational essence, enabling us to move forward. In a sense, it is through ritual that an idea emerges as action.

Despite the conclusion that the *Diné* culture is devoid of rhetorical practice, there is clear evidence that the *Diné* do engage in an activity where individuals are persuaded to consider some avenues rather than others in order to induce cooperation, problem solve, and clarify misunderstandings. According to David Brugge, the earliest record of such an activity was held in 1840 in order to solicit peace between the *Diné* and the Mexican government headquartered in Jemez, New Mexico. Brugge is quick to note that this tribal assembly known as *naach'id* is "poorly known from ethnographic accounts" (186). The reason for this lack of information regarding *naach'id* is its connection to ceremonial and sacred wisdom, and it is consequently kept from non-*Diné*, traditionally.

However, in 1868, the *Diné* signed a treaty with the Unites States ending hostilities between the two nations. Besides peace, the Treaty of 1868 established the need for a semiautonomous *Diné* government based on that of the Western, democratic model. As the *Diné* established the Navajo Tribal Council, foundational law, and the peacemaker program, *naach'id* became the ideological context for *Diné* tribal laws and enforcement of those laws. In essence, the tribal government, while still maintaining the ceremonial significance of *naach'id*, applies these sacred ideas pragmatically in a judicial manner. For scholars, the end result is that never before has information regarding *naach'id* been more available.

Simply defined, a *naach'id* is a "tribal assembly," characterized by being "held in the winter[, and] . . . involved both political functions such as making of war and peace and ceremonial procedures including dancing, and that all or most members of the tribe were present simultaneously during portions of the assembly" (Brugge 186). In the *Diné* language, *naach'id* means "handling or managing." *Diné Bizaad* is a complex language where each verb not only tells you what is done but how it is done and what it is done with. According to the "Peacemaking" page of the Navajo Courts website, *naachid* is "a process. . . . [I]t means the procedure of *naachid* in which the societal situation is recognized and confronted[,] . . . the way human beings and creatures solve problems at a particular time in the history of the *Diné*" ("*Bitsé Siléi*" 3). Like the rhetoric of Aristotle, *naachid* is characterized as a process or procedure of perceiving a particular situation rooted in a unique moment—its own moment.

What is managed is not the problem, which is secondary, but the means by which that problem is solved. The basis for *naach'id* is *bitsé siléi*. According to the text of the *Bitsé Siléi*, *bitsé* means:

> That which is in front or ahead, or in the forefront. *Siléi* means that which lies before. *Bitsé Siléi* together may mean putting into descriptive words what someone at the head of the line has seen in order to lay down a road. It may mean that which is put down, like a path, to be perceived and followed. *Bitsé Siléi* is foundational essence.

The uniqueness of moment requires the observer to consider the present in light of the past but realize that, while similar, they are not the same. In other words, to solve the problem, the participant must be *akoninizin*. *Akoninizin* requires an awareness of situational similarities and differences in how each rhetorical constraint contradicts and complements the other elements in the discourse situation.

The path suggested by *bitsé siléi* is not a linear path. Instead, explicit logical argument takes the form of a circle. As Brugge suggests, *naach'id* is not separate from, but part of, the larger ceremonial system that includes the more well-known ceremonies like the Blessing Way, Enemy Way, and Night Chant. In order to discern the logic of *Diné* argument, *naach'id* must be considered in its own philosophical context.

At the heart of *Diné* metaphysics is the idea of *nahagha*. Gary Witherspoon calls this concept a "large and significant category of Navajo behavior which non-Navajos least understand, and thus constitutes a major dimension of the estrangement that divides Navajos and non-Navajos" (*Language* 13). Without a proper understanding of *nahagha* as the foundational structure of *Diné* thought, it is easy to dismiss *Diné* discourse as lacking logical argument.

Nahagha, and its verb form *naaghaii,* is one of more than 350,000 ways to conjugate the verb "to go." *"Naa"* or *"Na"* refers to the repetition of an act or condition that leads to the restoration of a condition (Witherspoon, *Language* 21). *Nahagha* can be glossed simply as "ritual." The basis for all *Diné* discourse behavior is the act of continually going about and returning: repetition, continuation, the revolutions that restore and maintain the life cycle. The *Diné* do not practice a linear logic, which they perceive as both accusatory (it is directed toward an individual) and pointless since its trajectory is directed outward toward infinity with no clear end point (think of an academic department meeting). Instead, *Diné* logic is circular and recursive, always returning to the point at hand in order to restore the idea to its proper balance with the current situation.

The organizing model for all *Diné* society and discourse, therefore, is the circle. The *Diné* onto-cosmological view of the world is that of the series of concentric circles nested to infinity within the human being, the physical world, and on into the spiritual realm of things we can't see. All things have their proper place. In each quadrant of the circle, each "thing" has its power and yet must also yield its power to the next quadrant as the circle rotates. Within this semiotic compression and epistemological rotation, each element gains meaning from its relationship (both complementary and antagonistic) with the others. For example, *naach'id* is held in the winter. This placement is meaningful messaging because winter is in the Northern quadrant, which is the time of the elders. Elders reference wisdom but also the earth representing where you stand now and a time for reflecting on how you got here and where you will go next. It is also a time of sleep and, therefore, dreams and, consequently, the reassessment of the "day." Finally, the North is feminine, so one must be receptive and focused on change and continuity. Each participant, however, is aware that night will soon become day, and there is a movement toward the aggressive investigation and influence of the dawn.

The *Diné* recognize that analogies compressed into *naaghaii* should never be taken at face value and that meaning is determined by an active agent who experiences the world and is aware (*akoninizin*) of his/her personal feelings about that experience. This process of meaning-making is rooted in the three perspectives the *Diné* have regarding the universe (Burnside, Personal). The first is the sensed objective world of the five senses. This is the world experienced objectively with the senses. Second is the psychological/spiritual world, where feelings and opinions about those feelings reside. In this world, experiences are given meaning and those meanings come with subjective feelings about the ethical nature of those feelings. Finally, there is the world of ceremony where the sensed world and the spiritual world are made one when activities are performed mindfully (*Diné Binahagha*).

The process of *Diné Binahagha* can be compared to Aristotle's idea of artistic and nonartistic proof. According to Kennedy, Aristotle defines nonartistic proofs as "those that are not provided by 'us' but are pre-existing . . . and artistic [proofs as] whatever can be prepared by method and by 'us'; thus, one must use the former and invent the latter" (37). The focus of pure rhetoric is the transformation of artifacts found in the world through the structured use of reason and emotion into *pistis* (belief). However, this process is a messy one. In the movement from the objective world not provided by us and the one that emerges as a result of our experiences with the nonartistic, there is bound to be "confusion."

This cognitive dissonance between the world as it is and the world as experienced is called *anahoti* or disharmony. In both Western and *Diné* rhetoric, discourse both responds to and emerges from a particular ideological situation. For Bitzer, rhetoric emerges in response to "an imperfection marked by urgency . . . a defect, an obstacle, something waiting to be done, a thing which is other than it should be" (6). For the *Diné*, experience gains meaning from an idea of how things should be and an awareness of how they are not. Second, this unease can be positively mediated through discourse and is, therefore, attached to the prior knowledge or thoughts that are a foundation for language.

The convergence of foundational knowledge, opinion, and language place exigence within the first "presupposition of a rhetorical system" (Philipsen 137), which is the metaphysical. Philipsen defines the metaphysical as "presuppositions about the nature of reality" (133). But, metaphysics is about more than ideas of how things are or are meant to be. Wayne Booth looks not to the mere expression of metaphysics but to the essential warrants of these beliefs as they are used to arrive at a context for rhetorical exchange. He argues that ideas about reality are rooted in two assumptions. The first is that "the world as we experience it is somehow flawed" (161). The second assumption is that "[t]he flaws are seen in light of the unflawed, some truth, some notion of justice, or 'goodness,' or some possible purging of ugliness or ignorance; standards of judgment of the brokenness exist somewhere" (162).

Booth makes two important points here. First, all rhetoric bases its function in the idea of an *a priori* idea of order, truth, holiness, etc. Be it *hozho*, truth, or justice there is an ideal that operates both as the standard and the goal for rhetoric to consider in the process of problem solving. Second, Booth makes an important distinction between the "world" and experiences of the world. According to Booth, the world itself is not flawed. It is as it was meant to be. Rather, our experience of the world is flawed. For some reason, it is the observer who has fallen out of balance with the order of things and must find his/her way back. This disconnect between the sacred, objective world and the subjective experience of the objective world creates rhetorical exigence.

The key to mediating *anahoti* is found in the original, *a priori*, process of the universe. Creation was meant to unfold as *nizhonigo* "in an orderly and proper way" (Griffin-Pierce 83). The circle is the primary metaphor for *nizhonigo* because "[i]n a circle, there is no right or left, no beginning or end. Every point (or person) on the line on a circle looks to the same center as the focus. The circle is the symbol for Navajo justice because it is perfect, unbroken, and a simile of unity and oneness" (Yazzie 29). John Farella writes that the experience of the circle is "omnipresent, not just occasional. It is the experience of being part of something larger and grander than oneself, the direct experience of oneness (*nizhoni*)" (23). From this experience of *nizhoni*, the individual can "*nizhoni go silei*," "put things in their proper place."

In the center of this "perfect" process is *hozho*. *Hozho* is the ideal circumstance manifested in individual activity. According to *Diné* meta-narratives, *hozho* begins with the emergence narrative where the *Diné* seek their "place on the earth and . . . attune their lives to the rhythm, melodies, and cycles of the earth and sky" (Witherspoon, "Emergence" 258). Most often glossed as beauty or balance, *hozho* is a "cosmic concert" that expresses "the normal state of the fourth world [our current realm of existence], which is a state of beauty, harmony, health, happiness, and peace" (Witherspoon, "Emergence" 264). In other words, *hozho* is a mental state of peace cultivated through experience and maturity with the world. Chester Nez, in his memoir *Code Talker*, defines *hozho* as a balance "not only between individuals, but between each person and his world" (5). By achieving this level of harmony with the self, the self with the world, and the self with worldly circumstances, one is able to transcend one's former place of existence and emerge into the new existential plane.

In order to achieve the desired level of harmony with the universe, the *Diné* rely on ceremony where the sensed world and the spiritual world are made one when activities are performed mindfully (*Diné Binahagha*). This confluence of experiential feelings creates an exigence that demands mediation in order to return the agent to a state of balance. Rhetoric as ritual becomes the means of mediating the confusion created by experience, emotion, and history. Ceremony (*nahagha*) is a pragmatic method of slowing down the senses and the mind—becoming mindful and aware as information is arranged and allowed to emerge into its proper place.

This ritual process is similar to stasis where a moment of calm is created for reflection and consideration. For Farella, this moment of reflection is central to *Diné* philosophy. For me, *Diné* stasis reveals a rhetoric focused on producing change not only in an audience but also in the rhetor. Farella writes: "Ritual is used for the relatively major adaptions to life [ecological, social, personal]; it is invoked to aid in, define, and create major personal growth experiences" (184). As a constantly changing mind is brought to bear on an infinitely evolving world, a thoughtful, structured approach to meaning-making—moment to moment—becomes necessary for the agent to gain mastery, first of him/herself, and then of the situation.

Yet, ritual rhetoric is not a solipsistic pursuit. *Diné Binahagha* is deeply rooted in invention and must be understood as Karen Burke LeFevre has argued as a social act. The first step in rhetorical invention is finding the scene. In both *Diné* and Western rhetoric, this rhetorical scene is not found in an isolated individual but in an individual fully engaged in a community that shares the same semiotic system. In this sense, *Diné* rhetoric operates as Burkian rhetoric, where language is used as a "symbolic means of inducing cooperation in beings that by nature respond to symbols" (qtd. in Booth 8). Ritual rhetoric allows for a stabilization of signs through a discursive practice that allows for a maturing of meaning through the unified actions of the agents.

To stabilize the signs and symbols and bring them to epistemic maturity, the *Diné* value the viewpoints of others, especially elders who have laid the path ahead by keeping alive histories of traditional knowledge. The *Bitsé Siléí* remarks that a *Diné* "will never attribute knowledge to him or herself. He or she will always attribute the knowledge as having been gained through revelations from his or her elders." In *Diné* rhetoric, the individual must be aware of and able to navigate a complex kinship system that encompasses not just blood relationships, but also clan relationships, social relationships, and those nonhuman relationships that ground the individual within the harmony of the four sacred mountains. These semiotically constructed kinship relations provide "an ever present context for action and reflection" ("*Bitsé Siléí*"). This concept is expressed as *k'e*. *K'e* is the means by which all things are related. The *Bitsé Siléí* defines *k'e* as imposing "a duty . . . to instruct and guide one another. It emphasizes restorative justice and sharing that individuals living in disharmony are brought back into right relationships and into the community to reestablish order." To achieve harmony, even within the individual, requires a knowledge of "audience," capable of restoring balance.

Being engaged in a *naachid* rooted in *k'e*, an individual creates the harmony (*hozho*) that was present at the beginning. In characterizing *Diné* healing ceremonies, Donald Sandner writes that "the Navajo medicine man draws upon a fixed traditional body of symbolism (sand paintings, prayers, songs) and presents them to the patient, who must actively co-operate in the ritual" (261). A complex symbol system becomes the scene where the elders and the youth meet, share a common language and history, and cooperate to solve a problem. This realization of the role of others in transformative discourse is the first step in cognitive maturity since the individual realizes that the work cannot be done alone. The rhetor becomes aware of audience and the pragmatic fact that "rhetorical discourse produces change by influencing the decision and action of persons who function as mediators of change" (Bitzer 7). As Karen Burke LeFevre points out, invention is indeed a social act even when the agent acts as a single individual.

In this paper, I have outlined *Diné* rhetoric as I have come to understand it during the course of my research. During the last five years, I have come to realize how far Western rhetoric has strayed from its own epistemic promise. Aristotle defines rhetoric as discerning the available means of persuasion in all situations. The rhetor Lloyd Bitzer sees rhetoric as being the means by which we resolve urgent imperfections. In these definitions, rhetoric reflects an ethical, epistemological system that leads from awareness of disorder to the resolution of that situation. Western rhetoric has descended into a practice where the knowledgeable lead the unaware by limiting access to knowledge in an increasingly information-saturated system. The unaware, on the other hand, willingly surrender their epistemic responsibility for the sake of personal convenience. Rhetoric as a means to reveal *pistis* becomes little more than a cynical exercise in changing the mind of another, for the personal gain of the rhetor, at all cost.

The goal of ritual rhetoric is to alter reality by bringing into existence a discourse of such a character that the audience, in thought and action, is so engaged that together they become mediators of change. In writing about *Diné* ceremony, Farella writes that the purpose of any ritual is to restore the individual to *hozho*. He then comments that "parts of a person commonly mentioned in restoration rituals include... *bin* (his mind), *bizaad* (his speech), *bigaat* (his moving power or characteristic way of moving)" (97). These elements requiring restoration are easily compared to Aristotle's essential activities of humankind. These were *theoria* (production of ideas), *poiesis* (the production of words and signs), and *praxis* (the production of action). Exigence, dissonance, and *anahoti* occur when an individual has lost his/her connection with the creative process. In order to regain balance, the individual must regain the ability to think, speak, and perform those foundational ideas of truth or beauty in the context of the circle. In the end, ritual rhetoric restores the right thinking that produces right speech and, consequently, induces right action. This generative perspective of rhetoric validates ideas about foundational essence by manifesting it in the ideal actions of the individual and corroborated by the community.

Most people are familiar with the iconic cliff dwelling ruins that blanket the Four Corners region of the Southwestern United States. In *Diné* tradition, these ancestral Puebloans, called Anasazi, serve as a cautionary tale about those who would trade the epistemology of ritual for the authority of an elite group of leaders. According to the story, when the Anasazi replaced ritual with the authority of the priesthood, society collapsed and was scattered by *Nilch'i*, the Holy Wind. For us, there is a lesson here. In the oldest of Western rhetorical tradition, there is a demand that rhetoric be an active rhetoric. Equally as old are those who would reduce this essential human activity to one of trickery, while keeping the power of discourse for themselves. For the *Diné*, the remedy for this *anahoti* is simple: we must never surrender our responsibility to participate in the process of knowing; we must always be aware of the needs of others and the demands of the situation; and, most importantly, we must never forget that to be human requires working together as equals to solve problems. Sometimes, this responsibility requires that we question and correct those whom we most respect and admire. But, as the mythologist Joseph Campbell once remarked, there can be no coming to consciousness without pain.

WORKS CITED

Aristotle. *Poetics and Rhetoric.* Trans. W. Rhys Roberts. New York: Barnes and Noble Classics, 2005. Print.

Bernays, Edward. "The Engineering of Consent." *The Annals of the American Academy of Political and Social Science* 250 (Mar. 1947): 113-20. Print.

"*Bitsé Siléí.*" *The Navajo Nation Peacemaking Program.* Navajo Courts, 28 July 2008. Web. 1 Feb. 2012.

Bitzer, Lloyd. "The Rhetorical Situation." *Philosophy and Rhetoric* 1 (Jan. 1968): 1-14. Print.

Booth, Wayne. *The Rhetoric of Rhetoric.* Malden: Blackwell, 2004. Print.

Brugge, David M. "Documentary Reference to a Navajo Naach'id in 1840." *Ethnohistory* 10 (Spring 1963): 186-88. Print.

Burke, Kenneth. *A Rhetoric of Motives.* Berkeley: U of California P, 1969. Print.

Burnside, Francis Kee. Personal communication. 16 Mar. 2010.

Driver, Tom. "Transformation: The Magic of Ritual." *Readings in Ritual Studies.* Ed. Ronald L. Grimes. Upper Saddle River: Prentice Hall, 1996. 170-87. Print.

Farella, John R. *The Main Stalk.* Tucson: U of Arizona P, 1984. Print.

Griffin-Pierce, Trudy. *Earth is My Mother, Sky is My Father.* Albuquerque: U of New Mexico P, 1992. Print.

Kennedy, George. *Comparative Rhetoric.* New York: Oxford UP, 1997. Print.

LeFevre, Karen Burke. *Invention as a Social Act.* Carbondale: Southern Illinois UP, 1987. Print.

Nez, Chester. *Code Talker.* New York: Penguin, 2011. Print.

Philipsen, Gerry. "Navajo World View and Culture Patterns of Speech: A Case Study in Ethnorhetoric." *Speech Monographs* 39.2 (1972): 132-39. Print.

Sandner, Donald. *Navajo Symbols of Healing.* Rochester: Healing Arts, 1991. Print.

Scott, Robert L. "On Viewing Rhetoric as Epistemic." *Professing the New Rhetorics.* Ed. Theresa Enos and Stuart C. Brown. Englewood Cliffs: Prentice Hall, 1994. 307-18. Print.

Witherspoon, Gary. "Emergence Narratives." *American Indian Religious Traditions: An Encyclopedia, Volume I.* Ed. Suzanne O'Brien and Dennis Kelley. Santa Barbara: ABC-CLIO, 2005. 258-65. Print.

---. *Language and Art in the Navajo Universe.* Ann Arbor: U of Michigan P, 1997. Print.

Yazzie, Robert. "Life Comes from It: Navajo Justice." *The Ecology of Justice* 3.8 (1994): 29-31. Print.

34

REFRAMING DISCIPLINE

Rhetoric's Shared Disciplinary Identifications

Tonya Ritola

While the field of rhetoric and composition and the field of communication occupy different disciplinary spaces within the academy, the two fields have much to learn from one another. Organizations such as the Rhetoric Society of America and the Alliance of Rhetoric Societies, as well as journals such as *Rhetoric Society Quarterly* and *Rhetoric Review*, provide spaces for shared inquiry between the two fields; however, because rhetoric is split primarily between these two disciplines, it remains, as Carolyn Miller suggests, "a house divided" (qtd. in Norton 21).

As a result, the historical trajectory of rhetoric's lineage presents a professional problem for rhetoricians whose theoretical commitments traverse monolithic disciplinary boundaries. While Richard McKeon worked valiantly in 1971 to establish rhetoric as an architectonic art, one endemic to all academic disciplines—and thus a legitimate field of study—rhetorical theorists must, at the end of the day, choose a rhetorical pathway within a specific discipline if their work is to be intelligible to academic discourse communities. Because rhetoric is often considered a meta-discourse, as opposed to a defined discipline, rhetorical scholars who study "rhetoric" must often justify their object of study by identifying themselves not with rhetoric proper but with established academic fields that give them credence.

While disciplinary identification enables scholars to develop sanctioned professional identities, its function as an academic imperative creates a separation within rhetorical studies, by casting rhetoric and composition (hereafter rhet-comp) and communication as two distinct disciplines. The irony, however, is that both disciplines ask similar questions, draw on similar theorists, and explore similar rhetorical concepts. Particularly in the past decade, scholars such as Sharon Crowley, Maureen Daly Goggin, Michael Leff, Steven Mailloux, and Louise Wetherbee Phelps, along with organizations such as the Rhetoric Society of America and the Alliance of Rhetoric Societies, have developed shared scholarship and theoretical spaces for cross-disciplinary conversations about rhetoric's history and formation.

These conversations have created the need for rigorous scholarship in regard to rhetoric's genealogy. This need is obvious enough: rhetoricians' identification with a particular field falsely theorizes rhetoric's development (Lauer; Norton). The shared histories among disciplines such as rhet-comp and communication necessitate a wider theoretical perspective that accounts for the complexity of rhetoricians' disciplinary and theoretical commitments.[1] Focusing specifically on the scholarship produced in the past decade, my research revealed four specific disciplinary markers that bind our disciplines together: disciplinary anxiety, rhetorical traditions, pedagogy, and shared scholarship.

These markers are not artificial. If we examine the recorded cross-disciplinary exchanges from the 2000, 2001, and 2003 volumes of *Rhetoric Society Quarterly* (*RSQ*), the selected papers from the 2000 Rhetoric Society of America (RSA) Conference published in *Professing Rhetoric*, the collected papers from the 2003 Alliance of Rhetoric Society (ARS) Conference, the American Society for the History of Rhetoric's 2005 publication of *The Viability of the Rhetorical Tradition*, and the numerous surveys of PhD programs in rhetoric published in *RSQ* and *Rhetoric Review* (in both English and communication departments), we will notice, without question, that the prominent crossovers fit into these categories.[2] I argue that these markers are important because they provide us with tangible ways to rethink rhetorical studies within the context of both fields, without having to divide our lines of inquiry. More importantly, these markers designate a specific point of consensus that scholars from both fields identify as the binding agents of the two disciplines (Leff and Lunsford 59; Zarefsky 27; Graff and Leff 11).

Disciplinary Anxiety

Much of the scholarship exploring the relationships between rhet-comp and communication follows a similar organizational pattern: debate the status of rhetoric as a discipline first, examine the individual instantiations second, and establish the common ground/point of intersection third. Because "rhetorical theory and criticism" is a subset of communication and "rhetoric and composition" is a subset of English studies, the impulse to debate rhetoric's disciplinary status appears logical. After all, its primary gatekeepers have not achieved the level of disciplinary autonomy as, say, the fields of mathematics or psychology. While independent programs in rhetoric, rhetorical studies, and/or speech do exist, we often find rhetorical studies a mere concentration within the larger disciplines of English and/or communication (Phelps and Ackerman 193).

As a result, many scholars interested in bridging the rhetorical divide between rhet-comp and communication must first tackle their own fragmented disciplinary histories in order to create the intellectual space for interdisciplinary dialogue. However, it is precisely the need to reify rhetoric's disciplinary identity that enables rhetoric scholars from rhet-comp and communication to participate in productive, vibrant exchanges on the history, current status, and future of rhetorical studies in higher education.

This anxiety is presented most clearly in the 2000 and 2001 volumes of *RSQ*, which featured four articles concerning the "rhetorical paths in English and communication studies," the first of which was presented by Steven Mailloux. In this article, "Disciplinary Identities," Mailloux advocated for "renewed dialogue among rhetoricians studying Literature, Composition, and Communication" (5). His purpose in the article was to encourage the development of "a multi-disciplinary coalition of rhetoricians" who would create thoughtful, well-documented accounts of the theories, practices, and evolution of rhetorical studies (23). Mailloux received four responses to his article, two in 2000 from communication scholars and two in 2001 from rhet-comp scholars.

Communication scholars Michael Leff and William Keith each criticized Mailloux's disciplinary account of communication history, showing how Mailloux got certain aspects "wrong." For Keith, the major difference for rhetoricians in both fields is the traced history of rhetorical alliances. For communication, Keith argues that rhetoricians find their roots in the work of Richard Whately, whereas rhetoricians in rhet-comp find their roots in Alexander Bain (104). His concern is that a unified rhetorical orientation is simply not possible between the disciplines, but I argue that Mailloux's goal was not to oversimplify the histories by offering a grand narrative of disciplinary origin but, instead, to trace the major connections through the lens of a "rhetoric of science." In contrast to Keith, Leff's response to Mailloux's article was gracious. He first criticized Mailloux's overemphasis on the importance of Charles Woolbert's 1916 identifications of rhetoric with science but then agreed with Mailloux's reflection on the hermeneutical reading of disciplinary histories (Leff 86). At the end of the article, Leff laments the incoherence of communication's disciplinary research and suggests that rhet-comp's self-awareness as a discipline is one that communication should strive for (92). In each of these responses, disciplinary anxiety reveals a major cross-disciplinary touchstone for the renewed dialogue Mailloux encourages, in part because pinning rhetoric to a singular tradition or school of thought is impossible since it is a particular function of all discourse.

Rhetoric and composition scholars Thomas Miller and Martin Nystrand each raised separate but important concerns for Mailloux's disciplinary call. First, Miller suggested that rhetoric scholars should work pragmatically to understand the power implied by the institutional location of rhetoric, which is often at the "margins" of the academy (108). Then, he encouraged rhetoricians to "look beyond traditional disciplinary identifications" and reaffirm their commitments to the public identity of rhetoric so that institutional reform and civic engagement become the stronghold for rhetorical investigation in both fields (115). Nystrand, however, was not concerned with strengthening institutional partnerships between rhet-comp and communication and, instead, took issue with Mallioux's dismissal of rhet-comp's affinity toward science in the 1970s. For Nystrand, Mailloux overlooked the prominent influence of the scientific method in the works of Mina Shaughnessy,

Janet Emig, and Linda Flower and John Hayes (93). Nystrand argued that rhet-comp gravitated toward scientism in response to national shifts in research in order to develop strong professional and disciplinary identities. For Nystrand, this shift made a significant contribution to the current status of the field.

Again, each of these responses signals a sense of disciplinary anxiety: the need to re-establish, first, rhetoric's importance as a field of study and, second, the need to revise the confused accounts of disciplinary development for both rhet-comp and communication. This anxiety drives much of the scholarship we see from 2000 to 2001 in *RSQ*. The desire to understand rhetoric's disciplinary identifications and to demarcate the boundaries of the discipline are natural tasks for rhetorical scholars, but the anxiety itself signals a larger cultural problem: the need to make the study of rhetoric relevant as the increasingly corporatized university prioritizes science-based disciplines, as opposed to humanities-based disciplines, based on the assumption that science-based disciplines accrue more funding for universities while generating substantial disciplinary knowledge (Goggin 64; Zarefsky 28). Rhetoric, then, as a hallmark of a liberal arts education, must be justified so as to remain viable in a changing institutional environment.

The same year Mailloux published "Disciplinary Identities" in *RSQ*, the RSA hosted its ninth biennial conference where more than two hundred rhetoric scholars met in Washington, DC. Many of the papers presented at this conference were collected in a volume titled *Professing Rhetoric*, published in 2002. Two major articles stand out in this collection: Nancy McKoski's "The Politics of Professing Rhetoric in the History of Composition and Communication" and Janice Norton's "Sleeping with the Enemy: Recoupling Rhetorical Studies and Rhetoric and Composition," both of which examine the relationship between rhet-comp and communication. Sharon Crowley ("Communication Skills and a Brief Rapprochement of Rhetoricians"; *Composition in the University*) contends with McKoski's account of progressive education in 2004, so I will not critique McKoski here. However, McKoski's piece represents one attempt to account for the highly politicized aftermath of World War II and its influence on composition and communication curricula. She argues that the influence of rhetoric, through the lens of social sciences, actually produced conservatism in the field of rhet-comp in the 1960s, undercutting the progressive agenda of the '40s and '50s, and she marginally attempts to draw disciplinary connections (18). Following McKoski's article, however, we find Norton's comprehensive examination of the "disciplinary fragmentation" existing between rhet-comp and communication (26). Norton surveys the institutional relationships between the two fields and develops several cross-disciplinary categories that rhetoricians, regardless of disciplinary identifications, should consider. Like other scholars, such as Maureen Daly Goggin and Martin Nystrand, Norton does not argue for a "unified discipline" but rather a series of disciplinary considerations that rhetoricians should take up, including the politics of "creating full professors," "feminist theory," "doing criticism, and "civic space" (27). For Norton, bringing the two fields together under particular disciplinary considerations is one way to overcome the "ignorance" the two fields have for one another (26). From these two essays, disciplinary anxiety remains at the forefront of the conversation, but Norton works to overcome this anxiety by shifting the focus on the actual elements that bind us. In this way, *Professing Rhetoric* demonstrates only a subtle shift in cross-disciplinary conversations, but this shift is important.

Rhetorical Traditions

The year following the publication of *Professing Rhetoric*, another major event occurred: the inaugural meeting of the Alliance of Rhetoric Societies. The meeting took place in September of 2003 at Evanston, Illinois, where 125 rhetoric scholars from a variety of fields met to discuss the theories, institutional locations, and practices of rhetoric, as well as the possible areas of collaboration for rhetoric scholars (Zarefsky 27). The results of this conference were so important that *RSQ* devoted a special 2004 issue to share the conference discussions.

Included in this collection are the participants' reflections on rhetorical traditions. Even though classical rhetoric is clearly one unifier of the two disciplines, a place we can point to in order to understand our shared rhetorical traditions, the concept of tradition is undoubtedly complex. If rhetoric is to increase its interdisciplinary status and seek a wider international scope, the "tradition" must be untangled in order to move forward.[3] Patricia Bizzell and Susan Jarratt's contribution, "Rhetorical Traditions, Pluralized Canons, Relevant History, and Other Disputed Terms: A Report from the History of Rhetoric Discussion Groups at the ARS Conference," outlines how conference participants debated the function of the tradition in rhetorical scholarship. Rather than working to identify a singular tradition as a basis for both disciplines, scholars worked to develop "conceptual bases for pluralizing the rhetorical tradition" (21). These conceptualizations primarily took into account multicultural rhetorics, transnational rhetorics, excluded rhetorics, and polyvocal rhetorical histories. The point for these scholars was to acknowledge a shared history of rhetoric while valuing its fundamental plurality in order to capture the rhetorical tradition in its varied instantiations.

This discussion is critical for modern rhetorical studies because it demonstrates the need for increasing the international and local scope of rhetoric aside from the iterative scripts that focus solely on the Western tradition, beginning with Plato and Aristotle and moving through a strictly canonical lineage. The importance of a rhetorical tradition is not undermined in this conversation, but it is complicated, and with good reason. If we, as rhetoric scholars, reimagine the rhetorical tradition so that we account for its multiplicity, then our potential to establish cross-disciplinary relationships increases, as we can forego debates concerning our origin and sidestep the impulse to establish a point of origin or creation story for the history of rhetoric. This touch-stone is particularly important for our future work on shared histories, since any discussion of disciplinarity, undoubtedly, hails the rhetorical tradition.

Further, *The Viability of the Rhetorical Tradition,* a book largely composed of papers delivered at the American Society for the History of Rhetoric con-ferences held in 2000-2001, chronicles different concerns than those men-tioned above, namely, the "dilemma" that a loss of a coherent "rhetorical tradition" presents for rhetoric scholars (Graff and Leff 12). In this collection, writers from rhet-comp and communication explore the relationship between classical rhetoric and each discipline, the function of civic education, the rec-lamation of rhetoric's disciplinary status, and the necessity of creating mutu-ally dependent relationships in an effort to create a coherent understanding of rhetorical traditions. This publication is worth noting because, while it puts into practice Mailloux's earlier call for collaboration, it also unsettles some of the major pathways between rhet-comp and communication by calling into question the coherence of rhetoric as a discipline.

Introducing us to the collection, Richard Graff and Michael Leff present us with the following dismal view of the rhetorical tradition: "The almost infinite sprawl of rhetorical practices encourages a splintering of interests, and without a tradition against which we can measure our innovations, we may lose the minimum level of coherence necessary to sustain an academic community" (12). This fear makes sense: if rhetoric is everywhere, present in multiple disciplines without a unifying "tradition" (and thus no apparent connection to the history of intellectual thought), then its ability to craft an intelligible disciplinary identity is lost. However, by examining the practices of both theory and teaching, the writers bring us back to a common link: ped-agogy. They write:

> [T]radition can be conceived as practices transmitted through time. Thus, we might discover a sense of tradition consistent with contempo-rary interests by viewing our subject, or some important part of it, as practices that have occurred within a community. . . . To do this . . . we suggest looking at the teaching of rhetoric[,] . . . the history of teaching writing and speaking. Whatever else we are or do, we all teach rhetoric, so the practices of past teachers clearly constitute something we can claim as our history. (25)

In their view, by equating the rhetorical tradition with the practices involved in teaching writing and speech, we can locate "a stable reference for a histor-ical tradition," one that "does not lock us into grand narratives or perspec-tives that move us outside a local context" (27).

I cannot overemphasize the importance that the call to teaching reveals for our shared disciplinary identities. Rhetoricians' abilities to create shared scholarship and cross-disciplinary relationships through the tradition of teaching position us in the same disciplinary field. After all, as Mailloux reminds us in the closing of the collection, "Academic disciplines are institu-tionalized sets of practices, theories, and traditions for knowledge production and dissemination" ("Using Traditions" 181). By generating new knowledge, crafting new disciplinary histories, and collaborating on our fundamental ties, we can begin to institutionalize the discipline of rhetoric in different ways and overcome the challenges that divide us. Of course, this process will take time, and although it might appear a pipedream to some readers—particularly those who celebrate the disciplinary divide, there is a strong contingency of rhetoricians who value this kind of intellectual work. My biggest hope is that we continue to support this line of inquiry, not to unify the disciplines but to enrich them.

Pedagogy

As noted above, the most obvious disciplinary marker for the disciplines is pedagogy. In a carefully constructed and elegant conclusion to the 2004 volume of *RSQ*, Michael Leff and Andrea Lunsford position pedagogy as a distinct marker of both fields. First, Leff and Lunsford refer to Jeffrey Walker's response in his plenary address titled "On Rhetorical Traditions: A Reply to Jerzy Axer," in which Walker states, "The teaching, the production of rhetorically habituated selves in an educational theater devoted to enacting and experiencing a dream of civic life, is what has always distinguished, and still distinguishes, what we do" (10-11). For Walker, the "teaching tradition" promulgated by classical rhetoric does, in fact, bind rhetoricians, and while others have signaled the importance of pluralizing our conception of the rhetorical tradition, teaching is a powerful thread that sutures our varied disciplinary locations. To this tradition, Lunsford observes that performance goes hand in hand with pedagogy. She writes:

> In retrospect, I realized that every keynote address touched not only on pedagogy but also on performance: the performance of teaching; the performance of civic duty and discourse; the performance of student speaking and writing; the performance of disciplinarity . . . . [T]he focus on performance and pedagogy seemed perfectly to bridge the rhetoric/composition and communication traditions to which most participants belonged. (Leff and Lunsford 55-56)

This quotation signals a shift in thinking: if both fields are united through the traditions of teaching and performance, then our traditions align in more ways than one: we do not simply find our connected histories in classical rhetoric or a unified tradition; instead, we can look at the ways in which our rhetorical practices bring us together. However, Lunsford also demonstrates caution in her reply when she states that "our [rhetoricians'] positions in different institutional spaces continue to divide us, as do our differing research traditions" (Leff and Lunsford 57). Lunsford's point is clear: while we have established bridges for cross-disciplinary unions, the placement of rhetoric programs, particularly graduate programs, tend more often to be located in English departments, rather than communication departments. More specifically, in communication departments in which rhetorical theory and criticism is a subset of the field, rhetorical criticism has its own history and development that is entirely separate from rhet-comp.[4]

Despite this fact, Michael Leff's response to Lunsford offers rhetoricians hope when he writes:

> [W]e can regard the teaching tradition as the river—as the unifying referent for a vast and diverse enterprise whose pursuit pushes us outward in many directions, encourages us to explore previously uncharted territory, and also forces us to return to and reconsider ground that we have covered earlier. (Leff and Lunsford 61)

When we consider the teaching tradition as a river, which I find an apt metaphor, we can discard our disciplinary anxiety and revel in the rhetorical practices that bring both disciplines together. That is, we can celebrate the plurality of our traditions by emphasizing how our rhetorical practices exemplified in the art of teaching bring us together. A thoughtful way to do this is to take the suggestion of Gerard A. Hauser and create "structure(s) that can collect and facilitate dialogue on models of courses, course sequences, and modes of instructing" (45). Hauser presents this view in his article "Teaching Rhetoric: Or Why Rhetoric Isn't Just Another Kind of Philosophy or Literary Criticism," which appeared in the 2004 *RSQ* special edition, and he cites the ARS as an important professional organization that will allow rhetoricians to cross the disciplinary divide. As a result, Lunsford and Leff's concluding thoughts on the teaching tradition speak to Hauser's call for dedicated scholarship, professional meetings, and organized structures to reinstate the significance of the teaching tradition to the rhetorical scholarship. And finally, when Lunsford closes the 2004 issue by charging rhetoricians to develop "[a] view of rhetoric as an art that is strategically agentive, deeply performative, devoted to ethical action and to developing *all* student's abilities," she forces us to realize that we do, in fact, have a "a strong ground on which to build a common rhetorical project" (Leff and Lunsford 67). In this way, the scholars identity the teaching tradition as the most important touchstone, and it is worth mentioning that Brian Jackson thoughtfully takes this charge in his 2007 *RSQ* article "Cultivating Paideweyan Pedagogy: Rhetoric Education in English and Communication Studies." Since teaching is "what makes rhetoric rhetoric," this touchstone is the most profound articulation rhetoricians examine in rhet-comp and communication's shared disciplinary histories.

Shared Scholarship

Aside from the work of Steven Mailloux, the most carefully articulated exploration of rhetoricians' desire for shared scholarship appeared in David Zarefsky's 2004 article "Institutional and Social Goals for Rhetoric," which recounts in detail, the exchanges and the recommendations of the ARS conference. In his conclusion, Zarefsky presented a series of recommendations developed by the workgroups, which included the following: overcoming the binary between rhet-comp and communication through the continued development of shared scholarship and continued professional alliances, the creation of "rhetoric centers" that would allow for cross-disciplinary research and also increase the public presence of rhetoric, and increased emphasis on internationalizing rhetoric, which would foster stronger international relationships among rhetoric scholars worldwide (35).

These recommendations reveal rhetoricians' desire to further expand the access to available rhetorical scholarship and, more importantly, to promote the production of scholarship that transgresses disciplinary boundaries. In doing so, "the case for rhetoric" will be easier to make to both institutional and public audiences. By building a strong international and national coalition of rhetoric scholars regardless of disciplinary affiliation, rhetoric's power as a discipline will prosper. In my research, this conference presents the most careful articulation of rhetoricians' strong desire to produce shared scholarship. In this way, shared scholarship is a major touchstone for rhetoric's future agenda. However, as Leff reminds us, "crossing disciplinary boundaries is never easy, and if we are to succeed, we must not only continue the conversation but must also listen carefully and learn much more about the aspirations, idiosyncracies [sic], and anxieties of our rhetorical neighbors" (92). This project is one way we might begin this journey.

The Visibility Project

Chronicling the four major areas that link rhet-comp and communication only provides us with part of the picture of how scholars articulate the shared histories of both fields. Another important piece of this puzzle is the continued work in both *RSQ* and *Rhetoric Review* to publish surveys of PhD programs, which catalogue the courses offered in rhetoric, the development and disbandment of programs, and the institutional locations of rhetoric programs. These surveys are important because they are a necessary form of scholarly research that is needed to understand the disciplinary history of rhet-comp and communication. More specifically, these surveys provide us with a map for understanding the relationship between rhetoric programs and institutional location (see, for example, Skeffington). Unfortunately, the research demonstrates that most rhetoric programs are housed in English departments, and while studies in rhetorical theory and criticism do, in fact, happen in communication departments, the available research concerning these programs pales in comparison to that of rhet-comp. Perhaps this is the reason why Leff laments the disciplinary incoherence for rhetoric within the larger field of communication in 2000.

Regardless, communication scholars knowledgeable in disciplinary history need to model the work accomplished by rhet-comp scholars in English, particularly the work of Louise Wetherbee Phelps, who, more so than any other scholar, has systematically organized a way to chronicle existing rhetoric programs in rhet-comp and to gain national recognition of these programs by collecting institutional data, organizing numerous consortiums, and obtaining "a code series to rhetoric and composition/writing studies in the federal Classification of Instructional Programs (CIP)" (Phelps and Ackerman 180). The US Department of Education uses CIP codes to track the available programs of study in higher education. Realizing that rhetoric was typically subsumed under the larger discipline of English, Phelps in partnership with the Consortium of Doctoral Programs in Rhetoric and Composition (established in 1993) developed "The Visibility Project" in order to gain national recognition for the field of rhet-comp and to establish its rightful place as "an emerging discipline." This kind of institutional scholarship is important for showing the primacy of rhetoric in higher education, and I think that, through a similar approach in communication, rhetoric's national reputation as legitimate and vibrant field of study will only be strengthened. Right now, communication's CIP code for rhetoric is "Speech Communication and Rhetoric" (09.0101), but I have not discovered available scholarship on the development of this code or a comprehensive list of programs that are assigned with this code (National Center for Education Statistics). By making this information available, communication can recognize its own disciplinary frequency and begin to develop strategic ways for increasing its public visibility.

Phelps and Ackerman argue, in their 2010 article "Making the Case for Disciplinarity in Rhetoric, Composition, and Writing Studies: The Visibility Project," that "[e]xternal validation matters; disciplinary status can't be willed from within, nor can it be solely written into existence" (182). By publishing the origins of the visibility project, Phelps and Ackerman provide a powerful example of how rhet-comp's former "schizophrenic behavior" as theorized by John Schilb, can be refocused through powerful disciplinary efforts to make rhet-comp a nationally intelligible field of study (402). While the work of the Visibility Project is not complete (for instance, the goal is to eventually transform rhet-comp from an "emerging field" to "an established field"), it provides rhetoricians with a hopeful success story for realizing rhet-comp as a discipline—not a fraught interdiscipline, but as an actual, reputable discipline. I share this story in order to help assuage the disciplinary anxiety rhetoricians expressed in the previous decade and to show communication scholars one way to improve rhetoric's public presence. The code exists. Now, let's make it more visible for a wider variety of audiences.

Moving Forward

The shared scholarship between rhet-comp and communication has positioned our scholarly gaze to four major touchstones, and while there is still much scholarly work to be accomplished, I will end with a short list of recommendations in order to encourage readers to consider how they might contribute to the ongoing scholarly conversations that reframe rhetoric's disciplinary identities.

1. The RSA and ARS will continue to thrive, as the organizations provide rhetoricians with shared spaces for exploring the importance of the rhetorical tradition, the disciplinary status of the disciplines, the emphasis both fields place on pedagogy, and the opportunity to develop shared scholarship. As a result, we need to continue recruiting new members of the field to participate in these organizations, not in opposition to the National Communication Association or the Conference on College Composition and Communication but rather in tandem with both.

2. If pedagogy is a major point of emphasis for scholars in both fields, then we need to do more critical work on the history of each field's curricula. Clearly, Sharon Crowley and Thomas Miller have started this project, but one way we might fully understand the pedagogical connections we share is through a concentrated study of the first-year course in both disciplines, since that is one disciplinary similarity both fields share. To do this, we need additional archival research that reconstructs the development of undergraduate rhetoric courses in both fields. Clearly, rhet-comp has produced sound historical scholarship on this topic, and communication has initiated the same project. Now, we need to look at the curricular developments side-by-side to see the connections in our evolution.

3. Communication should consider constructing its own visibility project in order to garner continued national respect as a discipline. Right now, communication has a valid CIP code, so by expanding the already available resources, communication can widen its public audience and national reputation. In addition, communication should begin mapping its genealogy in public forums. For example, rhet-comp faculty and graduate students at Graduate Center of the City University of New York (CUNY) created a Writing Studies Tree (writingstudiestree.org) to map out the relationships of rhet-comp scholars. This tree is a visible representation of mentor relationships, institutional affiliations, and scholarly collaborations. Creating such a visible project between both fields, for example, can help us to see how wide the network of rhetorical scholarship extends. Finally, the fact that the 2012 RSA conference featured a supersession on Rhetoric's Critical Genealogy, including scholars from both disciplines, means that the visible work has started; we just need to keep going.

4. Rhetorical scholars should continue to publish scholarship on our shared disciplinary history. In no way does this paper advocate for an erasure of disciplinary divides, nor does it advocate collapsing the two fields. Instead, it advocates for disciplinary cross-talk that will enrich our lines of inquiry. The more work we do to show our shared connections, the more force we have for developing rhetorical education in this country and retaining rhetoric's viability as an academic discipline.

NOTES

[1] This project continues an investigation initiated at the 2011 RSA Summer Institute titled "Rhetoric's Critical Genealogies," led by Vanessa Beasley, Jim Jasinski, Chuck Morris, and Kirt Wilson.

[2] It is worth noting that the inaugural meeting of the Alliance of Rhetoric Societies, held in 2003, explored four major areas: rhetorical tradition, rhetorical agency, disciplinarity, and pedagogy. While these categories provide a strong entry point for considering the prominent areas of overlap, "rhetorical agency" does not appear as a common theme throughout the literature on shared disciplinarity. Instead, "rhetorical agency" is subsumed under the larger category of pedagogy, where civic engagement and rhetorical education are explored. In this way, "rhetorical agency" is theorized through the lens of education. As a result, I focus on the four touchstones above because they appear in multiple publications.

[3] While "the rhetorical tradition" is honored by both fields, Zarefsky's article demonstrates that scholars in both rhet-comp and communication were not necessarily aware of the rhetorical tradition throughout the first half of the twentieth century; hence, the "return to rhetoric" in the 1960s is where we can locate the deliberate invocation of the rhetorical tradition in both fields.

[4] Four years ago, after I attended the 2009 RSA Summer Institute on Rhetorical Criticism, I experienced a slight identity complex, as I had never been introduced to the words *rhetoric* and *criticism* at the same time. I affiliated criticism with literary studies and rhetoric with rhet-comp. The conjoining of the two words was new to me. So, when my colleagues from my PhD program joined the institute for the weekend workshops, I took a poll, asking them if they knew what "rhetorical criticism" was. No one did.

WORKS CITED

Bizzell, Patricia, and Susan Jarratt. "Rhetorical Traditions, Pluralized Canons, Relevant History, and Other Disputed Terms: A Report from the History of Rhetoric Discussion Groups at the ARS Conference." *Rhetoric Society Quarterly* 34.3 (2004): 19-25. Print.

Crowley, Sharon. "Communication Skills and a Brief Rapprochement of Rhetoricians." *Rhetoric Society Quarterly* 34.1 (2004): 89-103. Print.

---. *Composition in the University: Historical and Polemical Essays.* Pittsburgh: U of Pittsburgh P, 1998. Print.

Goggin, Maureen Daly. "The Tangled Roots of Literature, Speech Communication, Linguistics, Rhetoric/Composition, and Creative Writing: A Selected Bibliography on the History of English Studies." *Rhetoric Society Quarterly* 29.4 (1999): 63-87. Print.

Graff, Richard, and Michael Leff. "Revision Historiography and Rhetorical Tradition(s)." *The Viability of the Rhetorical Tradition.* Ed. Richard Graff, Arthur E. Walzer, and Janet M. Atwill. Albany: State U of New York P, 2005. 11-30. Print.

Hauser, Gerard A. "Teaching Rhetoric: Or Why Rhetoric Isn't Just Another Kind of Philosophy or Literary Criticism." *Rhetoric Society Quarterly* 34.3 (2004): 39-53. Print.

Jackson, Brian. "Cultivating Paideweyan Pedagogy: Rhetoric Education in English and Communication Studies." *Rhetoric Society Quarterly* 37.2 (2007): 181-201. Print.

Keith, William. "Identity, Rhetoric, and Myth: A Response to Mailloux and Leff." *Rhetoric Society Quarterly* 30.4 (2000): 95-106. Print.

Lauer, Janice. "Composition Studies: Dappled Discipline." *Rhetoric Review* 3.1 (1984): 20-29. Print.

Leff, Michael. "Rhetorical Disciplines and Rhetorical Disciplinarity: A Response to Mailloux." *Rhetoric Society Quarterly* 30.4 (2000): 83-93. Print.

Leff, Michael, and Andrea A. Lunsford. "Afterwards: A Dialogue." *Rhetoric Society Quarterly* 34.3 (2004): 55-67. Print.

Mailloux, Steven. "Disciplinary Identities: On the Rhetorical Paths between English and Communication." *Rhetoric Society Quarterly* 30.2 (2000): 5-29. Print.

---. "Using Traditions: A Gadamerian Reflection on Canons, Contexts, and Rhetoric. *The Viability of the Rhetorical Tradition.* Ed. Richard Graff, Arthur E. Walzer, and Janet M. Atwill. Albany: State U of New York P, 2005. 181-194. Print.

McKeon, Richard. "The Use of Rhetoric in a Technological Age: Architectonic Productive Arts." *Rhetoric: Essays in Invention and Discovery.* Ed. Mark Backman. Woodbridge: Oxbow P, 1987. 1-24. Print.

McKoski, Nancy. "The Politics of Professing Rhetoric in the History of Composition and Communication." *Professing Rhetoric: Selected Papers from the 2000 Rhetoric Society of America Conference.* Ed. Frederick J. Antczak, Cinda Coggins, and Geoffrey D. Klinger. Mahwah: Lawrence Erlbaum, 2002. 13-20. Print.

Miller, Thomas. "Disciplinary Identifications/Public Identities: A Response to Mailloux, Leff, and Keith." *Rhetoric Society Quarterly* 31.3 (2001): 105-17. Print.

National Center for Education Statistics. "Detail for CIP Code 09.0101." *The Integrated Post-Secondary Education System (IPEDS).* Institute of Education Sciences, U.S. Department of Education, 2010. Web. 8 Mar. 2012.

Norton, Janice. "Sleeping with the Enemy: Recoupling Rhetorical Studies and Rhetoric and Composition." *Professing Rhetoric: Selected Papers from the 2000 Rhetoric Society of America Conference.* Ed. Frederick J. Antczak, Cinda Coggins, and Geoffrey D. Klinger. Mahwah: Lawrence Erlbaum, 2002. 21-28. Print.

Nystrand, Martin. "Distinguishing Formative and Receptive Contexts in the Disciplinary Formation of Composition Studies: A Response to Mailloux." *Rhetorical Society Quarterly* 31.3 (2001): 93-103. Print.

Phelps, Louise Wetherbee, and John M. Ackerman. "Making the Case for Disciplinarity in Rhetoric, Composition, and Writing Studies: The Visibility Project." *College Composition and Communication* 62.1 (2010): 180-215. Print.

Schilb, John. "Getting Disciplined?" *Rhetoric Review* 12.2 (1994): 398-405. Print.

Skeffington, Jillian K. "Situating Ourselves: The Development of Doctoral Programs in Rhetoric and Composition." *Rhetoric Review* 30.1 (2010): 54-71. Print.

Walker, Jeffrey. "On Rhetorical Traditions: A Reply to Jerzy Axer." Meeting of the Alliance of Rhetoric Societies. Northwestern University, Evanston. 12 Sept. 2003. Plenary address.

Zarefsky, David. "Institutional and Social Goals for Rhetoric." *Rhetoric Society Quarterly* 34.3 (2004): 27-38. Print.

CONTRIBUTORS

Matthew Abraham is Associate Professor of Writing, Rhetoric, and Discourse at DePaul University in Chicago. His articles on the life and legacy of Edward Said, the question of Palestine, and academic freedom have appeared in *JAC, Cultural Critique, South Atlantic Quarterly,* and *College Composition and Communication.* He is the winner of the 2003 Rachel Corrie Award for Courage in the Teaching of Writing and is currently writing a book entitled *Out of Bounds: Academic Freedom and the Question of Palestine.*

Dominic J. Ashby is a doctoral candidate in Composition and Rhetoric at Miami University in Oxford, Ohio. His research interests include comparative rhetoric, Japanese rhetoric, and WAC/WID. His dissertation, "Enacting a Rhetoric of Inside-Outside Positionalities: From the Indexing Practice of *Uchi/Soto* to a Reiterative Process of Meaning-Making," studies the interplay of inside and outside in Japanese rhetoric and its applicability to broader rhetorical study. An article drawing from this work is forthcoming in a special issue of *Rhetoric Society Quarterly.* Research on this project was funded by an Academic Challenge Dissertation Fellowship from Miami University.

Michelle Ballif is Associate Professor of English at the University of Georgia and Managing Editor of *Composition Forum.* Her teaching and research interests focus on the history and historiography of rhetoric, particularly the intersections between classical rhetoric and contemporary continental theory. She is the author of *Seduction, Sophistry, and the Woman with the Rhetorical Figure,* coauthor of *Women's Ways of Making It in Rhetoric and Composition,* and editor of a number of volumes on the history and historiography of rhetoric, including *Theorizing Histories of Rhetoric.*

Geoffrey W. Bateman is Assistant Professor of Peace and Justice Studies at Regis University in Denver, Colorado. As one of the founding members of the Community Writing Center project, he's worked for the past four years consulting directly with writers at The Gathering Place, a daytime, drop-in refuge for women, children, and transgender individuals experiencing homelessness or poverty. His scholarship on queer rhetorics and community-based learning has appeared in *Reflections: A Journal of Public Rhetoric, Civic Writing, and Service Learning,* and he's coeditor of *Don't Ask, Don't Tell: Debating the Gay Ban in the Military.*

Katherine Bridgman is a doctoral candidate in Rhetoric and Composition at Florida State University. Her research currently focuses on social protest, mobile media, embodiment, and transnationalism.

Bryan Carr is a doctoral candidate at the Gaylord College of Journalism and Mass Communication at the University of Oklahoma. He studies the construction and representation of identity in popular culture and mass media as well as interactive media. He teaches audio production, race and gender in the media, video games as a communicative and narrative medium, and radio performance and operations. He has received awards for his academic and professional work, including the Association for Education in Journalism and Mass Communication's 2012 Minorities and Communication Division Top Student Paper award. In his free time, he enjoys consuming pop culture.

Karen Ching Carter is a doctoral candidate in English with a concentration in rhetoric, composition, and linguistics at Arizona State University. She holds an MA in Writing, Rhetoric, and Discourse from DePaul University and a JD from the University of Denver. Her primary interests lie in Asian American rhetoric, especially in rhetorical performance. She also has a research interest in institutional rhetoric and its impact on diverse populations.

Dale Cyphert is Associate Professor in the Department of Management at the University of Northern Iowa. Her work in rhetorical theory focuses primarily on processes of normative change. Current projects explore the contrasting and evolving norms in virtual organizations, rural communities, and the economic discourses of sustainability and corporate citizenship. Cyphert teaches in the MBA program and serves as the director of the college's Professional Readiness Program.

Elizabeth Tasker Davis is Assistant Professor of English at Stephen F. Austin State University in Nacogdoches, Texas, where she teaches courses on eighteenth-century literature, literary satire, and composition pedagogy. She has published articles on eighteenth-century female novelists, eighteenth-century rhetoric, and feminist research methods in *South Atlantic Review*, *The Sage Handbook of Rhetoric*, *Rhetoric Review*, and *Peitho* and is currently writing a manuscript about eighteenth-century British women's rhetoric and coediting a collection about the literary activities of the Sheridan-Lefanu family. Davis also serves as the current president of the Coalition of Women Scholars in the History of Rhetoric and Composition.

Erik Doxtader is Professor of Rhetoric at the University of South Carolina and a senior research fellow at the Institute for Justice and Reconciliation in Cape Town. Interested in classical and contemporary questions of discovery, including the ways in which rhetoric's potential shapes subjectivity, recognition, human rights, and ethical life, Doxtader has published numerous books and essays on transitional justice, the rhetorical dynamics of reconciliation, and human rights discourse. His 2009 book, *With Faith in the Works of Words:*

The Beginnings of Reconciliation in South Africa, was awarded the Rhetoric Society of America's annual Book Award.

William Duffy is Assistant Professor in the English Department at Francis Marion University, where he primarily teaches courses in argument, composition pedagogy, and professional writing. His work has been published in *Rhetoric Review* and *Enculturation*, as well as in several edited collections, including the 2008 RSA conference volume, *The Responsibilities of Rhetoric*.

Jason A. Edwards is Associate Professor of Communication Studies at Bridgewater State University. He is the author of *Navigating the Post Cold War World: President Clinton's Foreign Policy Rhetoric* and editor, along with David Weiss, of *The Rhetoric of American Exceptionalism*. Additionally, his scholarship has appeared in *Rhetoric and Public Affairs, Presidential Studies Quarterly, Communication Quarterly, Southern Journal of Communication*, and the *Howard Journal of Communications*.

Brian Gogan is Assistant Professor of English at Western Michigan University, where he teaches courses in the Rhetoric and Writing Studies Program. His scholarship on Baudrillard and rhetoric has appeared in *Rhetoric Review*, the *International Journal of Baudrillard Studies*, and the collection *Who Speaks for Writing: Stewardship in Writing Studies in the 21st Century*. He is currently working on a book-length project, *Jean Baudrillard: Rhetoric and Exchange*, which examines Baudrillard's relevance as a rhetorical theorist.

David M. Grant is Assistant Professor in the Department of Languages and Literatures at the University of Northern Iowa, where he teaches courses in the theory and practice of writing, literatures of the environment, and literatures of Native American peoples, and he administers the campus writing program. His writings on the environment and rhetoric have appeared in *JAC, Kairos,* and *PRE/TEXT.* He is currently researching the "animating myths" of composition studies in order to provide a place for dialogue between composition and communication studies about rhetoric. He would like to thank the American Craft Council and Geoff Sirc for their invaluable assistance with this paper.

Randall Iden is a lecturer in the Department of Communication at Lake Forest College and at Northwestern University. He holds a PhD in Communication Studies from Northwestern University and a JD from the University of Pennsylvania Law School. His research interests include the rhetoric of economics, public sphere theory, and public argumentation.

Edward Karshner is Associate Professor of English at Robert Morris University. Since receiving his PhD in Rhetoric and Philosophy from Bowling Green State University in 2000, he has researched comparative rhetoric firsthand in the highland jungles of southwest China and the southwestern deserts of the United States. His interests are primarily in the metaphysical contexts of thinking and speaking in early esoteric traditions and their implications for current theories regarding communication.

Jerry Won Lee is a doctoral candidate in the Department of English at the University of Arizona (Tucson). His research investigates, among other things, the intersections of nationalist/state ideologies and rhetorical action, and the practice of English in global contexts. He has taught previously at California State University, Long Beach. He would like to thank Theresa Enos, Adela C. Licona, Kenny Walker, and Juan Gallegos for their suggestions for revision on earlier versions of this project.

Kaitlin Marks-Dubbs is a doctoral candidate at the University of Illinois, Urbana-Champaign. Her research focuses on digital technology; writing across media; and gender, sexuality, and body studies. She has presented her work at conferences such as the Computers and Writing Conference, the Conference on College Composition and Communication, and the Thomas R. Watson Conference, in addition to the Rhetoric Society of America Conference. Kaitlin's teaching focuses primarily on courses in informatics, and business and technical writing.

Keith D. Miller is Professor of English at Arizona State University. His most recent book is *Martin Luther King's Biblical Epic: His Great, Final Speech*. His essays have appeared in *College English, College Composition and Communication, Rhetoric Society Quarterly, PMLA*, and *Journal of American History*. In 2007, his essay on "I Have a Dream" won the Theresa Enos Award for Best Essay of the Year in *Rhetoric Review*. He is currently writing a book about *The Autobiography of Malcolm X*.

Janice Odom is Assistant Professor of English at Georgia Gwinnett College. She received her PhD from the University of Iowa in Communication Studies, specializing in rhetorical studies, with a dissertation on Luce Irigaray. She previously taught at Arizona and Valdosta State Universities. Her affiliations are with the Rhetoric Society of America and the National and Southern States Communication Associations. Her research interests include rhetorical, visual, psychoanalytic, and feminist theory and criticism, and she has published on a range of subjects from French feminism to Jackson Pollack to Kenneth Burke.

Nicholas S. Paliewicz is a doctoral student at the University of Utah. He studies environmental rhetoric and critical/cultural studies with a focus on public sphere deliberation. Currently, he addresses the cultural and discursive hegemony of industry in the Salt Lake Valley. Using rhetorical field methods he evaluates the rhetorical efficacy of local environmental organizations targeting Rio Tinto's Kennecott Utah Copper. Additionally, Nicholas maintains an interest in global warming arguments and post-9/11 visuality. He has taught courses on basic communication, argumentation and debate, and rhetorical/argumentative writing. He also assists Utah Forensics and hopes to complete his PhD program in 2015.

Heather Palmer is Associate Professor of Rhetoric, Writing, and Women's Studies at the University of Tennessee in Chattanooga. Her research and teaching interests are rooted in gender and the history and theory of rhetoric, focusing specifically on feminine *ethos*. At present, she is analyzing gendered rhetoric in a collection of hagiographies about Byzantine transvestite nuns. She is also currently working on a project about bestial rhetorics as a practice of the epideictic in Pentecostal snake handling.

M. Karen Powers is Associate Professor of English at Kent State University at Tuscarawas, where she teaches courses in writing/rhetoric and American literature. Her research coalesces around the public work of rhetorical historiography, sociocultural difference, and the politics of institutions, especially the research university.

Katie Rose Guest Pryal is Clinical Assistant Professor of Law at the University of North Carolina School of Law (Chapel Hill), where she teaches legal writing, argumentation, reasoning, and advocacy. She earned her law degree from University of North Carolina School of Law and her PhD in Rhetoric and Composition from University of North Carolina at Greensboro. She is the author of *A Short Guide to Writing About Law* and *Core Grammar for Lawyers*.

Shawn D. Ramsey is Visiting Assistant Professor at the University of North Carolina at Greensboro. He teaches introduction to rhetoric, as well as introductory academic writing. His research interests include the history of rhetoric in the Early and High Middle Ages, as well as continental nineteenth-century rhetoric. He has articles forthcoming in *Advances in the History of Rhetoric*, *Rhetoric Society Quarterly*, and *Rhetoric Review.*

Andrew Nicholas Rechnitz is a doctoral candidate at the University of Texas at Austin, with concentrations in rhetoric and digital literacies and literatures. His research interests include digital media theory, sophistic pedagogy, critical theory, continental philosophy, and histories of rhetoric. This presentation is part of a dissertation that engages Gorgias, Jacques Rancière, and Paul de Man in order to challenge the *logos* of the standard "rise-and-fall" narrative concerning the relationship between rhetoric and democracy.

Tonya Ritola is Assistant Professor of English at Georgia Gwinnett College. She received her PhD in English, with a focus on rhetoric and composition, from the University of North Carolina at Greensboro. Her teaching experience includes undergraduate and graduate courses in rhetoric, developmental writing, professional writing, and writing-center theory and practice. She is working on a book project, *Institutional Narratives and Writing Program Administration*, and she has presented papers at regional and national conferences, including the Rhetoric Society of America, the Conference on College Composition and Communication, and the International Writing Centers Association Conference.

Jacqueline Jones Royster is Dean of the Ivan Allen College of Liberal Arts at the Georgia Institute of Technology. She holds the Ivan Allen Jr. Dean's Chair in Liberal Arts and Technology and is Professor of English in the

School of Literature, Media, and Communication. She is the author of several books and articles in rhetorical studies, women's studies, and literacy studies. Her most recent book publication is a coauthored volume with Gesa E. Kirsch, *Feminist Rhetorical Practices: New Horizons in Rhetoric, Composition, and Literacy Studies.*

Jessica L. Shumake is a doctoral candidate in the Rhetoric, Composition, and the Teaching of English Program at the University of Arizona. She earned an MA in Philosophy from the University of Windsor. Her dissertation research examines the intersections of visual-spatial and publics theory through an archival study of the rhetorical tactics of the multimedia artist, writer, and activist David Wojnarowicz. Her work on the rhetorical dimensions of space, publics, and archives has been published in *TOPIA: Canadian Journal of Cultural Studies.*

Laura A. Sparks is a doctoral candidate and Culbertson Fellow in composition, literacy, and culture at Indiana University, Bloomington. She has served for two years as an assistant director for the Composition Program's first-year writing course and for four years as a participant in the English Department's digital pedagogy initiative. She researches the rhetoric of torture and currently writes on intersections of rhetoric, torture, and temporality in the context of interrogational torture.

M. Elizabeth Thorpe is Visiting Assistant Professor in the Communication Department at The College at Brockport. A native of Texas, she received her BA in English from Baylor University, her MA in English at Texas A&M University, and her PhD in Communication with an emphasis in rhetoric and public affairs at Texas A&M University, as well. Her research interests focus on American constitutive rhetoric, specifically the construction of the idea of "American," itself. Much of her work is historical in nature with a focus on the Cold War.

Jill M. Weber is Assistant Professor of Communication Studies and the coordinator of the oral communication skills initiative at Hollins University. This essay developed from her dissertation. She would like to thank Thomas W. Benson for his comments on earlier drafts of this essay.

Malinda Williams is a lecturer in the University of Denver Writing Program. She has a PhD in Literary Studies from the University of Denver's English Department with an emphasis in literature of the Americas, Caribbean and Latino/a literature, and critical race theory. Her research interests include the intersections between literature, rhetoric, and constructions of race; issues and locations of diversity; and community-based research and writing.

Sue Carter Wood is Associate Professor and directs the Rhetoric and Writing Doctoral Program in the English Department at Bowling Green State University. She teaches courses in the history of rhetoric, women's rhetorical practices, US composition history, and grammar in the context of writing. A frequent presenter at meetings of the Rhetoric Society of America, she has published articles and book chapters on nineteenth-century US rhetorics.

K. Hyoejin Yoon is Associate Professor of English at West Chester University of Pennsylvania. She has published on emotion in composition studies, critical pedagogy, and Asian American rhetoric. Winner of the 2005 Elizabeth A. Flynn Award for most outstanding article in feminist rhetoric and composition, she is also a contributing author to *Representations: Asian American Rhetoric*, edited by LuMing Mao and Morris Young, which received honorable mention for the MLA Mina P. Shaughnessy Prize. The essay that appears here reflects a new area of historical and archival research on the first Chinese woman in the United States in the early nineteenth century.

David Zarefsky is Owen L. Coon Professor Emeritus of Argumentation and Debate, and Professor Emeritus of Communication Studies, Northwestern University. He was president of the Rhetoric Society of America in 2006–2007 and again in 2010–2011.

Name Index

347

SUBJECT INDEX